Englishmen
At War

A Social History In Letters 1450 – 1900

ERNEST SANGER

With a Foreword by
General Sir Anthony Farrar-Hockley

ALAN SUTTON

First published in the United Kingdom in 1993 by
Alan Sutton Publishing Limited
Phoenix Mill · Far Thrupp · Stroud · Gloucestershire

First published in the United States of America in 1993 by
Alan Sutton Publishing Inc · 83 Washington Street · Dover NH 03820

British Library Cataloguing in Publication Data

Sanger, Ernest
Englishmen at War: Social History in Letters, 1450–1900
I Title
941

ISBN 0-7509-0160-8

Library of Congress Cataloging in Publication Data applied for

Typeset in 10/12pt Palatino.
Typesetting and origination by
Alan Sutton Publishing Limited.
Printed in Great Britain by
The Bath Press, Avon.

Contents

List of Illustrations

Foreword

Reading other people's letters is a popular pursuit and one that is conscience free when the correspondence has passed out of currency. Letters of the past, like the journals of the day, are the stuff of history.

War letters have a special character. Nations in arms tend to reassess their values. Campaigns draw in great numbers of people who would otherwise have remained strangers, exposing them to extraordinary challenges and temptations. Threats to political power or life and limb draw out the best and worst in men and women. These circumstances stimulate letters of many kinds, official and personal, which, as a totality, illuminate the nature and outcome of such struggles.

The English have long been a warrior-nation. Their governments have tended to engage in military operations beyond their means but, with rare exceptions, have been supported in these ventures by the majority of the populace.

The letters selected for this book present a panorama of Englishmen at war from the outset of modern times to the end of the nineteenth century. At the beginning, the British Isles were disunited politically; by the end, they were contained within one kingdom. The span thus embraces internal wars with Scots and the Irish, and a civil war between English factions, as well as foreign and colonial wars, wars to defend the English shores, and wars abroad of conquest.

Those involved tell the story.

General Sir Anthony Farrar-Hockley

Acknowledgements

I wish to record my gratitude to the late Ursula Somervell who first started collecting war letters with me; to my old colleagues Charles Keeley and William Lough, and to Dr David Chandler, Head of War Studies at the Royal Military Academy Sandhurst, who read my manuscript and recommended many valuable amendments. I am also indebted to the authors, editors, publishers, and agents for their kind permission to reproduce letters included in their books; if I omitted to obtain any necessary authorization, I hope I shall be forgiven.

The author wishes to thank the following for giving their permission to use copyright material: B.T. Batsford for extracts from W. Baring Pemberton, *Crimean War Battles*, 1962, M. Edwardes, *The Battle of Plassey*, 1963, and C. Lloyd, *The Capture of Quebec*, 1959; Blackie & Son for an extract from J. Laffin, *Women in Battle*, Abelard-Schumann, 1967; Blackwell Publishers for extracts from T. Charles-Edwards and B. Richardson, *They Saw it Happen*, 1958, and C.N.R. Routh, *They Saw it Happen*, 1956; Frank Cass Publishers for an extract from G.E. Mainwaring and B. Dobrée, *The Floating Republic*, 1966; Curtis Brown & John Farquharson on behalf of the Estate of Sir Winston Churchill for an extract from W. Churchill, *From London to Ladysmith*, Longman, 1900; Leo Cooper for extracts from *Recollections of Rifleman Bowlby*, 1969; Laurence Pollinger on behalf of the Estate of Clemence Dane for an extract from C. Dane, *The Nelson Touch*, Heinemann, 1942; J.M. Dent for extracts from *Cromwell Letters*, ed. Th. Carlyle, 1908; Mr Byron Farwell for an extract from B. Farwell, *The Great Boer War*, Allen Lane, 1977; Robert Hale for an extract from B. Bevan, *Marlborough the Man*, 1975; David Higham Associates on behalf of Mr Christopher Hibbert for extracts from C. Hibbert, *The Great Mutiny*, Allen Lane, 1978; David Higham Associates on behalf of the Estate of B.H. Liddell Hart for extracts from the *Letters of Private Wheeler*, ed. B.H. Liddell Hart, Michael Joseph, 1951; Longman Group UK for extracts from C. Aspinall-Oglander, *Admiral's Wife*, 1940, and X.F. Walker, *Young Gentlemen*, 1938; Macmillan Publishing Company, New York for extracts from Earl of Birkenhead, *The Five Hundred Best English Letters*, 1931, P. Frischauer, *England's Years of Danger*, 1938, and *Letters of Queen Elizabeth*, ed. G.B. Harrison, 1935, all originally published by Cassell and Co., London;

Manchester University Press for an extract from A. Temple Patterson, *The Other Armada*, 1960; the Director, National Army Museum, London and the owner of the copyright in the writings of Brigadier F.A. Maxwell VC, for an extract from a letter; R.I.B. Library, Reed Book Services on behalf of Methuen & Co. for an extract from C. Isherwood, *Kathleen and Frank*, 1971; John Murray for extracts from *The Letters of Queen Victoria*, ed. A.C. Benson and Viscount Esher, 1907, F. Maxwell, *A Memoir*, 1921, J. Gore, *Creevey's Life and Times*, 1934, K.H.M. Diver, *Honoria Lawrence*, 1936, P. Magnus, *Kitchener*, 1958, and *Fields of War*, ed. Philip Warner, 1977; Oxford University Press for extracts from *Swift Correspondence*, ed. H. Williams, 1963, and R. Whitworth, FM Lord Ligonier, 1958; Random House UK for extracts from R.J. Minney, *Clive*, Jarrolds, 1931, E.C. Holt, *Opium Wars in China*, Bodley Head (Putnam), 1964, and K. Griffith, *Thank God we Kept the Flag Flying*, Hutchinson, 1974; Deborah Owen Literary Agency on behalf of Miss C.V. Wedgwood for an extract from *The King's War*, Collins, 1958.

Introduction

There is history in all men's lives,
Figuring the nature of the times deceased
SHAKESPEARE, HENRY IV, PART II

History is better written from letters than from histories
LORD ACTON

The purpose of this book is threefold – to provide: a) a continuous selective narrative for the general reader of the successive English wars from the middle of the fifteenth century to the end of the nineteenth, accompanied by brief summaries of the causes, principal actions and social features of the wars, as witnessed by our letter writers; b) a sourcebook for the student of history, with short details of the circumstances in which the letters were written and of the personalities involved; c) a socio-psychological study of English attitudes to war which are highlighted by significant quotations from the letters in the captions and comments, and by contemporary poetry (or prose) at the beginning of each chapter.

No attempt is made to cover any war completely, as this would be far beyond the compass of one volume; only some of the most important events and social features, and the most characteristic reactions that could be exemplified by letters, have been chosen to represent each period. The structure and pattern of every chapter, if read as a continuous story, accompanied by an analytical appraisal, should give the reader a fair conception of how war appeared to the English people during four and a half centuries.

The great diversity of individual views on the wars crystallize together a number of recurrent themes which are typical of permanent attitudes – albeit modified by changing circumstances – a kaleidoscope of English character and reactions in face of war. Letters 'bring out the hourly urgency and confusion through which contemporaries lived'.[1] It is fascinating to see how the figures of the past, humble and exalted alike, rise again before our eyes as witnesses of war:

---

1   C.V. Wedgwood, *The King's War*, Collins, 1958, p. 11.

Too few have troubled themselves over much with the minds and spirits of those involved, and those who have done so have tended to simplify and thus to distort, in order to argue a case and bolster a prejudice. The soul of man, in all its majesty and mystery, has been dwarfed by the war game.[2]

The strong feelings of the moment are evoked forcibly in all their infinite variety; no historian can equal the impact of living reality that letters convey, although they can impose a rationalized artificial order upon the chaos of reality, in the way admirals and generals do in their despatches. Few diaries or retrospective accounts, both of which tend to be either self-conscious or composed to build up an image for effect, can compete in genuineness with letters, freely written fresh from the scene of action for those nearest and dearest, although the global view of the event may sometimes be out of focus and some details unreliable:

Letters wrote in the scene and at the time of actions are with reason deemed the most proper means of conveying down to posterity just and authentick accounts, generally more enlivening than narrations purely historical, bringing us back to those times that we are in a manner present at them; so that they are often as entertaining as a poetic description, with this advantage, that they have truth on their side.[3]

Controversial historical events, and received ideas about them, may be illuminated and corrected by the frank testimony of letters in all their spontaneity:

Every letter will shed some light on the heart of bygone times, still animated by the passions then throbbing in every breast. Human nature, and the nature of each writer, is transparent in them all: the reader sees the very conscience of war.[4]

Foremost, war heightens the awareness of the inevitability of death, and battles spring to life again in the letters of the participants: they are imbued with the awesome elation which the immediate presence and fatality of death inspires while they carry out their well-rehearsed killing manoeuvre for which they have been conditioned, in defence or for the glory of the nation, or, more generally, just simply to survive.

A vast number of specialized studies of every aspect of war have been

---

2   J. Connell in J. Baynes, *Morale*, Cassell, 1967, p. 3.
3   T. Carte, *Collection of Letters*, I, 1739, III.
4   E. Warburton, *Memoirs of Prince Rupert*, I, 1849, p. 5 f.

published over the last thirty years. As far as I am aware, however, this is the first attempt to cover the whole period of English wars from the mid-fifteenth century up to the end of the nineteenth century during which letters were written and to concentrate on the display of characteristic attitudes among the infinite variety of Englishmen and -women's reactions to war.

The 333 letters in this book have been chosen from among many many thousands, published or in manuscript, the vast majority of which were dull, stereotyped, confused, badly written and lengthy. Every one of those chosen has a particular function in the framework of this book, and a great deal of pruning has been essential to bring out what is relevant to our story of English attitudes to war and to preserve continuity, clarity and interest. Some earlier editors of collections of old letters have tampered with them to 'improve' them to their taste and have modernized words and spelling; here the texts have been strictly preserved as they appear in the printed (and sometimes adapted) source or in the manuscript, without, however, being so pedantic as to insert constantly the usual three dots to mark cuttings when they do not fit in naturally. At the same time, the greatest care has been taken that omissions do not in any way modify the sense, and anything irrelevant or disfiguring, which would impair clearness, readability and enjoyment, has been left out. It would also have been narrow-minded to exclude completely letters written by Scots, Welshmen and Irishmen at a time when English character mingled with that of the other parts of the British Isles and widened to embrace them to a certain extent.

English attitudes to war were moulded by the off-shore island position under the protection the Channel provided: as long as the navy kept control of the narrow sea barrier the country could afford to be off its guard, neglect its armed forces, and begin its wars with defeats and disasters. The strong antipathy to a standing army which, it was felt, could threaten hard-won freedoms and the climate of toleration, impeded timely preparations. So, one reverse after another had to be endured undaunted, in the cheerful certitude that the last battle would be won.

The Englishman's 'easy-going opportunism and benevolent sense of superiority' resulted from this reluctance to go to war: he 'must be convinced that he is fighting for a principle, and is only too glad when the whole business is over'. Yet 'it is a curious paradox that this "insular" nation, so wedded to home and soil, has provided so many adventurers to all parts of the world', whose 'longing for home is ever present.'[5]

The frontier in wartime remained the coast from Brittany to Flanders, with the sea as the last defence line against superior continental armies. Francis Bacon stressed its strategic advantage: 'He that commands the sea is at great

---

5   J. Freeman, *Englishman at War*, Allen & Unwin, 1941, p. xv ff.

liberty, and may take as much and as little of the war as he will.' Drake emphasized in 1588 that 'the advantage of time and place in all martial actions is half the victory', and, much later, Admiral Fisher, taking the navy as a model, reminded Jellicoe in May 1916 – without success as it turned out – that 'Rashness in war is prudence. Prudence in war is criminal. War is "audacity and imagination"!', a view also propagated by Churchill.

The outlook of an island nation must necessarily be naval, versatile, makeshift and bold.

Insularity also explains the degree of incomprehension of the character of England's continental neighbours, particularly the French; so, almost permanent warfare became inevitable, until it ended with a second Hundred Years' War from 1689 to 1815. The painful experience of interminable conflict is expressed in an old song:

> War, like a serpent, has its head got in,
> And will not end so soon as't did begin.

Chance played an important role, particularly the hazards of the weather, not only at sea but also on land: the downpour before Waterloo may have saved Wellington who was always ready to admit the element of luck in the confusion of battle. The weather was also specified by Wavell who was intensely aware of what he called the 'actualities' of war even in modern conditions:

> The effects of tiredness, hunger, fear, lack of sleep, weather, inaccurate information, the time factor. The principles of strategy and tactics, and the logistics of war, are really absurdly simple; it is the actualities that make war so complicated and so difficult, and are usually neglected by historians.[6]

It is precisely these 'actualities' that can best be studied in letters. We constantly find them there; but it is the island mentality, focused on sea defences and the oceans of the world for trade and conquest ('Others may use the oceans as a road, only the English make it their abode' writes Edmund Waller in 1659) which is perhaps the most intrinsic factor among the recurring themes and attitudes permeating our war letters. A systematic list of these attitudes which characterize them throughout the centuries can be found at the end in the Conclusion.

Several excellent monographs have been devoted to the social history of the British sailor and soldier and no summary can be given here.

Conditions in the navy were even more appalling than in the army: 'Our naval glory was built up by the blood and agony of thousands of barba-

---

6   J. Connell, *Wavell*, Collins, 1964, p. 22 f.

rously maltreated men.'[7] It must not be forgotten, though, that many sailors were recruited from prisons: 'In a man of war', writes Lieutenant Edward Thompson in 1756, 'you have the collected filth of jails; condemned criminals have the alternative of hanging, or entering on board. There's not a vice committed on shore, but is practised here.' Yet these same ill-used seamen, however low their spirits may have sunk with hunger, disease and flogging, rallied at the instant of action, worthy heirs of the Norse pirates, and were dreaded for centuries by their enemies for their pugnacious fighting skill.

British soldiers, with a different task, drill, and tradition, were, in comparison, slower to get roused. They often first needed the stimulation of defeat to become martial: 'They are commonly fiercer and bolder after being repulsed than before; and what blunts the courage of all other nations commonly whets theirs – I mean the killing of their fellow soldiers before their faces,' writes a 17th century Chaplain.[8] Regimental brotherhood, even more than discipline, overcomes the instinct of self-preservation and leads to the acceptance of self-sacrifice; it is indeed a peculiarity of the English outlook on war that desperate heroic last stands, rather than victories, are glorified by the people and made into myths.

Proud consciousness of a long history of ultimate victory and a firm belief in the unfailing triumph of his just cause makes the British soldier never despair: refusing to accept defeat, he thereby always manages to retrieve himself in the end. Wavell has sung his praises:

> Above them all towers the homely but indomitable figure of the British soldier, the finest all-round fighting man the world has seen; he has won so many battles that he never doubts of victory, he has suffered so many defeats and disasters on the way to victory that he is never greatly depressed by defeat; whose humorous endurance of time and chance lasts always to the end.[9]

He adds that with the bluff and daring of the 'cat-burglar, gunman, poacher' he makes the ideal infantryman.

Grumbling, grousing and swearing all the time, without ever losing his sense of humour, the British soldier lets off steam, and this strengthens his staying power; he fights all the better for it, especially in defence: Londonderry, Waterloo and Ladysmith testify to his unyielding stubbornness. Despite his rigid drill, he tends to remain something of a Boy Scout on a jamboree; yet this happy-go-lucky amateurism is deceptive – light-hearted insouciance reinforces resilience and willingness to go on.

7   J.E. Masefield, *Sea Life in Nelson's Time*, Methuen, 1905, p. 127.
8   J. Laffin, *Tommy Atkins*, Cassell, 1966, p. 27.
9   A. Wavell, *Soldiers and Soldiering*, J. Cape, 1953, p. 124.

The superiority complex engendered by the island position, and a long record of final success, means that the forces available in war are always initially insufficient: 'The misfortune and vice of our country is that we believe ourselves better than other men,' wrote Admiral Shovell in 1702.[10] This disposition leads to defeats and bloody sacrifices in the early stages of war which are then, as for example the Battle of Corunna, turned into legends of glory.

Changing English attitudes to war can be followed through the centuries: from an arbitrary, almost sport-like affair, the natural occupation for gentlemen and mercenaries, the view of war became increasingly influenced by the growing nationalism of the reigns of Henry VIII and Elizabeth; later the ever recurrent concern about invasion led to war being considered as an instrument for the preservation of the balance of power on the continent. During the Napoleonic Wars for the first time a moral query emerged as to the rights of other nations to survive. At the same time, the desirability of war as such began to be questioned: 'We shall have war, because it is just the most absurd thing in creation', wrote a physician in 1803;[11] it was a new note that persisted. In the course of the nineteenth century, moral uncertainty began to gnaw at imperial self-confidence and at the old complacent idea that war was inevitable. The shock of the well-publicized sufferings of soldiers in the Crimea led to widespread doubts about the usefulness of war.

It is a long way from the soldiers of fortune locked in hand-to-hand combat, and from the unruly mob Wellington could still disdainfully call 'the scum of the earth', to the disciplined professionals of later nineteenth-century wars. From individual valour the path leads by way of national pride and patriotic glory to the defence of the ideals of freedom, justice and peace; but the emotional involvement with death's reflection on life and love remains the same through the ages.

---

10 J. Corbett, *England in the Mediterranean*, II, 1917, p. 479.
11 Dr J. Currie of Liverpool on the unexpected renewal of war. He had published an open letter to Pitt in 1793 to try to persuade him not to go to war with France. (*Creevey Papers*, ed. H. Maxwell, I, 1960, p. 12).

PART ONE

THE SIXTEENTH AND SEVENTEENTH CENTURIES

'God made them as stubble to our swords'

How merrily they forward march
Their enemies to slay!

JOHN PICKERING (HANGED 1537)

War seems sweet to such as little know
What comes thereby, what fruits it bringeth forth

GEORGE GASCOIGNE (*c.* 1525–77)

ONE

The Fifteenth-Century Background

They called us for our fierceness
English dogs
SHAKESPEARE, HENRY VI, PART I

And now the House of York . . .
Burns with revenging fire
SHAKESPEARE, HENRY VI, PART II

The Hundred Years' War (1337–1453) started as a plundering foray into France by English soldiers of fortune: 'They take delight and solace in battles and slaughter; covetous and envious are they above measure of other men's wealth,' writes Froissart, the French chronicler. Gradually, however, the English were passing from feudalism to national consciousness and organization, and this expansionist militarism was backed by a racial hatred of the French among ordinary people (the nobles followed only slowly), based on a popular feeling of proud insularity.

The first national war ended in failure and the conquest of France was never again attempted. The islanders turned their eyes to the oceans of the world instead, where, as seamen of the merchant navy they had acquired great skill, fighting as pirates or in the service of the king. It is fitting that a letter, witnessing this proud spirit of defiance on the sea by a small island nation, should open this collection.

1

'Drown them and slay them'
A NAVAL VICTORY IN THE HUNDRED YEARS' WAR (1449)

Robert Wenyngton[1] to Thomas Daniel, Esquire for the King's body.

[Isle of] Wight [25 May 1449]

Most reverend master,

We met with a flote of an hundred great ship of Prusse, Lubeck, Campe,[2] Rostock, Holland, Zealand, and Flanders, betwixt Guernsey and Portland; and then I came abroad the admiral, and bade them strike in the king's name of England, and they bade me skite[3] in the king's name of England; and then I and my fellowship said but he will strike down the sail, that I will oversail them by the grace of God, and God will send me wind and weather; and they bade me do my worst, because I had so few ships, and so small that they scorned me.

And as God would, we had a good wind; and then we armed us to the number of 2000 men in my fellowship, and made us ready to oversail them; and then they launched a boat, and set up a standard of truce, and came and spoke with me; and there they were yielded all the hundred ships to go with me into what port that me list and my fellows; but they fought with me the day before, and shot at us a 1000 guns, and quarrels[4] out of number, and have slain many of my fellowship, and maimed also.

Wherefore methinketh that they have forfeited both ships and goods at our sovereign lord the king's will, and so I have brought them, all the hundred ships, within Wight, in spite of them all. Ye saw never such a sight of ships taken into England this hundred winters; for we lie armed night and day to keep them in, to the time that we have tidings of our sovereign and his council; for truly they have done harm to me, and to my fellowship, and to our ships, more than £2000 worth harm.

And therefore I am advised, and all my fellowship, to drown them and slay them, without that we have tidings from our sovereign the king and his council.

I write in haste within Wight, on Sunday at night after the Ascension of our Lord.

By your own servant,
Robert Wenyngton

---

1   On 3 April 1449 royal letters were issued in favour of Robert Wynnyntone of Devonshire, who was bound by indenture to do the King service on the sea 'for the cleansing of the same, and rebuking of the robbers and priates thereof, which daily do all the noisance they can.' (J. Stevenson, *Letters of the Wars of the English in France*, I, 1858, p. 489.)
2   Kampen (now Gotham), a Hanse town in Holland until the mouth of the Yssel was sanded up.
3   An insulting rejoinder.
4   Square pyramids of iron, shot out of cross-bows.

The fear of invasion is one of the dominant themes right up to the Second World War: more numerous and better equipped continental armies were a constant threat, although an incursion was not quite as easy as imagined and rumours often turned out to be false. Small raids, though, causing damage, were made on the south coast in the Hundred Years' War.[5] The rumour in the next letter, pass on 'in right secret wise', proved to be without foundation; the danger from 'meddlers', forerunners of fifth-columnists, has always been easily suspected and exaggerated.

2

'There be many meddlers'
INVASION FEARS IN 1462

Sir Thomas Howes to his 'master', John Paston, country gentleman.

February 1462

Please your mastership, it was letten me weet in right secret wise that a puissance[6] is ready to arrive in three parts of this land, of six score thousand men, and their day, if wind and weather had served them, should have been here soon upon Candlemas;[7] at Trent to London ward one part of them, and another part coming from Wales, and the third from Jersey and Guernsey, wherefore it is well done ye inform mine Lord Warwick, that he may speak to the king[8] that good provision be had for withstanding their malicious purpose and evil will,[9] which God grant we may overcome them, and so we should I doubt not if we were all one; there be many meddlers, and they be best cherished which would hurt much if these come too, as God defend.

In 1455, two years after the English had been driven out of France (except Calais, held until 1558), the Wars of the Roses for the crown broke out between the Houses of Lancaster and York. They were fought by the unruly mercenaries who had returned home with their barons and felt no loyalty to either side, while the people looked on indifferently. The infantry, with long-bow and sword or bill, followed the mounted knights into suicidal battles which spelt the twilight of feudalism. Edward IV, the best soldier, had

---

5 Agnes Paston alarms her husband in March 1450 that it is dangerous to live on the coast: French corsairs had caused damage near Yarmouth and Cromer, and had even dared to advance inland, conducting themselves as if they were at home there.
6 Force.
7 2 February.
8 Edward IV.
9 As Henry VI was in Scotland and his queen had failed to get help from Louis XI in France, it was a false alarm.

emerged as the Yorkist victor at Towton in 1461. In the Battle of Barnet of 1471 which was fought in thick fog, the Earl of Warwick, 'the Kingmaker', was killed; he had helped Edward to the throne and then resentfully turned against him in favour of Henry VI.

3

'Be ye not adoubted of the world'
THE BATTLE OF BARNET (WARS OF THE ROSES), 1471

The courtier Sir John Paston (1442–79) sends his mother news of the battle in which his party, the Lancastrians, were beaten.

London, [18 April 1471]

Mother,

I recommend me to you, letting you weet, that blessed be God, my brother John is alive and fareth well, and in no peril of death; nevertheless he is hurt with an arrow on his right arm beneath the elbow; and I have sent him a surgeon, which hath dressed him, and he telleth me that he trusteth that he shall be all whole within right short time.

As for me, I am in good case, blessed be God. There was killed upon the field, half a mile from Barnet, on Easter day, the Earl of Warwick and other people of both parties to the number of more than a thousand.

I hope hastily to see you. All this bill must be secret. Be ye not adoubted of the world, for I trust all shall be well.[10]

---

10   On the same day – too late – Queen Margaret landed at Weymouth with an army, but Edward IV routed it at Tewkesbury on 4 May with Yorkist fury and entered London in triumph; Henry VI was at once put to death in the Tower.

Henry VIII (1509–47)

Fair blows the wind for France
MARLOWE, EDWARD II

Navy and Army in Action against France, 1512–13

The cannons have their bowels full of wrath,
And ready mounted are they to spit forth
Their iron indignation . . .
SHAKESPEARE, KING JOHN

After the Hundred Years' War, military intervention, under Wolsey's direction, was confined to sustaining the European importance of England in the contest between Spain and France. Henry VIII joined Spain in the Holy League of the Pope against France, and Admiral Sir Edward Howard made a number of damaging attacks on French vessels in the Channel, also landing in Brittany and Normandy: two great ships went down in flames side by side when the last gunner of the *Cordelière*, grappled by Howard's flagship, the *Regent*, lit the magazine.

1

'As cowards they fled'

Thomas Wolsey (*c.* 1475–1530), Dean of Hereford (Cardinal and Lord Chancellor in 1515), tells the Bishop of Worcester about the burning of the *Cordelière* and the *Regent*.

Farnham: 26 August [1512]
. . . Our folks, on Tuesday was fortnight, met with 21 great ships of France, the best with sail and furnished with artillery and men that ever was seen. And after

7

innumerable shooting of guns and long chasing one another, at the last the *Regent* most valiantly boarded the great carrack of Brest wherin were four lords, 300 gentlemen, 800 soldiers and mariners, 400 crossbowmen, 100 gunners, 200 tuns of wine, 100 pipes of beef, 60 barrels of gunpowder and 15 great brazen curtalls[1] with so marvellous number of shot and other guns of every sort. Our men so valiantly acquit themselves that within one hour fight they had utterly vanquished with shot of guns and arrows the said carrack, and slain most part of the men within the same. And suddenly as they were yielding themselves, the carrack was on a flaming fire, and likewise the *Regent* within the turning of one hand. She was so anchored and fasted to the carrack that by no means possible she might for her safeguard depart from the same and so both in fight within three hours were burnt, and most part of the men in them.

The residue of the French fleet, after long chasing, was by our folks put to flight and driven off into Brest haven. There were six as great ships of the said fleet as the *Regent* or *Sovereign*,[2] howbeit as cowards they fled.

Bad victualling, which was to be the bane of the Elizabethan navy, made the fleet increasingly ineffective and the French Admiral Prégent de Bidoux (called 'Prior John' by the English), with his superior ordnance, successfully retaliated and burnt Brighton in 1514.

2

SO MANY LEAKS BUT NO MEAT, BEER AND BISCUITS

Admiral Sir Edward Howard (*c.* 1477–1513) complains to Wolsey of the unpreparedness of the fleet for the expected battle.

Plymouth, in the *Mary Rose*, the 5th day of April 1513

Master Almoner,

In my heartiest wise I can I recommend me unto you, certifying to you that I am now in Plymouth road, with all the King's fleet.

Sir, I think our business will be tried within five or six days at the furthest, for an hulk that came straight from Brest sheweth for a certainty that there be ready coming forward a hundred ships of war, besides the galleys, and be pressed upon the first wind, and says that they be very well trimmed and will not fail to come out and fight with us.

Sir, these be the gladdest tidings to me and all my captains and all the residue of the army that ever came to us, and I trust on God and St George that we shall have a fair day on them, and I pray God that we linger no longer, for I assure you was never army so falsely victualled. They that received their proportion for two months' flesh cannot bring about for five weeks, for the barrels are full of salt. Also many came out of Thames with a month's beer, trusting that the victuallers should bring the rest, and

---

1 Short-barrelled cannon.
2 Henry VII's avant-garde ships, soon to be surpassed by the two versions of the unwieldy 1,500 ton *Great Harry*, relying on guns instead of grappling, but never tested in action.

here cometh none. I send you word for a surety here is not in this army together, one with another, past 15 days [supply]. In consideration to keep the army together, Sir, for God's sake, send by post all along the coast that they brew beer and make biscuits that we may have some refreshing to keep us together upon this coast, or else we shall be driven to come again into the Downs and let the Frenchmen take their pleasure, and God knoweth when we shall get us up so high westward again. I had ever, than that we should be driven to that issue, to be put all the days of my life in the painfullest prison that is in Christendom.

Sir, the *Katheryn Fortileza* hath so many leaks by reason of Bedell, the carpenter that worked in her at Woolwich, that we have had much to do to keep her above water; he hath bored a hundred auger holes in her and left unstopped, that the water came in as it were in a sieve. Sir, this day I have all the caulkers[3] of the army on her. I trust by to-morrow she shall be more staunch.

Sir, spare not to spend victual upon us. For, with God's grace, the fleet of France shall never do us hurt after this year.[4]

The bellicose young Henry, lusting for glory, seized the opportunity when the French army was engaged in Italy, to land at Calais on 1 July 1513, with 35,000 men armed with bows and bills, supported by 14,000 German and Swiss arquebusiers, pikemen and cavalry, and immediately laid siege to Thérouanne, a town south of Boulogne.

3

BEST WINE FOR THE ARMY

Humphrey Rudyng describes the siege to William Mocklow.

July 1513

On the 10th of July, Frenchmen in Terouenne [*sic*] made a great skrye[5] about midnight, and rung the bells in alarm, for Englishmen shot guns so fierce and so thick against the walls and the gates, and into the town, that they thought to have lost the town and to have been slain, man and child. That same night, the fairest young women within the town, many dozen in number, were slain by the falling of a house, whose death is greatly moaned amongst the best within the town. The walls of Terouenne are sore beaten with guns, and many houses are broken and destroyed. Our guns lie within birdbolt shot to the walls and our miners are near the walls. I trust that by St James's day the lord captain and the army shall drink wine in Terouenne of the best.[6]

---

3   Men to stop up the seams.
4   In the battle of 25 April, Howard, grappling Prégent's own galley from a row-barge with only seventeen men, went overboard and perished in the sea.
5   Sortie.
6   Thérouanne fell on 23 August after the defeat of the relief force in the Battle of Guinegâte a week earlier, which the French, in self-mockery, called the Battle of the Spurs, because, panic-stricken, their cavalry mainly made use of their spurs to get away.

The King and Two of his Katherines

I have been to you a true and humble wife,
At all times to your will conformable
KATHERINE OF ARAGON IN SHAKESPEARE'S HENRY VIII

While Henry, accompanied by Wolsey, was personally directing his campaign in Picardy, his first queen, Katherine of Aragon, was acting as regent and organizing the defence against the Scottish invasion.

4

'Horribly busy with making standards'

Queen Katherine of Aragon (1485–1536) tells Wolsey of her preparations for war with Scotland.

At Richmond, 13 day of August [1513]

Master Almoner,

I received both your letters and am very glad to hear how well the king passed his dangerous passage, the Frenchmen being present.

Ye be not so busy with the war as we be here encumbered with it. All his subjects be very glad, I thank God, to be busy with the Scots, for they take it for pastime. My heart is very good to it, and I am horribly busy with making standards, banners, and badges.

Katharina the Qwene

At Flodden, the Scots were routed by the seventy-year-old Thomas Howard, Earl of Surrey, and King James IV was killed with his nobles and 10,000 men: English bills proved to be more deadly than Scottish spears. Queen Katherine chides English hearts for their softness over the Scottish King's body.

5

THE SCOTTISH KING'S COAT FOR A BANNER

Queen Katherine of Aragon writes to Henry VIII after the victory of Flodden.

Woburn, September 16, 1513

Sir,

My Lord Howard hath sent me a letter by which ye shall see at length the great victory that our Lord hath sent your subjects in your absence.

My husband, I send your Grace the piece of the King of Scots' coat. In this your Grace shall see how I can keep my promise, sending you for banners a King's coat. I thought to send himself unto you, but our Englishmen's hearts would not suffer it. It should have been better for him to have been in peace than have this reward. All that God sendeth is for the best. And with this I make an end: praying God to send you home shortly, for without this no joy here can be accomplished; and for the same I pray.

Your humble wife and true servant,
Katherine

Thirty years later, in contrast, Katherine Parr pines away with no other thought but tender and affectionate longing for her warrior husband who had again invaded Picardy with 42,000 men. He had the over-ambitious aim of capturing Paris for power prestige but got no further than successfully laying siege to Boulogne, and revelling in the 'great noise and marvellous roar' of his 60 pounder cannon battering down the walls. The expediton cost £2 million which Henry raised by the confiscation and sale of monastic land, and debasement of the coinage. Katherine Parr, sweet-tempered and experienced in humouring husbands, indulges in perhaps excessive flattery: not surprisingly, as she had been frightened of marrying Henry ('better to be his mistress than his wife') and, in fact, only just escaped deadly heresy charges by her total submission.

6

A QUEEN'S HUMBLE PROTESTATIONS OF LOVE

Katherine Parr (1512–48) to Henry VIII.

Greenwich [1544]

Although the distance of time and account of days neither is long nor many of your majesty's absence, yet the want of your presence, so much desired and beloved by me, maketh me that I cannot quietly pleasure in anything until I hear from your majesty. The time, therefore, seemeth to me very long, with a great desire to know how your highness hath done since your departing hence, whose prosperity and health I prefer and desire more than mine own. And whereas I know your majesty's absence is never without great need, yet love and affection compel me to desire your presence.

Again, the same zeal and affection forceth me to be best content with that which is your will and pleasure. Thus love maketh me in all things to set apart mine own convenience and pleasure, and to embrace most joyfully his will and pleasure whom I love. God, the knower of secrets, can judge these words not to be written only with ink, but most truly expressed on the heart. Much more I omit, lest it be thought I go about to praise myself, or crave a thank; which thing to do I mind nothing less but a plain, simple relation of the love and zeal I bear your majesty, proceeding from the abundance of the heart. Wherin I must confess I desire no commendation, having such just occasion to do the same.

Even such confidence have I in your majesty's gentleness, knowing myself never to have done my duty as were requisite, and meet for such a noble prince, at whose hands I have found and received so much love and goodness, that with words I cannot express it.

Lest I should be too tedious to your majesty, I finish this my scribbled letter, committing you to the governance of the Lord with long and prosperous life here, and after this life to enjoy the kingdom of the elect.

From Greenwich, by your majesty's humble and obedient servant,

Kateryn the Queen, K.P.

Henry finds time to reply lovingly to his 'sweetheart', although rather busy with the storming of Boulogne.

7

THE KING'S RESPONSE

Henry VIII (1491–1547) to Katherine Parr.

Sept. 8, 1544

Most dearly and most entirely beloved wife, we recommend us heartily unto you, and thank you as well for your letter as for the venison which you sent and would have written unto you again a letter with our own hand, but that we be so occupied, and have so much to do in foreseeing and caring for everything ourself, as we have almost no manner rest or leisure to do any other thing.

We have won (and that without any loss of men) the strongest part of the town, which is the bray[7] of the castle – such a piece, and of such strength, as now that we have it in our hands we think 400 of our men within it shall be able to keep it against 4000 of our enemies, and yet it is much weaker to the castle side than it was outward to us.

At the closing up of these our letters the castle aforenamed, with the dyke, is at our commandment, and not like to be recovered by the Frenchmen again, as we trust, not doubting with God's grace but that the castle and town hall shall shortly follow the same trade, for we have three mines going besides one which hath done his execution in shaking and tearing off one of their greatest bulwarks.[8]

No more to you at this time, sweetheart, both for lack of time and great occupation with business, saving we pray you to give in our name our hearty blessings to all our children, and recommendations to our cousin Margaret and the rest of the ladies and gentlewomen, and to our Council also.

Written with the hand of your loving husband,[9]

Henry R.

---

7   Out-work.
8   Owing to the explosion of mines under the castle, the town was forced to surrender on the 14th, after a two-month siege.
9   This applies only to the postscript.

Some of the later English attitudes towards war appear in the century before the advent of Queen Elizabeth. The onslaught on France in the Hundred Years' War, for carnage and looting by a soldiery in high spirits led by their feudal lords, gave rise to sentiments echoed in later conflicts of pride as a nation at war. Hatred and contempt for the French could, conversely, turn into concern for the ill-prepared island sanctuary, arousing lingering invasion scares and spy-phobias. Above all a proud sea-faring people had found a natural outlet for martial defiance in piratical raids on the oceans which promised rich pickings.

T H R E E

Elizabeth I (1558–1603)

To arms my fellow soldiers! Sea and land
Lie open to the voyage you intend
GEORGE PEEL (*c.* 1558–97)

Elizabeth was a reluctant warrior queen: she regarded war as a stupid and wasteful calamity and, with machiavellian prevarication, struggled for twenty-seven years to keep an increasingly precarious peace. In the end she had to defend her crown and the national interest by supporting Dutch Protestant resistance to keep the invasion ports out of Spanish control. The war with Spain, waged without decisive purpose, dragged on for the last eighteen years of Elizabeth's reign and strained the resources of the country whose population of three and a half million was smaller than that of the United Provinces, less than half that of Spain and a quarter of that of France.

There was no royal standing army: home defence against rebellion and Scottish incursions was entrusted to militia conscripts among the yeomen farmers raised by the lord lieutenant in each shire. This self-reliant obligation to serve was felt to be part of liberty – a view which changed in the nineteenth century. Campaigns abroad were fought by professional soldiers who often proved to be undisciplined and mutinous: with the severance of feudal ties of loyalty to a liege lord, which had not yet been replaced by a firm bond with sovereign and state, men only enlisted reluctantly for lack of money to buy themselves off and often ran away at the first opportunity, especially as there was a constant shortage of funds for soldiers' pay and food.

Elizabeth's revenue, grudgingly accorded by her subjects who were much readier to give their lives than their money, was less than £300,000, which explains her parsimony and tolerance of piratry: Drake returned on the *Golden Hind* with more than a whole year's revenue, plundered in South America on a single voyage! He was also the founder of the English naval tradition, made possible by Henry VIII's creation of the Royal Navy for the fulfilment of England's new trading and naval aspirations and of Raleigh's prophetic vision of a colonial empire. The new royal dockyards of Woolwich and Deptford constructed, under Hawkins' direction, low-built manoeuvrable fighting ships with long-range culverins in the port-holes, from which 'broadsides' of concentrated firing power were dispatched – floating batteries, manned by sailors, which superseded the grappling tactics of 2,000 years of sea warfare by soldiers. Drake also broke down the feadalist class divisions ('I must have the gentlemen to hale and draw with the mariner') and this helped to raise the spirit of the Navy. Under its protection business could be carried on as usual at home in wartime, and the world was opened up for exploitation which shaped English character and history.

Prelude: '. . . any good wars'?

Adventurous young gentlemen, unlike soldiers, regarded war abroad as good sport – a view shared by Ensign Edmund Verney, fighting for the army of the states in Flanders in the 1630s, when he wrote home: 'We hear that you are likely to have war with France. Tis brave news. Twere sport for us to hear that all the world were in combustion, for then we could not want work. O tis a blessed trade!'[1]

The young Winston Churchill still took a similar attitude.

1

Robert Sidney (1563–1626) (later 2nd Earl of Leicester), aged seventeen, writes to his father, Sir Henry Sidney, from his continental tour.

Prag, 1st November 1580

My Duty most humbly remembered to your Lordship,

Yesterday I came hither, where I mean to stay a good part of the winter, and if I may, will learn to ride. My brother [Philip], in his last letter, put it to my choice, whether I would go next year into France or into Italy; I have chosen Italy, because it is not so far from hence, and afterwards into France; and so will do, if your Lordship shall think it good, and will give me leave. My brother likewise wrote that if there were any good wars I should go to them, but as yet I have heard of none. But before any such wars will be, I hope to hear further from your Lordship. . . .

Your Lordship's most humble and obedient son during life,
Robert Sidney

---

1   Camden Society, LVI (*Verney Papers*), p. 270.

The Campaign in the Netherlands against Spain (1586)

A famous fight in Flanders
Was foughten in the field . . .
Then courage, noble Englishmen,
And never be dismayed . . .
To fight with foreign enemies,
And set our nation free . . .

ANON. BALLAD: BRAVE LORD WILLOUGHBY

The assassination of William the Silent, the Spanish conquest of Antwerp and the seizure of English ships in Spanish harbours finally induced the Queen, after avoiding a decision for fifteen years, to send the anti-Spanish Earl of Leicester to the aid of the United Provinces. He went with a poorly trained and equipped expeditionary force of 5,000 foot-soldiers and 1,000 horsemen, hoping Philip II would come to terms.

Leicester got a triumphant reception with fireworks and banquets, and accepted the title of Governor and Captain General, contrary to the orders of a furious queen who had previously turned down the Dutch offer of sovereignty.

Due to the Queen's usual parsimony, and to dissension in her Council, the troops were kept short of funds[2] and supplies, and were justifiably discontented, on the grounds that irresponsible and corrupt captains were retaining their pay when it at last arrived; moreover, they either sent soldiers on dangerous missions, to augment their 'dead pay', or on plundering forays, to take their cut. Leicester himself, arrogant, quarrelsome, and lacking military experience and administrative skill, at once nearly doubled his own and the officers' pay, without ever sending any accounts to London. Hundreds of recruits ran away and a private who dared to ask Leicester to his face for his company's pay was rescued by them from being hanged.

2

'Our men run fast away'

Robert Dudley, Earl of Leicester (1533–88) tells Secretary of State Sir Francis Walsingham of his fears of 'foulest mutiny', owing to lack of pay for his troops.

---

2 Partly the fault of the Dutch who were always slow in paying those English troops who it had been agreed were their responsibility; so English funds had to be diverted to them.
3 Son-in-law, Sir Philip Sidney.

8 July [1586]

We have taken Axel, a town in Flanders, near Ternous. Your son Philip[3] with his bands had the leading and entering the town, which was notably handled, for they caused thirty or forty to swim over the ditch, and so get up the wall and opened the gate; yet, ere they could enter half their numbers, the soldiers were in arms, and came to resist our men, but they were overthrown, and most of them slain, being 600 as I hear, soldiers in that town, beside burghers. The Count Morrice[4] was there, and my Lord Willoughby,[5] and young Mr Hatton for his first nuseling.[6] God send we may hold it, victual is so hard to come by there; but all is done that can be possible.

I see we shall starve on every side. I hear now, that there is 10,000 pounds sent over by exchange, and other 10,000 in the midst of August; you wrote unto me that her Majesty had appointed 30,000 pounds to come over. It is no marvel our men run fast away. I am ashamed to write it, there was 500 ran away in two days, and a great many to the enemy.

There is of our runagates 200 brought again from the coast-side. Divers I hanged before the rest, and I assure you they could have been content all to have been hanged rather than tarry. Our old ragged rogues here hath so discouraged our new men as, I protest to you, they look like dead men. God once deliver me well of this charge, and I will hang too, if I take charge of men and not be sure of better pay aforehand. I assure you it will fret me to death ere long, to see my soldiers in this case, and cannot help them. I cry now, peace! peace! for never was there such a war, and a cause so slenderly countenanced; but God will help us I trust.

I will not now hold you longer; but, Mr Secretary, I tell you, if our people shall be no better relieved, by the Lord, I look for the foulest mutiny that ever was made, both of our men and these country soldiers, and I am sure I can do as much with them as ever any man could, and I do but wonder to see they do not rather kill us all than run away, God help us! . . .

The Queen seems fully aware of the defrauding of soldiers that went on in the Army and admonishes Leicester to see that they get what is due to them and to punish the guilty officers; but blinded by her affection, she does not suspect him personally and has long forgiven him for over-stepping his brief.

---

4 Maurice, Prince of Orange and Count of Nassau, succeeded his father as Stadhouder of the Netherlands.
5 Peregrine Bertie, the 'brave Lord Willoughby' of the ballad.
6 Christopher Hatton, one of Elizabeth's favourites, for his first nursing (earliest education).

3

'The poor soldier that hourly ventures life'

Elizabeth I (1533–1603) to the Earl of Leicester.

19 July 1586

Rob,

. . . If there be fault in using soldiers or making profit by them, let them hear of it without open shame and doubt not but I will chasten them therefor. It frets me not a little that the poor soldier that hourly ventures life should want their due, that well deserve rather reward: and look in whom the fault may duly be proved, let them smart therefor. And if the Treasurer be found untrue or negligent, according to desert he shall be used; though you know my old wont, that love not to discharge from office without desert; God forbid. . . .

Now will I end that do imagine I talk still with you, and therefore loathly say farewell, õ õ [two eyes – nickname for L.], though I ever pray God bless you from all harm and save you from all foes, with my million and legion of thanks for all your pains and cares. As you know, ever the same.

E.R.

As to dealing with a mutinous soldiery, Sir Henry Sidney, one of the ablest governors of Ireland, had shown a few years earlier how easily good leadership could restore their fighting spirit in face of the Irish rebels:

The private soldiers came to their officers, the officers to their captains, the captains to my councillors, and the councillors to me, and nothing in their mouths but home! home! home! or else we are all undone.

He summoned his troops to the market place and revived their courage with a speech supported by a tun of wine:

All my men's cowardish coldness was turned into martial-like heat, and nothing but 'Upon them, upon them! Lead you, and we will follow to the land's end or die by the way, and let us go by and by!' – 'Nay, soft, Sirs', quoth I, 'it is Sunday, and it is afternoon; we will go and hear evening prayer, sup and rest, and you shall be called, I warrant you, betimes in the morning, and so in the name of God we will advance forwards.' That evening and all the night there was nothing but singing, casting of bullets, drying of powder, filing of pikes.[7]

7   In Mona Wilson, *Sir Philip Sidney*, Duckworth, 1931, p. 298.

Manuscript illumination from a French version of the official Yorkist chronicle of the Battle of Barnet, 1471, sent by Edward IV to Charles the Bold of Burgundy. (*University Library, Ghent*)

VII ♣

The Spaniards dispatching
Messingers to the Prince of
Parma requiring him forthwith
to joyn himselfe with them.

III ♣

8 Fireships Sent by y English
Admirall towards y Spanish
Fleet in y Middle of y night
vnder the Conduct of Young
and Prowse.

II ♣

The Spaniards on sight of the
Fireships weighing Ancors
cutting Cables and betakeing
themselves to flight w a hide:
ouse noise & in great Confusion.

II ♦

The 2d Fight betweene y English
and Spanish Fleetes being the 23
of June 1588. wherein only Cock
an Englishman being w his litle
Vessell in y Midst of y Enemies died va:
liently. but y Spaniards much worsted.

King ♠

Drake and Fener w great
Violence set upon the Spanish
fleet gathering to gether
before Graveling.

VI ♠

More then halfe y Spanish

Fleet Taken and Sunck

VIII ♣

The third Fight betweene y Eng h
and Spanish Fleetes, being the
25 th of June 588. wherein the
English had again y better

V ♠

The Prince of Parma
coming to Dunkerk with his
Army but too late is received
by the Spaniards with reproach

X ♠

The Spaniards Consulting ~
and at last resolving to return
into Spain by the north Ocean
many of their Shipps being disabled

The Spanish Armada, 1588, from *Playing Cards of Various Ages and Countries* by C. Schreiber and A.W. Franks. (*Bodleian Library, Oxford*)

Leicester bungled the campaign despite some heroic exploits led by the bravest of his officers who knew how to rally their men: in the attempt to storm the fort of Zutphen, 500 English horsemen twice charged 3,000 Spanish cavalry under the walls.

4

A BRAVE LIEUTENANT

Leicester describes to Sir Francis Walsingham a gallant assault on a fort at Zutphen.

6 October [1586]

I thank God he hath given us this day a very happy sucess of the two principal forts here. We have taken one by a gallant and a thorough-fought assault, and for a quarter of an hour we did look for a very furious resistance, yet so it pleased God to daunt their hearts, and to animate those worthy soldiers who attempted it, as it was entered, and the enemy, as many as did abide, killed, the rest fled to the other fort.

There was one gentleman whom we all present did behold, that had the leading of all the rest that went to the assault, which was Mr Edward Stanley, Lieutenant to Sir William Stanley.[8] Since I was born I did never see any man to behave himself as he did. First climb the breach, a pike-length before and above any person that followed him, so did he alone maintain the fight, first with his pike, and afterward his sword, against at the least nine or ten, and every man either brake his pike upon his breast, or hit him with the shot of their musket, yet would he not back a foot, but kept himself in this sort without any one man to get up to him; we all gave him for lost if he had a hundred lives.

When he had long thus dealt most valiently and worthily, and none of his company easily could come to him, at length they all came so fast together as one bare up another even to the top of the breach, where that gentleman got a halberd and leapt among the enemies, and then the rest with him, in so resolute manner as they speedily despatched the enemy, and in the sight of all the town both placed their ensigns and made this fight. . . . This gentleman shall I never forget if I live a hundred year, for so worthily he did by God's goodness, as he was the chief cause of all the honour of this day, and he shall have part of my living for it as long as he lives.[9]

Also at Zutphen, Leicester's nephew, Sir Philip Sidney – soldier, statesman, poet, and 'the perfect gentleman' – was struck by a bullet in the thigh;

---

8 Sir William, Edward Stanley's father, was a typical adventurer of the time: he first fought for the Duke of Alva, then for fifteen years against the Irish rebels (although he was a Catholic); he was involved in the Babington plot against the Queen, and, like his son, showed great courage at Zutphen, but turned traitor soon after, surrendering Deventer to the Spaniards.

9 For this exploit, Leicester knighted Edward Stanley in the trenches, gave him £40 in gold and a patent of 100 marks annual pension out of his own pocket.

nursed by his wife, in advanced pregnancy, he died after twenty-six days of suffering cheerfully borne, keeping his sense of humour to the last by writing a poem on 'La cuisse rompue' and setting it to music.

5

'Thy necessity is greater than mine'

The poet and court favourite Sir Fulke Greville (1554–1628) tells of the heroism of his friend Sir Philip Sidney before he died of his wounds.

[October 1586]
When that unfortunate stand was to be made before Zutphen to stop the issuing out of the Spanish Army from a streict,[10] with what alacrity soever he went to actions of honour . . . the weather being misty, fell unawares upon the enemy, who had made a strong stand to receive them, near to the very walls of Zutphen, their muskets layed in ambush within their own trenches. . . .

An unfortunate hand brake the bone of Sir Philip's thigh with a musket shot. The horse he rode upon, was rather furiously choleric than bravely proud, and so forced him to forsake the field, and being thirsty with excess of bleeding, he called for drink, which was presently brought him; but as he was putting the bottle to his mouth, he saw a poor soldier carried along, who had eaten his last at the same Feast, ghastly casting up his eyes at the bottle. Which Sir Philip perceiving, took it from his head, before he drank, and delivered it to the poor man, with these words, Thy necessity is greater than mine. And when he had pledged this poor soldier, he was presently carried to Arnheim, where the principle Chirurgeons of the Camp attended for him. . . .

The Navy Tackles the 'Invincible Armada' (1588)

> Though cruel Spain and Parma
> With heathen legions come,
> O God! arise and arm us,
> We die for our home!
> JOHN STILL (1542–1607)

> So by a roaring tempest on the flood,
> The whole armado of connected sail
> Is scattered
> SHAKESPEARE, KING JOHN

Philip II hesitated for many years before embarking on war on a grand scale against Elizabeth's regime; in 1587 he was at last getting ready. However,

---

10   Obs. for strait.

Drake's devastating raid 'to impeach the gathering of the Spanish fleet' postponed the assembly of the Armada for another year. His four swift galleons put Don Pedro de Acuña's eight galleys to flight, as, being low in the water, they were more exposed to gunfire; then, despite covering fire from the shore batteries, Drake burnt about thirty of the finest Spanish ships, lying unready for action at Cádiz. Medina-Sidonia's swift arrival with 3,000 foot soldiers and 300 horsemen rescued Cádiz from being sacked, but Drake had captured the *San Felipe* with £114,000 in gold, jewellery, china, silk and spice, of which he passed £40,000 to the Queen (enough to furnish an army) and kept £17,000 for himself. Acuña sent him wine and sweetmeats with his congratulations, they exchanged prisoners, and Drake was off again.

Like Philip, Drake trusted in God's support for his cause; here he expresses his belief in the effectiveness of prayer.

6

SINGEING THE SPANISH KING'S BEARD

Sir Francis Drake (*c.* 1540–96) tells his 'very loving friend Mr John Foxe, preacher'[11] about his raid on Cádiz and asks for prayers.

> From aboard Her Majesty's good ship the *Elizabeth-Bonaventure*
> in very great haste this 27 of April, 1587

Mr Foxe,

Whereas we have had of late such happy sucess against the Spaniards, I do assure myself that you have faithfully remembered us in your good prayers, and therefore I have not forgotten briefly to make you partaker of the sum thereof.

The 19th of April we arrived within Cales [Cádiz] Road, where we found much shipping; but, among the rest, thirty two ships of exceeding great burthen, laden, and to be laden, with provision and prepared to furnish the King's Navy, intended with all speed against England; the which, when we had boarded and thereout furnished our ships with such provision as we thought sufficient, we burned; and, although for the space of two days and nights that we continued there we were still endangered, both with thundering shot from the town, and assaulted with the roaring canons of twelve galleys, we yet sunk two of them and one great argosy,[12] and still avoided them with very small hurt; so that at our departure we brought away four ships of provision, to the great terror of our enemies and honour to ourselves, as it might appear by a most courteous letter, written and sent to me with a flag of truce by Don Pedro, general of the galleys.

But whereas it is most certain that the King doth not only make speedy preparation in Spain, but likewise expecteth a very great fleet from the Straits and divers other places to join with his forces to invade England, we purpose to set apart all fear of

---

11   Author of the *Book of Martyrs*; he died before receiving this letter.
12   A 700 ton Genoese Levanter, armed wtih forty cannon.

danger, and by God's furtherance to proceed by all good means that we can devise to prevent their coming; wherefore I shall desire you to continue a faithful remembrancer of us in your prayers, that our present service may take that good effect as God may be glorified, his church, our Queen and country preserved, and the enemy of the truth utterly vanquished, that we may have continual peace in Israel.

Your loving friend, and faithful son in Christ Jesus,
FRANCIS DRAKE

A year later, the Armada, consisting of 130 ships (half of them for transport and stores only) with 19,000 soldiers and 7,000 sailors – oars replaced by sails, and mounting a superior number of heavy, short-range guns – was ready to sail under the reluctant commander, the Duke of Medina-Sidonia from Castile, who had no experience of sea warfare. His orders were to make contact with, and escort, the barges and transports of the Duke of Parma's invasion army of 16,000 seasoned troops, from Dunkirk across the Channel to Margate, whence they would march to London.

The intelligence service was on the alert.

7

'Lyghtnynge and Thunder clapp wilbe'

An English spy sent to Madrid, writes to his Government about the preparations of the Armada.

Madrid, 28 May 1588

My laste was owte of this towne of the laste of Aprill whiche I sent by waye of Italie, I havinge better commodytie for the place and tyme, whiche, presently, is full souspitious. This do I sende by the waye of Lion, whiche perhappes maye arryve before the other. My Jorney into Portugall, and the money I lefte to one there, coste me mutche, as in my former I wrote; synce whiche I have had more particular advises as herin I send yow. And althoughe I judge this Navie (nowe in a redynes under the castell of Belem expectinge wynde to sett sayle) maye be in your quarters before these come to your handes, yett woulde I omyt no occasion to wryte, seyenge that were heretofore I was in the number of the incredulous, yet nowe beinge in place where I maye here and see, I confes to be in the wronge; for nowe I am owte of dowte they will in very dede that waye: so that the Lyghtnynge and Thunder clapp wilbe bothe in a moment.

From Dunkerke is lately come to Lisbone a smale shipp with good spede, having passed in vij daies; she bringethe from the Duke of Parma certayne pilottes for the conducte of this Armye, and sayethe that upon all the couste of our lande she never sawe one sayle, and further awowethe that the saide Duke mutche slocytethe[13] the departure of the Armata. . . .

---

13   Sollicitates.

Here in this towne and countrey are grete prayers, processions, fastinges, and almes, for the happy success of this Armata. . . .

Yours to use,
B.C.

Four weeks before the Armada appeared off the Lizard, the Lord High Admiral, Charles Howard, was trying to rouse the Queen, who was still secretly negotiating with Parma (deceiving her on Philip's order), to the country's danger, and particularly to the 'villainous treasons' round her: he feared she might be assassinated. Fighting *for* queen and country was not yet a general patriotic conviction; rather, it was personal and national pride that stimulated the fighting spirit *against* the hated foreigner whether he was a merchantman to be robbed on the high seas or a galleon to be kept out of the Channel. There were even English troops in Parma's invasion army, commanded by noblemen, and English pilots steered the Armada through the Channel.

8

'For the love of Jesus Christ, Madam, awake'

Charles, Lord Howard of Effingham (1536–1624) to the Queen.

From aboard the *Ark*, ready to weigh [23 June 1588]
May it please your most excellent Majesty,

We have often put to the sea, and have been fain to run off and on the Sleeve[14] with contrary winds. . . .

It is very likely that this stormy weather hath parted the fleet. I hope in God we shall meet with them on the coast of France, for I have some intelligence that for certain they mean to come thither, and there to receive many Frenchmen into their ships.

For the love of Jesus Christ, Madam, awake thoroughly, and see the villainous treasons round about you, against your Majesty and your realm, and draw your forces round about you, like a mightly prince, to defend you. Truly, Madam, if you do so, there is no cause to fear. If you do not, there will be danger. . . .

I am now in haste, and long to set sail. I beseech the Almighty God to bless and defend your Majesty from all your enemies, and so I do most humbly take my leave.

The sea battle in the Channel from 21 to 27 July and the action at Gravelines on 28–9 July are shrouded in legend. The Armada was *not* superior to the English fleet: there were 197 English ships against 130 Spanish, with

---

14 The Chops of the Channel – the sea between Ushant and Scilly – always called 'Sleeve' by Howard after the French 'Manche'.

two and a half times the number of sailors, though their tonnage was roughly equal; the low-built English galleons were swifter and more manoeuvrable and, because of their length, could mount more long-range guns with
high muzzle velocity, but the Spanish ships were more heavily armed with
short-range guns; the Spanish seamen were equally brave but their leaders
quite rightly relied on tight formation discipline rather than daring free
attack, as their purpose was to act as escort for the invasion army and not to
fight sea battles; the wind gave the navy the weather-gauge for nine days but
their line-ahead tactics were unable to disrupt the impenetrable defensive
wall of the crescent; and the Armada was finally not scattered just by the
wind ('God breathed and they were scattered') – their gear was shot to
pieces when they were at the mercy of the navy, after squandering their
100,000 shot without result and unable to refurbish themselves.

The failure of the Armada was due to Philip's meticulous but unrealistic
planning and to his rigid orders from the remoteness of the Escorial: it was
precluded from attacking a port, and effecting a landing and anchorage,
essential for its maintenance. Above all, the junction with Parma was never a
practical possibility, although he had built canals for his 70 landing craft and
200 flat-bottomed barges, to pass from the Scheldt to Dunkirk without venturing out into the open sea: Justinus of Nassau kept him blockaded with his
light draught ships in the shallow waters of the West Scheldt and at Dunkirk
– inaccessible to the Armada – and, for extra safety, as Elizabeth did not trust
her Dutch allies, Lord Henry Seymour's squadron was keeping a relentless
watch outside. Philip had fatally disregarded Parma's advice to wait till he
had taken the deep-water port of Flushing, and Parma was not quite ready
anyway, while Medina-Sidonia was under the impression he had enough
fly-boats at his disposal.

So the majestic Armada sailed slowly (at two miles per hour) through the
Channel towards Calais, keeping its tight formation despite all attacks from
the inaccurate English long-range guns which could not penetrate the hulls
but battered masts and sails, while the navy would not be lured within range
of the Spanish 50 pounders.

At Gravelines, eight fire-ships, laden with blazing pitch and their guns
exploding when they got near, struck terror among the Armada and at last
succeeded in breaking it up in the gale: now the navy was able to close in
and wreak havoc, as the Armada had run out of ammunition. By the time the
navy had spent theirs too, four Spanish ships had been lost. A shift of the
wind to the south-west allowed the Armada to escape to the North Sea, pursued by Howard right up to the Firth of Forth. The storms did the rest and
fifty-one crippled Spanish ships perished on the Scottish coasts, where some
of the crews were massacred, and on the Irish coasts, where Lord Deputy
FitzWilliam executed 1,100 survivors. Medina-Sidonia succeeded, however,
in getting well over half the Armada safely back to Santander, with a third of
his men.

Lord Howard was later criticized for lagging behind the attack at Calais in his flagship, the *Ark*, and for not allowing the fleet to close in earlier, but it is clear from the next letter that he always acted wisely. The requirement of shot and powder had been underestimated by both sides.

9

THE BATTLE OF GRAVELINES

Captain Henry Whyte describes to Sir Francis Walsingham how the Armada was put to flight and how parsimony robbed the navy of the 'famousest victory'; he sacrificed his bark *Talbot* as a fire-ship and now goes 'a-begging'.

Margate, 8th August, 1588

My duty most humbly remembered:

If it seem unto your Honour that I have been slack in this duty, impute it, I beseech you, to the long sickness and indisposition that haunted me. When we heard of the arrival of the Spanish forces by sea upon the coast, weak as I was, I embarked myself to wait upon my Lord Admiral, who with all diligence addressed himself to go meet them; which the second day after he put from Plymouth he did.

The majesty of the enemy's fleet, the good order they held, and the private consideration of our own wants did cause, in mine opinion, our first onset to be more coldly done than became the value of our nation and the credit of the English navy; yet we put them to leeward, kept the weather of them, and distressed two of their best ships, whereof Don Pedro's was one. After that, our fleet increased daily; and as men and munition came, we plied them every day with more courage than other, until they came to an anchor before Calais, as your Honour may have heard. There it was devised to put them from their anchor, and seven ships were allotted to the fire to perform the enterprise; among the rest, the ship I had in charge, the Bark *Talbot*, was one; so that now I rest like one that had his house burnt, and one of these days I must come to your Honour for a commission to go a-begging.

Sunday, the 28th of July, at night, about one of the clock, the enterprise was undertaken, which took good effect, though not so good as was expected; for it drove two of their galleasses to be foul one of the other, so that the one plucked away the other's rudder, which afterwards drove into Calais haven aground upon the sands. The next morning, by the dawning, we found all the fleet put from their anchors, with the loss, by report of some of them that were afterwards taken, of 100 or 120 anchors and cables. Part of our fleet made haste to overtake the enemy; my Lord Admiral, with another part, lingered a space, to see what would become of those he sent to attempt the galleon.

As soon as we that pursued the fleet were come up within musket shot of them, the fight began very hotly. Myself was aboard the *Mary Rose* of the Queen's, with Captain Fenton, whose value for that day's service deserved praise. We had not fought above three hours but my Lord Admiral with the rest of the fleet came up, and gave a very fresh onset, which continued amongst us some six hours more; and truly, sir, if we had shot and powder sufficient to have given them two such heats more, we had utterly distressed them.

The next day it was decreed the Narrow Seas fleet should go back; and my Lord Admiral with the rest pursued the enemy, that fled before us with all the sail they could make, until he had brought them up well nigh as high as Berwick, having weakened their fleet, first and last, to our judgement of about twenty sail; so there rested of them whole, when we parted, to the number of fourscore sail, and all at liberty, if wind and weather hinder not, to practise in Scotland and attempt Ireland, if so they resolve not to return again this way, if weather serve as now it doth.

By this my simple relation, your Honour may see how our parsimony at home hath bereaved us of the famousest victory that ever our navy might have had at sea. . . .

The capture of Don Hugo de Moncada's great galleass, *San Lorenzo*, with eight hundred prisoners, by a mere one hundred sailors under Captain Amyas Preston in long-boats and pinnaces, was a daring feat of great bravery.

10

HOW THE GREAT GALLEASS WAS CAPTURED

Richard Thomson to Walsingham.

[n.d.]

At the break of day [29 July], my Lord and all the fleet setting sail after our enemies, we espied riding within shot of the town of Calais the greatest of the King's galleasses, the rest of the Spanish fleet being two leagues to leeward of her. My Lord Admiral began to go toward the galleass with his ship, the *Ark*, but finding the water to be shallow, other ships of less draught bare in with her and shot at her; whereupon she let slip and run the galleass aground hard before the town.

In our ship, which was the *Margaret and John of London*, we approached so near that we came on ground also; but afterwards came safely off again with the flood, being damaged by nothing but by the town of Calais, who, off the bulwarks, shot very much at us, and shot our ship twice through. And the like powder and shot did Monsieur Gourdan [Governor of Calais] bestow upon our countrymen, and make us relinquish the galleass which otherwise we had brought away to the great credit of our country, if Monsieur Gourdan herein had not showed his affection to the Spaniards to be greater than our nation, or seemed by force to wrest from us that which we had gotten with bloody heads.

My Lord Admiral, seeing he could not approach the galleass with his ship, sent off his long boat unto her with 50 or 60 men, amongst whom were many gentlemen as valiant in courage as gentle in birth, as they well showed. The like did our ship send off her pinnace, with certain musketeers, amongst whom myself went. These two boards came hard under the galleass sides, being aground; where we continued a pretty skirmish with our small shot against theirs, they being ensconced within their ship and very high over us, we in our open pinnaces and far under them, having to shroud and cover us; they being 300 soldiers, besides 450 slaves, and we not, at the instant, 100 persons.

Within one half hour it pleased God, by killing the captain with a musket shot, to give us victory above all hope or expectation; for the soldiers leaped overboard by heaps on the other side, and fled with the shore, swimming and wading. Some escaped with being wet; some, and that very many, were drowned. The captain of her was called Don Hugo de Moncada, son to the viceroy of Valencia. He being slain, and the most part of their soldiers fled, some few soldiers remaining in her, seeing our English boats under her sides and more of ours coming rowing towards her, put up two handkerchiefs upon two rapiers, signifying that they desired a truce. Hereupon we entered, with much difficulty, by reason of her height over us, and possessed us of her, each man seeking his benefit of pillage until the flood came that we might haul her off the ground and bring her away. . . .

During the Channel battle, Drake, always looking out for loot, searched the *Nuestra Señora del Rosario* he had captured for treasure, instead of keeping up with the action. He took Don Pedro de Valdés prisoner and handed him over to the Queen who confined him to a country house near London where he spent three years with hunting and parties, before being ransomed for £3000.

Even after the dispersal of the Armada, Parma's invasion army was still expected hourly. This caused Elizabeth to drive to Tilbury where four thousand soldiers under Essex and one thousand militia under Leicester had been hastily assembled – hardly a match for thirty-five thousand of the best soldiers in Europe! In her famous speech, the Queen succeeded in rousing their spirits by pledging with Shakespearian rhetoric: 'Resolved to live or die amongst you all . . . I myself will take up arms, I myself will be your general.'

11

THE SPANISH COMMANDER WILL WISH HIMSELF BACK AMONG HIS ORANGE TREES

Sir Francis Drake, still hoping to 'wrestle a pull' with the Duke of Parma, sends prisoners to Walsingham.

This last of July, 1588

I am commanded to send these prisoners ashore by my Lord Admiral. Let me beseech your Honour that they may be presented unto her Majesty. The one Don Pedro is a man of greatest estimation with the King of Spain, and thought next in his army to the Duke of Sidonia.[15]

We have the army of Spain before us and mind, with the grace of God, to wrestle a pull with him. There was never anything pleased me better than the seeing the enemy flying with a southerly wind to the northwards. God grant you have a good eye to the Duke of Parma; for with the grace of God, if we live, I doubt it not but ere it

15 Don Pedro de Valdés commanded the Andalusian squadron; Drake mixes him up with his cousin Diego Flores de Valdés who commanded the Castilian squadron in Medina–Sidonia's flagship *San Martin* as his chief of staff.

be long so to handle the matter with the Duke of Sidonia as he shall wish himself at St Mary Port among his orange trees.

God give us grace to depend upon him; so shall we not doubt victory, for our cause is good. . . .

The navy lost not a single ship in the nine days' running battle and less than one hundred sailors; but three thousand died subsequently of food poisoning. Lack of proper food was always the bane of the Elizabethan navy but the accusation that Elizabeth deliberately starved her fleet of victuals and ammunition cannot be upheld, although she hated war above all for the money it cost. She certainly did not seem to be much concerned that thousands of the sailors who had saved her realm should die of typhus, fever and scurvy, induced by the squalor of their overcrowded quarters and their diet of putrid salted beef and fish, maggoty biscuits and sour beer.

Not knowing the Armada's fate, the High Admiral warns that the danger is not yet over and asks urgently for victuals and munitions of which they are 'in great want' to be able to keep up their patrol.

12

'. . . or else we shall starve'

Lord Howard reminds Walsingham that 'security is dangerous', pleads for victuals and derides Spanish victory reports.

Margate road, the 8th August

Sir,

I bare with some of the ships into Margate road; where the rest be gone I do not know, for we had a most violent storm as ever was seen at this time of the year, that put us asunder athwart of Norfolk, amongst many ill-favoured sands; but I trust they do all well, and I hope I shall hear of them this night or to-morrow.

I pray to God we may hear of Victuals, for we are generally in great want; and also that I may know how the coast ships of the west shall be victualled; and also that order be taken for the victualling and for munition for the ships of London. I know not what you think of it at the Court, but I do think, and so doth all here, that there cannot be too great forces maintained yet for five or six weeks, on the seas; for although we have put the Spanish fleet past the Firth, and I think past the Isles, yet God knoweth whether they go either to the Nase of Norway or into Denmark or to the Isles of Orkney to refresh themselves, and so to return; for I think they dare not return with this dishonour and shame to their King, and overthrow of their Pope's credit.

Sir, sure bind, sure find. A kingdom is a great wager. Sir, you know security is dangerous; and God had not been our best friend, we should have found it so. Some made little account of the Spanish force by sea; but I do warrant you, all the world never saw such a force as theirs was; and some Spaniards that we have taken, that were in the fight at Lepanto,[16] do say that the worst of our four fights that we have had with them did exceed far the fight they had there; and they say that at some of our fights we had twenty times as much great shot there plied as they had there. Sir, I pray to God that we may be all thankful to God for it; and that it may be done by some order, that the world may know we are thankful to him for it.

Sir, I pray you let me hear what the duke of Parma doth, with some speed; and where his forces by sea are.

Sir, in your next letters to my brother Stafford I pray write to him that he will let Mendoza[17] know that her Majesty's rotten ships dare meet with his master's sound ships; and in buffeting with them, though they were three great ships to one of us, yet we have shortened them sixteen or seventeen; whereof there is three of them a-fishing in the bottom of the seas. God be thanked of all.

Sir, being in haste and much occupied, I bid you most heartily farewell.

Your most assured loving friend,
C. Howard

Sir, if I hear nothing of my victuals and munition this night here, I will gallop to Dover to see what may be there, or else we shall starve.

This gun battle between sailing fleets in which the English line-ahead tactics had, until Gravelines, been frustrated by the Armada's tight line-abreast strategy, was the prototype for more than two centuries' naval encounters, right up to Trafalgar.[18]

Elizabeth and Essex

Made proud by princes that advance their pride
Against that power that bred . . .

Possessed he is with greatness,
. . . imagined worth
Hold in his blood such swoln and hot discourse
SHAKESPEARE, JULIUS CAESAR AND TROILUS AND CRESSIDA

In 1591, Elizabeth sent her great favourite, the twenty-six-year-old handsome and hot-headed Earl of Essex, idol of the army with a strong popular following, to

---

16 The bloodiest naval battle of the century in which Philip's brother Don Juan of Austria, commanding the fleet of the Christian League, defeated the Turks in 1571.

17 Don Bernardino de Mendoza, Spanish ambassador in London, was expelled in 1584 for his involvement in the Throckmorton plot in favour of Mary Queen of Scots. An ambassador in Paris, he publicized a report he had received from Calais that the English fleet had been utterly defeated: a translation under the title of 'A pack of Spanish lies' caused great indignation in England.

18 For up-to-date evaluation of documentary evidence from English as well as Spanish sources, I am indebted to G. Mattingly, *The Defeat of the Spanish Armada*, J. Cape, 1959. C. Martin and G. Parker, P. Kemp, and D. Hart-Davis in their quarter-centenary books of 1988, also agree that the Armada failed for logistical and tactical reasons.

help the Huguenot Henry IV with four thousand men to wrest Rouen from the Catholic League. After entreating Elizabeth on his knees to entrust him the command of the expedition, he now immediately complains about being away from her. His flattery sounds exaggerated, but was, in the style of the period, perhaps more genuine than it seems to us now; in any case, the Queen loved adulation.

13

'The misery of absence'

Robert Devereux, 2nd Earl of Essex (1566–1601) tells the Queen how much he misses her.

[Before Rouen, August 1591]

Most dear Lady,

I must not let this second day pass without complaining to your Majesty of the misery of absence. I shall think my life very unpleasant till I have rid myself of this French action, that I may once again enjoy the honour, the pleasure, the sweetness which your presence is accompanied with. . . . I hope your Majesty shall presently have great honor by the service of your little troop; and I, as a reward of my service, to be soon at home at your Majesty's feet, whence nothing but death, or your inconstancy . . . can drive me. Nothing be it heard or seen that your Majesty be less than the greatest, the healthfullest, or the happiest, or other than a most gracious kind lady to your Majesty's humblest, faithfullest, and most affectionate servant,

R. Essex

Instead of getting on with the siege despite his lack of artillery, Essex indulged in displays of useless knightly chivalry, treating war as a romantic field sport; while he went falconing in enemy country or rode one hundred miles to Compiègne to show off his jewel-studded attire to Henry IV, his force was melting away through desertion. The Governor of Rouen turned down his personal challenge as incompatible with his office. Furious at Essex's inaction, Elizabeth ordered him home a month later and Rouen was relieved by Parma.

14

'My mistress is fairer than yours'

The Earl of Essex challenges Monsieur Villiers, Governor of Rouen.

[December 1591]

Having received a message from you by the trumpet of Mons. Jerponville that Chevalier Picart was ready to fight with me according to a challenge I had sent unto him, I answer that I sent Chevalier Picart this message by my drum upon my first arrival in France, that, saving the cause, I was his friend, having known him heretofore with Mons. Marchemont in England; but in this cause I would be glad to find him in the head of his troop with a pike in his hand. This I was ready the first day of our sitting down to have made good, not on foot, but on horseback, with my sword, where they that came up the hill saw me twice at the head of my troop: and as for your offer to make a match for me, I answer that I command an army wherein are many of Chevalier Picart's quality, and am lent to an absolute prince but if yourself will fight on horseback, or on foot, armed or in doublet, I will maintain that the King's quarrel is juster than the League's, that I am a better man than yourself and that my mistress is fairer than yours; and if you will not come alone I will bring twenty, the worst shall be a fit match for a Colonel, the meanest being a captain.

Five years after the Rouen fiasco, Elizabeth wanted to send Essex to relieve Calais. It was besieged by a Spanish army from Flanders and she could hear its bombardment of the city as she wrote the next letter, full of caution and affection. Calais fell the next day and Essex never left.[19]

15

'God cover you under His safest wings'

Elizabeth I to the Earl of Essex.

From the *Due Repulse*, where this day I have been, April 14, 1596
As distant as I am from your abode, yet my ears serve me too well to hear that terrible battery that methinks sounds for relief at my hands; wherefore rather than for lack of timely aid it should be wholly lost, go you on, in God's Blessed Name, as far as that place where you may soonest relieve it, with as much caution as so great a trust requires. But I charge you, without the mere loss of it, do in no wise peril so fair an army for another Prince's town. God cover you under His safest wings, and let all peril go without your compass. . . .

No Respite from War

> Let us be back'd with God and with the seas,
> Which he hath given for fence impregnable . . .
> In him and in ourselves our safety lies . . .
> Go levy men, and make prepare for war;
> They are already, or quickly will be landed . . .
> SHAKESPEARE, HENRY VI, PART III

---

19   Calais was taken by Edward III in 1347 and remained English for over two centuries. The Duc de Guise recovered it in 1557 but Elizabeth had thoughts of reconquering it; the Spaniards held it from 1596–8.

The epic last fight of the *Revenge*, the prototype of Hawkins' fast galleons and Drake's flagship against the Armada, was immortalized by Tennyson after Sir Walter Raleigh's account. Lord Thomas Howard, anchored off Flores Island in the Azores with six ships of the line, most of whose crews were sick, was surprised by Alonso de Bazan's twenty new escort vessels for the treasure fleet, and gave orders to retreat as quickly as possible. Sir Richard Grenville, captain of the *Revenge* and Howard's second in command, bravely but foolishly defied the Spanish fleet and got cut off: for fifteen hours his one hundred sailors held out against gun attacks from fifteen ships, sinking four of them, and assaults from fifteen thousand soldiers, killing two thousand of them. Grenville, though mortally wounded, wanted to split and sink his wrecked ship but the survivors, all wounded or sick, finally surrendered. Soon after, the Spanish fleet was damaged by violent gales which the English prisoners attributed to Grenville having sunk straight down to hell, raising all the devils to take his revenge.

One of the crew, first happy at sea and later miserable in prison, desperately appeals for ransom.

16

A SOLDIER ON THE LITTLE REVENGE: IN LOVE WITH THE SEA – ALMOST AS MUCH AS WITH HIS MISTRESS

Philip Gawdy writes affectionately to his brother shortly before the famous action.

> From aboard her Majesty's good ship the *Revenge*, 6th of July [1591]
> My sweetest and best beloved Brother,

The time hasteth and the Captain is ready to set sail. We stay and pray every day heartily for the Spanish fleet's coming. Since my last writing we have had some adventures. We watered at Flowers [Flores]. And I saw the dolphin course the flying fish whereof I saw one fly as far as young partridges will do at the first flight. I thank God we have good ships with us both of her Majesty's and otherwise. I never had my health better in my life thanks be to God. I like the sea and the sea life, and the company at sea, as well as any that ever I lived withal. The place is good and healthful to a willing mind.

Though there be some storms endured at sea, yet the end is honourable, and sweet, and pleasing to any that taketh the course, with which life I am greatly in love, almost as much as with my Mistress.

Commend me to thine own heart and most loving thoughts, and think sometime of him that daily museth, and nightly dreameth of thy well-doing. . . .

17

PRISONER IN THE CASTLE OF LISBON

Gawdy writes a diplomatic letter to his brother after the *Revenge* had been taken by the Spaniards, longing to be ransomed.

From the Castle of Lisbon, 9th of February [1592]

Good Brother,

The fortunes of wars have ever been doubtful and uncertain. For the place I now remain in was ever far unlooked for at my hands, and though I well know your estate to be very mean, and far unable to do me any good, yet in love I could not choose but write to you. . . .

Always my liberty was promised as the rest of our ship had, and when I expected the same and went for my pass I was sent to the Castle of Lyshborne [Lisbon] though they had sent others of the same ship far better than myself home for England. I have endured much sickness in this country, I thank God at this instant somewhat recovered. I am reported to be the son of the chief judge of London, or else of my Lord Mayor of London, or else of some other noble house. The untruth thereof is best known to yourself, our father being a poor man. They request a captain called Diogio Daller for me, whosoever best knoweth me will think it an unreasonable demand.

I was without any office in the ship and I hope that her Majesty will not be unwilling to further the cause of a poor man every way unable to help himself. I doubt not but that the God of Heaven will be merciful to me in whom is my only trust and that he will grant us a happy meeting, the sooner the better.

Your loving Brother and now a poor prisoner,

Ph. Gavdy[20]

The last years of Elizabeth's reign were full of anxiety and worry: poor harvests caused inflation, famine and riots, and opposition to the drafting of men for foreign wars. However, the danger of invasion became acute time and again, as Philip persisted in using his Western treasure for naval rearmament. The Spanish fleet had learnt how to repel English raids and Drake had shot his bolt: he and Hawkins, after quarrelling violently, both died during their unsuccessful expedition to the West Indies in 1595. A month earlier, the Spaniards had again dared to send small landing parties to Cornwall, burning Penzance.

---

20 Philip Gawdy was released by the Spaniards thanks to the Dutch merchant Lucas Phelip, who remained bound for him at Lisbon, on condition that he either returned a prisoner called Mathias de Frias in Raleigh's custody (who wanted £500 for him which was quite beyond Gawdy's means) or paid his ransom. When nine months later he had done neither, the Dutchman was imprisoned in his place, until Gawdy managed to raise the money.

18

A SPANISH RAID ON CORNWALL

Sir Nicholas Clifford reports to the Earl of Essex.

July 26th [1595]

My lord,

According to Sir Fr.Drake and Sir John Hawkins desire I have been with Sir Fr. Godolphyn in Cornwall, where, before our coming, the Spaniards, out of four galleys, had landed some 400 soldiers, which burnt Moldsey, a small village, and Newland, with Penzance, a very good town. For the town of Penzance, had the people stood with Sir Fr. Godolphyn, who engaged himself very worthily, it had been saved, but the common sort utterly forsook him, saving some four or five gentlemen. Further, it is reported, by prisoners whom they set ashore, that for want of fresh water, they would have landed again, with some 500 of Don Juan's best soldiers; but the wind shifting north they took the opportunity to avoid the fleet at Plymouth and retired. Had they landed again, the writer would have accompanied Godolphyn either to have buried them or ourselves.

The Queen wrote personally to comfort Lady Norris,[21] with a mixture of regal stylishness and afffectionate sympathy, whenever one of her six soldier sons was either killed or wounded. The mother responded with joyful acceptance of sacrifice in the Queen's service – she lost four sons in the Irish rebellion. Her eldest son, Sir John Norris, was one of the ablest military commanders but not politic enough to avoid quarrelling with people less competent but more powerful than himself; he died on active service in Ireland, of gangrene from his old wounds brought about, it was said, by a broken heart over what he felt was the Queen's disregard of his long, devoted service.

21 Lady Norris was the daughter of John Lord Williams who had treated Elizabeth kindly when he guarded her during her imprisonment at Woodstock in Queen Mary's reign and invited her frequently to his house at Rycote, Oxfordshire. Her husband, Sir Henry (later Baron) Norris, was the son of the Henry Norris who as alleged lover of Elizabeth's mother, Queen Anne Boleyn, had been executed in 1536. Elizabeth remained devoted to the family and addressed Lady Norris affectionately as her 'black crow' because of her dark complexion.

19

A SOVEREIGN'S SYMPATHY

Elizabeth I condoles with Marjorie, Lady Norris on the death of her son, Sir John Norris.

Given at our Manor of Richmond, the 22nd of September 1597

Mine own Crow,

Harm not thyself for bootless help; but show a good example to comfort your dolorous yokefellow.

Although we have deferred long to represent unto you our grieved thoughts, because we liked full ill to yield you the first reflection of misfortune, whom we have always sought to cherish and comfort; yet, knowing now that necessity must bring it to your ears, and nature consequently must move both grief and passions in your heart, we resolved no longer to smother either our care for your sorrow, or the sympathy of our grief for his love, wherin, if it be true that society in sorrow works diminution, we do assure you, by this true messenger of our mind, that nature can have stirred no more dolorous affection in you as a mother for a dear son, than gratefulness and memory of his services past hath wrought in us, his Sovereign, apprehension of our miss of so worthy a servant.

But now that Nature's common work is done, and he that was born to die hath paid his tribute, let that Christian discretion stay the flux of your immoderate grieving, which hath instructed you both by example and knowledge, that nothing of this kind hath happened but by God's divine Providence. And let these lines from your gracious and loving Sovereign serve to assure you, that there shall ever appear the lively characters of you and yours that are left, in valuing all their faithful and honest endeavours. More at this time we will not write of this unsilent subject; but have dispatched this gentleman to visit both your Lord and you, to condole with you the true sense of your love; and to pray you that the world may see, that what time cureth in weak minds, that discretion and moderation helpeth in you in this accident, where there is so just cause to demonstrate true patience and moderation.

ELIZABETH REGINA[22]

The year after his brilliant but empty success with combined operations against Cádiz, in which the city underwent a fortnight of sacking but the treasure fleet escaped – a feat of reckless courage, scornful bravado, and romantic chivalry, dimmed by greedy squabbles over the spoils of which the Queen was robbed by these gentlemen adventurers – Essex was again in

22 Two years later, when two other Norris sons were killed, Elizabeth wrote to the parents: 'We were loth to write at all, least we should give you fresh occasion of sorrow, but could not forbear, knowing your past resolution in like mishaps. . . . We propose ourselves as an example, our loss being no less than yours'. The Norrises have a life-size monument in St Andrew's Chapel in Westminster Abbey, with their six sons, 'a brood of spirited, martial men' (Camden).

command of the Islands Voyage of 1597 with 98 ships and 6000 soldiers. Owing to his disputes with Raleigh he let the Spanish treasure ships once more slip past at night off the Azores. Meanwhile, only gales stopped another Spanish Armada of 136 ships and 9000 soldiers from invading England, which was denuded of its fleet, and establishing a naval base at Falmouth. In the same year, Essex, as Master of Ordnance, was in charge of mobilizing the country levies against the renewed invasion threat.

20

'We eat ropes' ends and drink rain water'

The Earl of Essex on returning from the ill-starred Islands Voyage, sends disturbing news about the Spanish fleet to Secretary of State Sir Robert Cecil.

At Plymouth the 26th of October [1597]
I am so full of business as I cannot write to you at large. The news I bring is that I miss very few of her Majesty's fleet, but hope they will all be here this night. I parted company with Sir Walter Ralegh two days ago, and I think I saw him yesterday coming out of Scilly, for we saw a ship of the Queen's there which we made to be the 'Wastspight'. The news we find is that the Spaniards are upon the coast; upon which, if we do not bestir ourselves as never men did, let us be counted not worthy to serve such a Queen. For the country, by the grace of God, I will take order, and I will instantly out with as many ships as I can, but this hour the wind blows full up into the harbour and we were all in ere we had this news. But we do set ashore our sick men, take in fresh, and water, for though we eat ropes' ends and drink nothing but rain water, we will out that we may be partly th'instruments to make a final end of this proud nation that is destined to destruction. They are already in distress, and if we can get out, I hope none of them shall escape.

Although Philip died in 1598, the fear of a new Armada invasion still agitated the country and feverish preparations were made in London which was in the throes of panic.

21

'Cry of women, chaining of streets, and shutting of the gates'

John Chamberlain (1553–1627) informs his friend, the diplomat Dudley Carleton (later Secretary of State and Viscount Dorchester) at Ostend, of the latest news.

London, 1st August 1599
. . . Upon what ground or good intelligence I know not, but we are all here in a hurl as though the enemy were at our doors. The Queen's ships are all making ready, and

this town is commanded to furnish out 16 of their best ships to defend the river, and 10,000 men, whereof 6,000 to be trained presently, and every man else to have his arms ready. Letters are likewise going out to the bishops and their clergy and all the noblemen and gentlemen here – about to prepare horses and all other furniture, as if the enemy were expected within fifteen days. . . . That which makes me think all is in good earnest, is that Sir Francis Vere[23] is certainly sent for out of the Low Countries with 2,000 of his best soldiers. All this noise riseth upon report that the Adelantado[24] hath an armada ready at the Groyne of 30 galleys and 70 ships (though some say more) which makes us misdoubt that the besieging of your town is but in shew, to draw their men down to the sea side and this navy to convey them over hither. Howsoever it be, I would we were well rid of this brunt. . . .

9th August

Though here be little happened since I wrote last, but only scambling[25] provisions and preparations for war, yet because I cannot tell when I shall write again if any sudden alarm call us away, I think it not amiss to let you understand what was and is intended to be done. The news increasing daily of the Spaniards coming, and advertisements concurring from all parts, of their design for London (whereof the Adelantado himself gave out proud speeches), order was given for a camp to be raised. The rendezvous for Hertfordshire men was to be at Tottenham, and so forward to Tilbury. I mean (though I were never professed soldier) to offer myself in defence of my country, which is the best service I can do it. Twelve or thirteen of the Queen's ships are preparing in all haste, whereof the Lord Thomas Howard to be admiral, Sir Walter Raleigh vice-admiral, Fulke Greville rear-admiral.

The Earl of Cumberland to have charge of them [the Londoners] and the river, meaning to make a bridge this side Gravesend, and to this end got together all the lighters, boats, Western barges, cables, and anchors that were to be found, giving out that with 1,500 musketeers he would defend that bridge or lose his life upon it, but yesterday, after much turmoil and great charges bestowed, it was quite given over, and now they have an imagination of sinking certain hulks in the channel, if need should be.

Upon Monday, toward evening, came news (yet false) that the Spaniards were landed in the Isle of Wight, which bred such a fear and consternation in this town as I would little have looked for, with such a cry of women, chaining of streets, and shutting of the gates, as though the enemy had been at Blackwall. I am sorry and ashamed that this weakness and nakedness of ours on all sides should shew itself so apparently as to be carried far and near, to our disgrace both with friends and foes. Great provision is made for horse, as being the best advantage we are like to have if the enemy come. . . . But now, after all this noise and blustering, methinks the weather begins to clear somewhat, for our preparations begin to slack and go not on so headlong as they did, so that there may be hope all shall be well; and our rendezvous at Tottenham is put off for five days. . . .

23 General of the English troops in Dutch service who had, at Turnhout in 1597, inflicted the first defeat on the hitherto unbeaten Spanish infantry; at Nieuport in 1600, he again broke the tercios in a bloody battle.
24 Provincial governor appointed to administer England after its conquest, who accompanied the admiral.
25 Obs. for scrambling; here, collecting.

23rd August

The world is well amended here since I wrote last, and the storm that seemed to look so black almost quite blown over; yet our navy is gone to sea prettily strong and in good plight for so short warning. Our land forces are daily discharged by little and little, and this day I think will be quite dissolved.

The vulgar sort cannot be persuaded but that there was some great mystery in the assembling of these forces, and because they cannot find the reason of it make many wild conjectures, and cast beyond the moon; as sometimes that the Queen was dangerously sick. . . . The forces in the West country are not yet dismissed, for there if anywhere may be some doubt of danger. . . . And now in the midst of all this hurlyburly here is a sudden sound of peace, and that certain fellows are come from Brussels with commission from Spain.

The longest continuous war in modern English history dragged on for eighteen years until after Elizabeth's death. The Queen was weary of debts and discontent because of her desperate need of revenue and the lack of trade and employment. The restraints of finance dominated her reign: taxation, always inequitable, was only granted in wartime as an extraordinary measure by a reluctant parliament. This goes a long way to explain Elizabeth's parsimony (which was really a determination not to go bankrupt like Philip, despite all his treasure from the New World) and her financial participation in piratical ventures which were given an aura of bellicose, self-righteous patriotism. Elizabeth did not seek glory in war and was anxious, first to avoid, and later to end it, with a minimum of expenditure. What appears to us today as callous indifference to the suffering of soldiers and sailors would, at the time, cause no shock; corruption and plundering were also regarded as normal in war.

Unlike Sir Henry Sidney, the Earl of Essex did not humour soldiers who let themselves be routed by the Irish rebels: he executed the first two officers accused of cowardice and put the others in prison together with one in every ten of the soldiers. These were harsh dealings, considering that he himself was, at the time, secretly parleying and plotting with Hugh O'Neill, Earl of Tyrone, in flagrant disobedience to Elizabeth's urgent orders to get on with the fighting! The Queen angrily rebuked him when he pleaded that the Captains' Council of his demoralized army, which had shrunk to four thousand men, was opposed to action.

22

A SOVEREIGN'S DISPLEASURE

Elizabeth I to the Earl of Essex.

14th of September 1599

Having sufficiently declared unto you before this time how little the manner of your proceedings hath answered either our direction or the world's expectation, we are doubtful what to prescribe you at any time, or what to build upon your writing unto us in anything. For we have clearly discerned of late, what you have ever to this hour possessed us with expectation, that you would proceed as we have directed you; but your actions always show the contrary. . . . If sickness of the army be the reason, why was there not the action undertaken when the army was in a better state? If winter's approach, why were the summer months of July and August lost? . . . We must conclude that none of the four quarters of the year will be in season for you and that Council to agree of Tyrone's persecution. We have not a great cause to think that your purpose is not to end war, but loss of time, consumption of treasure, and, most of all, our people. . . . And therefore that you may prepare to remedy matters of weight hereafter, rather than to fill your papers with impertinent arguments, our Lord Lieutenant, we do tell you plainly, that we wonder at your indiscretion. . . .

Essex, however, had already agreed a truce with Tyrone on 6 September, and, stung by her criticism, told the Queen of this *fait accompli.* Without waiting for a reply, he proceeded to Nonsuch Manor with his captains and stormed into her room where she was just dressing.

Essex's execution was brought about by the final folly of his defiance of the Queen: he had sensed rightly that Elizabeth was jealous of his popularity and had determined to stop his growing influence. Yet his death cast a gloom over her declining years, when she was holding on precariously to the end. Recruiting for the army was a problem: officers from the aristocracy and gentry, looking for adventure, glory and loot, were plentiful, including the fraudulent captains who regarded the robbing of soldiers' pay as their hallowed privilege. Understandably, recruits would not readily enlist for being shipped abroad. Press gangs, directed by corrupt JPs, were lurking in London, sometimes grossly exceeding their instructions from the Lords of the Council, and proclamations had to be issued to release all respectable people and keep only the rabble found in bawdy play houses and bowling alleys. This is attested in a letter from Captain Barnaby Rich:

'Any idle fellow, some drunkard, or seditious quarreller, a privy picker, or such a one as hath some skill in stealing of a goose, these shall be presented to the service.'[26]

23

PRESSING EARLS AND 'CONY CATCHERS'[27] IN LONDON

Nicholas Squyer to John Willoughby.

Holborn, 17th May [1602]
Here hath been such a press in London for the Low Country that the like was never seen in England: they did press earls, barons, knights, justices of the peace and

26   G. Scott Thomson, *Letters from a Lieutenant in the 16th Century*, p. 46.
27   Cheats.

gentlemen, and all other sorts of men, taken up in the streets, and presently sent, some to Bridewell, and some to Leadenhall, and some to Christchurch, and some to other places appointed for them to stay some two or three hours, and so sent to the ships: they could not be suffered to go to their own houses or lodgings: but where there was a thousand pressed, there was not above three hundred did serve, but were sent back again, for there was complaints made to the Council, and so there was order taking that they should press none but such as dwelt within the city and suburbs: and these that were masterless men, cony catchers, and such like, that was the true meaning of the first press.

In the Elizabethan age some of the typical English attitudes to war become discernible. The Queen, who still saw sea-power as coastal defence and as a source of profit in the battleground of the high seas, shunned open hostilities as the country still lacked a sufficient economic base. She hated war for its wasteful expense and avoided it while supporting Dutch resistance as an obstacle to Spanish and French ambitions, but was inexorably drawn into it for the defence of her rule and, very much in the second place, of Protestantism. Once she was forced into action, despite her complex and procrastinating diplomacy, she showed great courage.

Soldiers of fortune like Essex combined romantic panache with military amateurism and a love of his men ('I find sweetness in their conversation and happiness in their friendship'). There were also competent professional generals like Sir Francis Vere, first to defeat the Spanish tercios and helping to forge Dutch independence. Violently individualist sea captains like Drake, out to smash Spanish hegemony, would take no orders from anyone. Hawkins' vision was of sea-power leading to trading supremacy, and Raleigh looked towards the colonization of America; but there were also prudent admirals like Howard, with a loyal feeling of responsibility.

Soldiers and sailors, many of whom had been pressed into the forces by unemployment, poverty and crime, combined a love of loot with a hatred of the foreigner, which gave them fierce pride and reckless courage in battle.[28] The civilian population, always subject to intense xenophobia and fear of invasion, delighted in heroic actions, especially with a tragic ending, and created legends which would see reality through a golden haze – quite unlike the actors in the war drama who, by and large, were guided by a practical outlook and instinct.

28 A Dutchman described Englishmen at war as 'bold, ardent, cruel, inconstant, rash, vainglorious and deceiving' (J.P. Kenyon, *Stuart England*, Penguin, 1978, p. 47.)

F O U R

The Civil War (1639–51)

In the body of this fleshly land,
This Kingdom, this confine of blood and breath,
Hostility and civil tumult reigns . . .
SHAKESPEARE, KING JOHN

Unnatural wars, where subjects brave their king
CHRISTOPHER MARLOWE, EDWARD II

Prelude: Sir Edmund Verney and the Scottish Rebellion (1639)

Crush your old limbs in ungentle steel.
For God's sake, go not to these wars!

My honour is the pawn,
And, but my going, nothing can redeem it
SHAKESPEARE, KING HENRY IV, PARTS I AND II

The First Bishops' War initiated the British Revolution: by replacing the nobles with bishops on the Scottish Privy Council, Archbishop Laud roused the Church Assembly in Glasgow to restoring Presbyterian government of the Church in defiance of the King, and the Scots invaded Northumberland and took Durham.

The conflict of loyalties in the Verney family may reflect the way in which the whole country was soon to divide, and exemplifies the sentiments which determined attitudes to the Civil War that engulfed England three years later.

No parental and brotherly relationship could be more loving than that of the Verney household at Claydon, Bucks. Yet old Sir Edmund rushed off to fight the Scots, despite his eldest son Ralph's entreaties and all the hardships the campaign was bound to cause him. His unquestioning loyalty to the King was all the more generous as he was opposed to his policy and voted in

Parliament against Laudian practices: 'I have no reverence for Bishops for whom this quarrel persists', he wrote. But he loved honour even above Bible and Parliament:

> I have eaten the King's bread and served him near 30 years, and will not do such a base thing as to forsake him; and chose rather to lose my life – which I am sure I shall do.

And so it happened later.

1

HONOUR ABOVE CONVICTION: A GOUT-RIDDEN VETERAN JOINS UP

Sir Edmund Verney (1590–1642) expresses his sorrow at parting from his son Ralph after leaving for the campaign against the Scottish Covenanters with rag-tag troops who inspired little confidence; he worries about his heavy armour and pot helmet.

York, April 1st 1639

Good Raphe,

Since Prince Henry's death I never knew so much grief as to part from you; and truly, because I saw you equally afflicted with it, my sorrow was the greater. But, Raph, we cannot live always together. It cannot be long ere by course of nature we must be severed, and if that time be prevented by accident, yet we must resolve to bear it with that patience and courage as becomes men and Christians; and so the great God of heaven send us well to meet again, either in this world or in the next. . . .

April 29

Our army is but weak; our purse is weaker; and if we fight with these forces & early in the year we shall have our throats cut; and to delay fighting long we can not for want of money to keep our Army together. . . . I dare say there was never so raw, so unskilful and so unwilling an Army brought to fight . . . truly here are many brave Gentlemen that for point of honour must run such a hazard. . . . For my own part I have lived till pain and trouble has made me weary to do so; and the worst that can come shall not be unwelcome to me; but it is a pity to see what men are like to be slaughtered here. . . .

Last night there came certain news that Aberdeen is delivered up too, without so much as a bloody nose; so that to me it seems apparent that they have only pretended to make a party for the King there to cozen him of arms, munition, and money, to weaken us and strengthen themselves; for they were 6000 men well armed, in a reasonable defensive town, well victualled, and yet never struck one blow for it. . . . So now all Scotland is gone. I would it were under the sea, for it will ask a great time, and cost much blood, to reduce them again. . . .

I am infinitely afraid of the gout, for I feel cruel twinges, but I hope to starve it away, for, God willing, I will drink but once a day. I pray put your mother in mind to send me those papers of powder I gave her to keep for me, for they are excellent to prevent the gout. As I came hither I was in so much hope of a peace that I bought a fine hunting nag by the way. I would I had my money in my purse again, for I fear I shall not hunt in haste again. . . .

I have not yet seen my armour, for it is at Newcastle, but I believe there is never a long gauntlet sent with it. It will kill a man to serve in a whole cuirass. I am resolved to use nothing but back, breast, and gauntlet. If I had a pot for the head that were pistol proof, it may be I would use it, if it were light; but my whole helmet will be of no use to me at all. I pray go or send about this the next day after you receive this letter. Say nothing to your mother, it may give her causeless fears. . . .

4th of June

. . . When my pot is done let it be quilted and lined, and sent to me, for here is no hope at all of peace, and we are like to have the worst of the war which makes the Scots insufferably proud and insolent, insomuch that every Englishman's heart is ready to break with rage against them here.

15th of June

. . . I hear nothing of my pot. I will now keep it to boil my porrage in. . . .

Farewell. Your loving father
Ed. Verney

2

Ralph Verney MP (1613–96), who later fought on the Parliament side, tries to stop his father from going on with the Borders expedition.

May 1639

Sir you know your years, your charge, your distracted fortune, your former life, were privilege enough to keep you back, without the least stain to your reputation; you may easily guess how this afflicts me, for if you go (knowing your forwardness) I shall never think to see you more, but with grief confess that never man did more wilfully cast away himself. – Till now I never had the least reason to suspect your affection. But when I see you thus hastily run to your own ruin, and as it were purposely to lose that life that is so much dearer to me than my own, how can I think you love me?

His father replied:

May 16

Raphe, I thank you for your good advice. It has both expressed your judgement and affection, and I pray let me entreat you to believe, I will neither seek my ruin, nor avoid any hazard when that little honour I have lived in may suffer by it. . . .

The Civil War broke out haphazardly in the summer of 1642 when Charles I turned down the nineteen propositions demanding Parliamentary sanction for appointments in the State, Church and Armed Forces. The new middle-class traders in the towns and ports, represented by Parliament, were no longer prepared to accept government based on the King's absolute power, which appeared unsympathetic to the rising capitalist commercialism. No attack on the King's person was advocated, only on his prerogatives, and, in the same way, the King claimed to restrain Parliament within its traditional scope in order to safeguard the people's liberties which he believed were entrusted to him by divine right.

The motivation of the conflict is too complex to be fully dealt with here; historians have tended to stress the aspect with which they are particularly concerned and debate about the nature and causes of this conflict will no doubt continue. It was, in some way, a clash between the forces of progress and those of tradition – for liberty against tyranny; and, equally, between the old feudal order and the new bourgeois capitalism – for liberty against exploitation; but, on the other hand, it was Parliament which rose in defence of government according to English tradition, threatened by a new and alien, continental type of absolutism. Mutual distrust created excessive fears: Parliament suspected a Royalist conspiracy to impose popery and the King's party feared a challenge to the monarchy; moderates were apprehensive of even their own side winning, to avoid 'courses of will and violence'.[1]

The fraticidal war which broke out was the largest England has ever known: both sides believed that God would grant their just cause a quick victory but the struggle lasted for four years and continued intermittently for another five. The Cavaliers who were defending a universal creed, inspired by sentiment, honour and glory, faced the Puritans who were fighting for popular and personal liberty, based on faith, truth and reason. By and large, most noblemen and the feudal rustic gentry with their retainers in the north and west, were facing the upstart landlord squires and the merchants and industrialists in the towns with their militia in the south and east, the Navy and most of the ports siding with them.

This ideological war about Church and State divided the whole country, including many families and friends, in numerous local skirmishes and sieges.[2] The initial advantage lay with the Royalists, as the hunting gentry soon learnt to be effective cavalrymen, and three quarters of the country was in the King's hands at the end of 1643; but constant lack of money prevented the creation of a regular army and the resulting increase in plundering alienated the population. On Parliament's side, the resources

---

1 A. Fletcher, *The Outbreak of the English Civil War*, 1981, p. 413 ff.
2 John Kenyon in *The Civil Wars of England*, 1988, has advanced the idea that it was the logic of war largely fought by mercenaries, rather than popular controversy, that kept on stirring up hostilities.

of the City of London and the rich towns began to tell once the Puritan army, always superior numerically, was fully trained, organized and disciplined. The solid power of Cromwell's East Anglian cuirassiers, the 'Ironsides', facing Prince Rupert's brilliant but volatile Cavaliers, was a decisive factor in the cavalry charges and close-range infantry fire by which the battles were fought.

In the same way as the rebellion created a modern regular army, the 'New Model', England was set on the path of an expanding economy (after the stagnation of the early 1640s) which, based on a capitalist agriculture and industry, led in conjunction with the revival of the Navy to the foundation of a great colonial empire, as well as to a constitutional monarchy, coupled with religious toleration and the rule of law:

> The transition from divine right of monarchy to the divine right of the nation had lasting consequences. The new English patriotism was closely associated with religion, with liberty and with the rise of the middle class.[3]

While Germany took well over a century to recover from the ravages of the Thirty Years' War, the English Civil War, although cruel and tragic with all its self-inflicted slaughter and devastation, ultimately had the positive effect of safeguarding the English way of life.

Roundheads: Commander and Sergeant

> *Cromwell, our chief of men . . .*
> *Guided by faith and matchless fortitude . . .*
>
> *What field of all the Civil War*
> *Where his were not the deepest scar?*
> JOHN MILTON AND ANDREW MARVELL, ODES TO CROMWELL

Cromwell, the practical man of action, was impatient with the slow wheels of the administration and, as instructor and captain of his troops, he wanted them to be 'honest sober Christians'. War provided the means for this late religious convert to prove God's support by military success: implicitly, might was right for him, as it demonstrated divine approval however it was obtained or exercised. God, he believed, always led the way: 'None climbs so high as he who knows not whither he is going'. Therefore he could square any cruelty – whether devastation, persecution or massacre – with his conscience. He had 'a pure and direct relationship with his Maker, and every

---

3   J.E.C. Hill, *God's Englishman*, Weidenfeld & Nicolson, 1970.

letter he wrote, every troop he organized, every garrison he strengthened, every village he occupied or skirmish he won was for him part of a psalm in action, a ceaseless glorifying of God'.[4]

3

'Raise all your bands'

Oliver Cromwell (1599–1658) stirs up the Cambridge Commissioners.

Huntingdon, 6th August 1643

Gentlemen,

You see by this enclosed how sadly your affairs stand. It's no longer disputing, but out instantly all you can! Raise all your bands; send them to Huntingdon; – get up what volunteers you can; hasten your horses.

Send these letters to Norfolk, Suffolk, and Essex, without delay. I beseech you spare not, but be expeditious and industrious! Almost all our foot have quitted Stamford: there is nothing to interrupt an enemy, but our horse, that is considerable. You must act lively; do it without distraction. Neglect no means!

4

'A plain russet-coated Captain' better than 'a gentleman'

Cromwell tells the Suffolk Commissioners that 'a few honest men are better than numbers'.

[Cambridge, September 1643]

Gentlemen,

I beseech you be careful what Captains of horse you choose, what men be mounted: a few honest men are better than numbers. If you choose godly honest men to be Captains of horse, honest men will follow them.

The King is exceeding strong in the west. If you be able to foil a force at the first coming of it, you will have reputation; and that is of great advantage in our affairs. God hath given it to our handful; let us endeavour to keep it. I had rather a plain rus-set-coated Captain that knows what he fights for, and loves what he knows, than that which you call 'a gentleman' and is nothing else. I honour a gentleman that is so indeed. . . .

---

4   C.V. Wedgwood, *The King's War*, Collins, 1958, p. 217

5

PREACHERS WILL FIGHT BEST

Cromwell rebukes Colonel Francis Hacker.

December 25, 1650

Sir,

I was not satisfied with your last speech to mee about Empson, that he was a better praecher then a fighter or souldier or words to that effect. Truly I thinke Hee that prayes and praeches best will fight best. I know nothing will give like courage and confidence as the knowledge of God in Christ will and I expect itt bee encouraged by all Chiefe Officers in this Army especially: and I hope you will doe soe. I pray receave Captain Empson lovinglye. I dare assure you hee is a good man and a good officer. I would wee had noe worse. I rest Your lovinge friend,

O. Cromwell

In contrast to the high-minded commander, a sergeant in the London Volunteers in the Earl of Essex's army is very much down to earth and vividly personifies the spirit of the Puritan forces early in the Civil War. When there were no skirmishes with the enemy, always fought with great gusto, pillaging was the order of the day: churches were robbed and defaced, Cavalier sympathizers plundered, and soldiers from different companies even stole from each other. Although aristocrats like the Earls of Essex and Manchester were Puritan generals, feeling against the gentry was running high, and looting had to make up for the lack of food and pay. In order to stop the disorganized rabble from alienating popular sympathies, ordinances for better conduct were promulgated, to restore a measure of discipline by imposing drastic penalties, from whipping and piercing the tongue with a red-hot iron to hanging and shooting. However, cruelty and devastation only rarely descended to the horrors of the Thirty Years' War which ravaged Germany at the time, and relative humanity – and even sometimes chivalry – prevailed within the compass of a very rough age.

6

'A dish of Cavaliers to supper'

Sergeant Nehemiah Wharton of the London Volunteers in the Earl of Essex's army tells George Willingham, merchant at the Golden Anchor in St Swithin's Lane, his peace-time employer, how keen they are to fight the Cavaliers like 'cannibals in arms'.

Coventry, Aug. 26, 1642

Worthy Sir,

Saturday I gathered a complete file of my own men about the country, and marched to Sir Alexander Denton's park, who is a malignant fellow, and killed a fat buck, fastened his head upon my halbert, and commanded two of my pikes to bring the body after me to Buckingham, with a guard of musketeers coming thither. With part of it I feasted my captain, and with the rest several lieutenants, ensigns, and sergeants, and had much thanks for my pains.

Monday morning we marched into Warwickshire with about 3000 foot and 400 horse, until we came to Southam. In the way we took two Cavalier spies. This is a very malignant town, both minister and people. We pillaged the minister, and took from him a drum and several arms. This night our soldiers, wearied out, quartered themselves about the town for food and lodging, but before we could eat or drink an alarum cried 'Arm, arm, for the enemy is coming', and in half an hour all our soldiers, though dispersed, were cannibals in arms, ready to encounter the enemy, crying out for a dish of Cavaliers to supper. Our horse was quartered about the country, but the enemy came not, whereupon our soldiers cried out to have a breakfast of Cavaliers. We barricaded the town, and at every passage placed our ordnance and watched it all night, our soldiers contented to lie upon hard stones.

Our enemies, consisting of about 800 horse and 300 foot, with ordnance, led by the Earl of Northampton, intended to set upon us before we could gather our companies together, but being ready all night, early in the morning we went to meet them with a few troops of horse and six field pieces, and being on fire to be at them we marched through the corn and got the hill of them, whereupon they played upon us with their ordnances but they came short. Our gunner took their own bullet, sent it to them again, and killed a horse and a man. After we gave them eight shot more, whereupon all their foot companies fled and offered their arms in the towns adjacent for 12 pence a piece.

From thence we marched valiantly after them into Coventry, where the country met us in arms and welcomed us, and gave us good quarter.

Northampton, Sept. 13th

. . . Certain gentlemen of the country informed me that Justice Edmonds, a man of good conversation, was plundered by the base blue coats and bereaved of his very beads, whereupon I immediately divided my men into three squadrons, surrounded them, and forced them to bring their pillage upon their own backs unto the house again: for which service I was welcomed with the best varieties in the house, and had given me a scarlet coat lined with plush, and several excellent books in folio of my own choosing; but returning, a troop of horse met me, pillage me of all, and robbed me of my very sword, for which cause I told them I would either have my sword or die in the field, commanded my men to charge with bullet, and by divisions to fire upon them, which made them with shame return my sword, and it being towards night I returned to Northampton, threatening revenge upon the base troopers. This night and the day following our company by lot watched the south gate, where I searched every horseman of that troop to the skin, took from them a fat buck, a venison pasty ready baked, but lost my own goods.[5]

5   In an earlier letter, Wharton had complained of 'great dissension between our troopers and
     foot companies, for the footmen are much abused and sometimes pillaged and wounded'.

Sabbath day morning Mr Marshall, that worthy champion of Christ, preached unto us. These with their sermons have already subdued and satisfied more malignant spirits amongst us than a thousand armed men could have done, so that we have great hope of a blessed union.

I received your letter with my mistress's scarf and Mr Molloyne's hatband, both which came very seasonably, for I had gathered a little money together, and had this day made me a soldier's suit for winter, edged with gold and silver lace. These gifts I am unworthy of. I have nothing to tender you for them but humble and hearty thanks. I will wear them for your sakes, and I hope I shall never stain them but in the blood of a Cavalier.

I conclude, until death remaining,
Your humble, thankful, and deeply engaged servant at command,
Nehemiah Wharton

Cavaliers: Knights and Sovereign

> *Then spur and sword, was the battle-word,*
> *And we made their helmets ring,*
> *Shouting like madmen all the while*
> *'For God and for the King!'*
> LORD BYRON, THE OLD CAVALIER

The Cavaliers, imbued with ancient and noble notions of honour and chivalry, fought for their King with desperate courage and loyalty. Sir Bevil Grenville, MP for Cornwall and only six years younger than Sir Edmund Verney, did not hesitate either to leave his wife and family to fight for his King: he served in Sir Ralph Hopton's crack Cornish infantry which attempted to march on London.

7

'The King's standard waves in the field'

Sir Bevil Grenville (1596–1643) explains to his old friend Sir John Trelawny, who had tried to persuade him not to leave for the war, why he must go.

[1642–3]

Most Honourable Sir,

I cannot contain myself within my doors when the King of England's standard waves in the field upon so just occasion – the cause being such as must make all those that die in it little inferior to martyrs. And, for mine own, I desire to acquire an honest name, or an honourable grave. I never loved my life or ease so much as to shun such an occasion, which if I should, I were unworthy of the profession I have held, or to succeed those ancestors of mine who have so many of them, in several ages, sacrificed their lives for their country.

Sir, the barbarous and implacable enemy (notwithstanding His Majesty's gracious proceedings with them) do continue their insolences and rebellion in the highest degree, and are united in a body of great strength. . . . I am not without the consideration (as you lovingly advise) of my wife and family; and as for her, I must acknowledge she has ever drawn so evenly in her yoke with me as she hath never pressed before or hung behind me, nor ever opposed or resisted my will. And yet truly I have not, in this or anything else, endeavoured to walk in the way of power with her, but of reason; and though her love will submit to either, yet truly my respect will not suffer me to urge her with power, unless I can convince with reason. So much for that, whereof I am willing to be accomptable unto so good a friend.

While I live, I am, Sir, your unfailing, loving, and faithful servant,

B.G.

Although Grenville had assured his family friend of his consideration for his wife, his heart is so absorbed by the fighting that he can find no affectionate word for her. Six months later, he was killed in the battle of Lansdown, near Bath, leading the legendary victorious charge of his pikemen up the ridge, in face of cannon salvoes and cavalry attacks.

8

SALUTE WITH BULLETS

Sir Bevil Grenville tells his wife about the Royalist victory at Bradock Down, near Liskeard, in which he led the van.

[19 January 1643]

For the Lady Grace Grenvil, at Stow.
The messenger is paid, yet give him a shilling more.
My dear Love,

It has pleased God to give us a happy victory for which pray join with me in giving God thanks.

We advanced yesterday from Bodmin and, about noon, came in full view of the enemy's whole army upon a fair heath between Boconnock and Braddock church. They were in horse much stronger than we, but, in foot, we were superior I think. They were possessed of a pretty rising ground which was in the way toward Liskerd: and we planted ourselves upon such another against them within a musket shot; and we saluted each other with bullets about two hours or more, each side being willing to keep their ground to advantage and to have the other to come over to his prejudice. But after so long delay, they standing still firm, and being obstinate to hold their advantage, Sir Ralph Hopton resolved to march over to them, and to leave all to the mercy of God and valour on our side. I had the van, and so, after solemn prayers at the head of every division, I led my party away, who followed me with so great courage both down the one hill and up the other, that it struck a terror in them, while the seconds came up gallantly after me, and the wings of horse charged on both sides. But their courage so failed, as they stood not the first charge of the foot, but fled in great disorder.

We have taken 600 prisoners, and without rest we marched to Liskerd, and took it without delay; and so I hope we are now again in the way to settle the country in peace.

Let my sister, my cousins of Clovelly, with your other friends, understand of God's mercy to us; and we lost not a man. So I rest

Yours ever,
Bevill Grenvil

In contrast, the young Earl of Sunderland was a reluctant soldier. He wrote to his wife: 'If there could be an expedient found to solve the punctilio of honour, I would not continue here an hour.' He strikes a different note when, from the trenches at the siege of Gloucester, he foreshadows senti-ments inspired by the First World War, such as love of home and the good company of fellow soldiers amid 'horrid spectacles'.

9

TINTAMARRE, HIDEOUS CRIES, AND SOLITARINESS

Henry Spencer, Earl of Sunderland (1620–43) writes with affectionate long-ing to his wife; he was killed four weeks later at the battle of Newbury.

Aug. 25th [1643]

My dearest Heart,

Just as I was coming out of the trenches, I received your letter which gave me so much satisfaction, that it put all the inconveniences of this siege out of my thoughts. At that instant, if I had followed my own inclinations, I had returned an answer to yours; writing to you, and hearing from you, being the most pleasant entertainment, that I am capable of, in any place; but especially here, where, but when I am in the trenches (which place is seldom without my company) I am more solitary than ever I was in my life; this country being very full of little private cottages, in one of which I am quartered. . . .

Our gallery will be finished within this day or two, and then we shall soon despatch our mine, and them with it. Many of the soldiers are confident, that we shall have the town, within this four days,[6] which I extremely long for, not that I am weary of the siege; for really, though we suffer many inconveniences, yet I am not ill

---

6   The mining attempt was flooded out by the rain, the heavy siege guns never made a breach, and Rupert's cavalry was driven back by musket shot and pike. On the approach of a relief force under the Earl of Essex, the siege of this key city of the Puritans was aban-doned after only four weeks by the much stronger Royalists, just when the defenders were running out of ammunition and intending to negotiate surrender.

pleased at this variety, so directly opposite to one another, as the being in the trenches with so much good company, together with the noise and tintamarre of guns and
drums, the horrid spectacles, and hideous cries, of dead and hurt men, is to the solitariness of my quarter; together with all the marks of peace, which often bring into
my thoughts how infinitely more happy I should esteem myself, quietly to enjoy
your company at Althorpe, than to be troubled with the noises, and engaged in the
factions of the Court, which I shall ever endeavour to avoid. . . .

I hope ere long you will let me have your company, and Popet's, the thought of
which is to me most pleasant, and passionately desired.

Sir Thomas Knyvett was one of the small band of Royalists in the Eastern
Counties taken prisoner during their insurrection at Lowestoft; he was tried
by a Parliamentary Commission, but Cromwell intervened on his behalf. He
had always opposed resorting to arms: 'They are extreame bad councellars
that shall excite the King to a Warr against his people.' He felt increasingly
alienated by a war which seemed to him unreal and shameful, and took to
strange signatures like 'Theophilus ye Nutcracker'.

10

'I glory in suffring for my conscience'

Sir Thomas Knyvett (1596–1658) writes to his wife Katherine at Ashwell
Thorpe, Norfolk, from his imprisonment at Cambridge where he is hoping to
'studdy like a pigg-hogg'.

23 March 1642

Dear Harte,

'tis no small comfort to me, in the midst of my Afflictions, to heare of thy Wellfare &
to receive such divine corialls from A sincere hart. I humbly thank god I have my
health very well yet. It hath been our good fortune hetherto to lighte into the hands of
gent: that have treated us very fayer & with much curtesy. . . . God Allmighty fram &
temper the harts of both sides to a peac'able way, And send a happy
Accommodation, before distruction and ruine rages to farr in this Kingdome. . . . We
heard the last night the Commissioners have some designe to remove us to Jesus
Colledg. If we shall fall into this happiness, thers some of us will studdy like pigg-
hoggs. . . . I hope the mallice of our neighbores will not streatch to the utter ruine of
us. . . . Deer hart, be patient and cheerly. . . . I glory as much in suffring for my conscience & a good cause as any can doe. . . . God Allmighty Bless you & yor & my
stock. The same God, I hope, will bring us together againe. Far'well,

Thy faithfull loving husband
Thomas Knyvett

Two years later he wrote: 'This History to after Ages will seeme rather a
Romancy, the faingned thing in a matter really Acted; And, then my opinion,

twilbe much more for the credit of the Nation to have it so constred then deer'ly beleev'd, for the best excuse that can be made for us must be a fit of Lunacy . . .'

Prince Rupert, the King's nephew, was the dashing hero of the Cavaliers: tall, dark and handsome, he galloped into battle on a black horse at the head of his cavalry, dressed in scarlet and silver lace. From the age of fourteen he had gloried in war with all its cruelty and chivalry. The lightning impetuous charges this seasoned campaigner in his early twenties had learnt from the Swedes were irresistible until Cromwell found the answer through training and discipline of his 'New Model' cavalry. The Puritans believed that the 'diabolical Prince' was in league with the devil and used his white poodle, 'Sergeant Major General' Boye, who could make himself invisble, to collect intelligence in their lines.

Here Rupert challenges the Earl of Essex, the staid and uninspiring veteran Parliamentarian commander, in a style which, ironically, bears a pale resemblance to Essex's father's when he wrote to the Governor of Rouen, and with a similar result: Essex replied that he 'feared not to meet the Prince in a place that he should appoint' but no duel took place.

11

'Your friend till I meet you next'

Prince Rupert (1619–82) challenges the Earl of Essex to a duel.

23 September 1642

My Lord,

. . . I shall be ready, on his [Majesty's] behalf, to give you an encounter in a pitched field, the Dunsmore Heath, 10th October next. Or, I shall expect private satisfaction as willingly, at your hands for the same, and that performed by a single duel.

I know my cause to be so just that I need not fear; for what I do is agreeable both to the laws of God and men.

In the interim I am your friend till I meet you next,
Rupert

In the summer of 1645 the King resolved to go to Scotland, dreaming of a grand alliance between the Earl of Montrose, the Presbyterian Covenanters and the Irish Confederates, which would win the war for him. When Prince Rupert wrote to warn him that such a plan was illusory, he replies with his characteristic unshakeable reliance on God's help for the cause of the legitimate sovereign against his rebel subjects, although he realises that 'as a mere soldier and statesman' he must be resigned to facing ruin. His honour as King, he feels, obliges him to ignore all wishes of his subjects which he considers contrary to his rights.

12

'God will not suffer rebels to prosper'

King Charles I (1600–49) writes to Prince Rupert with a serene rejection of all compromise.

[Summer 1645]

. . . As for your opinion of my business and your counsel thereupon, if I had any other quarrel but the defence of my religion, crown and friends, you had full reason for your advice; for I confess that speaking either as a mere soldier or statesman, I must say there is no probability but of my ruin. Yet as a Christian I must tell you, that God will not suffer rebels and traitors to prosper, nor this cause to be overthrown. And whatever personal punishment it shall please him to inflict upon me must not make me repine, much less give over this quarrel. And there is as little question that a composition with them at this time is nothing else but a submission, which, by the grace of God, I am resolved against, whatever it cost me, for I know my obligation to be, both in conscience and honour, neither to abandon God's cause, injure my successors, nor forsake my friends. . . . He that will stay with me at this time must expect and resolve either to die for a good cause or (which is worse) to live as miserable in maintaining it as the violence of insulting rebels can make him. . . .

Divided Loyalties: Enemies Correspond

All were Englishmen and pity it was that such courage should be spent in blood of each other
BULSTRODE WHITELOCKE (1605–75)

Families were broken up by sons and fathers or brothers joining opposite sides, and life-long friends faced each other as enemies. As a rule, however, ties of blood and affection remained intact and a spirit of generous respect from one countryman to the other prevailed in letters exchanged between them.

To the great sorrow of Sir Edmund Verney, his eldest son Ralph had joined the Parliamentarian army and they had stopped writing; but Ralph's brother, Mun, a gallant Cavalier 'tooth and nail for the King's cause', yet expresses to Ralph in loving terms his grief that he is fighting for the enemy.[7]

---

7 But Ralph, who always put conscience before interest, went into exile rather than sign the covenant, lost his estates, and was, after his return, imprisoned by Cromwell for alleged royalist plotting; Charles II made him a baronet.

13

LOVING BROTHERS AS ENEMIES

Edmund (Mun) Verney assures his 'sweet brother' Ralph of his unimpaired love.

[1642]

Brother,

What I feared is proovd true, which is your being against the King; give me leave to tell you in my opinion tis most unhandsomely done, and it grieves my hearte to think that my father allready and I, who soe dearly love and esteeme you, should be bound in consequence (because in duty to our King) to be your enemy. I heare tis a greate greife to my father. . . . I am soe much troubled to think of your being of the syde you are that I can write no more, only I shall pray for peace with all my hearte, but if God grant not that, yet that He will be pleased to turne your hearte that you may soe expresse your duty to your King that my father may still have cause to rejoice in you.

When he received no reply, Mun wrote again:

I beseech you let not your unfortunate silence breede the least distrust of each other's affections, although I would willingly lose my right hand that you had gone the other way, yet I will never consent that this dispute shall make a quarrel between us, there be too many to fight with besides ourselves. I pray God grant suddaine and firme peace that we may safely meete in persone as well as in affection. Though I am tooth and nayle for the King's cause, and endure soe to the death, whatsoever his fortune be, yet sweet brother, let not have my opinion (for it is guyded by my conscience) nor any report which you can heare of me, cause any diffidence of my true love to you.

An old family friend writes to Ralph about her and her neighbours' apprehensions of his army and of the international situation.

14

'i hope i shall be safe hear'

Eleanor Countess of Sussex writes to Sir Ralph Verney, offering him eight pots of jelly.

[1642]

. . . ther was somethinge rede from your parlyment to have all the tranede bandes in a redines. They are all in great fear at Sentorbones [St Albans], and ever hose [house] the say have bought armes and gons to defend them. i hope i shall be safe hear, though i have nether. It is ill nues to hear ther is a pese betwixt Spane and frince, suer the will com uppon us, and help eyrlande. i pray God keepe us from the misyres that other nasyons have sufferede by ware. i am very glade to hear your father is so will agane. i have presented him with some ihely [jelly] and there is eyght pots for you and your lady, how i beceche you to rember me most affecynatly. . . .

Later she writes about Ralph's father who seems to have been deeply torn by the conflict between the convictions he shared with his prodigal son and his honour and loyalty to the King:

. . . He is a most sade man. i pray God may do well, i fear his trubles togather will made an end of him. Now lett me intrete you as a frende that loves you most hartily, not to write passynatly to your father, but ovour com him with kaindness; he is infinetly malincoly, for many other things i belive besides the difference betwixt you.

Sir Edward Sydenham succeeded Sir Edmund Verney as Knight Marshal of the King's Horse (motto: 'Give Caesar his due'). When Verney was killed bearing the standard in the battle of Edgehill (his hacked-off hand was found to grasp it even in death), Sydenham sends a letter of condolence to Ralph; with human dignity in face of bereavement, he ignores the fact that they are enemies now.

15

THE DEATH OF THE STANDARD BEARER

Sir Edward Sydenham tells Sir Ralph Verney how his father died.

[28 October 1642]
For all our greaty vyctorie I have had the greatest loss by the death of your nobell father that ever anie freind had. . . . He himself killed two with his owne hands, whereof one of them had killed povre Jason (his servant) and brocke the poynt of his standard at push of pike before he fell. He would nither put on armes or buff cote, the day of battell, the reason I know not; the battle was bloody on our syde, for our hoorss raun away at the first charge. The Kinge is a man of the least feare and the greatest mercie and resolution that I ever saw, and had he not been in the fylde, we might have suffired.

God in mercie send us peace and although our loss be as great as a sonn can loose in a father, yitt god's chyldren must beare with patience what afflycktion soever he shall please to laye upon them. . . .

My humbell sarvise to your sad wyfe. G of his infinite mercie comfort you bothe which shall be the prayers of your freind and sarvant.

Personal friendship and respect for loyally held conviction bridged the opposing camps when two commanders, who had been comrades in arms in the German wars twenty years before, correspond across the lines.

16

'I detest a war without an enemy'

Sir William Waller (*c.* 1597–1668), the Puritan general, writes to Sir Ralph Hopton, the Royalist general, nobly lamenting that he cannot grant him the requested interview; they were soon to fight each other in the battle of Lansdown.

[1643]

Sir,

The experience which I have had of your worth, and the happiness which I have enjoyed in your friendship, are wounding considerations to me when I look upon this present distance between us: certainly, Sir, my affections to you are so unchangeable, that hostility itself cannot violate my friendship to your person; but I must be true to the cause wherein I serve – where my conscience is interested all other obligations are swallowed up. . . . That Great God, who is the searcher of all hearts, knows with what a sad fear I go upon this service, and with what a perfect hate I detest a war without an enemy. . . . We are both on the stage and must act those parts that are assigned to us in this Tragedy, but let us do it in the way of honour and without personal animosity; whatsoever the issue of it be, I shall never resign that dear title, of

Your most Affectionate Friend and faithful servant,
William Waller

The same Puritan general, who treated his adversaries with such courtesy and humanity, sent a trumpeter from Salisbury to Bruton to deliver a message to his hard-drinking flamboyant opponent, nicknamed 'the jovial lad', couched in the cavalier spirit which would appeal to him. They met at Shaftesbury afterwards, 'with such displays of splendour and good fellowship on both sides that the country people thought this could be nothing less than the peace treaty to end the war'.[8]

17

'You are the jolliest neighbour'

Sir William Waller proposes to Lord George Goring an exchange of prisoners; Goring was himself exchanged later, after being captured and lingering in the Tower for nine months.

8   Wedgwood, op. cit., p. 427 f.

[c. 1643]

Noble Lord,

God's blessing be on your heart, you are the jolliest neighbour I have ever met with: I wish for nothing more but an opportunity to let you know, I would not be behind in this kind of courtesy. In the mean time, if your Lordship please to release such prisoners as you have of mine, for the like number and quality that I have of yours, I shall esteem it as a great civility, being your Lordship's most humble and obedient servant,

William Waller

The Earl of Denbigh's son was a former ambassador in Venice who had fallen out of favour with the Queen and had changed sides. Fighting for the defenders in Prince Rupert's attack on Birmingham, he was allowed under a flag of truce to see his mortally wounded father, who at sixty had shown singular courage, but he came too late. He sent a letter of condolence to his mother who now appeals to him 'to leave those that murdered your dear father'.

18

'God and nature claim it from you'

The Countess of Denbigh, the Queen's first lady of the bedchamber, writes to her son, Basil, the second Earl of Denbigh, that his error has now become 'monstrous and hideous'; this had no effect, as two months later he became Commander-in-Chief for the Associated Midland Counties.

[April 1643]

My dear Son,

I am much comforted with the receiving of your kind letter in this time of my great sorrow for the loss of my dear husband, your dear father, whose memory I shall ever keep with sorrow and a most tender affection, as he did deserve from me and all the whole world. God make me able to overcome this my affliction! I beg of you, my first-born son, whom I do so dearly love, to give me that satisfaction which you now owe me, to leave those that murdered your dear father – for what else can it be called? When he received his death-wound for saying that 'he was for the King' they showed no mercy for his grey hairs, but swords and shots, a horror for me to think of. O my dear Jesus! put it into my dear son's heart to leave that merciless company that was the death of his father; for now I think of this party with horror, before with sorrow. This is the time when God and nature claim it from you. Before, you were carried away by error, now it seems monstrous and hideous. The last words your dear father spoke, was to desire God to forgive you and to touch your heart. Let your dear father and unfortunate mother make your heart relent – let my great sorrow receive some comfort. If I receive joy, you shall receive blessing and honour. Think, if I may be so happy as to obtain this my desire of you. . . .

Your loving mother,
S. Denbigh

Sir Thomas Fairfax summoned Prince Rupert to surrender Bristol, which he was besieging by land and sea, in a letter full of dignified sympathy for a former fellow fighter in the Protestant cause in the Thirty Years' War, who, according to his deeply held conviction, had been sadly misled.

19

'This unnatural war'

Sir Thomas Fairfax (1612–71) to Prince Rupert.

September 4, 1645

Sir,

For the service of the Parliament I have brought this army before the City of Bristol, and do summon you in their names to surrender it, with all the forts. I take into consideration your Royal birth, and relation to the Crown of England, your honour, courage, and the virtue of your person, and the strength of that place which you may think yourself bound and able to maintain.

Sir, the Crown of England is and will be where it ought to be, we fight to maintain it there; but the King, misled by evil Counsellors or through a seduced heart, hath left his Parliament and his people, under God the best assurance of his crown and family. The maintenance of this schism is the ground of this unhappy war on our part, and what sad effects it hath produced in the three kingdoms is visible to all men. . . .

Sir, if God makes this clear to you as he hath to us, I doubt not but he will give you a heart to deliver this place. And if, upon such conviction you should surrender it, and save the loss of blood or hazard of spoiling such a city, it would be an occasion glorious in itself and joyful to us, for the restoring of you to the endeared affection of the Parliament and people of England – the truest friends to your family it hath in the world.

So let all England judge whether the burning of its towns, ruining its cities, and destroying its people be a good requisits from a person of your family, which hath had the prayers, tears, purses, and blood of its Parliament and people in this unnatural war.

Your Highness's humble servant
Thomas Fairfax

Unimpressed, Rupert tried to gain time by negotiating, but six days later Fairfax gave the order for the assault at 2 a.m.; in a fierce pike battle on the palisades all Royalists in Prior's Hill Fort were killed. Rupert asked for terms to save his remaining garrison of 2500 men; Fairfax paid him 'all fair respects' and allowed him to retire to Oxford with his army, although he had refused to swear he would never fight Parliament again.

There were rumours of an understanding between Rupert and Fairfax: persuaded by his favourite, Lord Digby, who hated Rupert and wanted to impeach him for high treason to succeed him as lieutenant-general, the King believed Rupert was betraying him in league with his brother Maurice in London, and preparing a coup at Oxford. He sends him a bitter letter of dismissal.

20

THE KING BANS PRINCE RUPERT

Charles I accuses his nephew of treason and tells him to leave England;
Rupert submitted to the King's order in affirmation of his loyalty.

[September/October 1645]

... Though the loss of Bristol be a great blow to me, yet your surrendering it as you did is of so much affliction to me, that it makes me forget not only the consideration of that place, but is likewise the greatest trial of my constancy that hath yet befallen me; for what is to be done, after one that is so near to me as you are both in blood and friendship, submits himself to so mean an action (I give it the easiest term). . . . You assured me that, if no mutiny happened, you would keep Bristol for four months. Did you keep it four days? Was there anything like mutiny? More questions might be asked, but now I confess to little purpose. My conclusion is, to desire you to seek your subsistence (until it shall please God to determine of my condition) somewhere beyond the seas, to which end I send you herewith a pass.

Rupert insisted on an enquiry and the Council of War fully rehabilitated him in opposition to the King. Rupert left with his faithful cavalry and this spelt the end of the King's army; Charles' suspicion of Rupert's loyalty had dealt a final blow to his cause. Although Rupert had apologized for his alleged errors to obtain a reconciliation, it took the King another two years until, musing upon his past actions, he at last recognized the injustice he had done to his nephew. He now tries to make amends.

21

A KING'S APOLOGY

Charles I, imprisoned at Hampton Court, expresses his regret to Prince
Rupert for accusing him of treason for the surrender of Bristol.

[September 1647]

Nephew,

Amongst many misfortunes, which are not my fault, one is, that you have missed those expressions of kindness I meant you. . . . Excuse me if I only say this to you now, that, since I saw you, all your actions have more than confirmed the good opinion I have of you. Next to my children I shall have most care of you. . . .

Your most loving Uncle and constant faithful Friend
Charles R.

It is unlikely that the King ever became aware that by not following Rupert's counsel he threw away the chances he had of winning the war: Rupert had advised him to march on London immediately after the battle of Edgehill, to storm Gloucester regardless of losses, and avoid fighting at Naseby.

Women in Arms

With musket on her shoulder, her part she acted then,
And everyone supposed that she had been a man;
Her bandeliers about her neck and sword hang'd by her side,
In many brave adventures her valour has been tried
ROXBURGH BALLAD (1655)

Like Lady Sussex, Sir Ralph Verney's north-country aunt is a faithful Royalist who nevertheless writes to her Parliamentarian nephew to describe her anxieties; the difference is that she gets flustered and defiant in turn, and describes the rising anger of women in the north as an enclosure was pulled down by what we would now call hooligans 'to make themselves merry'.

22

'The women in this country begin to rise'

Mrs Eure warns Sir Ralph Verney to take heed of women who are up in arms against 'this very vermin'.

May 1642

. . . O that the sweet Parliament would come – with the olive branch in its mouth, it would refresh and glad all our hearts here in the north. We are so many frighted people; for my part if I hear but a door creak I take it to be a drum, and am ready to run out of that little valour I have. . . .

The women in this country begin to rise; there hath been a hundred with the King, and above, to have these grievances redressed, and he hath given them so good content that they say he is as proper a man as is in England. I wish you all to take heed of women, for this very vermin have pulled down an enclosure which some of them were put in prison for it by the justices, that had their pipe to go before them, and their ale and cakes to make themselves merry when they had done their feats of activity. I write you this news to let you see what brave spirits is in the north. I wish all were well ended, for things stand in so ill a condition here as we can make no money of our coalpits. If rents fail and those fail too, we shall be in a hard case. . . .

Your faithful and loving Aunt

Like the formidable Countess of Derby who defied Fairfax for several months in the famous siege of Lathom House, her family stronghold,[9] Lady Brilliana was left in charge of Brampton Bryan Castle in Herefordshire by her husband Sir Robert Harley when he left to organize the militia in London. She sent the family plate for the cause, not forgetting to enclose a wholesome home-baked cake for him. Her affectionate motherly concern was directed to her eldest son Ned, who, although only eighteen and rather delicate, was a captain of horse under general Waller.[10]

23

LADY BRILLIANA DEFENDS HER CASTLE

Lady Brilliana Harley (c. 1600–43) writes to her son Edward about her fears while she is getting the garrison ready for the siege.

13 Dec. 1642

My dear Ned,

My heart has been in no rest since you went. I confess I was never so full of sorrow. I fear the provision of corn and malt will not hold out, if this continue; and they say they will burn my barns; and my fear is that they will place soldiers so near me that there will be no going out. My comfort is that you are not with me, lest they should take you; but I do most dearly miss you. I wish, if it pleased God, that I were with your father. I would have writ to him, but I durst not write upon paper. Dear Ned, write to me, though you write upon a piece of cloth, as this is. I pray God bless you, as I desire my own soul should be blessed.

June 11, 1643

O! my dear Ned – that I could but see you! I live in hope that the Lord will give me that comfort, which I confess, I am not worthy of. I hear from a good hand that you are ready to come out of London. The Lord in much mercy go with you and make you to do worthily; and dear Ned, believe my heart and soul is with you.

I am exceedingly beholding to Colonel Massy.[11] I sent to him to desire him to send me an able soldier, that might regulate the men I have, and he has sent me one that was a sergeant, an honest man, and I think an able soldier; he was in the German wars. He came to me on Thursday last, but your brother has the name of the command.

---

9   She refused to surrender despite a bombardment by mortar shells and fireballs, and Fairfax pronounced it 'ignoble and unmanly to assault a lady of her high birth and quality in her own house' (M. Bence-Jones, *Cavaliers*, Constable, 1976, p. 137).
10 Three years afterwards he became a general, opposed Cromwell as a presbyterian and was imprisoned when he declared himself for the King; later he was governor of Dunkirk.
11 Lieutenant-Colonel Edward Massey, after changing sides, Governor of Gloucester during the siege, and later a Major-General.

Honest Petter is come out of prison. He was grievously used in Ludlow. Turks could have used him no worse; Lieutenant Colonel Marrow would come every day and kick him up and down, and they laid him in a dungeon upon foul straw. He is very glad he has come home again, and so am I. The Lord in mercy bless you, and give you a comfortable meeting with

Your most affectionate mother,
Brilliana Harley

The castle was unsuccessfully besieged by the Royalists in the summer of 1643 for six weeks, but, worn out by anxiety, Lady Brilliana died a few weeks later. In a second siege, the servants surrendered the castle which was burnt down.

When the Civil War came, Queen Henrietta Maria, the daughter of Henry IV of France, turned her energies from court amusements to raising arms, money and soldiers in France, appealing to Richelieu, and even the Pope, for support of the Royalist cause. She had tremendous courage and was always chiding the King for his mistakes and procrastination. She only spent one and a half years of the Civil War in England, during which she held court in splendour at Merton College, Oxford. Her intrigues, fervent catholicism, and attempts to bring over foreign armies proved fatal to Charles.

The Queen was condemned for high treason by Parliament in May 1643 and left York for Newark soon after. She gloried in riding at the head of her army and sharing the soldiers' camp life which she compared with Alexander the Great's!

24

'Her she-majesty generalissima over all'

Queen Henrietta Maria (1609–69) reports to Charles I on her march from York towards Oxford, obviously pleased with herself in charge of an army; at Stratford she was the guest of Shakespeare's daughter.

Newark, June 27, 1643

My dear Heart,
I received just now your letter by my Lord Saville,[12] who found me ready to go away. I carry with me 3,000 foot, 30 companies of horse and dragoons, six pieces of cannon,

---

12 Thomas, first Viscount Saville, the King's treasurer, was imprisoned in 1642 on suspicion of plotting to seize the Queen, but, after vindicating himself, he was pardoned by the King, shortly before being sent with his letter to the Queen.

and two mortars. Harry Jermyn[13] commands the force which goes with me, as colonel of my guard, Sir Alexander Lesley the foot under him, Gerard the horse, and Robin Legge the artillery, and her she-majesty generalissima over all, and extremely diligent am I, with 150 waggons of baggage to govern in case of battle. Have a care that no troop of Essex's army incommode us. I hope that for the rest we shall be strong enough, for at Nottingham we had the experience that one of our troops had beaten six of theirs, and made them fly. I have received your proclamation or declaration, which I wish had not been made, being extremely disadvantageous to you, for you show too much apprehension, and do not do what you had resolved upon.

Farewell, my dear heart[14]

Women occasionally disguised themselves as soldiers or sailors, usually to remain secretly with their lovers; sometimes the moment of truth came when they were wounded in battle and stripped by the doctor. They seemed to enjoy army life and showed as much courage in battle as the men.

25

A WOMAN SOLDIER

Lieutenant-Colonel Roger Sawrey reports to William Clarke, secretary to General Monck, the unmasking of a girl soldier in disguise.

Citadel at Ayr, April 6, 1657

I with my company got very well to Ayr where we found all things in good order, only a young person who is discovered to be a woman; her name she saith is Ann Dimack of Keale in Lincolnshire. She hath been with us but one muster, and saith that her father and mother being dead she lived with her aunt, and fell in love with one John Evison. Her friends were against it, and would by no means yield to their marriage, nor had she any way of accomplishing her end left, but by putting herself into man's habit, and they went as two brothers. Coming with John by sea the said John was cast away, and she, keeping still her man's habit, came to Carlisle, and there listed herself for a soldier by the name of John Evison, and there she continued until she came to this garrison, and never was known to any. And I can perceive nothing

---

13   Henry Jermyn, first Earl of St Albans, the Queen's secretary and colonel of her bodyguard. He went to France with the Queen in 1644 and proposed paying for French aid by handing over the Channel Islands. A gambler, *bon-viveur* and the Queen's favourite, he was said to have married her secretly in exile; 'more Frenchman than an Englishman', said Charles II.

14   A year later, the Queen was nearly captured at Exeter, and, abandoning her new-born baby, she fled to France from Falmouth, although suffering acutely from puerperal sepsis; her Dutch ship was tossed about in the storm and pursued and fired on by a Parliamentary vessel, under orders to sink it. Despite illness and sea-sickness, her courage was unimpaired; standing on deck, facing the elements and the enemy, she pronounced proudly: 'Queens of England are never drowned'.

but modesty in her carriage since she hath been with us. If you think it necessary you may acquaint my Lord General with it, with my respects to yourself and lady.

The Battles

To slay or be slain
By the men they knew in the kindly past,
Of their own blood and speech and race,
Comrades or neighbours all!
RUDYARD KIPLING, EDGEHILL FIGHT

Edgehill

The Civil War mostly consisted of hundreds of local skirmishes and sieges, and the fortunes of war were in a constant flux. There were never more than 140,000 under arms and half the country stayed neutral. The first major battle was fought at Edgehill on 23 October 1642 between the King, who after ceremoniously firing the first cannon shot 'engaged himself in the place of the greatest danger', and the Earl of Essex, who, at the age of fifty-one, bravely stopped the rout of his infantry by swinging a pike at the head of them. Around 11,000 Royalists opposed 13,000 Puritans, but Rupert's cavalry soon broke the enmy's and galloped off in hot pursuit, giving Essex a chance to maul the King's infantry until Rupert returned at dusk. The battle was bloody but indecisive and the accounts from both sides differ widely, which is not surprising, as the battlefield was enveloped in smoke from the black powder being used. Essex lost 4,000 men and 300 prisoners, and escaped to an alehouse after his coach and money-box had been captured; he and his soldiers were accused of giving no quarter, 'barbarously hacking and hewing' the wounded and abandoning their own without surgeons, 'horribly crying out upon the villainy'.[15] Essex managed to get back to London with his army in time to protect it against the Royalists.

26

A CAVALIER VICTORY?

Lord Bernard Stuart (1623–45), Commander of the King's Lifeguard, gives his version of the battle.

28 October 1642

We marched on Sunday morning from Edgcot to Edghill which is five miles to fight with them there. After our men were put into battalia and the cannon planted we

---

15 Sir Patrick Wemyss in a letter to the Duke of Ormonde. (T. Carte, *Collection of Letters*, I, 1739, p. 9 ff.)

gave fire with our cannon and then charged them with both wings of our horse. They stood still all the while upon the hill expecting the charge and that we were fain to charge them uphill and leap over five or six hedges and ditches. Upon our approach they gave fire with their cannon lined amongst their horse, dragoneers, carabines and pistols, but finding that did nothing [to] dismay the King's horse and that they came more roundly to them with all their fire reserved, just when our men charged they all began to turn head and we followed in execution upon them for four miles together. . . . A great many of them saved their lives by getting our word For God and King Charles. Had our reserve of horse not mistaken but stood still in their place they were commanded, we had given them as absolute a defeat both of horse and foot as ever was given.

It was equally divided by these foot till night. A troop of their reserve did charge among our foot where they did a great deal of hurt. . . . Prince Rupert hath forced the Earl of Essex and his men to retire into Warwick with so much haste that the Prince hath 30 of his carriages, set fire on four carriages of powder. . . . The King hath taken Banbury yesterday and the castle which held within both 1,500 men and a troop of horse. This day he is gone for Woodstock and tomorrow for Oxford and marches straight for London.

27

'To stop false rumours'

The Revd Adoniram Bifield (1615–60), a regimental chaplain, tells Isaac Pennington, Lord Mayor of the City of London, that they 'beat the enemy out of the Field'.

Warwick Castle, 24 October 1642 at 2 a.m.
Yesterday, being the Lords day, it pleased God to make my self the first instrument of giving a certain discovery, by the help of a prospective Glasse from the top of an Hill, when the two Armies were drawn into Battalia; about two a clock in the afternoon, a very sore and fierce Battail began, which continued about four houres in mine own sight and hearing, much blood was shed, and a gallant spirit expressed by our Infantry. But the left Wing of our Horse being charged by the King's right Wing, was suddainly put to flight so that the right Wing in which your Son was placed, did the best service for the Chevalry. We had beat the enemy out of the Field – some say that Rupert is slain.

A few of our waggons were burned and plundered by the Enemy, who wheeled about in our Rere, but our Musquetiers played bravely up on them in the mean time, and recovered our Waggons again, and six pieces of Ordnance which we had lost.

All this hath God enabled our Army to perform, though the Common soldiers have not come into bed, but lodged in the open field, in the wet and cold nights, and most of them scarse eate or drank at all for 24 hours together, nay, I may say for 48, except fresh water where they could get it.

For my own part, after I had discharged my duty as far as I was enabled, by passing from Regiment to Regiment, and Troop to Troop to encourage them, at the latter end of the fight, not knowing what the issue of things might be, in the darksome Evening; while it was yet light, I rid to Warwick amongst hundreds of drawn swords, and yet was saved from the least touch of blood thirsty hand. . . . Have send this letter to stop the mouth of false rumours. . . .

Marston Moor

This was the biggest and closest battle of the war, fought by 18,000 Cavaliers (crying 'God and the King!') against 27,000 Roundheads (crying 'God and Religion!') in a storm of hail and thunder, between sunset and midnight on 2 July 1644. Cromwell surprised his enemies who had dispersed for supper, but Sir Thomas Fairfax's Yorkshire Puritans were defeated on the right wing by Lord Goring's Yorkshire Cavaliers in a fractricidal carnage of countrymen. Prince Rupert, after first driving back Cromwell's 'Ironsides', rashly exposed his flank to Leslie's Scots and got routed for the first time; this saved the Puritan infantry in the centre which was in a critical state. Rupert escaped to Lancashire with 6,000 men, but the Northern Cavalier army had been destroyed.

28

'God made them as stubble to our swords'

Oliver Cromwell tells his brother-in-law, Colonel Valentine Walton, about the battle and breaks to him the news of the death of his son, 'a glorious saint in Heaven'.

[Leaguer before York] 5th July 1644

Truly England and the church of God hath had a great favour from the Lord, in this great victory given unto us, such as the like never was since this war began. It had all the evidences of an absolute victory obtained by the Lord's blessing upon the Godly Party principally. We never charged but we routed the enemy. The left wing, which I commanded, being our own horse, saving a few Scots in our rear, beat all the Prince's horse. God made them as stubble to our swords. We charged their regiments of foot with our horse, and routed all we charged. I believe, of 20,000 the Prince hath not 4,000 left. Give glory, all the glory, to God.

Sir, God hath taken away your eldest son by a cannon-shot. It brake his leg. We were necessitated to have it cut off, whereof he died.

Sir, you know my own trials this way:[16] but the Lord supported me with this, that the Lord took into the happiness we all pant for and live for. There is your precious child full of glory, never to know sin or sorrow any more. He was a gallant young man, exceedingly gracious. God give you His comfort. Before his death he was so full

---

16   Captain Oliver Cromwell, 'the joy of his father', had recently died of smallpox.

of comfort that he could not express it, 'It was so great above his pain.' This he said to us. Indeed it was admirable. A little after, he said, One thing lay upon his spirit. I asked him, What that was? He told me it was, that God had not suffered him to be any more the executioner of His enemies.

At his fall, his horse being killed with the bullet, and as I am informed three horses more, I am told he bid them, Open to the right and left, that he might see the rogues run. Truly he was exceedingly beloved in the Army, of all that knew him. But few knew him; for he was a precious young man, fit for God. You have cause to bless the Lord. He is a glorious saint in Heaven; wherein you ought exceedingly to rejoice. . . . Let this public mercy to the Church of God make you to forget your private sorrow.

29

'Gone to the bone-setter'

Arthur Trevor, a Cavalier, describes the battle to Lieutenant-General Marquis of Ormonde as inconclusive, but ends with a message in cypher which belies his account and admits total defeat.

July 10, 1644

. . . In the fire, smoke and confusion of that day, the runaways on both sides were so many, so breathless, so speechless, and so full of fears, that I should not have taken them for men; both armies being mingled, both horse and foot; no side keeping their own posts.

In this horrible distraction did I coast the country; here meeting with a shoal of Scots crying out 'Weys us, we are all undone'; and so full of lamentation and mourning, as if their day of doom had overtaken, and from which they knew not whither to fly: and anon I met with a ragged troop reduced to four and a Cornet; by and by with a little foot officer without hat, band, sword, or indeed anything but feet and so much tongue as would serve to enquire the way to the next garrisons, which (to say the truth) were well filled with the stragglers on both sides within a few hours, though they lay distant from the place of the fight 20 or 30 miles.

I shall now give your Excellence the short of the action. The armies faced one another upon Hessam-Moor, three miles from York, about 12 of the clock, and there continued within the play of the enemy's cannon until 5 at night; during all which time the Prince and the Marquis of Newcastle were playing the orators to the soldiers in York, (being in a raging mutiny in the town for their pay) to draw them forth to join with the Prince's foot; which was at last effected, but with much unwillingness. The enemy perceiving the advance of that addition to the Prince's army, instantly charged our horse, and mingled with very great execution on both sides. On the left wing the enemy had the better of us, and on the right wing, where the Prince charged, we had infinitely the better of the enemy; so that in truth the battle was very doubtful, as in the number of the slain as well as the success of the day. . . . This, my Lord, is what can be punctually said of this encounter; each side being retired with a broken wing and gone to the bone-setter.

[Postscript in cypher in the original:]

The horse of P. Rupert and Lord Byron were totally routed; all their cannon taken; the Marquis of Newcastle fled unto Scarborough, and some say unto France; P. Rupert's forces of foot destroyed; yet he keeps the field with 5000 horse and 2000 foot, but will shortly march to Chester. The fault is laid wholly upon the Marquis of Newcastle.[17]

Naseby

In this battle on 14 June 1645, Cromwell's 'New Model' Army, the first standing army with a firmly disciplined cavalry and infantry of greater mobility and fire-power (flint-lock instead of match-lock), inflicted the most decisive defeat on the Royalists. Cromwell wrote:

> When I saw the enemy draw up and march in gallant order towards us, and we a company of poor ignorant men, to seek how to order our battle – the General[18] having commanded me to order all the horse – I could not (riding alone about my business) but smile out to God in praises, in assurance of victory, because God would, by things that are not, bring to naught things that are. Of which I had great assurance: and God did it.

Cromwell knew, however, that his army had 6,500 horse and 7,000 foot soldiers facing 4,000 and 3,500 respectively – a 2:1 superiority.[19] He went into one of his laughing ecstasies, as four weeks later at Langport, where he exclaimed: 'To see this, is it not to see the face of God?'

The King, resplendent in gilt armour, rode into battle on his fine horse at the head of the infantry in the centre, to shouts of 'Queen Mary!', and pushed back the opposing infantry, while Rupert's horse on the right wing routed Ireton's. Yet he made, once again, the fatal mistake of leaving the battlefield in a reckless pursuit: Cromwell's 'Ironsides', after putting Langdale's Northern Horse to flight on the other wing, were thus able to attack the exposed left flank of the King's infantry, supported by Okey's dragoons of the reserve, emerging from behind a hedge. By one o'clock the disaster was complete: all the Royalist infantry and artillery were lost, and the Puritans took 5,000 prisoners and £100,000 worth of gold, silver and jewels, not to

---

17 An unjustified accusation: Newcastle headed a troop of gentlemen volunteers in the battle with conspicuous bravery, but held no command. Weary of being a general, he sailed to Hamburg and later lived in Paris and Antwerp, devoting himself to horsemanship and writing comedies about human folly.

18 Sir Thomas Fairfax, organizer of the 'New Model' Army, was Commander-in-Chief, heading gallant charges and personally capturing a standard; like Cromwell, he was also seen to be 'highly transported'.

19 Wedgwood, op. cit., p. 452.

speak of hundreds of coaches with ladies, wives, and prostitutes – the ordinary women defending themselves against massacre with knives and forks. Naseby marked virtually the end of the Civil War.

In the next letter, Cromwell ends with a wise plea for religious toleration (in opposition to Presbyterian autocracy), omitted from publication by the Commons, but slipped in again by the Lords who revealed the attempt to suppress it.

30

CROMWELL ADMONISHES PARLIAMENT ON LIBERTY OF CONSCIENCE

Oliver Cromwell describes the battle of Naseby to William Lenthall, Speaker of the House of Commons, and draws a lesson from it.

14th June 1645

Sir,

Being commanded by you to this service, I think myself bound to acquaint you with the good hand of God towards you and us.

We marched yesterday after the King, who went before us from Daventry to Harborough; and quartered about six miles from him. This day we marched towards him. He drew-out to meet us; both armies engaged. We, after three hours fight very doubtful, at last routed his army; killed and took about 5000, also about 200 carriages, all he had; and all his guns. We pursued the enemy even to the sight of Leicester, whither the King fled.

Sir, this is none other but the hand of God; and to Him alone belongs the glory, wherein none are to share with him. The General[18] served you with all faithfulness and honour: and the best commendation I can give him is, that I daresay he attributes all to God, and would rather perish than assume to himself. Which is an honest and a thriving way: and yet as much for bravery may be given to him, in this action, as to a man. Honest men served you faithfully in this action. Sir, they are trusty; I beseech you in the name of God, not to discourage them. I wish this action may beget thankfulness and humility in all that are concerned in it. He that ventures his life for the liberty of his country, I wish he trust God for the liberty of his conscience, and you for the liberty he fights for.

Drogheda

In one area Cromwell did not practise what he preached: while professing, 'I meddle not with a man's conscience', he did not hesitate to persecute Catholics. In 1649, he went as Commander-in-Chief and Lord Lieutenant to subdue Ireland with 12,000 men, in a campaign of a ruthlessness reminiscent of the Thirty Years' War but not of the Civil War in England. He regarded the Irish as primitive, superstitious savages whose massacre of English settlers in 1641 had to be avenged by murdering the population in the cities, thereby opening a way for systematic colonization. In the storm of Drogheda, all the surviving garrison of 2,000 were massacred (including Sir Mun Verney, a regimental commander who, on behalf of the Cavaliers, had proclaimed: 'We give no quarters, but put all to the sword'), the churches burnt together with priests and refugees, and the women hiding in the vaults stabbed. After repeating this performance three weeks later at Wexford, Cromwell commented:

> I was intending better to this place than so great a ruin . . . yet God would not have it so; but, by an unexpected providence in His righteous justice, brought a just judgement upon them; causing them to become a prey to the soldier.[20]

31

'Put them all to the sword'

Oliver Cromwell describes the massacre to Lenthall and justifies it.

Dublin, 17th September 1649

Upon the 10th inst., we began the storm; and after some hot dispute we entered, the enemy disputing it very stiffly with us. Our men that stormed the breaches were forced to recoil; they made a second attempt and became masters both of their retrenchments and the Church. Divers of the Enemy retreated into the Mill-Mount: a place very strong and difficult of access. The Governor, Sir Arthur Ashton,[21] and divers considerable officers being there, our men getting up to them, were ordered by me to put them all to the sword: and indeed, being in the heat of action, I forbade them to spare any that were in arms in the Town: and, I think, that night they put to the sword about 2000 men; about 100 of them possessed St Peter's Church-steeple whereupon I ordered [it] to be fired, when one of them was heard to say in the midst of the flames: 'God damn me, God confound me; I burn, I burn.'

The next day, the other two Towers were summoned. When they submitted, their officers were knocked on the head; and every tenth man of the soldiers killed; and the rest shipped for the Barbadoes. . . . I am persuaded that this is a righteous judgement of God upon these barbarous wretches, who have imbrued their hands in so much innocent blood; and that it will tend to prevent the effusion of blood for the future, which are satisfactory grounds to such actions, which otherwise cannot but work remorse and regret.

---

20 In Peter Young, *Oliver Cromwell*, Batsford, 1962, p. 102.
21 His wooden leg was said to be full of gold coin, but the eager soldiers found two hundred gold pieces sewn in his belt, for which there was a scramble.

Dunbar

Prince Charles landed in Scotland in June 1650 after being proclaimed Charles II by the Scots. On 3 September, at Dunbar, Cromwell's 11,000 men beat 20,000 Scots thanks to his superior tactical skill, killing 3,000 and taking 10,000 prisoners. Cromwell had never faced such odds before: 'This is the Lord's doing and it is marvellous in our eyes'; even Leslie, the Scottish general, acknowledged in the defeat of the Presbyterian Covenanters 'the visible hand of God'. An eyewitness wrote:

> We carried on as with a divine impulse. He [Cromwell] did laugh so excessively as if he had been drunk, and his eyes sparkled with spirits.[20]

32

THE SCOTS ARE ROUTED

Oliver Cromwell sends an account of the battle to Lenthall.

Dunbar, 4th Sept. 1650

. . . There was a very short dispute at sword's point between our horse and theirs. My own regiment, at the push of pike, did repel the stoutest regiment the Enemy had there. The horse in the meantime did, with a great deal of courage and spirit, beat back all oppositions; charging through the bodies of the Enemy's horse, and of their foot; who were, after the first repulse given, made by the Lord of Hosts as stubble to our swords. . . .

The best of the Enemy's horse being broken through and through in less than an hour's dispute, it became a total rout; our men having the chase and execution of them near eight miles. We believe that upon the place and near were about 3000 slain. . . .

Worcester

Exactly one year later, Cromwell's final battle in the Civil War spelt the end of the independence of Scotland: it was incorporated in the Commonwealth and Charles II fled to France.

33

FINAL VICTORY

Cromwell tells Lenthall.

Worcester, 4th Sept. 1651

. . . This Battle in the end became an absolute victory, – and so full an one as proved a total defeat and ruin of the Enemy's Army. . . . What the slain are, they are very many: – and must needs be so; because the dispute was long and very near at hand; there are about six or seven thousand prisoners taken. The dimensions of this mercy are above my thoughts. . . .

The Tragedy of Defeat

Early or late,
They stoop to fate,
And must give up their murmuring breath
When they, pale captives, creep to death
JAMES SHIRLEY (1596–1666), DEATH THE LEVELLER

Defeat in war is always tragic, when all the sacrifices and all the effort turn out to have been in vain, but doubly so in a civil war when there is no united nation to save the loser from ruin, when a man's own compatriots condemn him to suffer the supreme penalty for fighting for a cause firmly believed in, relying on God's help.

The King surrendered at Newark in May 1646 to take refuge in Scotland, and, according to persistent assumption, was sold by his hosts to Parliament for £400,000. Negotiations with Parliament failed because, even in face of death, Charles, bravely and without losing faith, upheld the convictions of his conscience. He was sentenced to death as 'a tyrant, traitor, murderer, and public enemy', and beheaded on 30 June 1649. The King's dignified political testament, to guide the future Charles II, was written two days before he was taken to Hurst Castle to await his trial; it shows his belief that the sober English nation was 'under some infatuation' and 'another Parliament would remember how useful a King's power is to a people's liberty'.

34

THE BEATEN KING KEEPS HIS BELIEF IN DIVINE RIGHT

Charles I nevertheless advises the Prince of Wales to affect only prerogative which is for the good of the people, to keep the peace.

Newport, November 29th, 1648

SON,

By what hath been said, you may see how long we have laboured in search of peace. Do not you be discouraged to tread those ways, to restore yourself to your right; but prefer the way of peace. Show the greatness of your mind, rather to conquer your enemies by pardoning than punishing. If you saw how unmanly and unchristianly this implacable disposition is in our evil willers, you would avoid that spirit. Censure us not, for having parted with too much of our own right; the price was great; the commodity was security to us, peace to our people. And we are confident another Parliament would remember how useful a King's power is to a people's liberty.

Of how much have we divested ourself, that we and they might meet again in a due Parliamentary way to agree the bounds for Prince and people! And in this, give belief to our experience, never to affect more greatness, or prerogative than what is really and intrinsically for the good of your subjects (not satisfaction of favourites). And, if you thus use it, you will never want means to be a father to all, and a bountiful Prince to any you would be extraordinarily gracious to. You may perceive all men trust their treasure, where it returns them interest; and if Princes, like the sea, receive and repay all the fresh streams and rivers trust them with, they will not grudge, but pride themselves, to make them up an ocean.

These considerations may make you a great Prince, as your father is now a low one; and your state may be so much the more established, as mine hath been shaken. For subjects have learnt (we dare say) that victories over their Princes are but triumphs over themselves; and so, will be more unwilling to hearken to changes hereafter.

The English nation are a sober people; however at present under some infatuation. We know not but this may be the last time we may speak to you or the world publicly. We are sensible into what hands we are fallen; and yet we bless God we have those inward refreshments, that the malice of our enemies cannot disturb. We have learnt to own ourself by retiring into ourself, and therefore can the better digest what befalls us; not doubting but God can restrain our enemies' malice, and turn their fierceness unto his praise.

To conclude, if God give you success, use it humbly and far from revenge. If He restore you to your right upon hard conditions, whatever you promise, keep. Those men which have forced laws which they were bound to observe, will find their triumphs full of troubles. Do not think anything in this world worth obtaining by foul and unjust means. You are the son of our love; and, as we direct you to what we have recommended to you, so we assure you, we do not more affectionately pray for you (to whom we are a natural parent) than we do, that the ancient glory and renown of this nation be not buried in irreligion and fanatic humour: and that all our subjects (to whom we are a political parent) may have such sober thoughts as to seek their peace in the orthodox profession of the Christian religion, as it was established since the Reformation in this kingdom, and not in new revelation; and that the ancient laws, with the interpretation according to the known practices, may once again be a hedge about them; that you may in due time govern, and they be governed, as in the fear of the Lord.

C.R.

The Navy sided with Parliament but one third later revolted under the shock of the King's execution. This Royalist squadron under Prince Rupert, who, after the end of his military career at the age of twenty-six, soon mastered seamanship, menaced trade in the Channel, while the Parliamentary Navy was paralysed by mutiny, owing to poisonous food, plague, flogging, and arrears in pay.

Finally, the Navy drove Rupert to Lisbon, right into the Tagus; the King of Portugal, however, forbade them to attack. In revenge, they captured six and burnt three ships of the Brazil fleet, and tried to kidnap Rupert while he was hunting. In retaliation, Rupert sent a sailor, disguised as a Portuguese, to smuggle a time-bomb, hidden in an oil-barrel, on board the *Leopard*; had it not been discovered, the ship would have blown up. A mean trick, one might say, for a once great and chivalrous commander – and so was his attack on a few sailors, who were mingling peacefully with his own on shore – due, no doubt, to his being mercilessly hounded after the Royalist defeat. When his squadron was later destroyed at Cartagena, which he had reached after slipping away from Lisbon, Rupert fled across the Atlantic to the West Indies in the one solitary ship he had left.

35

HOW PRINCE RUPERT'S VINDICTIVE RUSE WAS FRUSTRATED

A Parliamentarian seaman writes home.

From aboard *The Happy Entrance*, riding before the mouth of the river of Lisbon

May 13 1650

. . . On Saturday Prince Rupert sent a Portugal boat amongst our fleet, having in her two negros belonging to the Portugals, and one Englishman in Portugal habit, belonging to Prince Rupert his ship; the boat having in her, bread, oil, onions, oranges and lemons, and such like trade to sell, and a small cask fitted wtih fireworks at one end, and oil at the other; and it went with such a device, that at the handing of it into the ship, they in the boat pulling at a string, which was fast to the spring of a pistol within the cask, it should take fire, and blow up and burn the ship.

This boat was aboard of the *Leopard* our Vice-Admiral; but through God's good providence to us, they were disappointed of their purpose and intent by the Englishman blurting out some English words unawares, which was taken notice of, and thereby mistrusted; so taking him upon suspicion of treachery he presently bid the men that came into the boat to take heed to themselves, for there was fireworks in the boat, and confessed that they were come purposely to blow up the ship, and that Prince Rupert had promised him an hundred pounds for so doing.

At that time Prince Rupert with some of his wicked crew being ashore to see their plot take effect, but perceiving his men to be taken, and themselves frustrated of their design, in a most furious rage came down to the waterside, where some of the *Bonaventure*'s men were filling water, Prince Rupert asked them who they were for? The men answered they did belong to the Parliament ships, he calling them dogs fell upon them, firing their pistols, and running at them their swords, killed three of them, two were mortally wounded, and three of them carried aboard prisoners, and were most barbarously used, and kept in chains.

Many splendid Cavaliers were either disabled in the war or rode home ingloriously at the end, facing a precarious future of impoverishment. No wonder their regretful thoughts were dwelling in melancholic nostalgia on the past.

36

'Thump-Thump-up your stairs like a knocker'

William Blundell (1620–98), a crippled, prematurely aged Cavalier, writes to his sister-in-law that it was 'a great pity' he ever went to war.

Crosby, 27th February 1651

Sister Margaret,

I think it is full time either for me to go to Haggerston or for you to come to Crosby, otherways we may shake hands in fancy at this distance, and bid farewell old acquaintance. I have seen all the world twice over at the least since you and I saw one another.

I remember there was a young fellow not far from Haggerston that told a friend of ours who would gladly have drawn him to the wars, that it was a great pity so gude a like man as he should be knocked o' th' head. And truly I have just such thoughts upon my own metamorphosis. For you well remember what a pretty straight young thing, all dashing in scarlet I came into Haggerston when you saw me last. But now, if you chance to hear a thing come Thump-Thump-up your stairs like a knocker, God bless us, at midnight, look out confidently: a gross full body of an ell or more in the waist, with an old peruke clapped on a bald pate, do not you fear for all that. The thing is no goblin; but the very part we talk on. 'By my truly', you will say, 'and that is a great pity.' And by my troth, sister, it is so; but we will talk more of this when you see it. . . .

I am your most affectionate brother,
W.B.

The 'Great' or 'Martyr' Earl of Derby regarded rebellion in Lancashire as 'a personal affront to the House of Stanley, a revolt of ungrateful and treacherous bondsmen against their rightful lord' (C.V. Wedgwood). After Marston Moor, he withdrew with other Royalist fugitives to the Isle of Man, which he governed as hereditary sovereign lord, and was determined to hold out there.

37

'His Majesty's most loyal servant'

James Stanley, 7th Earl of Derby (1607–51) rejects indignantly, twelve days after the King's execution, General Henry Ireton's proposal that he should surrender the Isle of Man in return for the repossession of his estates in England.

Castletown, July 12, 1649

I received your letter with indignation and scorn and return you this answer: that I cannot but wonder whence you should gather any hopes from me, that I should, like you, prove treacherous to my sovereign, since you cannot but be sensible of my former actings in his late Majesty's service; from which principles of loyalty I am no whit departed. I scorn your proffers, disdain your favour, and abhor your treason; and am so far from delivering this island to your advantage, that I will keep it to the utmost of my power to your destruction. Take this for your final answer, and forbear any further solicitations; for, if you trouble me with any more messages on this occasion, I will burn the paper and hang the bearer. This is the immutable resolution, and shall be the undoubted practice of him, who accounts it his chiefest glory to be

His Majesty's most loyal and obedient servant,
DERBY

On his return to Lancashire in August 1651 as commander of the local insurrection army, fighting in the cause of Charles II, the Earl of Derby was wounded and defeated at Wigan and captured at the battle of Worcester. He was court-martialled and sentenced to death as a traitor at Chester, and his appeal for pardon, although supported by Cromwell, was rejected.

38

'In heaven we shall be for ever free from plunder'

Letter left on the table by the Earl of Derby 'To his Lady in the Isle of Man', Charlotte, Countess of Derby, when he attempted to escape from prison.

[Chester, autumn 1651]

My dear Heart,

The King is dead or escaped in disguise,[22] all the Nobles of the party killed or taken, save a few; and it matters not much where they be. The common soldiers are dispersed, some in prison, some sent to other nations. I escaped a great danger at Wigan; but met with a worse of Worcester, being not so fortunate as to meet with any that would kill me. Lord Lauderdale and I were not thought worth killing; but we had quarter given us.

I thought myself happy in being sent prisoner to Chester, where I might have the comfort of seeing my two daughters; but I fear my coming here may cost me dear; but whatsoever come of me, I have peace in my own breast, and no discomfort at all but the sense of your grief and that of my poor children. . . .

The Son of God whose blood was shed for our good, preserve your lives, that we may meet once more on earth, and at least in the kingdom of heaven, where we shall be for ever free from all rapine, plunder, and violence. And so I rest everlastingly,

Your most faithful,
Derby

Derby was recaptured after his attempt to escape and executed at Bolton. He may have been 'narrow-minded, vain and silly' (C.V. Wedgwood), but his

---

22 Charles II wandered as a fugitive in disguise for six weeks and then embarked at Shoreham for Normandy.

farewell letter to his wife and children, in which he advises her (who had proved to be a more competent commander than her husband in her heroic defence of Lathom House) to accept conditions of surrender of the Isle of Man for the sake of finding safety and rest from war, is a moving testimony of the tragedy of defeat in the Civil War and shows him as a man 'of great honour and clear courage' (Clarendon). 'Among the sufferers for King Charles I none cast greater lustre on the cause' (Walpole).

39

'I must away to the fatal stroke'

The Earl of Derby sends a farewell letter to his wife and children three days before his execution in which he regrets the vanities of his life.

Chester, October 12th, 1651

My dear Heart,

I have heretofore sent you comfortable lines, but alas! I have now no word of comfort, saving to our last and best refuge, which is Almighty God, to whose will we must submit.

The Governor of this place, Colonel Duckenfeld, is General of the Forces which are going now against the Isle of Man, and however you might do for the present, in time it would be a grievous and troublesome business to resist, wherefore my advice, notwithstanding my great affection to that place, is, that you would make conditions for yourself and children, servants, and people there, and such as came over with me, to the end you may go to some place of rest where you may not be concerned in war,[23] and taking thought of your poor children, you may in some sort provide for them; then prepare yourself to come to your friends above, in that blessed place where bliss is, and no mingling of opinions.

I conjure you, my dearest heart, by all those graces which God hath given you, that you exercise your patience in this great and strange trial. If harm come to you, then I am dead indeed; and until then I shall live in you, who are truly the best part of myself. When there is no such as I in being, then look upon yourself and my poor children; then take comfort, and God will bless you.

I acknowledge the great goodness of God, to have given me such a wife as you; so great an honour to my family, so excellent a companion to me, so pious, so much of all that can be said of good. I must confess it impossible to say enough thereof. I ask God pardon, with all my soul, that I have not been enough thankful for so great a benefit, and when I have done anything at any time that might justly offend you, with joint hands I also ask your pardon.

---

23 Colonel Robert Duckenfield, after failing to save Derby's life, occupied the Isle of Man twelve days after the Earl's execution with the help of a local insurrection; the Countess retired peacefully to Knowsley.

Oh, my dear soul, I have reason to believe that this may be the last time that ever I shall write unto you. . . . Oh, my dear, again I ask you to take comfort; when you so do, rejoice thereat, I beseech you, as doing me a great favour; and for my sake, keep not too strict, too severe a life, but endeavour to live for your children's sake. . . . I draw near the bottom of the paper, and I am drawing on to the grave, for presently I must away to the fatal stroke, which shows little mercy in this nation, and as for justice the Great Judge judge thereof.

I have no more to say to you at this time than my prayers for the Almighty's blessing to you, and my dear Mall, Ned, and Billy. Amen: sweet Jesu.

Your faithful
Derby

My dear Mall, Ned, and Billy,

I remember well how sad you were to part with me, but now I fear your sorrow will be greatly increased to be informed that you can never see me more in this world; but I charge you all to strive against too great a sorrow; you are all of you of that temper that it would do you much harm. My desires and prayers to God are that you may have a happy life. Let it be as holy a life as you can, and as little sinful as you can avoid or prevent.

I can well now give you that counsel, having in myself, at this time, so great a sense of the vanities of my life, which fill my soul with sorrow; yet I rejoice to remember that when I have blessed God with pious devotion, it has been most delightful to my soul, and most be my eternal happiness.

Love the Archdeacon; he will give you good precepts. Obey your mother with cheerfulness, and grieve her not; for she is your example, your nursery, your counsellor, your all under God. There never was, nor ever can be, a more deserving person. I am called away, and this is the last I shall write to you. The Lord my God bless and guard you from all evil: so prays your father at this time, whose sorrow is inexorable to part with Mall, Ned, and Billy.

Remember
Derby

The attitudes engendered by the Civil War are in a different category from those generated by war against a foreign enemy. Members of the same family and friends of long standing found themselves on opposite sides through conviction, loyalty, or just circumstances. In one way, this fratricidal, ideological conflict was sometimes even more cruelly fought, evoked deeper hatred and led to pitiless carnage, at its worst when instigated by Cromwell's religious ecstasies. On the other hand, this 'war without an enemy' was thought to be unnatural and individual bonds could remain unimpaired across the lines through respect for honestly professed conviction; some combatants felt they had been fatally caught up on the stage of war in a tragedy in which they had to act out honourably their allotted parts against their own countrymen. The farewell letters of the King and his faithful retainer before their execution gave vent to sentiments of noble poignancy. A few women bravely conducted the defence of their castles, others took part in campaigns disguised as soldiers, or just voiced their grievances in the turmoil.

FIVE

The Dutch Naval Wars (1652–74), 1688 Invasion, and Wars of William III (1688–97)

Who never beheld so noble a sight,
As this so brave, and bloody sea-fight
JOHN DRYDEN (1631–1700)

During the first part of the seventeenth century, half of Britain's carrier trade was lost to the increasingly prosperous Dutch whose merchant fleet dominated the Atlantic and Indian Oceans and poached fishing grounds in the North Sea. The Navy failed to protect merchant shipping, even in the Channel, and Turkish pirates from Algiers roamed right up to Devon and Cornwall, capturing thousands of sailors as slaves.

The Navigation Act of 1651, limiting foreign ships in English ports, hit this lucrative Dutch ascendency. To enforce it, the Navy, after its sad neglect, was now doubled under Commissioner Robert Blake, one of three 'generals at sea', by the addition of forty-one new warships, paid for by funds exacted from the beaten Cavaliers. This challenge to Dutch naval supremacy, and the conviction of Parliament that war would be beneficial to commerce, inevitably led to conflict on the high seas to resolve this rivalry: it was purely a fight for naval power to guarantee economic profit and there was no threat to the country or its religion. The aggressive nationalism of the Puritans and the sailors' inveterate hatred of the foreigner meant that war was welcomed: 'The Dutch have too much trade and the English are resolved to take it from them', wrote General Monk.

Prelude: 'Keep foreigners from fooling us' (Blake)

England's honour, once her pride,
Rome's terror, Dutch annoyer,
Truth's defender, Spain's destroyer
GEORGE HARRISON, EPITAPH ON BLAKE (1657)

For the Dutch, who were more dependent on trade than agricultural Britain, this was a vital issue and the first clash occurred over pride and prestige. On 18 May 1652, Admiral Martin van Tromp appeared with forty-two ships off Dover and suddenly bore down on Blake's mere twenty, refusing to salute the English flag as requested. Blake who wrote 'it is not for us to mind state affairs but to keep foreigners from fooling us', attacked at once, drove the Dutch to the coast of France with the loss of two of their ships, and then proceeded to destroy the Dutch herring fleet.

1

A DUTCH PROVOCATION

Robert Blake (1599–1657) tells the Speaker of the action for the honour of the flag which opened the First Dutch War; he accuses the Dutch of seeking 'to brave us upon our own coast' and causing the first breach.

From aboard the *James*, three leagues off the Hydes [Hythe], 20th May 1652

I have dispatched away the express to your Honours to give you an account of what passed yesterday between us and the Dutch fleet, being in Rye Bay. I received intelligence that Van Tromp, with 40 sail, was off the South Sand-head, whereupon I made all possible speed to ply up towards them, and yesterday, in the morning, we saw them at anchor in and near Dover Road. Being come within three leagues of them, they weighed and stood by a wind to the eastward, we supposing their intention was to leave us to avoid the dispute of the flag.

About two hours after they altered their course and bore directly with us, Van Tromp the headmost; whereupon we lay by and put ourselves into a fighting posture, judging they had a resolution to engage. Being come within musket-shot I gave order to fire at his flag, which was done thrice. After the third shot he let fly a broadside at us. We continued fighting till night; then our ship being unable to sail by reason that all our rigging and sails were extremely shattered, our mizen-mast shot off, we came with advice of the captains to an anchor about three or four leagues off the Ness [Dungeness], to refit our ship, at which we laboured all the night.

What course the Dutch fleet steers we do not well know, nor can we tell what harm we have done them, but we suppose one of them to be sunk, and another of 30 guns we have taken, with the captains of both. We have received above 70 great shot in our hull and masts, in our sail and rigging without number, being engaged with the whole body of the fleet for the space of four hours, and the mark at which they aimed. We must needs acknowledge a great mercy that we had no more harm, and our hope the righteous God will continue the same unto us if there do arise a war between us, and they being first in the breach, and seeking an occasion to quarrel and watching, as it seems, an advantage to brave us upon our own coast.

Van Tromp sent a protest to Blake after the action, which Blake rejected with stinging self-righteous indignation. If we compare Blake's attitude with

Drake's, we notice the same pugnacious assertiveness; but the unscrupulous Elizabethan privateer, greedy for loot, has been succeeded by a conscientious patriotic Puritan.

2

'This great insult'

Blake answers back to Admiral van Tromp.

In the Downs, May 30th, 1652

Sir,

It is not without great astonishment that I have read yours of the 23rd May sent to me by your messengers, wherein though representing yourself as a person of honour, you introduce many gross misstatements; and this, just after having fought with the fleet of the Parliament of the English Republic, instead of employing the customary forms of respect, which the occasion demanded, and which you yourself have hitherto employed, and having thought fit to commit an act of hostility (which you yourself style a falling out with the Republic) without receiving the slightest provocation from her servants, who are thus assailed by you at a time when your Government and their Ambassadors were engaged in negotiations with Parliament, and in need of the friendship of the Republic of England. But God (in whom we trust) having frustrated your purposes, to your own destruction, and seeing that we have taken some of your ships, you have thought well to demand the same of us again, as though your former proceeding had been nothing but a salute (as you assert), and failing this to follow up your former insults by your present letter; to which the only meet answer that I can return is that I presume Parliament will keenly resent this great insult and the spilling of the blood of their unoffending subjects, and that you will moreover find in the undersigned one ever ready to carry out their commands.

Your humble servant,
Rob: Blake

About Social Conditions in the Navy

There are no men under the sun that fare harder and are so abused on all sides as we poor seamen, without whom the land would soon be brought under subjection
EDWARD BARLOW (ORDINARY SEAMAN FOR 48 YEARS)

For eight years, Blake dealt blow after blow to Prince Rupert, the Dutch, the French, the Spanish, and the Barbary pirates, and established for the first time the Navy in the Mediterranean, in a spectacular revival of English sea-power, based on discipline, courage and new ideas. He created a tradition unbroken until the Second World War. This he achieved in face of a continuation of the shortages and appalling conditions which had hampered Elizabeth's Navy.

3

'We walk in darkness, and see no light'

Blake paints a grim picture of food supply at Lisbon for Lord Protector Cromwell.

> Aboard the *George*, in Cascais Road, August 30th, 1655
> . . . Our condition is dark and sad; our ships extreme foul, winter drawing on, our victuals expiring, all stores failing, our men falling sick through the badness of drink, and eating their victuals boiled in salt water for two months' space; the coming of a supply uncertain (we received not one word from the Commissioners of the Admiralty and Navy by the last) and though it come timely, yet if beer come not with it, we shall be undone that way. We have no place or friend, and our mariners (which I most apprehend) apt to fall into discontents, through their long keeping abroad. Our only comfort is that we have a God to lean upon, although we walk in darkness, and see no light. . . .

At times the long-suffering patience of the sailors was exhausted and rebellion flared up.

4

MUTINY OVER BACK-PAY

Captain Thomas Thorowgood tells Navy Commissioner Thomas Smith how he was nearly torn to pieces.

> Portsmouth, December 13th, 1652
> These are to give your worship notice that on Saturday I tendered our sailors down six months' pay, which they refused to take, saying that they would have all or none, and railed upon your worship and the rest of the owners, saying that you had received all the ships' pay of the State, and that your worship and myself went about to cheat them of their wages, and swore they would have it all or else the ship would lie here and rot; and they are grown to such a height that they will not be at my command, but do what they please, for on Saturday night they were singing and roaring, and I sent my servant to bid the boatswain to be quiet and go to their cabins; but they would not, so I went down myself and desired them to give over and go to their cabins; but they told me they would not be under my command, so I struck one of them, and the rest put out the candle and took hold of me as though they would have torn me to pieces, so that I am almost beside myself, not knowing what to do. I could wish with all my heart that the ship were at London, and you knew how to deal with them.

'Parliament Joan' had been the Florence Nightingale of the Civil War; although pensioned, she volunteered again on the outbreak of the Dutch

War. When she had spent all her own savings for the relief of the sick and wounded, she urged the authorities to send her the necessary funds.

5

'I have laid out my monies'

Elizabeth Alkin ('Parliament Joan') appeals to Robert Blackbourne, Secretary to the Admiralty Committee, for repayment of her expenditure on the sick and wounded.

> Harwich, 2nd July 1653
>
> Sir, you have sent me down to Harwich with five pounds, but believe me, it hath cost me three times so much since my coming thither. I have laid out my monies for divers necessaries about the sick and wounded here; it pities me to see poor people in distress. A great deal of monies I have given, to have them cleansed in their bodies and their hair cut, mending their clothes, reparations, and several things else, so that I have spent both the money I had of you and my own money; and besides I am owing for my diet. I go often to Ipswich to visit the sick and wounded there, so that in coming and going money departs from me. I was necessitated to get 20s. of the Mayor of Harwich, and he is at a great want of monies himself. I pray you, sir, send me some money speedily, for I stand in great need thereof for the satisfying of my diet and reckonings I am owing.
>
> So wishing you much happiness – I rest, sir,
> Yours ready in any service to be commanded,
> Elizabeth Alkin

John Evelyn, the famous diarist, who had corresponded with Charles II in cypher during his exile, was appointed commissioner for the care of the sick, wounded and prisoners after the Restoration. He found himself in charge of not only 1,500 sick and wounded English sailors but also 25,000 prisoners, 'without one penny of money and above £2000 indebted'. The proceeds from the sale of the cargo of an Indian prize ship which Admirals Monck and Sandwich, straining their authority, had passed on to him in compassion, provided only temporary relief. A raging plague epidemic was decimating the prisoners who were weakened by the lack of food, and Evelyn was the only commissioner staying at his post and showing concern.

6

'Let us not be barbarians'
PRISONERS DYING OF HUNGER

John Evelyn (1620–1706) entreats Sir William Coventry, Secretary to the Duke of York, to relieve starvation.

2 October 1665

. . . Having lost all our servants, officers, and most necessary assistants, [we] have nothing more left us to expose but our persons, which are very moment at the mercy of a raging pestilence; who, having adventured their lives for the public, perish for their reward, and die like dogs in the street unregarded. Our prisoners (who with open arms, as I am credibly informed by eye-witnesses, embraced our men, instead of lifting up their hands against them) beg at us, as a mercy, to knock them on the head; for we have no bread to relieve the dying creatures. Nor does this country afford gaols to secure them in, unless Leeds Castle may be had; if at least half of them survive to be brought so far, to starve when they come there. As for the pittance now lately ordered us, what will that benefit to our numbers and the mouths we are to feed? – I beseech your Honour, let us not be reputed barbarians; or if at last we must be so, let me not be the executor of so much inhumanity; when the price of one good subject's life is (rightly considered) of more value than the wealth of the Indies. . . .

Six months later Evelyn conceived the revolutionary idea of setting up a hospital for sailors. In the following extract he tries to sell it by stressing its economic and humanitarian advantages. It was another twenty-eight years, however, before the Royal Hospital for Seamen at Greenwich was opened, with Evelyn as treasurer. Chelsea Hospital was opened in 1682.

7

AN INFIRMARY WOULD SAVE MONEY

Evelyn tells the diarist Samuel Pepys, surveyor-general of the victualling office and energetic reformer of abuses, why he thinks an infirmary for sick and wounded seamen should be built at Chatham.

26 March 1666

. . . In less than eight months time there will be saved, in the quarters of 500 men alone, more money than the whole expense (of building etc.) amounts to; 500 men's quarters at 1s. coming to £25 per diem. Now, 500 sick persons quartered in a town at the victuallers and scattered alehouses (as the custom is), will take up at least 160 houses, there being very few of those miserable places which afford accommodation for about two or three in a house; with, frequently at greater distances, employ of chirurgeons, nurses, and officers, innumerable; so as when we have been distressed for chirurgeons, some of them walked six miles every day, by going but from quarter to quarter, and not being able to visit their patients as they ought: whereas, in our hospitals, they are continually at hand.

At six-pence each, the sick shall have as good, and much more proper and wholesome diet, than now they have in the ale-houses, where they are fed with trash, and embezzle their money more to inflame themselves, and retard and destroy their cures out of ignorance or intemperance; whiles a sober matron governs the nurses, looks to their provisions, and the nurses attend the sick. By this method, likewise, are the almost indefinite number of chirurgeons and officers exceedingly reduced; the sick dieted, kept from drink and intemperance, and consequently, from most unavoidably relapsing. . . . Our accounts better and more exactly kept. A vast and very considerable sum is saved to his Majesty. . . .

Some Attitudes to War

If Providence prosper us with a good gale,
The Dutch, nor the Devil shall ever prevail
ANON. ON THE VICTORY OVER THE DUTCH IN 1665

In November 1652 van Tromp forced Blake to withdraw into the Thames and the story went round (probably just a joke) that van Tromp had fastened a broom to his masthead as a symbol of sweeping the Navy off the sea. Yet three months later, Blake, although outnumbered by over 3:1, fought off van Tromp's convoy fleet in a persistent three-day running fight near Portland, until, with reinforcements, he drove the Dutch from Beachy Head to Cape Gris Nez where only the night saved them from complete destruction. They lost nine men of war and thirty to forty merchant ships, but Blake, for good measure, doubled their losses in his report. His reference to God's help echoes Cromwell's.

8

THE SCORE IS 17:1?

Blake and Admiral Richard Deane tell the Council of State about the Battle of Portland.

From aboard the *Triumph* near the Isle of Wight, February 22nd, 1653
The 18th inst. about six in the morning we espied the Dutch Fleet, between Portland and the Casquets and consisting of about 200 merchant ships, and 80 men of war. They were in the wind of us some two leagues, and came down upon us. We were some 25 sail together, the rest astern and much to leeward by reason of which we were engaged very long before the rest could come up to our relief. We fought the whole day till the evening parted us. We kept sight of them that night and the next morning we came up with them again (the wind being West, they steering up the Channel homewards) and continued fighting until the dark night parted us.

We kept fair by them all the night, and the next morning we began with them again, and pressed so hard upon them that divers of their ships, both men of war and merchant men began to fly off from their body towards the coast of France, insomuch that in the evening they had not above 35 men of war left and 100 merchant ships. We were in the wind of them over against Blackness [Gris Nez] in France, bore directly in for the French shore, so near that we durst not follow them, it being nigh a lee shore, and most of the great ships had their masts, yards, and sails in such a condition as they were ready to fall down every hour, we thought it the best way to come to an anchor. Thus your Lordships see what the Lord hath done for us, and how far He brought us. We have taken and destroyed about 17 of their men of war and have not lost any one ship as we know of, only one that was so torn that she was not fit to keep the seas and therefore we took out the men and sunk her. Yet we are miserably torn and have very many men slain and wounded, and therefore humbly desire provisions, chirurgeons, and all things needful. We are now hasting to Portsmouth, and the Isle of Wight for our refitting. . . .

After ten years of peace on conclusion of Blake's war, the Second Dutch Naval War – the first entirely colonial struggle – began after the seizure of New Amsterdam (re-named New York) by the three warships of Captain Robert Holmes and the 450 soldiers of Colonel Richard Nicolls, in the name of the Duke of York as colonial proprietor; rivalry in the West African slave trade and the prohibition of Dutch commerce with the West Indian and American colonies were also points of dispute. The Dutch captains were the better sailors and more daring, but the Navy successfully combined naval and military ideas, as the crews were a mixture of 'tarpaulins' (old sea dogs) and former soldiers.

The Duke of York (later James II) was Lord Admiral at the battle of Lowestoft, assisted by Prince Rupert who later succeeded him (before retiring into commerce as head of Hudson's Bay Company). They blew up Admiral Opdam's flagship and the Dutch lost thirty ships, but Cornelius van Tromp, Martin's son, managed to make a skilful withdrawal with the remnants of the Dutch fleet, for which, despite his victory, the Duke of York was blamed, and subsequently dismissed.

The following report of the battle mainly deplores the burning and drowning of so many enemy sailors, 'the saddest sight I ever beheld', and voices outrage about the 'barbarous villany' of refusing quarter, perpetrated by an 'inhuman rogue' of an English fire-ship captain.

9

COMPASSION FOR THE ENEMY

Sir Allen Apsley (1616–83), Keeper of the King's hawks and Hampton Court park, sends his wife an account of the victory at Lowestoft.

3rd June 1655

I know this letter will be welcome to thee, because it will inform thee that by God Almighty's favour I am well, which is a blessing I think I have received from Him for thy virtue's sake. . . .

The battle began about half an hour past three in the morning. They continued a fierce fight from that time till about four in the afternoon, at which time Updam's ship blew up with all her men. Not long after they began to fly towards their own coasts, but still fighting; which continued as long as we could see. Four of their great ships being foul of one another, a fireship of ours ran in amongst them and in a moment set them all on fire. And to see so many poor souls leaping from the fire to the sea, and swimming there as thick as ears of corn together, was the saddest sight I ever beheld. I think our ketches saved about 120 of them.

A rascal that commanded a fireship did the most barbarous villany in the world. There being three or four great ships of theirs foul of one another, the poor men seeing the fireship come up sent out their boat and begged for quarter. This inhuman rogue runs in amongst them and sets them all on fire, and burned and drowned 500 men.

We have taken divers of their great ships, burned some more than those I have mentioned, and chased them all this morning as soon as it was light till 12 at noon, about which time those that escaped got into the Texel, which were about 48. The rest of them were either burned or taken or dispersed about the sea out of our sight.

This is the greatest victory that ever the English won, and our seamen say it is the most dreadful battle that ever was fought. Their Admiral blown up with all his men. . . .

Sir Thomas Browne, physician at Norwich and author of *Religio Medici* (a transitional book between medievalism and rationalism in which scripture and nature are treated as parallel areas of revelation), models his attitude to war entirely on the great classical writers when he sermonizes his sailor son and praises him for his scholarly bent; but he does not forget to ask for 'a box of the Jesuit's powder at easier rate' from Cádiz. Thomas, serving in the *Marie Rose* as a lieutenant, was soon to perish at sea.

10

COURAGE THROUGH ARISTOTLE

Dr (later Sir) Thomas Browne (1605–82) gives learned advice to his son at Portsmouth before his departure for Tangier.

[Spring 1667]

Dear Son,

I am very glad you are returned from the Straights mouth once more in health and safety. God continue his merciful providence over you. I hope you maintain a thankful heart and daily bless him for your great deliverances in so many fights and dangers of the sea, whereto you have been exposed upon several seas, and in all seasons of the year.

When you first undertook this service, you cannot but remember that I caused you to read the description of all the sea fights of note, in Plutarch, the Turkish history, and others; and withal gave you the description of fortitude left by Aristotle. . . . To give you your due, in the whole course of this war, both in fights and other sea affairs, hazards and perils, you have very well fulfilled this character in yourself. . . .

He that goes to war must patiently submit unto the various accidents thereof. To be made prisoner by an unequal and overruling power, after a due resistance, is no disparagement; you cannot forget many examples thereof, even of the worthiest commanders in your beloved Plutarch. God hath given you a stout, but a generous and merciful heart withal; and in all your life you could never behold any person in misery but with compassion and relief: so you have laid up a good foundation for God's mercy, and, if such a disaster should happen, He will, without doubt, mercifully remember you.

I like it, that you are not only Marti but Mercurio, and very much pleased to find how good a student you have been at sea, and particularly with what sucess you have read divers books there, especially Homer and Juvenal. Having such industry adjoined unto your apprehension and memory, you are like to proceed [not only] a noble navigator, but a great scholar, which will be much to your honour and my satisfaction and content.

I am much pleased to find that you take the draughts of remarkable things where e'er you go; for that may be very useful, and will fasten themselves the better in your memory. You are mightily improved in your violin, but I would by no means have you practise upon the trumpet, for many reasons. Your fencing in the ship may be against the scurvy, but that knowledge is of little advantage in actions of the sea.

When you are at Cales [Cádiz], see if you can get a box of the Jesuit's powder at easier rate, and bring it in the bark, not in powder. Enquire farther at Tangier of the mineral water you told me, which was near the town, and whereof many made use. Take notice of such plants as you meet with, either upon the Spanish or African coast; and if you know them not, put some leaves into a book.

The merciful providence of God go with you.

Your loving father,
Thomas Browne

While the Treaty of Breda was being negotiated, Admiral De Ruyter sailed up the Thames and the Medway, despite the forts and the boom, where, after the Great Plague and Fire in the City of London, the Navy was laid up defenceless for lack of money. The Dutch, guided by English pilots who with three thousand other English sailors had deserted to them because they had received no pay for years, bombarded the English warships lying at Chatham, spreading panic and destruction.

The young philosopher John Locke, who had just settled down as secretary and physician in the Strand townhouse of Anthony Ashley Cooper (later Earl of Shaftesbury and Lord Chancellor), takes a sceptical view of the many suppositions being bandied about.

11

THE DUTCH IN THE MEDWAY

John Locke (1632–1704) sends Mr Strachy news of the naval disaster at Chatham, trying to sort out truth from rumour.

15 June 1667

I believe report hath increased the ill news we have here; therefore, to abate what possibly fear may have rumoured, I send you what is vouched here for nearest the truth. The Dutch have burned seven of our ships in Chatham, viz. the *Royal James, Royal Oak, London, Unity, St Matthias, Charles V*, and the *Royal Charles*, which some say they have towed off, others that they have burned. One man of war of theirs was blown up, and three others they say are stuck in the sands; the rest of their fleet is fallen down out of the Medway into the Thames. It was neither excess of courage on their part, nor want of courage in us, that brought this loss upon us; for when the English had powder and shot, they fought like themselves, and made the Dutch feel them; but whether it were fortune, or fate, or anything else, let time and tongues tell you, for I profess I would not believe what every mouth speaks. It is said this morning the French fleet are seen off the Isle of Wight. I have neither the gift nor heart to prophesy, and since I remember you bought a new cloak in the hot weather, I know you are apt enough to provide against a storm. Should I tell you that I believe but half what men of credit and eye-witnesses report, you would think the world very wicked and foolish, or me very credulous. Things and persons are the same here, and go on at the same rate they did before, and I, among the rest, design to continue.

In 1670 Charles II concluded the Treaty of Dover with Louis XIV for the partitioning of Holland, in support of his finance and crown, and because of the commerical rivalry with the Dutch; a secret clause referred to the restoration of the Catholic religion. The resolute Dutch flooded their country to halt the French invaders and, on 28 May 1672, surprised the combined navies of England and France, anchored in Sole Bay, Suffolk. Admiral De Ruyter burnt Lord Sandwich's flagship, the *Royal James*, and the latter was drowned, while the French fleet was keeping away from the fight.

The heavy casualties caused great distress, and popular opposition to a war, as it was understood, for the territorial designs and Catholic aspirations of Louis XIV, was growing. The naval war was the talk of society ('how handsomely Mr Digby died') but one of the many lady admirers of the attractive Earl of Chesterfield would have preferred to walk with him 'by a river side or in a grove' and quite forget about war!

12

THE LADY IS FOR LOVING AMID 'DISMAL NEWS OF DEATH'

An unknown Lady R. writes to Philip Stanhope, second Earl of Chesterfield, after the battle of Sole Bay.

[June 1672]

My Lord,

. . . We hear nothing but dismal news of death from the Fleet. Love has no employment but weeping and everybody's business is to enquire after the volunteers. Am not I happy that amidst all these glooms can sit in my closet and write to you. . . .

I imagine you have an account of the war from your friends of the other sex, and that they have told you how handsomely Mr Digby died. If you have not better intelligence than mine I will constantly inform you of all we know here in every kind. At this time the sea is our theme, and we discourse of what is done there in all places. Do we not pass our time very ill? Pray imagine if I should not have reason to be better pleased if I were walking by a river side or in a grove with you, and that neither of us thought of anything in the world besides. But then we might chance to fall in love again and that would be more disquiet to

Your ever faithful humble servant

When the Cavalier Parliament realized that the war against Holland was not carried on for naval supremacy, they withdrew from it. Charles was forced to reverse his policy, and war with France, which presented the real threat, became a possibility.

In the following extract, the actress Nell Gwynne, mistress of Charles II, chatters along in her irresistibly open and vulgar warmhearted manner, seasoned with a pinch of down-to-earth cynicism: the only meaning war has for her is the return of a lover she is longing for – the handsome (married) 'Lory' Hyde, younger son of the former Lord Chancellor, the Earl of Clarendon, and brother-in-law of the later James II, who was at the Hague negotiating the Peace Treaty of Nimeguen which was to end the Dutch Wars. He was a hot-tempered alchoholic and an arrogant intriguer, who rose to become First Lord of the Treasury and Earl of Rochester, but had, no doubt, his attractions.

13

WHY NELL GWYNNE IS FOR WAR

Nell Gwynne (1650–87) has 'a thousand merry conseets' for Lawrence Hyde.

[c. 1678]

Pray Deare Mr Hide forgive me for not writeing to you before now for the reasone is I have bin sick thre months & sinse I recovered I have had nothing to intertaine you withall nor have nothing now worth writing but that I can holde no longer to let you know I never have ben in any companie wethout drinking your health. for I loue you with all my soule. the pel mel [Pall Mall] is now to me a dismale plase sinse I have uterly lost Sr Car Scrope[1] never to be recourd agane for he tould me he could not live allwayes at this rate & so begune to be a littel uncivil, which I could not sufer from an uglye baux garscon. . . . We are a goeing to supe with the king at whithall & my lady Harvie. the King remembers his sarvis to you. now lets talke of state affairs, for we never caried things so cunningly as now for we dont know whether we shall have pesce or war, but I am for war and for no other reason but that you may come home.

---

1   Sir Carr Scrope, Bart., was a member of the gay fashionable set at the court of Charles II and wrote witty epigrams; he was small and of delicate health and died at the age of thirty-one.

I have a thousand merry conseets, but I cant make her write um[2] & therfore you must take the will for the deed. god bye. your most loueing obedunt faithfull & humbel sarvant

E.G.[3]

The Dutch Invasion of 1688

> *The common people swarm like summerflies;*
> *and whither fly the gnats but to the sun? . . .*
> *Commanded always by the greater gust:*
> *This is the lightness of you common men*
> SHAKESPEARE, HENRY VI, PART III

During the three years of his rule, James II, a Catholic convert full of contradictions, embarked on a policy of toleration for popish dissenters, but he had no intention of turning England into a Catholic absolute monarchy like France, or becoming Louis XIV's puppet, however much he may have admired him. His lack of political aptitude, and of consideration for popular dread of popery, did not allow his aim to establish a mere equality of Churches to be understood. He was widely regarded as a submissive tool of Louis' designs, although, in fact, he had turned down the alliance he was offered. Therefore, after the birth of an heir and the trial of the seven bishops, political and ecclesiastical leaders invited William of Orange, Stadhouder General of the United Provinces and husband of James' Protestant daughter Mary, to save Protestantism in England. As James had fallen out with Louis just then and the latter was busy sending his army to the Rhine against the Empire, while keeping his superior fleet inactive, William could risk shipping an invasion army over to England.

The following sequence of letters gives a fascinating day-to-day account of the gradual but inexorable swing of public opinion in face of the Dutch invasion, and shows how quickly the unthinkable can become accepted by everyone. Patriotic reactions of contemptuous scorn for the invader, and sentiments of loyalty to the King, soon evaporated under the impact of fear of being caught on the wrong side, with the bitter memory of the Civil War still fresh. All William had to do was to avoid hostilities and wait to give public opinion time to rally to him peacefully.

James, who as Duke of York had led the Navy into many a brave battle,

---

2 Nell Gwynne dictated her letters to an amanuensis, as she could not write, and just initialled them E. (Eleanor) G.

3 War could also work in the opposite direction; six years later, Nell Gwynne wrote to Mrs Jennings, Sarah Churchill's mother: 'Here is a sad slaughter at Windsor. The young men taking their leaves and going to France, and although they are none of my lovers, yet I am loath to part with the men.' (B. Bevan, *Nell Gwynne*, Hale, 1969, p. 134.)

but had not expected an invasion by his own son-in-law, seemed paralysed: at Salisbury, in command of a loyal army double the size of William's, with many Catholic officers and Irish soldiers he had recruited, he panicked when his lack of resolution resulted in a tide of defections, and finally fled to France in terror of the memory of his father's execution.

The attitude of Lord Dartmouth, Commander-in-Chief of the Navy, a close friend of James' for twenty years whose loyalty to him was in no doubt, appears all the same somewhat ambiguous. He probably knew that some of his captains intended to desert to the opposing Admiral Herbert, who, after dismissal for refusing to vote for the repeal of the Test Act, had gone to Holland to organize the rebellion; also, he never received any definite orders from James to intercept the invasion fleet of 50 warships and 500 transports, carrying 14,000 men, which was blown down the Channel by an east wind past the Navy (peacefully bottled up in the gunfleet) to effect an unopposed landing near Torbay. Dartmouth, who would not risk taking any initiative himself, then handed the Navy to William, as his wife had urged him to do, without a shot being fired, amid protestations of undying loyalty to the King.

When William reached St James' Palace on 18 December, after James' pathetic flight, 'all the world hastened to see him' and contrary to original intentions, he was to be declared joint sovereign with Mary.

14

READY TO MEET THE 'MONGREL INVADERS'

An unnamed correspondent (probably a cousin in the Civil Service) reports to John Ellis, Secretary of the Revenue in Ireland, about preparations against the imminent invasion by the Prince of Orange.

London, October 2nd, 1688

The Advices from Holland continue to give us the same account of the Dutch Fleet, that it lies off of Goree, and is three or four hundred sail strong in capital men of war and bylanders for the transportation of troops. Their Army is said to be about 18 or 20,000 strong, made up of High and Low Dutch, of refuged Frenchmen, English fugitives and rebels, and such like medley. Earl Maxfield is to command all the horse, and Colonel Sidney[4] the foot, and our late Admiral Herbert the fleet; and if fame be true he is to carry the standard of England. According to the Dutch computation, this Army will have conquered England, Scotland, and Ireland, in six weeks time; and so far are they from making any secret of it, that they make it their public brag, and it is

---

4 Henry Sidney (later Earl of Romney), general of the British regiment in Dutch service, was an intriguer in William's confidence who conveyed the conspirators' invitation to him.

the common talk and vapouring of their carmen and fishermen about their streets. But we hope they reckon without their host, and that England and its old renown, is not yet sunk so low as to be made a prey to such mongrel invaders.

We hear that many Noblemen and others have prayed and had his Majesty's Commission to raise men in their Countries for the public defence. His Majesty is said to have resolved to march in his own royal person (whom God preserve) as soon as they are landed, and all the Court and his Ministers are preparing to attend him. The City is unanimously resolved for the common defence, and the London apprentices seem eager for an opportunity to try their loyalty and briskness against those new pretended invaders. The Lord Dartmouth is gone down the river to hasten the Fleet together. . . .

15

THE ADMIRAL'S WIFE IS ANXIOUS

Barbara, Lady Dartmouth, expects 'the Dutch every moment to take us away' and her husband to 'bear the brunt of them first'.

Oct. 14th

I am very glad to hear my dearest dear heart that you are so well and cheerful; it is all I have in this world to satisfy my dejected spirits, in this melancholy state I am in, expecting the Dutch every moment to take us away, but all that I could freely submit to, were you not to bear the brunt of them first. Indeed when I think of that, it is insupportable to me, God Almighty in his infinite mercy deliver me out of it by bringing us together again. . . .

16

THEY HAVE SAILED

King James II (1633–1701) tells Lord Dartmouth 'tis next to madness'.

Whitehall, Oct. 26th

You will find by Mr Pepys' letter to you the intelligence I have had of the Prince of Orange having sailed out with all his fleet and land soldiers on Friday; what damage they received by the storm of Saturday night I do not yet know. The express who brought the letters tells me that he heard as he passed by Ostend they were on Monday seen still on the coast of Holland. You can best judge by the winds which have been since, what they can do, and by that, how to govern yourself, in such a blowing season as this is, if what is said of their coming out with so small a quantity of victuals and water be true 'tis next to madness. . . .

The Civil War, 1639–51. *England's Arke Secured,* a Parliamentarian propaganda print showing the two Houses and the Assembly on an ark preserved amid a tempest drowning Royalist leaders; the six medallions represent the Puritan generals. *(Ashmolean Museum, Oxford)*

Above, flight of James II to France after his defeat by William III in the Battle of the Boyne, 1690, pictured below. (*Courtesy of the National Gallery of Ireland*)

17

THEY HAVE LANDED

Anon writes to Ellis, with 'hope for good success' against the starving invaders.

6th Nov.

We hear the Dutch fleet (500 sail) was put into Torbay, Exmouth, and Dartmouth: all conclude they design to Bristol, but will take Exeter and other places in the way. We here are in good heart, though in some hurry, and hope for good success. Our enemies having fed these two months upon a biscuit, two herrings, and a pint of Dortz Engelze a-day, we hope to find their noble courage much cast down. When anything occurs, and that I have a minute's time, I shall give you part of it. A Counter-Declaration is sent to the press.

18

THE WEST COUNTRY IS 'UNCONCERNED AT THEIR BEING THERE'

13th Nov.

It is said the Prince of Orange is now settled at Exeter as his head quarters. The 6000 pair of shoes which he bespoke at Exeter are not yet ready, and so we know not what way they intend to take. Others think that the bespeaking these shoes was but a trick to drill on time, till they could see if any part of England would come into them; but we are assured that their allies come on but slowly, all the West being quiet, and almost unconcerned at their being there, while they pay for what they have. Some of the scurf and meaner part run in to them as they would to see a show, but generally retreat the next day; most of our Western people having ever since Monmouth's[5] time been much troubled with dreams of gibbets.

The Dean and Chapter as well as the Bishop ran away at their coming into Exeter, and so would most of the inhabitants, but that it happens to be a great fair time there.

They stop and rifle all Mails and Letters that pass that way, as if they looked for money and bills of exchange, and not letters of news. Some tell us they begin to plunder and imprison, notwithstanding they have promised the contrary, having taken violently £300 from the Collector of Excise, and thrown him into prison.

Some few of the Maltsters and Butchers of Buckinghamshire (most commonly those that owe more than they can pay) are missing, and supposed to have run away in hopes of plunder, not to pay their creditors.

Great endeavours are used to prevail with the lads of London to be troublesome under the pretence of pulling down the Popish Chapels in Lime Street, Bucklersbury, and St John's: some scores of them have rendezvoused these two last nights, but

---

5   The Puritan Rebellion in the West Country in 1685, led by the Duke of Monmouth, was suppressed with much bloodshed and execution.

upon beat of drum, and appearing of any small part of the Militia, have scampered away, and by flight provided for their safety. The Lord Mayor and Lieutenancy of the City, as well as the Officers of the County of Middlesex keeping a strict eye to the least motion that is made by these young mutineers.

19

UNCERTAINTY, RUMOURS, AND DISLIKE OF WAR

22nd Nov.

The winds have continued so loud and violent of late that we could not expect to hear of any action between the Fleets. Besides we are told the Dutch Fleet is dispersed by the late storm; above 30 sail being driven to the Westward towards Lands End. His Majesty's Fleet rides by Westwards of Portsmouth, not many leagues from Torbay.

His Majesty is in good health at Sarum, and reviews some part of his troops daily, who are cheerful and brisk. People please themselves here with a conceit as if Admiral Herbert had met with a French Squadron, and had at one dash sunk nine or ten of them, which is every whit as true as that an army of 50,000 French are already landed at Dover.

Though there never was more occasion of inquiry for busy impertinent people that gad about all day long for coffee and news, yet never was less certainty of what passes in the world; most people affecting to disguise the truth, and there being at present about the City many engines that are made use of to spread what most suits the humour of some party; yet the City of London was never more quiet, every man minding his business and securing their debts, and the generality of the soberer and the richer sort have expressed their dislike of these proceedings, which are like to perpetuate and entail war upon the nation. . . .

20

'A great alteration in most people's faces'

Admiral George Legge, Baron Dartmouth (1648–91) urges King James II for whom he is 'in so great perplexity', to call Parliament and give orders to the fleet.

Aboard the *Resolution* at Spithead, Nov. 28th

Your Majesty will easily believe with what grief of heart I write this to find what usage your Majesty hath received, and indeed I find a great alteration in most people's faces since my coming in hither not for want of loyalty in most of your Commanders, but the daily impressions they receive make them stand amazed. For God's sake, Sir, call your great council and see which way a Parliament may be best called for I fear nothing will give a stop but that, and if it may be acceptable to you or a real service you will soon have the thanks and approbation of your whole fleet with assurance of standing by your Majesty in it, but this your Majesty can best judge of, and I hope you will excuse the thoughts of a faithful servant for such I have ever been, and by the blessing of God will persist in it till my life's end.

I have been endeavouring ever since my arrival here to refit your fleet, and I hope it will prove serviceable to you and I earnestly beg what orders you have farther for me. . . .

Sir, I am daily sensible you have reason to mistrust mankind but if you should have hard thoughts of me it will break my heart for I am and will be just to my life's end. I am in so great perplexity for you that I am able to say no more.

21

THE KING IS 'GOING TO TAKE HORSE'

James II tells Lord Dartmouth of his decision to withdraw from England 'till this violent storm is over'.

Whitehall, Dec. 10th

My affairs are, as you know, in so desperate a condition that I have been obliged to send away the Queen and the Prince, to secure them at least, whatsoever becomes of me, that I am resolved to venture all rather than consent to any thing in the least prejudicial to the crown or my conscience, and having been basely deserted by many officers and soldiers of my troops, and finding such an infection got amongst very many of those who still continue with me on shore, and that the same poison is got amongst the fleet, as you yourself own to me in some of your letters, I could no longer resolve to expose myself to no purpose to what I might expect from the ambitious Prince of Orange and the associated rebellious Lords, and therefore have resolved to withdraw till this violent storm is over, which will be in God's good time, and hope that there will still remain in this land 7000 men which will not bow down the knee to Baal, and keep themselves free from associations and such rebellious practices. I know not whether any of the fleet under your command are free to continue serving me; if they are, their best course will be to go to Ireland, where there are still some that will stick to me. . . . I may say, never any Prince took more care of his sea and land men as I have done, and been so very ill repaid by them. I have not time to say more being just a going to take horse.

22

'Very suddenly all declaring for the Prince of Orange'

Anon tells Ellis that the royal family has fled.

Dec. 11th

I am now to tell you that the Queen and Prince of Wales went down the River yesterday morning, and 'tis believed gone for France, and the King went this morning about the same time; I hear hardly any body with him. God preserve him in health.

But here all people are wondering. The Prince of Orange will be in Oxford this night. The people in the city are searching all Roman Catholic houses for arms and ammunition: and this day they are about the Strand and other places. The Duke of Northumberland has put out all Papists out of his Troop of Guards, and so they say they will out of all the Army. . . .

This night I was frightened with the wonderful light in the sky, and 'twas the Rabble had gotten the wainscot and seats of a Popish Chapel in Lincoln's Inn Fields, and set it on fire in the middle of it. Until we knew what it was we guessed it to be a great Fire. Here is a very great Guard, both Militia and the Army. You will hear very suddenly all declaring for the Prince of Orange, now 'tis believed he will be here very soon. . . .

23

THE RABBLE IS LET LOOSE

Lady Dartmouth advises her husband to change sides while there is still time.

Dec. 12th

I know my dear heart this juncture of time is very amazing to every body throughout this nation and must be so particularly to you upon all accounts, and more in the discharge of so great a trust as you have in your hands which is now thought to be the nation's since the King is withdrawn. . . . I hope dear you will be so wise to yourself and family as to do what becomes a reasonable man who I am sure is left in the most deplorable condition of any subject. Therefore pray consider it well in your own thoughts, and then no one is better able to judge than yourself what is fit to be done to acquit you, for as hitherto, I do not find the protestant interest dissatisfied with you and the other I look upon as quite extirpated. Lord Chancellor[6] is prisoner in the Tower, and the rabble ready to pull him to pieces before he be brought to public justice. Indeed this town has been mighty unquiet since the King's departure, by pulling the chapels down and houses of papists and ambassadors, so that everybody is in great frights and wish for the Prince of Orange's coming to quiet things. . . .

Dec. 15th

. . . I believe you may not hear of the miserable condition the King lies in at Faversham in the hands of the rabble, who will not part with him or suffer any creature to go near him; they say he resolves not to return; the rabble rifled his

---

6   The notorious Lord Chief Justice George Jeffreys sentenced 320 rebels to death for high treason and 800 to be sold in slavery, in his highly illegal 'bloody assizes'. Both Kings he served despised him but found him useful; James II made him a Baron and Lord Chancellor. On 12 December he tried to escape abroad, disguised as a sailor, but, as a chronic alcoholic, could not help going ashore to an alehouse where he was recognized and seized, together with 35,000 golden guineas and a lot of silver he had extorted from his victims. He died in the Tower before being tried.

pockets and took away all from him.[7] I never knew so sad a time; God look upon us in mercy; it hath pleased God to take away your mother yesterday after a lingering illness, who is happy to be out of the world. . . .

Your brother Will went with his regiment to the Prince of Orange upon the first news of the King's absenting.

24

SEAMEN DRAW SWORDS OVER THE KING'S HEAD

A gentleman of the King describes to a friend in London the capture of James II, disguised as a monk, at Faversham, in the course of his flight to France. Rescued from a mob of irate seamen by Lord Feversham, James returned to London, but on William's advice made his final escape on 23 December.

12 Dec.

. . . Seamen about 11 at night took a Customhouse boat, in which proved to be the King in disguise; the seamen treated him very roughly, though incognito, called him old hatchet-faced Jesuit. He was detained at sea all night, brought up to Faversham and within a quarter of an hour after he was in the inn, fully discovered. To conceal himself, he called for bacon and eggs, as if were some ordinary man in his diet, whereas he takes no meat that is the least salted.

He declared he never designed to oppress conscience, alter the government or destroy the subjects' liberties; and at last asked me plainly, 'What have I done? What are the errors of my reign?' He said the Prince of Orange fought his crown and life, and if he were delivered up, his blood would lie at our doors, for he seemed persuaded they would murder him. . . . Whilst he insisted upon going off, begging, praying, tempting, arguing, persuading, reproving, etc., which was above three hours, the rage of the seamen took fire apprehending he would prevail with some to let him escape secretly. . . . They cried out one and all, 'We'll rather die than he shall go off', broke into scornful huzzas, doubled their guard, loaded their muskets and more than twenty swords were drawn over his head and some threats passed. . . .

Next day Captain Crayford came from Sheerness, declaring the resolution to deliver up the Prince, upon the hearing of which he said he would consent to anything to prevent bloodshed, but seemed extremely afflicted thereat. He was really very melancholy at times and often shed tears. . . .

---

7   James was taken by fishermen as his hoy was putting out from Sheppey, brought to Faversham, and escorted by 'seamen and rabble' to the Mayor's house where he was detained. (See next letter.)

25

THE NAVY GOES OVER

Lord Dartmouth reproaches the King for withdrawing and informs him that he sent to the Prince of Orange.

Dec. 17th

It is impossible for me to express the grief and anxious cares I am in for your Majesty, and the news of your withdrawing was the greatest surprise of my life, for I did think it impossible ever to enter into anybody's thoughts that had the least inclination of duty to your Majesty to give you so pernicious and destructive counsel as to go away yourself, and if your Majesty had been drove to such a desperate course (which was morally impossible at least in my thoughts) as to absent yourself, Sir, could you have been with more honour and safety than your own fleet who would always unanimously (I dare say) have protected and defended your sacred person from any violence or unhallowed hands. But this looks like so great mistrust of me that many could witness it hath almost broke my heart.

In the most unsupportable calamity of my life what could I do but send to the Prince of Orange when I found the whole nation did, and receive orders from the Lords which were communicated to the fleet and removed all Roman Catholic Officers. I have had yet no return from the Prince of Orange, but I hope all will end in your Majesty's happy re-establishment; but withal my confusion is so great that I am only able to beg God Almighty's protection of your Majesty and to deliver you out of all these troubles which shall not only be the prayers but hearty endeavours of a heart that never studied anything but your real service and will ever do to my unfortunate life's end.

26

WILLIAM TAKES CHARGE

William, Prince of Orange, (1650–1702) sends firm orders to Lord Dartmouth but signs as 'affectionate Friend'.

Windsor, Dec. 16th

My Lord,

I received your letter of the 12th and am glad to find you continue firm to the Protestant Religion and Liberties of England, and that you resolve to dispose the fleet under your command to those ends; to which not only the fleet, but the army and the nation in general have so frankly concurr'd. Neither shall my care of the honour and dignity of this nation be wanting in matters of disputes between the two fleets as you seem to apprehend; I therefore send you such orders as are necessary to prevent that, and useful to this Kingdom. As to the methods you have taken to purge the fleet from papist officers, I approve very much of it, and as to all other matters in general, I shall refer them to the ensuing parliament. I expect your speedy compliance with the orders I send you here enclosed, and when you have brought the fleet to the Boy in the North [*sic*] I desire to see you that I may have your advice, not only relating to the fleet, but the public in general. I am

Your affectionate Friend
Prince d'Orange[8]

Some Aspects of the Wars of William III

Come list and enter into pay,
Then o'er the hills and far away . . .
GEORGE FARQUHER (*c.* 1678–1707), THE MERRY VOLUNTEERS

In the 'Glorious Revolution' consent was achieved through moderation without bloodshed and the rivalry between King and Parliament resolved at last. As it was the new King's purpose to save Holland and Protestantism from Louis XIV, rather than impose strong rule on England, political and religious freedom prevailed, which alone could lead to world supremacy in trade, colonies and naval power, as well as science and industry, in the course of the next two centuries. But nine years of William's reign were taken up with warfare to consolidate his rule over Scotland and Ireland, and preserve England, and Protestantism, from Jacobite restoration and, above all, the threat of French domination.

The unyielding defence of Londonderry by the Ulster Protestants in the legendary 105-day siege gave William time to take his army to Ireland to reduce the insurrection.

27

'We would not yield'

George Holmes describes to William Fleming how stubbornly the garrison held out in spite of bombing, starvation and fever.

Strabane, 16 November 1689
On the 12th of April last the Irish army appeared before our city; we burned all our suburbs and hewed down all our brave orchards, making all about us as plain as a bowling-green. About the 18th of April King James came within a mile of our walls, but had no better entertainment than bullets of 14, 16 and 22 pounds weight. He sent us a letter under his own hand, sealed with his own seal, to desire us to surrender,

8   Lord Dartmouth was imprisoned in the Tower in 1691, suspected of treasonable correspondence with James about handing over Portsmouth to the French, and died there of apoplexy before being tried.

and we should have our own conditions. The messenger was a lord with a trumpet, and out of grand civility we sent three messengers, all gentlemen; but two of them ran away from us, and the other came again. In short, we would not yield.

Then we proceeded, and chose captains and completed regiments, made two governors. We had 116 companies in the city. All our officers fled away, so we made officers of those that did deserve to be officers. I was made captain. And then we began to sally out, and the first sally that we made we slew their French general and several of their men with the loss of nine or ten of our men, which was the greatest loss that ever we lost in the field. Every day afterward we sallied out and daily killed our enemies, which put us in great heart; but it being so soon of the year, and we having no forage for our horses, we was forced to let them out, and the enemy got many. The rest of them died for hunger.

About the 20th of May the enemy gave us a general onset on all sides, but was so defeated that we were not troubled with them again for a week. . . . One night one of them knocked at our gate and called for faggots to burn it with. This being in the dead of the night and our men being gone off their posts we were in some danger. The drums beat alarm, and we got a party together and sallied out at another gate, fell upon them and put them to rout.

They played abundance of bombs (the weight of many of them was near three hundredweight), which killed many people. One bomb slew seventeen persons. I was in the next room one night at my supper (which was but mean), and seven men were thrown out of the third room next to that we were in, all killed, and some of them in pieces. Into this city they played 596 bombs, which destroyed many of our people and demolished many of our houses. Cannon bullets flew as fast as you could count them, and as soon as we took up their bullets we sent them back again post paid. Thus men, horses, and all went to destruction.

But at last our provision grew scant and allowance small. One pound of oatmeal and one pound of tallow served a man a week; sometimes salt hides. I saw 2s. a quarter given for a little dog, horse blood at 4d. per pint; all the starch was eaten, horse flesh was a rarity, and still we resolved to hold out.

Four days before we got relief from England we saw a great drove of cows very near us, and we were very weak, but we resolved to sally out, and in order thereto we played our great guns off the walls and sallied out on our enemy. I led the forlorn hope, which was about 100 men of the best we had, with which I ran full tilt into their trenches, and before our body came up we had slain 80 men, put many to the rout. We got arms enough and some beef, but durst not stay long, not above half an hour. This vexed our enemies much; they said we took them asleep. I praise God I had still my health, and has yet.

After the ships came in with provision to us our enemies thought it was in vain to stay any longer. . . . In the siege we had not above 60 men killed, except with the bombs. But I believe there died 15,000 men, women and children, many of which died for want of meat. But we had a great fever amongst us, and all the children died, almost whole families not one left alive. This is a true account of the siege of Londonderry. . . .

William, although a better diplomat than soldier, was victorious on the Boyne on 1 July 1690, when James, fearing encirclement, fled with his Irish cavalry and French infantry as soon as the Dutch Blue Guards and French

Huguenots crossed the river. At Beachy Head the day before, however, the Earl of Torrington (Admiral Herbert) was forced to retreat into the Thames with his 37 English and 22 Dutch sail of line, when the 70 French ships under Tourville turned windwards and caught the Dutch between two fires.

Mary, physically weak and of pious and generous disposition, was always anxious for William's safety when he was campaigning; her love (despite his lack of attraction) and loyalty (against her own father) had always been absolute. In her loneliness, and nostalgia for the informality and devoutness in Holland, she wrote to William every day, confessing: 'My heart is not made for a kingdom and my inclination leads me to a retired life.' Four years later she was to die of smallpox at the age of thirty-two.

28

ANXIETIES OF A QUEEN FOR HER SOLDIER HUSBAND

Queen Mary II (1662–94) writes to King William III, then campaigning in Ireland.

Whitehall, 22 June 1690

The news which is come to-night of the French fleet being upon the coast, makes it thought necessary to write you. . . . I am so little afraid, that I begin to fear I have not sense enough to apprehend the danger; for whether it threatens Ireland, or this place, to me 'tis much at one, as to the fear; for as much a coward as you think me, I fear more for your dear person than my poor carcass. What I fear most at present is not hearing from you. Love me whatever happens, and be assured I am ever entirely yours till death.

29

JOY AT THE VICTORY OF THE BOYNE

July 7

How to begin this letter I don't know, or how ever to render to God thanks enough for his mercies, – indeed, they are too great if we look on our deserts; but, as you say, 'tis his own cause', and since 'tis for the glory of his great name, we have no reason to fear but he will perfect what he has begun. For myself in particular, my heart is so full of joy and acknowledgement to that great God who has preserved you, and given you such a victory, that I am unable to explain it. . . .

I am sorry the fleet has done no better, but 'tis God's providence, and we must not murmur, but wait with patience to see the event. I was yesterday out of my senses with trouble. I am now almost so with joy. . . .

With the hopes to see you, for which I am more impatient than can be expressed; loving you with a passion which cannot end but with my life.

30

'I must grin when my heart is ready to break'

Aug. 26

My poor heart is ready to break every time I think in what perpetual danger you are; I am in greater fears than can be imagined by any who loves less than myself. I count the hours and the moments, and have only reason enough left to think, as long as I have no letters all is well.

I believe, by what you write, that you got your cannon Friday at farthest; and then Saturday, I suppose, you began to make use of them. Judge, then, what cruel thoughts they are to me, to think what you may be exposed to all this while. I never do anything without thinking now, it may be, you are in the greatest dangers, and yet I must see company upon my set days; I must play twice a week, – nay, I must laugh and talk, though never so much against my will. I believe I dissemble very ill to those who know me, – at least, 'tis a good constraint to myself, yet I must endure it. All my motions are so watched, and all I do so observed, that if I eat less, or speak less, or look more grave, all is lost in the opinion of the world. So that I have this misery added to that of your absence and my fears for your dear person, that I must grin when my heart is ready to break, and talk when it is so oppressed I can scarce breathe. . . .

I can neither sleep nor eat. I go to Kensington as often as I can for air, but then I can never be quite alone; neither can I complain, – that would be some ease; but I have nobody whose humour and circumstances agree with mine enough to speak my mind freely. Besides, I must hear of business, which, being a thing I am so new in, and so unfit for, does but break my brains the more, and not ease my heart. . . .

This morning Lord Marlborough went away.[9] As little reason as I have to care for his wife, yet I must pity her condition, having lain-in but eight days; and I have great compassion for wives, when their husbands go to fight. . . .

After Beachy Head a French regiment had landed for a few hours in Devon; in the spring of 1692 a large-scale invasion was planned. James' French-Irish army of 24,000 under Marshal Bellefonds was poised with transport vessels to be convoyed across the Channel by Tourville's 44 ships of the line. At Spithead, 63 English and 36 Dutch ships under Admiral Russell lay ready for them, and at La Hogue, Rear-Admiral Shovell broke Tourville's rigid line and Rear-Admiral Carter doubled it from the rear. Tourville was forced to seek refuge under the protection of the fort batteries on the French shore, but Admiral Rooke burnt six of his ships under the nose of the forts and nine others were destroyed. This spelt the end of the French invasion plans and they now took to highly successful piratical sallies in which they captured altogether 4,000 English ships.

---

9   He had left for Ireland, to reduce Cork and Kinsale.

31

LA HOGUE

Richard Haddock gives his father, Admiral Sir Richard Haddock, a terse account still written in the heat of action; he succeeded him later as Comptroller of the Navy.

[23 May 1692]

Honoured Sir,

This is to acquaint of our engaging with the French and of our having got the victory. We met them at sea, May 19. There was about 60 sail. We fought them from 11 to 9 at night; since which, have been in pursuit of them. There is run ashore, in Sherbrook [Cherbourg] Bay, Tourville with three more capital ships, which are now burned and have chased fourteen sail more in the Hooke [La Hogue], where we now are. Sir Cloudesley Shovel is going in with the third rates and fire-ships to destroy them. We have been so unfortunate as lose Rear Admiral Carter in the fight. I am very well and have received no wound; only a small splinter hit me on the thigh, but did no damage.

I remain your dutiful Son,
Richd Haddock

When, on 8 June 1694, an Anglo-Dutch fleet, commanded by Admiral Lord Berkeley and carrying 7,000 soldiers, sailed into Camaret Bay off Brest to effect a large-scale amphibious landing – one of a series of raids on the French coast – it was surprised by withering fire from the fort guns and four newly installed batteries. In the confusion of the landing operation by 1,500 men under Lieutenant-General Tollemache (rumoured to be Cromwell's son), some of the boats collided or got stranded on the rocks, and only half the soldiers ever reached the shore; they found eight companies of marines and militia waiting for them in well-prepared entrenchments. After three hours' desperate fighting and the slaughter of eight hundred men, the raid had to be called off and many who could not refloat their boats in the low tide were taken prisoner. Tollemache died of his wounds after the return of this disastrous expedition.

32

CAMARET BAY

An eye-witness describes how the landing attempt was repulsed.

Neptune, June 1694

My Lord Berkeley was left here with 18 English and 11 Dutch ships of the line, and 12 fireships, six frigates, and five bomb vessels. We directed our course to Brest, and on the 7th inst. we anchored in the evening with our fleet towards Brest Sound, keeping out of shot of the shore, but were entertained with bombs from the land on Camaret side, also from both sides going into Brest Sound, and along the north shore almost as far as St Matthew's Point, and although we were out of gun shot, yet to my wonder the bombs reached where we rid, which I am confident was two miles and a half; if one of the great shells fall into one of our ships and burst, it will quite disable if not destroy her.

The 8th inst. in the morning, we embarked all our land forces in our boats and tenders in order to land them in Camaret Bay; but discovering there were forts and batteries of guns and lines and trenches all near where were intended to land, we sent seven frigates to batter the aforesaid fortifications, the better to facilitate the landing of the soldiers. The ships that went on this service were commanded by my Lord Carmarthen, who placed them with a great deal of skill, and performed his duty with much bravery and hazard.

Between 3 and 4 this afternoon four or five hundred of our soldiers landed (most of them grenadiers), and Lieut.-Gen. Talmash landed with them; but they were so warmly received by the enemy that Talmash was shot through the thigh, and with difficulty was brought off; and the rest not being able to advance by reason of the entrenchments and fortifications and number of horse and foot upon the shore, in so much that most of our men that landed were either killed or taken prisoners, the rest of our soldiers returned on board, we having lost five of our well boats which were grounded and left on shore, which the enemy burnt upon the retreat of the soldiers. I am pretty well satisfied the French knew of our coming, where we intended to land, they being more particularly fortified at that place. . . .

This suspicion appears to have been justified by the following letter by Marlborough which, admittedly, is only a contentious translation of an alleged copy of a lost original, though corroborated by James' papers.

John Churchill was a highly ambitious, coldly calculating intriguer, obsessed with money and position. As a young man of twenty-one of rather girlish beauty, he shared a mistress with Charles II, the amorous Duchess of Cleveland (who gave him £5,000 when he jumped out of the window on the sudden arrival of the King), and his devoted sister Arabella, mistress with four children of the later James II, also contributed to his early promotion. He had an uncanny sense of timing and guessing opponents' intentions which later made him such a brilliant general, and was totally unscrupulous in pursuit of his interests. He had given a pledge to Admiral Herbert that he would defect to William when James, in his trust, made him a Lieutenant-General; after first urging him vainly at Salisbury to attack William's inferior army, he immediately assessed the consequences of such irresolution and absconded in the same night with four hundred cavalrymen to join William, leaving behind a self-justification addressed to James II, claiming that he was 'actuated by a higher principle' of the 'inviolable dictates' of his conscience and 'a necessary concern' for his religion; he was even credited with plans to seize and stab the King. Then, on conclusion of William's campaign in Ireland, he started a secret correspondence with James at St Germain, to cover himself against all contingencies like a true man of his age. In January

1692 he was dismissed on suspicion of plotting and taking bribes, and then spent six weeks in the Tower on a put-up charge which he was able to refute.

Two years later, in revenge, and without the slightest consideration for King and country, he (among others) sent intelligence to James about the forthcoming attack on Brest, which gave Vauban, Louis' fortification expert, a month to prepare and drown the English raid in blood. The fact that Tollemache was Churchill's successor and rival in the army he wished to eliminate was an additional incentive. Treason, for Churchill, was justified by its success, in the same way as deception in battle: life was warfare for him, with no holds barred. This explains why, with his prodigious gift for the chess game and finessing of war, he became, with Wellington, the greatest English general, and also why, more so than Wellington, he finally failed as a politician.[10]

33

MARLBOROUGH'S DOUBLE-CROSSING

The Earl (later Duke) of Marlborough (1650–1722) transmits secret intelligence to ex-King James at St Germain through a Jacobite agent.

3rd May [1694]

It is only today that it came to my knowledge what I now send you, which is that the Bomb Vessells and the dozen regiments now encamped at Portsmouth are to be commanded by Talmashe and are designed to burn the harbour of Brest, and to destroy all the ships of war there. This would be of much advantage to England, but no consideration could or ever shall prevent me from informing you of what I think may be for your service. . . . I must conjure you for your own interest to let no one know it but the Queen and the bearer of this letter. Mr Russell[11] sails tomorrow with 40 ships, the rest not being yet paid; but it is said that in ten days the rest of the fleet will follow and at the same time the land forces. . . .

To conclude the first part of this book, before taking up the glorious (and tragic) tale of Marlborough's victories, let us turn once again to the English soldier who was the patient victim of the ambitions, quarrels and treasons of the great.

---

10 I have followed Bryan Bevan's assessment of Marlborough (Hale, 1975); other historians, like D. Chandler, have felt he should be awarded the benefit of the doubt.

11 Admiral Edward Russell (later Earl of Orford) commanded the fleet, part of which he diverted to Brest. Like Churchill, he intrigued against his senior colleague, the Earl of Torrington (Edward Herbert) to ruin his reputation by defeat in battle, and was ready to betray William in the same way as James. Also Godolphin, first lord of the Treasury, had sent intelligence about the Brest raid to James: treason in high places for self-interest, however detrimental to the country, was not uncommon.

The army was a rag-bag of many countries, commanded at times by foreigners like the Colonel of the Huguenot Cavalry, De Ruvigny, who became the Earl of Galway, or the German Protestant Schomberg, Marshal of France and then created a Duke in England; in the same way, the Roman Catholic Duke of Berwick was a French general. Nobles and gentlemen bought and sold their commissions like a business (£5,000 for a colonelcy in the Guards!) and often lacked any military qualifications; the only professionals were the NCOs, the backbone of the army. Service conditions were sordid and brutal, with hardly any medical provision.[12] Soldiers tended to be addicted to drink and unwilling to work hard, but it was observed that,

> they stand by one another, and are often seen to die together. They are spirited enough, and have plenty of boldness in warlike exploits, though not very amenable to military customs. In Naval Warfare they are not considered to have any equals.[13]

Impressment was the only way the ranks could be filled, apart from dire necessity, like unemployment, debt and imprisonment. Edmund Verney, Sir Ralph's eldest son, who was a recruiting officer for the war against France, complained in a letter that he could not find any decent volunteers, only 'gaolbirds, thieves and rogues', and that the 'overflowing scum of our nation is listed':

> The drums beat up at Alesbury for volunteers but not a man came in to list, whereby it plainly appears, the spirit of the nation is down. . . . I myself frighted most of the young fry into holes and cellars, with only walking up and down the streets, being taken for a Press-Master.[14]

It therefore became imperative to organize impressment with systematic ruthlessness and guile to find soldiers for William's campaign in Flanders which was dragging on inconclusively. One of the victims describes his experience.

---

12 C. Barnett, *Britain and her Army*, Penguin, 1974.
13 Robert Flud, *Metaphysica*, freely translated in C. Field, *Old Times Under Arms*, W. Hodge, 1939, p. 9 f.
14 *Verney Papers*, IV (1904), p. 237.

34

AN UNWILLING SOLDIER

Richard Welsh, a tavern handyman, writes a pathetic letter (many previous ones had been suppressed) to his wife Christiana, who later became a famous woman soldier.

[1692]

Dear Christian,

It was my misfortune to meet Ensign C-m, formerly my schoolfellow. We went, at his request, and took a hearty bottle at the tavern, where he paid the reckoning; having got a little too much wine in my head, I was easily persuaded to go on board a vessel that carried recruits, and take a bowl of punch, which I did in the captain's cabin, where pretty much intoxicated, I was not sensible of what was doing upon deck. In the interim, the wind sprang up fair, the captain set sail with what recruits were on board, and we had a quick passage, that we reached Helvoet Sluys [Holland] before I had recovered from the effects of liquor.

It is impossible for me to paint the despair I was in, finding myself thus divided from my dear wife and children, landed on a strange shore, without money or friends to support me. I raved, tore my hair, and cursed my drunken folly, which had brought upon me this terrible misfortune, which I thought in vain to remedy by getting a ship to carry me back, but there was none to be found. The ensign did all he could to comfort me, advised me to make a virtue of necessity, and take on in some regiment. My being destitute and unknown, compelled me to follow his advice, though with the greatest reluctance, and I am now a private sentinel of foot, where I fear I must pass the remainder of a wretched life, under the deepest affliction for my being deprived of the comfort I enjoyed while blessed with you and my dear babies: if Providence, in his mercy, does not relieve me. . . .

Your Unfortunate, but ever loving husband
Richard Welsh

This touching letter had a sequence which is typical of the reaction of a great many soldiers' wives who opted to share the hardships and hazards of war with their husbands and give their services as sutlers or nurses. A quota of about 5 per cent limited the number of volunteers, but a few women enlisted as soldiers in disguise.

Christiana ('Kit'), on hearing from her husband, joined the army in order to find him. She was wounded in battle, invalided out, captured, imprisoned, fought a duel for the honour of a girl friend, returned home, enlisted again in 1702 with the Scots Greys with whom she fought at Nimeguen and at the siege of Venlo, and with Marlborough at Schellenberg, where she was again wounded, and at Blenheim: 'We spared nothing, killing, burning and destroying all that we could not carry off,' she wrote. At last she discovered her husband in the process of making love to a Dutch woman! After being wounded at Ramillies, she was found out to the great merriment of the regiment and became a sutler, tending the battle wounded. When she took refreshment to her husband at Malplaquet, she found him dead. Three months later she married a grenadier comrade of his who also died shortly afterwards. Kit was received by Marlborough and Queen Anne, given a pension and ended her days as an out-patient of Chelsea Hospital.[15]

In the second half of the seventeenth century a certain change in attitudes to war becomes discernible: notice began to be taken of the appalling conditions in which sailors in particular were living, fighting and dying and against which they sometimes mutinied. Even the treatment meted out to prisoners was no longer thought to be acceptable. At the same time, the admirals continued to display aggressive pride and boastful challenge in face of the enemy, supported by popular feeling. Loyalty seemed to become less absolute both among the great and the people at large: the traumatic memory of the Civil War contributed no doubt to the amazingly rapid swing in favour of the Dutch invaders, albeit for the preservation of the Anglican religion.

---

15   J. Laffin, *Women in Battle*, Abelard-Schuman, 1967, p. 83 f. Like Kit, Phoebe Hessel from Stepney served in the infantry for many years, including Fontenoy where she was wounded, and 'Mother Ross' fought at Ramillies next to her husband as 'the prettiest fellow'.

PART TWO

THE EIGHTEENTH CENTURY

'We are the cox of the seas'

Now, France, thy glory droopeth to the dust
SHAKESPEARE, HENRY VI, PART I

S I X

The War of the Spanish Succession (1701–14)

When Charles II, the last Habsburg on the Spanish throne, died in 1700, there were three claimants: the Austrian Habsburgs, the Elector of Bavaria and the French Bourbons. Louis XIV obtained the crown for his grandson, the Duc d'Anjou (Philip V of Spain), whereupon Austria went to war with France, joined by England and Holland, to curb this threatening extension of French dominance. Initially, Louis XIV was in a strong position, being allied to the Spanish Netherlands, Italy, and Bavaria: his armies stood in the Dutch fortresses, on the Danube, on the Po, and on the Spanish Mediterranean coast, and by 1704 Vienna was threatened by a pincer movement down the Danube from Bavaria and over the Alps from Italy.

The Soldier-Lover: Marlborough to his Wife

Can you ever love me, I think it would make me immortal
JOHN TO SARAH

John Churchill, Duke of Marlborough, who, as a young officer, had fought for Louis XIV against the Dutch, shared with Prince Eugene of Savoy the command of the Allied forces opposing him. Now in his fifties, and on the threshold of fame still to be won, 'the Old Corporal', as he was nicknamed affectionately by his soldiers, could at last put his gifts to full use in the strategy and tactics of warfare: planning every detail patiently and carefully, he kept the enemy guessing as to his intentions until delivering the decisive stroke with perfect timing where it would have the strongest effect. He analysed the enemy general's character and reactions and this insight and anticipation allowed him to conduct his battles with the calm serenity of a superior chessplayer and the deadly execution of a duellist's feinting attack or swift riposte. Above all, like most great generals right up to the Second

113

World War, he conceived war in terms of movement and surprise rather than static rigidity and convention.

His letters to Sarah, his beautiful, brilliant but forceful and shrewish wife (Field Marshal Wolseley called her 'a torpedo in petticoats') who held Queen Anne under her sway, show him in a quite unexpected light: one calculating schemer wrote to another with utter devotion and melting romantic adoration like a love-sick youth and not an ageing general married for twenty-five years.

1

MARLBOROUGH S'EN VA-T-EN GUERRE

Marlborough (1650–1722) parts with 'a heavy heart' from his wife Sarah.

May 15, 1702

It is impossible to express with what a heavy heart I parted with you when I was by the water's side. I could have given my life to have come back, though I knew my own weakness so much that I durst not, for I knew I should have exposed myself to the company. I did for a great while, with a perspective glass look upon the cliffs, in hopes I might have had one sight of you. We are now out of sight of Margate, and I have neither soul nor spirits, but I do at this minute suffer so much that nothing but being with you can recompense it. If you will be sensible of what I now feel, you will endeavour ever to be easy to me, and then I shall be most happy; for it is you only that can give me true content. I pray God to make you and yours happy; and if I could contribute any thing to it with the utmost hazard of my life, I should be glad to do it.

Indeed, Sarah too, domineering, hot-tempered and arrogant as she was, sometimes driving John to despair when she treated him unkindly (perhaps in a lovers' tiff or out of coquetry, which we can only guess), was capable of writing to him with the deepest affection. We have, unfortunately, only one love letter from her which she sent to John when he was in the Tower in 1692 – all the others were burnt at her insistence to guard her secrets:

Wherever you are, whilst I have life, my soul shall follow you, my ever dear Lord M., and wherever I am I should only kill the time wishing for night that I may sleep and hope the next day to hear from you.[1]

Having been indifferent to his fate and only concerned 'to leave a good name behind', John was 'transported' when he received a 'dear dear letter' from Sarah.

---

1   W. S. Churchill, *Marlborough*, I, Harrap, 1933, p. 130.

2

HOPES OF HAPPY RETIREMENT

Marlborough tells Sarah she has preserved his life by writing kindly to him.

Hague, April 24 [1704]

Your dear letter of the 15th came to me but this minute; it is so very kind, that I would in return lose a thousand lives if I had them to make you happy. Before I sat down to write this letter, I took yours that you wrote at Harwich out of my strong box and have burnt it; and if you will give me leave it will be a great pleasure to me to have it in my power to read this dear dear letter often, and that it may be found in my strong box when I am dead. I do this minute love you better than I ever did before. This letter of yours has made me so happy, that I do from my soul wish we could retire and not be blamed. What you propose as to coming over, I should be extremely pleased with; for your letter has so transported me, that I think you would be happier in being here than where you are; although I should not be able to see you often. But I am going up into Germany, where it would be impossible for you to follow me; but love me as you do now, and no hurt can come to me. You have by this kindness preserved my quiet, and I believe my life; for till I had this letter, I have been very indifferent of what should become of myself. I have pressed this business of carrying an army into Germany, in order to leave a good name behind me, wishing for nothing else but good success. I shall now add, that of having a long life, that I may be happy with you.

Six weeks later, on his march to the Danube, John writes wistfully about the beauty of the countryside and, after his victory at Schellenberg, he deplores the political necessity of devastating so many fine places right up to Munich.

3

'I shall never be happy till I am quiet with you'

Marlborough writes to Sarah that it is contrary to his nature to make the German people suffer.

Weinheim, June 2, 1704

I am now in a house of the Elector Palatine that has a prospect over the finest country that is possible to be seen. I see out of my chamber window the Rhine and the Neckar and his two principal towns of Mannheim and Heidelberg, but I should be much better pleased with the prospect of St Alban's[2] which is not very famous for seeing far.

---

2   The Marlboroughs lived at St Albans before being presented with Blenheim Palace.

July 30

The succours [35,000 reinforcements under Tallard] which the elector expects have given him so much resolution, that he has no thoughts of peace. However, we are in his country, and he will find it difficult to persuade us to quit. We sent this morning 3000 horse to his chief city of Munich, with orders to burn and destroy all the country about it. This is so contrary to my nature that nothing but absolute necessity could have obliged me to consent to it, for these poor people suffer for their master's ambition. There having been no war in this country for above 60 years, these towns and villages are so clean, that you would be pleased with them.

You will, I hope, believe me, that my nature suffers when I see so many fine places must be burnt, if the elector will not hinder it. I shall never be easy and happy till I am quiet with you.

Blenheim (near Ulm in Swabia) opens Marlborough's bunch of glorious victories during the second part of his fifties when he reached his peak. His letters from the battlefields have been aptly described as laying 'his victories like roses at his wife's feet'.[3]

Always concerned about the impression he made personally on his soldiers as part of leadership, he rode into battle most conspicuously on a white horse, in a shining scarlet uniform with his garter ribbons, not out of hot-blooded vanity, as he wrote to Sarah, but to 'deserve and keep the kindness of this army I must let them see that when I expose them I would not exempt myself'.

At Blenheim, Marlborough's brilliant strategic surprise march to the Danube attained its tactical fulfilment: lateral feint attacks enabled him to cross the river Nebel which protected the weaker enemy centre. Anticipating correctly Marshal Tallard's moves, he placed his infantry between two lines of cavalry in an unconventional way: he allowed the French cavalry to break through his first line of cavalry, only to be shattered by the concentrated flint-lock muskets of the three-deep thin line of his infantry, who finished the job with their mounted sword-bayonets – a revolution in infantry fighting which proved most effective against the hitherto dominant cavalry. Then his second-line cavalry surged forward, completed the rout of the enemy cavalry with their swords, and proceeded to cut down the infantry they had encircled. The 52,000 Allied troops inflicted a decisive defeat on 60,000 Frenchmen, with casualties 3:1 and 11,000 prisoners taken, including the Marshal, while the remnants of the French army fled to the Rhine without halting. French military reputation had lost its aura, Bavaria was conquered and Vienna saved.

John's first thought, even before the battle ended, was for Sarah. He sent her a longer account the next day.

---

3   S. Reid, *John and Sarah*, 1914, p. xxi.

4

'You will be infinitely pleased'
BLENHEIM

Marlborough pencils a hasty note to Sarah on a slip of paper, torn from a memorandum book, with a bill of tavern expenses on the back.

August 13, 1704

I have no time to say more, but to beg you will give my duty to the queen, and let her know her army had a glorious victory. M. Tallard and two other generals are in my coach, and I am following the rest. The bearer, my aide-de-camp, Colonel Parke,[4] will give her an account of what has passed. I shall do it in a day or two, by another more at large.

August 14

Before the battle was quite done yesterday, I writ to my dearest soul to let her know that I was well, and that God had blessed her majesty's arms with as great a victory as has ever been known; for prisoners I have above 8000 men and near 1500 officers. In short, the army of M. de Tallard is quite ruined. . . .

I am so very much out of order with having been seventeen hours on horseback yesterday, and not having been able to sleep above three hours last night, that I can write to none of my friends. However I am so pleased with this action, that I can't end my letter without being so vain as to tell my dearest soul, that within the memory of man there has been no victory so great as this; and as I am sure you love me entirely well, you will be infinitely pleased with what has been done.

There was great rejoicing in England: for the first time since the Hundred Years' War an army commanded by an English general had decided the fate of Europe and curbed 'the exorbitant power of France', spreading a new confidence. Letters of congratulation were pouring in.

5

'I am giddy with joy'

Mrs Burnet, wife of the Bishop of Salisbury, (author of the *History of My Own Time*), congratulates the Duchess of Marlborough.

August 1704

I cannot defer letting your grace know the joy I see in every one I meet. The common people, who I feared were growing stupid, now show greater signs of satisfaction

---

4 Daniel Parke became Lieutenant-General and Governor of the Leeward Islands, where he was murdered in 1710 by colonists in an insurrection against his strong-arm regime.

and triumph, than I think I ever saw before on any good success whatever; and after the first tribute of praise to God, the first cause of all that is good, every one studies who shall most exalt the Duke of Marlborough's fame, by admiring the great secrecy, excellent conduct in the design, and wonderful resolution and courage in the execution. . . . How much blood and treasure has been spent to reduce the exorbitant power of France, and to give a balance to Europe; and when, after so long a struggle, the event remained under great uncertainty, to have the glory to break the chain, give the greatest blow to that tyranny that it ever had, have an emperor to owe his empire to the queen's armies, as conducted by his grace, are splendours that outshine any reward they can receive. I do not wonder you are all joy – I am really giddy with joy, and if I rave, you must forgive me.

The bishop said he could not sleep, his heart was so charged with joy. . . .

At Ramillies (near Namur in Brabant), Marlborough gained another great victory with his cavalry. By feinting manoeuvres, he made Villeroi shift troops to his left wing and then attacked the right, rolling up the French lines; he had a narrow escape, however, when his horse fell in the cavalry mêlée. The French army, having lost 15,000 men, fled in disarray and was relentlessly pursued for 20 miles to Louvain. The arc of frontier fortresses began to surrender in panic and, on entering Brussels, Marlborough wrote: 'It really looks more like a dream than truth.' The French occupation of the Netherlands had come to an end.

In the following letter, Marlborough expresses his belief, in terms reminiscent of Cromwell, that he was God's chosen instrument to preserve the liberties of England and Europe. He managed to combine unscrupulous Machiavellism with an apparently sincere religious faith, in the same way as avaricious cupidity with generous humanity.

He complains about headaches which were probably due to high blood pressure caused by excessive fatigue – early symptoms of the paralytic strokes he suffered ten years later; it is no wonder that physical and mental exhaustion in the quest of fame make him long for peace and quiet.

6

'My blood is so heated'
RAMILLIES

Marlborough, writing to Sarah after the battle, praises God for his 'very visible' protection.

Brussels, May 16 [1706]

I have been in so continued a hurry ever since the Battle of Ramillies, by which my blood is so heated, that when I go to bed I sleep so unquietly that I cannot get rid of my head-ache, so that I have not as yet all the pleasure I shall enjoy by this great victory. . . . I bless God that he has been pleased to make me the instrument of doing so much service to the queen, England, and all Europe, for it is most certain that we have destroyed the greatest part of the best troops of France. My dearest soul, I have now that great pleasure of thinking that I may have the happiness of ending my days in quiet with you.

I have appointed next Sunday for the army to return thanks to God, for the protection he has been pleased to give us. For on this occasion it has been very visible, for the French had not only greater numbers than we, but also all their best troops. I hope the queen will appoint a speedy thanksgiving day at St Paul's, for the goodness of God is so very great, that if he had suffered us to have been beaten, the liberties of all the allies had been lost. The consequences of this battle are likely to be greater than that of Blenheim, for I have now the whole summer before me. . . .

Louis XIV offered peace terms in 1709, including a stop to aid for Philip V, and Strasbourg and the French fortresses along the Netherlands border, but Marlborough still dreamt of taking Paris and the government insisted that Louis must himself eject his grandson from Spain which he obviously could not agree to do. Louis was now able to appeal to the patriotism of the French people and of his hungry, ill-equipped soldiers to defend the threatened French soil. At Malplaquet, near Mons, the French army offered stubborn resistance in this last and bloodiest pitched battle of the war: Marlborough took Villars' strong entrenchments in the centre by a surprise attack through the woods after some brilliant manoeuvring, but he only gained a pyrrhic victory – the Allies suffered well over 20,000 casualties against probably less than half the number on the French side. Villars managed to effect an orderly retreat and was able to report to Paris that another such victory would annihilate the enemy.

Marlborough, now in his sixtieth year, was ill from battle fatigues and distress at the terrible price of victory, but anxieties about court intrigues and disputes with Sarah also weighed heavily on his mind.

7

'Never another battle'
MALPLAQUET

Marlborough writes to Sarah, weary of war and hoping for peace.

11 Sep. 1709

I am so tired that I have but strength enough to tell you that we have had this day a very bloody battle. At first we beat their Foot, and afterwards their Horse. God Almighty be praised, it is now in our power to have what Peace we please, and I may be pretty well assured of never being in another battle, but that now nothing in this world can made me happy if you are not kind.

I have every minute an account of the killed and wounded which grieves my heart, the numbers being considerable, for in this battle the French were more obstinate than in any other war. I hope and believe it will be the last I shall see, for I think it impossible for the French to continue the war.

Marlborough's short account is supplemented here by a more detailed description of this most murderous see-saw battle of the war. The fiercest fighting occurred in the Wood of Taisnières.

8

'Such a butchering the oldest generall never saw'

Lieutenant-General George Hamilton, 1st Earl of Orkney (1666–1737), who opened the attack at the head of his thirteen infantry battalions, flanked by cavalry, and took 1,300 officers and 12,000 men prisoner, gives his brother, the Duke of Hamilton, a graphic description of the bitter battle.

16th Sept. 1709

Dear Brother,

Tuesday night orders were given that all the army should say prayers at four o'clock for success. It was a great fogg next morning [11 Sept.] till six, which was very advantageous to us in making our disposition. It was hardly seven when we marched to attack; and it really was a noble sight to see so many different bodies marching over the plain. My orders were to bring my right to the wood, and to advance my line up to their entrenchments. As the others beat them from their retrenchments, such a fire of musquety and cannon I believe no man alive ever heard, and great execution was done on both sides with our artillery. Finding the fire come so thick out of ye wood upon my flank, I sent in the 1st battalion of Guards and my own battalion, which very soon redrest matters there again. They beat the enemy from their retrenchments, but still they regained them again, with such a butchering that the oldest generall alive never saw the like.

It was about one o'clock that my 13 battalions got up to the retrenchments, which we got very easily. I verily believe that these 13 battalions gained us the day, and that without firing a shot almost. For, after it was master of all these retrenchments upon the top of the hill, where there was ouvertures to lett squadrons of horse form thro', our horses marched up. The enemy were in two lines on the other side of the retrenchment, and there was Boufflers at the head of the Maison du Roy and gens d'arms.[5] I took care not to fire even when they came pretty near; as our horse got on the other side, their horse came very near ours. Before we got 30 squadrons out they came down and attacked; and there was such pelting at one another that I really never saw the like. We broke through them, particularly four squadrons of English. Jemmy Campbell[6] at the head of the grey dragoons, behaved like an angell, broke through both lines. . . .

---

5   Marshal Boufflers with the Household Cavalry and Life Guards.

6   Lieutenant-Colonel Sir James Campbell, although under Prince Eugene's orders not to move, led his Scots Greys in a sudden charge right through the enemy positions at the most critical moment of the battle and thereby tipped the scales; he was afterwards thanked by Prince Eugene for his disobedience.

At first we pushed them, but it did not last long; for they pushed back our horse again so much that many of them run thro' our retrenchments. The gens d'arms advanced out; the right of my foot gave them such a fire that it made all that body retreat prodigiously; and then our horse pressed them again. However, more squadrons went out, and sometimes they gained a little ground, and were as fast beat back again. . . . I realy believe, had not ye foot been there, they would have drove our horse out of the field. Nay, after near two hours battle with the horse, they brought back a very great body of their foot, who had been retreating for some time, and were coming all along to the left, where my foot were; and some of them run quite away, tho' I both gave fair and foul language. However the others we got to stand firm. . . . [Orkney omits describing the final retreat of the French and their pursuit.]

I bless God I had no manner of hurt. As to ye killed and wounded, depend upon it, no two battles this war could furnish a like number. If you had seen the field as I did ye day after, in many places they lye as thick as ever you saw a flock of sheep. . . . I hope in God it will be the last battle I may ever see. A very few of such would make both parties end the war very soon. The French are very proud they have done so well. I do not believe they have lost so many as wee. . . . God send us a good peace and a happy meeting. Adiu, dear brother.

On 9 October, Mons, the last great fortress in French hands, surrendered, Brabant and Flanders were conquered and the way to Paris lay open. Queen Anne, at long last, freed herself from Sarah's domination, which resulted in the fall of the Whig pro-war government and in Marlborough's disgrace, and finally led to the Peace of Utrecht.

Naval Epilogue: the Conquest of Gibraltar

While Marlborough broke the power of Louis XIV on land, the Navy took the dominant strongpoints of the Western Mediterranean and reduced French naval and commercial capacity. In 1702, Sir George Rooke had landed 13,000 troops which occupied Puerto de Santa Maria, and attacked a Spanish treasure fleet off Vigo, convoyed by a French squadron; he sank or captured 24 French warships and 17 Spanish galleons with £2 million worth of bullion.

The successful three-day assault on Gibraltar in July 1704 was an afterthought when the intended attack on Toulon had to be abandoned because of the arrival of the Brest fleet. It was not realized at the time what a key role Gibraltar might play in the future. After a naval bombardment by Admiral George Byng, Prince George of Hesse-Darmstadt landed with 1,800 marines and cut off the land side. Two days later the castle was breached and the Spanish Governor surrendered.

All subsequent attempts by the French fleet and land forces to retake Gibraltar were repulsed by the Prince's garrison in sieges relieved by Admiral Sir John Leake. In the course of the next three years, Barcelona, Cartagena, Alicante, Majorca and Ibiza were taken, and, advancing from

Lisbon, the Allies even occupied Madrid for a time; the most important base, Minorca, fell to General Stanhope and Admiral Whitaker. The Western Mediterranean had become a British sea, wrested from France and Spain, with world-wide repercussions. British naval, commercial and financial power had overtaken France's.

9

HOW GIBRALTAR WAS STORMED

Captain (later Admiral Sir) Edward Whitaker who commanded the landing operation and hoisted the English flag on the bastion, reports to Sir Richard Haddock, Comptroller of the Navy.

On board HMS *Dorsetshire*, in Gibraltar Bay, July 29th [1704]

Sir,

July 21st we anchored here in the Bay, and about four in the afternoon landed about 2000 marines, Dutch and all. I commanded the landing with three captains more; all which was done with little opposition. About forty horse came down from the town, which was all; and they run away so soon as our guns began to play upon them. We landed about two miles from the town, in the Bay, and marched directly to the foot of the hill, where they posted themselves within musket shot of the gates; so cut off all manner of communication from the land. We hove into the town this evening about 17 shells. The Prince of Hesse landed with us and immediately sent a summons to the Governor, which did not return any answer till the next morning, and then the Governor said he would defend the town to the very last. Then Admiral Byng, who commanded the cannonading, began to draw up all his ships in a line before the town; but, it proving little wind, could not get in with them all, so that we did little this day. There was three small ships in the old mole, one of which annoyed our camp by firing amongst them, having about ten guns lying close in the mole and just under a great bastion at the north corner of the town. I proposed to Sir George [Rooke] the burning her in the night. He liked it; accordingly ordered what boats I would have to my assistance; and about 12 at night I did it effectually, with the loss of but one man.

July 23, at four this morning, Admiral Byng began to cannonade which made a noble noise, being within half shot of the town. After about two hours continual firing, I went to Sir George and gave him my opinion that the mole might be attacked. He immediately made the signal for all the boats in the fleet, and gave me the command of the attack; but some of the boats got ashore before I could reach them, with little or no opposition. Several of our men got into the Castle; upon which it blew up. We had killed between forty and fifty men. Most of all the boats that landed first were sunk; about a hundred or two wounded; upon which, all that remained came running down and leaped into the water, being so mightily surprised. I landed within a minute after the accident, and rallied our men. We went over a breach in the wall but one at a time, and took possession of a bastion of eight guns within less than half musket shot of the town wall; and there we pitched our colours. Soon after, Admiral

Byng came ashore to me and sent in a drummer with a summons, who returned in about two hours with a letter in answer that they would surrender the next day; which they accordingly did. I believe I had with me, at the first onset, between two and three hundred men; but we grew in a very little time to near 1000. This was the manner we took Gibraltar, which I hope we shall maintain.

Your most hearty humble Servant and kinsman to serve, whilst

Edwd Whitaker

For light relief, a frivolous letter from Swift, teasing the Governor of Virginia who had been taken prisoner by a French privateer and was later exchanged for the French bishop of Quebec, may conclude this chapter.

10

A PRISONER WITH THE LADIES OF PARIS

The satirist Dean Jonathan Swift (1667–1745) pulls the leg of Colonel Robert Hunter, 'Gentilhomme Anglois à Paris', about his exploits in 'gay Paree'.

London, Jan. 12, 1709

. . . 'Tis a delicate Expedient you Prisoners have of diverting your selves in an Enemye's Country, for which other men would be hanged. I am considering whether there be no way of disturbing your quiet by writing some dark Matter, that may give the French Court a jealousy of you. I suppose Monsieur Chamillard[7] or some of his Commissaries must have this Letter interpreted to them before it comes to your hands; and therefore, I here think good to warn them that if they exchange you under six of their Lieutenant-Generals, they will be Losers by the Bargain. But that they may not mistake me, I do not mean as *Viceroy de Virginia*, mais comme le Colonel Hunter. I would advise you to be very tender of your Honour, and not fall in Love because I have a Scruple whether you can keep your *Parole*, if you become a Prisoner to the Ladyes. At least it will be a scandal for a free Briton to drag two Chains at once.

I presume, you have the Liberty of Paris and fifty miles round, and have a very light pair of Fetters, contrived to ride or dance in, and see Versailles, and every Place else except St Germains.[8] I hear the Ladyes call you already *Notre prisonnier Hunter, le plus honnête garzon du monde*. Will you French yet own us Brittons to be a brave people? Will they allow the Duke of Marlborough to be a great General? Or are they all as partiall as their Gazetters? . . .

'Tis a loss you are not here to partake of three weeks Frost, and eat Gingerbread in a Booth by a Fire on the Thames. . . .

---

7   Louis XIV's Secretary of State for War.
8   Then the palace of the Queen Dowager of James II and the Stuart Pretender.

SEVEN

The Spanish War, the War of the Austrian Succession, and the Jacobite Rebellion (1739–48)

We must not only arm to invade the French
But to lay down proportions to defend
Against the Scot . . .
SHAKESPEARE, HENRY V

In 1739, the tension between the competitive colonial empires was heightened by the determination of skippers to partake in the profitable West Indian trade by brazen smuggling, and attempts to suppress it by brutal Spanish custom officials, often lining their own pockets. The seemingly insignificant incident of Jenkins' Ear in 1731, (the master-mariner of an English brig had one ear cut off by the captain of a guardacostas at Havana who plundered his brig as a reprisal for trading with colonists in the West Indies) was blown up out of proportion by the war party to whip up public indignation a full seven years later when a Parliamentary enquiry on the ear pickled in brandy was staged. Sir Robert Walpole, the unpopular champion of peace,[1] was forced into war with Spain by the outcry which ensued. Insulted pride and hatred for the foreigner boiled over, but the belief that there were easy pickings to be had in the Spanish colonies, promising rich plunder, lurked no doubt behind nobler passions.

---

1   An enlightened statement like: 'Other nations must be supposed to have honour as well as we, and all nations generally have a great opinion of their courage and power' could have hardly endeared him to the general public whose bellicose instincts had been aroused.

The Naval War: 'We are the Cox of the Seas'

Two skinny Frenchmen and one Portugee
The British sailor can beat all three
CONTEMPORARY DOGGEREL

Admiral Vernon was sent to the Caribbean with only six ships and orders to destroy the Spanish bases. He captured Porto Bello in the Isthmus of Panama on 22 November 1739, after driving away by naval fire the crew of two hundred guns in the castles commanding the harbour entrance and sending in his sailors and marines to storm them by climbing up through the embrasures. Here is a splendid letter from an impressed seaman, one of the earliest from the lower deck, written in the flush of victory, breathing English patriotism and bellicose revengeful contempt for Spaniards and Frenchmen. It was echoed by the people at home who went mad with joy.

1

'We are the Cox of the Seas – true british spirit revives'

Henry Roberts writes exuberantly to his wife about the taking of Porto Bello.

[November 1739]

My Dear Life,

When I left you, hevens noes it was with an akin hart for i thout it very hard to be hauld from you by a gang of rufins but hover i soon overcome that when I found that we were about to go in ernest to rite my natif contry and against a parcel of impodent Spaniards by whom I have often been ill treted and god nows my heart I have longed this fore years past to cut of some of their Ears and was in hopes i should haf sent you one for a sample now but our good Admiral God bless him was to merciful we have taken Port Belo with such coridge and bravery that I never saw before, for my own Part my heart was rased to the clouds and woud ha scaled the Moon had a Spaniard been there to come at him, as We did the Batry. Jack Cox is my mesmate you know he was always a hevy arsed dog and sleepy headed but had you seen him clime the Wals of the Batry you would never forget him for a cat coud not xceed him in nimbleness, and so in short it was with all of us i belefe i myself cod now overcum ten Spanards for i remember when I was in Spain that the Spanards calld the Englis Galen den mare[2] but we shall now make them kno that we are the Cox of the Seas for our Admiral is of true Game breed had you se us english Salor, now what altration what contnances what bravry can xceed us tha tell us we shall meet a French squadron by ann by but i wish it may be so And by G-d well jurch em. Our dear cok of an Admiral has true english blood in his vains; and thank god all our captins and officers have to a Man now we ar in ernes but lying in harbors and letting our timber rot and our Provision to be devoured with Rats; was bad as I haf sene.

2   Scum of the sea.

When our Canons had left of firing by order our men coud hardly forbear going on. My dere I have got some token of Suces to show you I wish I could have sent some of them to you. Our dear Admiral ordered every man some Spanish Dollers to be immediately given[3] which is like a Man of Honour, for i had rather have ten dollers in hand than to have 100 for sefen Years together and perhaps compond it at last for – owed me by – i am and so is every man of us resolved either to lose our lifes or conker our enemys. true british spirit revives and by G-d we will support our King and contry so long as a drap of blood remains. Jo Wilks is so good a Sailor as the best of um, and can now bear a hand with an Able Sailor and has vowed never to take a Shittle in hand[4] till we have reduced the pride of Spain help them who will the more the better, true blews will never flinch.

I cant help mentoning the Solders we took with us from Jamaca who were as harty as ever took Musket in hand and behaved with glorious coridge but all for the honour of England, I wish we coud se one of those Plundrers the garda costaes especially him by whom I was once met with when i lost 16 months wages if i did not cut of the captains ears may i be damd. my dear I am well getting money Wages secure, and all Revenge on my Enemies, fiteing for my King and contry.

i am Your for ever,
Henry Roberts

This success revived hopes of conquest of the Spanish Main and Indies which Cromwell had already entertained: Vernon sailed with a great fleet of 15,000 sailors and a landing force of nearly 10,000 soldiers under Brigadier-General Wentworth to attack Cartagena, the most important city in the Spanish Main. Initially he seemed on the way to repeating his success when batteries were silenced, forts stormed, and ships taken.

2

THE ATTACK ON CARTAGENA

Admiral Edward Vernon (1684–1757) (nicknamed 'Grog' after his grogram cloak because he introduced the dilution of rum with water to stop drunkenness) sends the first good news to his wife.

Princess Caroline, in the Harbour of Cartagena, 31st March 1741

My Dear,

After the glorious success it has pleased Almighty God so wonderfully to favour us with, I cannot omit laying hold of the opportunity of an express I am sending home to acquaint you of the joyful news.

---

3   Admiral Vernon forbade the usual pillaging, but, instead, distributed several thousand dollars of the town's public funds entirely among the lower deck, contrary to prevailing prize regulations; naturally, this further increased his popularity.

4   Lead a carefree life.

The first attack was by three of my 80-gun ships on the forts of St Jago and St Philip; we drove the enemy out of them in less than an hour, and secured a descent to the army. My gallant sailors twice stormed and took two batteries on the opposite side of the harbour; the one of 15-, the other of five 24-pounders, which the General complained of to me galled his army; they having remounted guns and repaired it after our first destroying it.

On the propitious 25th March, the General sent me word he intended to storm Boca Chica Castle; upon which, I sent all my boats manned and armed to land at those destroyed batteries a third time, for making a diversion on that side, to favour their storming it. But the enemy was under such consternation, that our troops marched into the castle over the breach without having a single shot fired at them, and about ten at night my gallant sailors stormed St Joseph's fort without the ceremony of a breach, from whence the enemy had been firing partidge-shot at our men through the bushes, but with little injury to them; they would not stand the assault, but deserted the fort, leaving only three drunken Spaniards behind them. Flushed with this success, my officers finding the Spaniards burning and sinking their ships, part of the boats were detached, to try what could be saved; and they boarded and took the Spanish admiral's ship, the *Gallicia*, with the flag flying, and in her the captain of the ship and 60 men, who, not having boats to escape, gave us the opportunity of saving this ship, which they had orders to sink likewise. Besides the admiral's ship taken, of 70 guns, they burnt the *St Philip*, of 80 guns, and sunk the *St Carlos*, *Africa*, *Conquistador* and *Dragon*, of 60 guns each, the only remaining men-of-war here. . . .

I have only time to send you my sincerest love and affection for you and blessing to our dear boys.

I am, my dearest, Your most affectionate husband,
E. Vernon

Vernon, however, had rejoiced too soon, and the siege was bungled: the admiral fell out with the general, exasperated by his slowness and incompetence, while their forces were in the grip of a severe outbreak of yellow fever. When Wentworth was at last ready to storm San Lazaro hill fort, his decimated troops were beaten off with heavy loss of life. On 17 April they re-embarked to try their luck in Cuba, but their attack met the same fate there.

Thus ended the War of Jenkins' Ear, the preamble of a wider conflict. The war extended to France, Britain's colonial rival in America and India, suspected of plotting with Spain to recover Gibraltar and commercial privileges lost in the Treaty of Utrecht; in fact, a secret Bourbon compact had been concluded.

At Finisterre, on 3 May 1747, Admiral Lord Anson, who had raided the Spanish Pacific coasts in the early 1740s but had returned with only his flagship *Centurion* after four years of circumnavigation, engaged La Jonquière's joint convoy, destined for the reconquest of Louisbourg and for reinforcing the French bases in India. He captured six of the nine French battleships and four of the eight armed Indiamen with £300,000 worth of cargo; the rest escaped in the night. This was the most important naval success since La Hogue and the planned French offensive in America and India was cut short.

Victory is viewed, quite naturally, in a different light by the seaman and the captain's wife: flushed with exuberance, the sailor vastly exaggerates figures of prisoners and booty, exults in patriotic pride and dreams of £1,000 for himself.

3

'Sixtie waggen loades of Mony'

A young sailor on board the *Centurion* gives a jubilant account of the battle to his brother at Winchester, delighting in the enemy decks being 'flotted with blood'.

Plymouth, May 16, 1747

Dear Brother,

Here comes joy enuff, we have the grate fortune to meet the French fleet with 35 sail of Marchant Men a going to Canedee, with ten Sail of Men of Warr, all ships of the Line. Our captane being the Devile of a man run in amongst the hole fleet; wee fought the French Admaril and thre more men of warr biger than ourselves, the halve of one hour before the fleet came up with us; we have so destroyed them and kild them so fast, there decks were flotted with blood. The Ingagement held from two a clock till almost six, and then they all struck, and we have taken all their Marchant Men. Such a Battell ever was nown in all the hole world; Shot and Ball flew like hail from the Heavens. I bless God I am still alive. In one of the Ships was found thre Milyon of Money, in the other about 16 Milyon. In all it is to be computed sixtie waggen loades of Mony; and for the French Warr, it is all damnd for this trick, for there is 10,000 prisoners, and five ships of the line, two of them are like Tours, grate ships of 90 guns; we shot the Admaril in the Ingagement. I cannot tell you half a quarter of the news. But, dear brother, this will crush the French for ever, and all there desines are sent on one side. If wee have justice done us, we shall have a thousand pound a man. . . .

Our Captane is now with the King with this joyfull newes; all England ought to be glad and sing and drink for sixmonths for this gloryus action which we have done. Dear brother, pray drink this health with joy. As for the priveteers we have taken a dozen; Damn the French; Drink, dear brother, for we dress mutton in Clarrett.

'The accomplished Mrs Boscawen', on the other hand, co-founder of the 'Blue-stocking Assemblies' of London society, bathes in the glory of her husband's 'individual self'. At Finisterre, he fought against four or five enemy ships single-handed with the *Namur*, and greatly contributed to the capture of ten ships with their Admiral Hocquart, his prisoner for the third time, although himself severely wounded. As a result, 'Old Dreadnought', as his sailors called him, was promoted to Rear-Admiral of the Blue at only thirty-six; he was to win many more victories against the French in the Mediterranean, North America and India.

4

'Mon vainqueur'

Mrs Frances Boscawen writes to her husband with exalted adulation.

George Street, Monday, 18th May 1747

I ask your forgiveness, my hero – for that is your justest appellation – that I did not write to you on Saturday. But unless you had seen how I was besieged and beleaguered that whole day, you can hardly excuse me. . . .

To-day, I have seen two letters and as they say their noble Captain (whom they seem ready to worship) is well, I trust in God I shall likewise see him so. I long for that pleasure beyond all expression. I do not intend (and may Providence favour me!) to be brought to bed before you come. The presence of so great a man may spread a happy influence, and inspire the child with some of his heroic virtue. Indeed, my love, I can't express how much I reverence your virtues. 'Tis not your courage alone – that, perhaps, is common to most of your men – but the magnanimity, the serene presence of mind, the coolness and calmness in the midst of so horrid a conflict – in fact all the various excellencies and perfections of conduct, with which you – YOUR INDIVIDUAL SELF – have achieved for this Nation an event of more consequence, more solid benefit and advantage, than any (the victory of Culloden only excepted) that have been performed since the time of the Duke of Marlborough, your uncle, whose bravery and conduct you have equalled rather than imitated. I must not wish you his honours, since I should share them, but I wish you his length of days, his prosperous children and every blessing which he enjoyed. You have not so handsome a wife, but I think you have an honester woman and more sincerely attached to you and more likely to be a comfort and friend to your children. . . .

His Majesty is vastly delighted with this glorious event; talks much of you and says your wound is exactly such a one as he should wish for. (God send it be no more, says your careful wife!) What a secret *mon vainqueur* has made of it. I beseech you take care of yourself and do not hurry in your journey so as to fatigue yourself. You have had fatigue enough. 'Tis high time you had some rest and reposed yourself on the faithful breast of your tender and affectionate wife.

Boy Campaigners: the Brothers Wolfe

How youngly he began to serve his country . . . [5]
SHAKESPEARE, CORIOLANUS

Boys used to start their naval or military careers very early: James Wolfe, later of Quebec fame, begged his father, who was adjutant-general in

---

5   The Wolfe boys were by no means unusual in joining up so young: midshipmen enlisted at around twelve, from Rodney and Nelson right up to Jellicoe and Mountbatten, and ensigns were often mere infants, to augment the pay of their father officers: Gen. Sir John Boscowen Savage first joined up at two.

Vernon's ill-fated Cartagena expedition, to let him sail with him at the age of thirteen and tries to cheer up his understandably anxious mother; but he soon fell ill and had to be left behind at Portsmouth.

5

A FAREWELL LETTER TO MAMMA

James Wolfe (1727–59), later Major-General, comforts his mother, Lady Cathcart.

Newport, Isle of Wight, August 6th, 1740

Dear Madam,

Papa and I are just now going on board, but I believe I shall not sail this fortnight; in which time, if I can get ashore at Portsmouth or any other town, I will certainly write to you, and when we are gone by every ship I meet, because I know it is my duty. Besides, if it was not, I would do it out of love, with pleasure.

I am sorry to hear that your head is so bad, which, I fear, is caused by your being so melancholy; but pray, dear Mamma, if you love me, don't give yourself up to fears for us. I hope, it if please God, we shall soon see one another, which will be the happiest day I ever shall see. I will, as sure as I live, if it is possible for me, let you know everything that has happened, by every ship; therefore pray, dearest Mamma, don't doubt about it. I am in a very good state of health, and am likely to continue so.

Your most dutiful, loving and affectionate Son,
J. Wolfe

After being commissioned in the Marines at the age of fourteen, James was sent to Flanders at fifteen as an ensign in the 12th Foot to fight the French. He finds the long march from Ghent to the Main rather tough going, confessing that he overestimated his strength, but assures his mother that he is nevertheless 'in the greatest spirits in the world'.

6

'Aching hips and knees'

Ensign James Wolfe, sixteen, writes to his mother from his first campaign.

St Tron, in the Bishopric of Liège,
February 12th, 1743

. . . This is our fifth day's march; we have had very bad weather all the way. I have found out by experience that my strength is not so great as I imagined; but, however, I have held out pretty well as yet. To-morrow is a very bad road to Tongres, so if I can I will hire a horse at this place, and march afoot one day and ride the other, all the rest of the journey. I never come into quarters without aching hips and knees; and I assure you the wisest part of the officers got horses at Ghent.

We have lived pretty well all the way, but I have already been glad to take a little water out of a soldier's flask, and eat some ammunition bread. I am now quartered at the head man of the town's house, one of the civilest men I ever met in my life. The people where I was billeted refused to let me in, so I went to the townhouse and complained, and this gentleman took me and another officer that was with me to his house. I'm in the greatest spirits in the world; I have my health pretty well, and I believe I shall be very well able to hold it out with a little help of a horse. . . .

James's younger brother, Ned, who was an ensign in the same regiment, also finds campaigning rather uncomfortable, particularly as they only have one horse between them. His Latin, still the universal language at the time, came in handy for scrounging a square meal.

7

'Latin for a good dinner'

Ensign Edward Wolfe, fifteen, reports to his father, Major-General Lord Cathcart, from the march to the Main.

Bonn, April 7th, 1743

Dearest Sir,

I am sent here with another gentleman to buy provisions, for we can get none upon our march but eggs and bacon and sour bread; but I have lived upon a soldiers ammunition bread, which is far preferable to what we find upon the road. We are within two leagues of the Rhine, which we shall pass the 14th, and then encamp. I have no bedding, nor can get it anywhere; not so much at this place, where the Elector's Court is, which I think a little extraordinary. We had a sad march last Monday; I was obliged to walk up to my knees in snow, though my brother and I have a horse between us. . . .

I have often lain upon straw and should oftener had not I known some French, which I find very useful; though I was the other day obliged to speak *Latin* for a good dinner, which if I had not done, I should have gone without it. Most people talk that language here. We send for everything we want to the priest, and if he does not send what he has, we frighten him pretty much. The people are very malicious here and very poor, except the priest and burgermaster, who live upon the republic; but I have had the good luck to be billeted at their houses, where there is everything good but their bread.

We are here at the worst time, for they kill no meat because it is Lent. They say there are many wolves and wild boars in the woods; but I never saw any yet, neither do I desire. Now I think I may end troubling you with my nonsense; but I flatter myself that you have a pleasure in hearing from,

Dear Sir, Your dutiful and affectionate Son,
Edward Wolfe

Ten weeks later, at the battle of Dettingen, their regiment saw the hardest fighting and suffered the heaviest losses, and, in the next year, Ned, now a lieutenant like his brother, and nicknamed 'the old soldier' for his bravery, was mortally wounded. After his death James regrets he had not spent more time with Ned who 'pined' for him, praises his soldierly virtues with a touch of condescension, and comments wryly, and with a slight feeling of guilt, on how sorrow soon loses its sting.

8

POOR NED KILLED AT SIXTEEN

Lieutenant James Wolfe, seventeen, condoles with his mother on Ned's death.

Ghent, October 29th, 1744

Poor Ned wanted nothing but the satisfaction of seeing his dearest friends to leave the world with the greatest tranquillity. It gives me many uneasy hours when I reflect on the possibility there was of my being with him some time before he died, and not apprehending the danger the poor fellow was in. I know you won't be able to read this paragraph without shedding tears, as I do writing it; but there is a satisfaction even in giving way to grief now and then. 'Tis what we owe the memory of a dear friend.

Though it is the custom of the army to sell the deceased's effects, I could not suffer it. We none of us want, and I thought the best way would be to bestow them on the deserving whom he had an esteem for in his lifetime. To his servant – the most honest and faithful man I ever knew I gave all his clothes. I gave his horse to his friend Parry, with the furniture; I know he loved Parry, and I know for that reason the horse will be taken care of. His other horse I keep myself. I have his watch, sash, gorget, books, and maps, which I shall preserve to his memory.

He was an honest and a good lad, had lived very well, and always discharged his duty with the cheerfulness becoming a good officer. He lived and died as a son of you two should, which, I think, is saying all I can. I have the melancholy satisfaction to find him regretted by his friends and acquaintances. His Colonel is particularly concerned for him, and desired I would assure you of it. There was in him the prospect (when ripened with experience) of good understanding and judgment, and an excellent soldier.

There was no part of his life that makes him dearer to me than that where you have often mentioned – *he pined after me*. It often makes me angry that any hour of my life should pass without thinking of him; and when I do think of him, that though all the reasons I have to lament his loss are now as forcible as at the moment of his departure, I don't find my heart swell with the same sorrow as it did at that time. Nature is ever too good in blotting out the violence of affliction. For all tempers (as mine is) too much given to mirth, it is often necessary to revive grief in one's memory.

One brother had time to become a major-general and legendary hero, dying at his moment of triumph at the age of thirty-two, the other – equally gifted and brave – met his end, unsung, at only sixteen.

The Battles: Dettingen, Fontenoy, Laffeldt

Sound trumpets! – let our bloody colours wave!
And either victory, or else a grave
SHAKESPEARE, HENRY VI, PART III

Frederick the Great's invasion of Silesia started the War of the Austrian Succession in which England, the Netherlands and Saxony supported Maria Theresa's right to the integral inheritance of her father Charles VI's lands under the Pragmatic Sanction, against Prussian, Spanish and Bavarian claims which were supported by France.

The Allied army under King George II was outmanoeuvred by Marshal Noailles and blocked between the Main and the French-dominated hills at Dettingen on 27 June 1743, but Grammont's impatient premature charge, before Noailles had completed his encirclement, allowed the Allies to break through and defeat the French with heavy losses; they had to abandon all German soil. Dettingen was the last battle commanded by a King of England, with his son, the Duke of Cumberland, at his side.[6] Wolfe, then still only sixteen, was acting adjutant in the most critical sector.

9

THE BATTLE OF DETTINGEN

Ensign James Wolfe gives his father a most mature account, showing early professional circumspection.

Höchst, July 4th, 1743

This is the first time that I have been able to write. The fatigue I had the day we fought and the day after made me very much out of order, and I was obliged to keep my tent for two days. Bleeding was of great service to me, and I am now as well as ever.

The army was drawn out between a wood and the river Main, near Dettingen, in five lines – two of foot and three of horse. The cannon on both sides began to play about nine in the morning, and we were exposed to the fire of theirs (said to be above 50 pieces) for near three hours. The French were all the while drawn up in sight of us and the fight began about one. The *Gens d'Armes*, or Mousquetaires Gris, attacked the first line, composed of nine regiments of English foot, and four or five of Austrians, and some Hanoverians. They broke through the Scotch Fusiliers, but before they got to the second line, out of 200 there were not 40 living, so they wheeled and about 20 of them escaped to their army. These unhappy men were of the first families in France. Nothing, I believe, could be more rash than their undertaking.

The second attack was made on the left by their Horse against ours which fired

---

6   When Cumberland was wounded, he told the surgeon to attend first a French officer whose wound was more serious – reminiscent of Sir Philip Sidney.

their pistols, which, if they had let alone, and attacked the French with their swords, being so much stronger and heavier, they would certainly have beat them. Their excuse for retreating – they could not make their horses stand the fire!

The third and last attack was made by the Foot on both sides – our men in high spirits, and very impatient for fighting. The Major and I, before they came near, were employed in begging and ordering the men not to fire at too great a distance, but to keep it till the enemy should come near us; but to little purpose. The whole fired when they thought they could reach them, which had like to have ruined us. We did very little execution with it. So soon as the French saw we presented they all fell down, and when we had fired they got up, and marched close to us in tolerable good order, and gave us a brisk fire, which put us into some disorder and made us give way a little, particularly ours who were in the hottest of it. However, we soon rallied again, and attacked them with great fury, which gained us a complete victory, and forced the enemy to retire in great haste. When they retreated, several pieces of our artillery played upon them, and made terrible havoc; at last we followed them, but too late, they had almost all passed the river. One of the bridges broke, and in the hurry abundance were drowned. A great number of their officers and men were taken prisoners. Their loss is computed to be 6–7000 men, and ours 3000.

His Majesty was in the midst of the fight; and the Duke behaved as bravely as a man could do. He had a musquet-shot through the calf of his leg. I have several times the honour of speaking with him just as the battle began, and was often afraid of his being dash'd to pieces by the cannon-balls. He gave his orders with a great deal of calmness, and seemed quite unconcerned. The soldiers were in high delight to have him so near them. A horse I rid at the first attack was shot in one of his hinder legs, and threw me; so I was obliged to do the duty of an adjutant all that and the next day on foot, in a pair of heavy boots. I lost with the horse, furniture and pistols which cost me ten ducats; but three days after the battle got the horse again, with the ball in him, and he is now almost well again, but without furniture and pistols. . . .

Letters written by simple soldiers or sailors have a directness of feeling and freshness of expression which is lacking in the polished and considered epistles of the officers; even the spelling adds spice to the ruggedness of description. After Wolfe's factual analysis, showing the future general's ability to sum up the situation as a whole, the footboy catches all the atmosphere of the confused reality of battle.

10

Balls 'the size of your light puddings'

Sam Davies, footboy to Major Honeywood, describes his part in the battle to his friend Abraham Debart, drawer at the White Hart Inn, Colchester.

Hanau, June 26, 1743

Friend Abraham,

I hope these few lines will find you very well and Mrs Ann and my old Mrs and Mrs Wallis my young mistress and my young Mr Joseph and all my old fellow-servants, as I am and have been ever since I came into this country. This is a very pleasant country we are now in. We have had a battel with French [that] lasted five ours, the first they played upon our baggage for about two ours with there cannon, and then we play upon there army and they upon us. There balls was from three lbs. to six lbs. and twelve lbs. each; our rigement was upon the left wing next the river, and they playing upon us all the time. The sarvents of the rigement went into the rear with their led horses. We stayed there till the balls came flying all round us. Then seven horses fell apeace, then I began to star about me, the bals came whisling about my ears. Then I saw the Oysterenns [Austrians] dip and look about them, for they doge the balls as a cock does a stick, they are so used to them. Then we sarvants began to get of into a wood for safete, which was about 400 yards from ware we stood. When we got into the wood we placed ourselves against the largest trees, gest as I had placed myself, a 12 pounder came, puts a large bow of the tree upon my head, the Ball came within tew yards of me. Then I began to stear indeed, it was about the size of your light puddings, but a great deal hevyer.

Then we took fresh quarters, to the baggage of the whole army. We had not been there but a littel while, but the hussers were coming to take it, whilst the tow armies was swurd in hand, then the baggage made all the haste they could away. I having good luck had a horse that would not follow. Jist as I had let him goe the word came to halt. Cornet Car came to me. Sam, says he, your master is dead, so of all my troubels that was the worst; I takes my horse and tyes him to a cart, then I went to see for my master. So when I came a littel higher in the field I saw Laftanet Lee, he told me my master was taken by the French. I liked that better than the other. When I came a littel higher I saw some of our men lay on the ground, some dead, some wounded, some without arms, some without legs. I saw one Fryer of our Rigement that came from the oyspeatal but that morning, he was afoot, the other men asked him to fech them some water from a well that was by them. He had been several times and as he was going agin a Cannon ball came, and went into his Back, takes his left Breast away and his Hart gumpt on the ground.

Then I rides further up and at last they finds my Master on the ground naked for two Freanch men had striped him of his Cloes, Watch, and Money and left him for dead under a Tree. Sam was riding by him and did not know him. My Master happened to open his Eyes, saw Sam going close by him, calls him as well as he could considering he lay four ours naked upon the Cold grund. Thay got him to a village ware the King was, got him into a Bed and now he is bravely, thank God for it. He has six Wounds, two cuts on the Head, a stab under his right Arm with a bagnet. One Ball went in at his Body, out at his Back, another Ball in at his Back – our Rigement is above half killed and wounded, for never any Men in the Field behaved as well as they did, so carry all the Honour. The King is meghtely pleased with them. But our English Army drive the Freanch so that some could not get fast eenuf over the Brige, but took to the Water and so were drounded.

We have got 3000 of the Queen's Hussers a coming to help [keep] the freanch Hussars from our baggage. Those fellows have nothing but what they ketch, they ride upon small light cattel that goos light, they plunder and take all they come any, kill all they can of our Army. They have two pr of Pistolles and a Simmeter but when the Queen's Hussars come, they will soon put an End to thoase Gentlemen. The Queens are the finest in all the Wourld.

But there is one thing I forgot that I was got out of Sight of any Body in the Wood.

Up comes a man a horseback to me, he had no Saddell nor no Pistolls so I did not mind him. He asked me for to give him my led Horse in Freanch, I told him no. At that he draws out a Sword, and runs it at me. Oh, thinks I, what sort of usige is this. So I takes out a Pistoll and shot him through the Shoulder. At that he makes of and I maks to the baggage. Thank God he did not hurt me, it went through my Grete Cote soo no more at present.

Pray send me all the news you can out of the Town. . . .

Your most sincere friend
S. Davies

After these contrasting battle accounts, it is interesting to complete them by throwing a glance behind the scene. A Guards officer, who was not himself involved in the fighting – very human in his concern for his 'coming stomach' in an age of strong English carnivorous appetites – comments on the scarcity of food, except at Field Marshal the Earl of Stair's princely table (a septuagenarian who as a result of his audacity was nearly taken prisoner). He tells of the shameful abandonment of the Allied wounded who were left for the French to care for while victory was being celebrated with a *Te Deum*, 'feu de joie', and gin for the men and brandy for the officers. He also recounts the bravery of some and cowardice of others.

11

'I wish I could partake of some strawberries with Molly'

Lieutenant-Colonel Charles Russell, First (now Grenadier) Guards, describes to his wife some features of life in the army during the campaign.

Aschaffenburg, June 15, 1743

I am resolved to omit no opportunity of scribbling away and telling you how well I am. I thank God I sleep well and have a very coming stomach, so much that when I came off guard, believing my mess would provide ill in my absence, I was glad to accept of an invitation at my Lord Stair's, who really lives like a prince; and my messmates had scarce any dinner and no bread. Provisions are very scarce here, bread especially, and I have to set a man to watch at the baker's for the opening of the ovens, in order to get any. . . . We never have a table cloth, but each carries a napkin of his own. We have, whenever we can rest in a place, a good soup and 'boulée' with a fowl or two sometimes in it, and some roast mutton or beef every day. This has been only since I came among 'em that we live so well; hope 'twill last. . . .

I have also taken a soldier's son from being almost starved, have clothed him, and being a smart boy of about 11 years old, find him extremely useful, being never from my tent but when sent on errands, which are not a few.

My blessing to my dear babies. I wish I could partake of some strawberries with Molly. . . .

We are, I thank God, now encamped where our men and we have great plenty of all kind of provisions and now are finely refreshed after the great fatigue we have all undergone, lying three nights together upon the ground, two of which were extremely wet, and no straw; and yet I thank God I never was better in my life; bread and brandy was my food, and the men absolutely for near 48 hours had nothing but gin to subsist upon. . . . To our great shame be it spoken, we left the field of battle the next day and the village where our sick and wounded lay, without taking proper care to bring 'em with us; so that when we came hither, the French seized upon 'em as prisoners of war, and lucky for 'em took care of 'em, which was more than we had done, and what had not the appearance, of our side, of being victorious. . . .

Sunday, June 26
We have had divine service, and have been returning thanks for our late victory. The order was for the whole line to sing *Te Deum* and in the evening we are to have a *feu de joie*. . . .

Nothing but the hand of Providence could have saved us, if you knew all, though the second cause must be ascribed to the bravery of our foot, and one or two regiments of Hanoverians and Austrians. The latter are so fond of our men that they never meet one but clap him on his back and cry *Brave homme*. The behaviour of all our horse officers was commendable, but the private men, especially of that regiment called the Blues, was scandalous; one General officer had ordered some platoons of his regiment to present and was going to fire upon the latter cavalry, but in consideration of the officers of that corps prevented it. . . .

The battle of Fontenoy was fought by the French on 11 May 1745 to stop relief for nearby Tournai which they were besieging. Again, the French occupied a strong strategic position and, despite the conspicuous bravery of the young Duke of Cumberland and his troops, he succumbed in the end to the tactical manoeuvres of the old fox, the great Marshal Maurice de Saxe, who trapped them between converging artillery. Cumberland then made an astonishing charge in parade step at the head of his infantry, over open ground in face of enemy fire, punctuated by the beating of drums. The Guards Brigade found itself facing the Gardes Françaises, and Captain Lord Charles Hay stepped forward, lifted his hat to the enemy, took a sip from his pocket flask, and exclaimed: 'We hope you will stand till we come up to you and not swim the river as you did at Dettingen.' The surprised Gardes Françaises responded to his subsequent three cheers likewise; whether the French were asked and declined to fire first, as legend relates, or not, the British volleys mowed down 50 officers and 760 men, and the rest fled. Was it sheer bravado or a ruse? Louis XV who was with his army, stood his ground at this critical moment, and Saxe, despite being laid up with dropsy, swung himself on his horse and led a cavalry charge which stopped the English advance at the price of over 7,000 killed on each side, and turned the battle in his favour.

12

BOWING TO CANNON BALLS
BUT NOT TO BULLETS BUZZING LIKE BEES

Charles James Hamilton, sixteen, son of the poet Lord Binning, gives a graphic account of the battle to his aunt Grizel, Lady Murray.

12th May 1745

Dear Aunt,

I have not had time to sleep this six days but what I got on the ground, and nothing to cover me but the skies.

We have had a most bloody battle with the French; yesterday we begun at five in the morning and left off at two in the afternoon, all which time the French kept cannonading us; I was forced to be very civil and made a great many bows to the balls, for they were very near me, for both my right and left hand men were killed, and all round me there were men and horses tumbling about, but thank God none touched me. We could do nothing but stand there and be knocked on the head, for they had a great many batteries and three times the number of cannon that we had, and besides that they were entrenched up to the ears that we could not hurt them. The foot were very sadly cut to pieces, for the French put grape shot into their cannon and cut them down just as if they were shearing corn. . . . I longed for them to come to it sword in hand, but they durst not do it. I had my horse shot just in the knee with musket ball, and I am afraid he will be always lame. I was forced to go off the field and get my other horse. I did not regard the small bullets after the cannon balls in the least, though they came buzzing about me like bees, but at last we were obliged to retreat for there was no standing their cannon as they were entrenched, for we could not see anything scarce but their bits of white paper in their hats, but I hope we shall be revenged of them for this trick.

I just writ this to let you know I am well. I recollected that I must die some time or other, and if my time was not come I was as safe there as any where else. Pray my duty to mama, Grand-mama, love to my brothers and sisters, and am dear Aunt your most dutiful nephew

C.J.H.

The Duke was widely commended for his great courage, rousing his men in the heat of battle by the example of Marlborough's victories. His aide-de-camp sings his praises.

13

CUMBERLAND 'A TRUE HERO'

Captain Joseph Yorke (later General Baron Dover, 1724–92), writes to his father, Lord Chancellor the Earl of Hardwicke, the day after the battle.

Ath, May 12th, 1745

My Lord,

The Providence of the Almighty led me thro' the utmost perils in following my Royal Master. He is a true hero. The right wing did more than can be expected from men; three times they put the enemy to flight, and were as often forced to retreat again by reason of strong intrenched batteries of cannon which played upon us, without discontinuing an instant, for above seven hours from both flanks. At last, after losing a great number of men and officers, the left not advancing with the same ardour that the right did, it was thought proper to retire.

I never saw or heard of such behaviour as the Duke's: he rode everywhere, he encouraged the wavering, he complimented the bold, he threatened the cowards. In the midst of the greatest dangers, in the heat of the action, whilst death stared him on every side in the face, he delivered his orders with a readiness and coolness worthy of himself: had the nation seen him they would have adored him.

With my humble duty to Mama, I have the honour,

Joseph Yorke

Yorke lost his best friend in the battle, the only son of Sir John Vanbrugh, the dramatist and architect of Blenheim Palace, and describes his last hours with intense grief.

14

'He died in his calling like a Hero'

Captain Yorke laments to John Jones the death of Charles Vanbrugh.

[May 1745]

. . . How to break it to his poor mother God above only knows; and yet, yet it must be done. Alas, those who knew him best must feel it most. I cannot comfort anyone, tho' I wish it; to say I have lost the only one in all my acquaintance with whom I had made so strict a friendship, is what makes my blood freeze with horror. My support, my comfort, my adviser, my everything is gone. After having suffered with unparalleled heroism and sweetness of temper 20 hours of the most racking torture, the Almighty of His goodness took him to Himself. For some time we had hopes, but we found yesterday the ball so fixed to the main bone of the thigh that it was in vain to attempt the taking it out: however, with the assistance of the best surgeon in the army we made an incision upon the part yesterday, but without success. I saw him a few hours before he died and kissed him, I was sure for the last time, and so it happened; for at 12 o'clock last night he was freed from misery and left his friends in despair. The last words he spoke was his concern for his mother and his regret in leaving me: nothing else affected him in dying. Judge then what I suffer! But poor Lady Vanbrugh, let the news be told her in the softest manner that it can and when she can bear it – tell her his dearest friend performed the last sad friendly office he could do him, to see him decently buried. . . .

His enemies felt the effects of his courage in the day of battle: with 40 men he routed a whole French Battalion; but alas! his friends feel the loss too deeply now. . . . Pray let me know how my poor Lady does: what, what will she do? . . . Adieu! Comfort yourselves! He died in his calling, in the eye of his Prince and like a Hero for his Country. I can no more. . . .

When glorious or sad tales of heroism reached the ladies at home, they were apt to get effusively dramatized by them.

15

'True romance heroes'

Lady Sarah Cowper, writing to Mrs Dewes, gives her own theatrical versions of the bravery of the Duke of Cumberland and the tragic death of litle Molesworth.

Midgham, June 5th, 1745

. . . His R.H., (*whose care was universal*), was in every part of the field where he saw the men dispirited and giving way, calling out, 'Don't you know me, my country men? Will you leave me? I don't ask you to do anything without me: all I beg you is to *share my danger.'* When the retreat was determined he showed the same spirit and diligence to preserve the order of the march, and to give all possible assistance to the wounded. He was one of *the last* that left the field, so that he did not reach the camp till three next morning, and great part of the army did not know what was come of him. While the army was retreating, and he looked round and saw the numbers lost in the action, and had accounts brought him of particular persons killed or wounded, he lost all command over his passions, and burst into a violent fit of crying! I own these tears of generosity and humanity make him appear *much greater* to me even than all the instances of his courage. . . .

Three young men are killed whom I am much concerned for, Mrs Sabine's second son, a very brave and fine young man, and Shaw Cathcart, a *true romance hero*, insensible of danger – these are a loss to the public; but I am *much more touched* with little Molesworth's death. I have known him ever since he was five years old; he was a youth of sixteen, a very sober boy, and a good scholar, and capable of making his fortune in a learned way, but nothing could persuade him from being a soldier. I saw him the day the Duke gave him his commission; he was quite fuddled with joy, his father went abroad with him. It happened there was a vacancy in the guards, and the Duke advanced him to it the day before the battle. Just before the engagement, Lord Albemarle said to Molesworth, 'Keep you son at home to-day; his commission is *not signed*, so that he really *has no post in the guards*, and it will be no disgrace to him that he is absent; he may avoid the danger of this battle, and will gain some experience against another': the boy *cried*, and said *'if he was not fit to fight he ought not to have a commission'*, went to the battle, and after it was missing. After several days' search his father thought him dead, and was returning home, when a note was given him on the road, with these words: '*Robert Molesworth is living,* slightly wounded, and a *prisoner at Lisle.'* Mr Molesworth writ this to his wife, and afterwards a further account came that he was fallen into the hands of a French Colonel, who was very humane, mightily pleased with him, and treated him like his own child; the mother was transported with this good news. Mr Molesworth went to Lisle, had leave to take care of him, found the wound they thought so slight had proved incurable, and the boy, after lingering a week, *died in his father's arms!* . . .

At the battle of Laffeldt on 2 July 1747 in which 90,000 Allied troops (10,000 of them British) were facing 125,000 Frenchmen, the Anglo-Hanoverian contingent bore the brunt. Cumberland was nearly taken prisoner when, as usual, he was trying to rally his wavering ranks; his popularity was beginning to wane, though, as he was said to be treating his soldiers 'rather like Germans than Englishmen'. His general of horse was Sir John Ligonier, one of the 70,000 French Huguenots who had found refuge in England after Louis XIV's revocation of the Edict of Nantes. Ligonier had risen in the army under Marlborough, been knighted on the battlefield of Dettingen by the King for breaking Grammont's cavalry as a major-general of the Horse, and saved the British Foot at Fontenoy by his skilful retreat when his plan of attack had been bungled. The brilliant cavalry charge he led at Laffeldt at the age of sixty-seven at the head of four regiments became 'the talk of Europe' and saved the infantry from being routed by Saxe's horse, although the French gained a pyrrhic victory. His mount fell in the mêlée, however, and he was taken prisoner.

As a French renegade, Ligonier knew he could face execution, but he was deeply moved when Louis XV received him generously and with full honours, as was the custom of the times with prominent prisoners. After Saxe had introduced him as having 'by one glorious action disconcerted all his projects', the King even complimented him. He was invited to supper and to watch the *feu de joie* as his personal guest and was commissioned to convey a peace offer to the British government which was turned down. Even when finally the balance between British superiority at sea and that of the French on land led to the Peace of Aix-la-Chapelle, it brought only a short respite in the struggle between Britain and France which continued throughout the eighteenth century.

While war roused violent chauvinist passions in the forces and at home, the main protagonists tended to regard it almost like a joust – rather than the bloody massacre it was – which would not impair their chivalrous non- partisan attitudes towards each other. This explains the French King's action, as well as the fact that a Frenchman, however idolized he was by the army and the aristocracy at whose dinner parties and hunts he shone as a man of English fashion, with a string of actresses to his bow, could become an Earl and Field Marshal.[7]

7   Ligonier's promotion was spectacular but not unique (see p. 108).

16

MERIT ABOVE NATIONALITY

General Sir John Ligonier (1680–1770) gives Prince William of Hesse an account of his reception by Louis XV after being taken prisoner at Laffeldt.

[July 1747]

I hasten to tell you of the good treatment I received from the King – I was far from expecting such a thing. The soldier who captured me, would have had his head broken if I had still had a loaded pistol. He knocked off my hat and taking his off to salute me, said, 'General, you are my prisoner and I bid you welcome.' He had six others with him and I gave him my purse. Without dismounting they led me off towards the King, who was quite close, being in the thick of the fight. On the way some of the Household Provost guards, whom I recognised by their uniform, pressed in on me and I thought, seeing my situation, they were going to kill me. But when I came to the King, he greatly reassured me, saying, with a charming smile, 'Well, General, we will have the pleasure of your company at supper tonight.' Wherupon a musketeer was commanded to accompany me to my quarters, and a moment later came an officer, who said 'Sir, the King bids me bring you good news. Your carriage and equipment which were captured, are here and it is the King's orders that you have them back.' I thought I was dreaming, for the idea of being executed returned again and again to my mind. However, the King was very gracious to me that evening and paid me every attention at table, which set an example to the others. At the end, when I took leave of his Majesty, mustering all the French vocabulary I could still remember, the King said to me, 'M. Ligonier your captivity will not be harsh, for you know that I am a kind hearted man.' At that my heart swelled and I could only answer by putting a knee to the ground, and the King stretched out to me his beautiful gloveless hand, on which I planted, I swear you, a very warm kiss mingled with some tears. The King of France is a great and good King believe me, who have the good luck to serve such an admirable Prince.

Threats of Invasion

England, being empty of defence,
Hath shook and trembled
SHAKESPEARE, HENRY V

Horace Walpole, son of the statesman Sir Robert, confined by lifelong gout to his villa at Strawberry Hill on the Thames at Twickenham, is considered the best English letter writer. After visiting the British envoy, Sir Horace Mann, in Florence, he corresponded with him for forty-four years, without ever meeting him again. His comments on current events are formulated with brilliant insight, wit and style, obviously with an eye to publication. Although he fully appreciated the political necessity of war and was as anxious as anyone to preserve England victoriously, he felt himself 'more a universal man than Englishman', this prevented him from being carried away by the war fever which gripped people from time to time, and kept him always aware of the bitter reverse side of war and its terrible inhumanity.

Early in 1744, as the following letter confirms, frantic preparations were being made to prevent being taken by surprise by the French invasion force which lay ready at Dunkirk to be convoyed across the Channel by the Brest fleet, and to intercept it by naval attack.

17

'All is at stake'

In the following two letters Horace Walpole (1717–97) tells Sir Horace Mann about counter measures, a fifth columnist, and the vain glory of bloodshed.

Feb. 23, 1744

I write to you in the greatest hurry, I am this moment come from the House. There is no doubt of the invasion: the young Pretender is at Calais, and the Count de Saxe is to command the embarkation. Hitherto the spirit of the nation is with us. Sir John Norris[8] was to sail yesterday to Dunkirk, to try to burn their transports; we are in the utmost expectation of the news. The Brest squadron was yesterday on the coast of Sussex. We have got 2000 men from Ireland, and have sent for two more. The Dutch are coming: Lord Stair is general. Nobody is yet taken up – God knows why not! We have repeated news of Matthews[9] having beaten and sunk eight of the Toulon ships; but the French have so stopped all communication that we don't yet know it certainly; I hope you do. 300 arms have been seized in a French merchant's house at Plymouth. Attempts have been made to raise the clans in Scotland, but unsuccessfully.

My dear child, I write short, but it is much; I could not say more in ten thousand words. All is at stake; we have great hopes, but they are but hopes! I have no more time: I wait with patience for the event, though to me it must and shall be decisive.

18

ANOTHER MARLBOROUGH NOT WORTH ONE LIFE

March 22

I am sorry this letter must date the era of a new correspondence, the topic of which

---

8   Admiral and Commander-in-Chief of the Fleet at Spithead ('Foulweather Jack').
9   Admiral Thomas Matthews sailed from Hyères to intercept the Toulon fleet.

must be blood! Yesterday came advice a declaration of war with England was to be published in two days. Politically I don't think it so bad; for the very name of war, though in effect on foot before, must make our governors take more precautions; and the French declaring it will range the people more on our side than on the Jacobite; besides, the latter will have their communication with France cut off. But, my dear child, what lives, what misfortunes, must and may follow all this! As a man, I feel my humanity more touched than my spirit – I feel myself more a universal man than an Englishman! We have already lost seven millions of money and 30,000 men in the Spanish war – and all the fruit of all this blood and treasure is the glory of having Admiral Vernon's head on alehouse signs! for my part, I would not purchase another Duke of Marlborough at the expense of one life. How I should be shocked were I a hero, when I looked on my own laurelled head on a medal, the reverse of which would be widows and orphans. How many such will our patriots have made!

The embarkation at Dunkirk does not seem to go on, though, to be sure, not laid aside. We received yesterday the particulars of the Mediterranean engagement from Matthews. We conclude the French squadron retired designedly, to come up to Brest, where we every day expect to hear of them. If Matthews does not follow them, adieu our triumphs in the Channel – and then! If England is ever more to be England, this sure is the crisis to exert all her vigour. We have all the disadvantage of Queen Elizabeth's prospect, without one of her ministers. . . .

When, after some delay, the invasion forces finally sailed, gales drove the ships out of the Channel and wrecked the Dunkirk transports. The attempt, like so many before and after, had to be given up.

In 1745, however, with the British army fighting the French in the Netherlands and the Scots rebels in the North, and the Channel coast denuded of defenders, the chances of effecting a successful landing appeared more propitious than ever: embarkations from Dunkirk and Calais were expected at any moment, and a converging movement from South and North seemed imminent. No wonder the old ladies became frightened.

19

THE FRENCH ARE COMING TO 'EAT US ALL UP ALIVE'

'Gran', an old retainer of the Granville family, living at Fulham, to her friend Martha at Calwich.

August [1745]

Indeed, my good friend Martha, it has been a deadly while I have taken to answer your kind letter, but what can a body do with one eye, and that a very bad one. Moreover, my hand shakes like any aspen leaf, and I have not been well all summer. I have a pain in my shoulder on one side, and a pain in my elbow on the other; much pain and very lame of my knees, and ankles; when I walk, it is like an elephant, without bending a joint. O how I grunt and groan night and day! but you do not know what it is to be old! You are capering about in your fine cardinals, and things, like a girl of twenty. I suppose you are about getting a young husband. I was told so, and much good may it do you, if he gives you a hearty thrashing now and then. . . .

Well, I wish you would let me know what master is doing! Surely, I thought, he would have been in London before now, and have got a new gown on purpose, thinking to see all the prime youth of Staffordshire reviewed in Hyde Park, with Colonel Granville at the head of them – such a day! So I went; but when I found it was the Norfolk Militia, how I was mortified, though they were fine men, and very fine officers! But what did I care for them? I wanted to have seen master! and now they tell me your militia are not yet raised. Good luck! good luck! I really believe in my heart master do not care if the French come and eat us all up alive. Are there not flat boats – I know not how many thousands – ready to come every day? and when they once set out they will be with us as quick as a swallow can fly, almost; and when they land we have nobody to fight them, because you *will not raise* your militia. For my part I dare not got to the Thames, for fear they should be coming; and if I see one of our own boats leaden with *carrots*, I am ready to drop down, thinking it one of the French. . . .

Ten battalions of infantry were rushed over from the Netherlands, seven of them Hessian and Dutch mercenaries on whom the defence of England now largely depended. Cumberland followed them. Even then the available forces were quite insufficient to meet the dual threat. One worried politician of the war party informs another of the precarious situation.

20

INVASION IS IMMINENT

Thomas Pelham-Holles, Duke of Newcastle (1693–1768), to the Duke of Devonshire.

Whitehall, December 15th, 1745

. . . By all our Advices from Dunkirk, the Preparations, which have been for some Time past making there for an Embarcation are now in such Forwardness that there is the greatest Reason to apprehend they will very soon attempt to put to sea. Their Destination seems to be some part of our Southern and Eastern Coast. But I hope, by the Blessing of God, they will be intercepted by the great number of Vessels that are stationed for that Purpose. By the last Advices, it looks as if they would not come with less than 12,000 men. They have a considerable Number of Vessels for Transports in Dunkirk, and have taken up a great Quantity of Fishing Boats, and small Boats, in order, as it is said, to fling over men into Sussex or Kent. We have a great Number of Ships of all sorts at sea, but are very poorly provided for our Defence at Land, not having, at present, above 6000 Men in and about London. For which Reason, we sent for Ligonier to come up with all the Troops from Lichfield with the utmost Expedition, and for the Duke to follow with His, as soon as possible.

The sending for the greatest part of the Duke's Army hither immediately was absolutely necessary for the Defence of the Capital against the intended Invasion; and at the same time I am afraid the Rebels will be able, either to remain in the North West Part of England, or to go into Scotland, and join the new Force which is getting together there, as they please. . . .

Orders were sent for bringing over immediately the 6000 Hessians; and they are to go directly to Edinburgh. It is evident we have not Force enough, effectively to suppress the Rebellion at home, and to defend ourselves from the Attempts of our Enemies abroad.

All foreign Affairs are in as bad a way as possible. . . .

Admiral Vernon alerts Deal that Irish troops are ready at Calais to cross over.

21

SIGNALLING THE ALARM

Admiral Vernon to Admiral Norris at Deal Castle.

Norwich, in the Downs, December 20 [1745]

As from the intelligence I have procured last night, of the enemy's having brought away from Dunkirk great numbers of their small embarkations, and many of them laden with cannon, field-carriages, powder, shot, and other military stores, the Irish troops being marched out of Dunkirk towards Calais, I can't but apprehend they are preparing for a descent from the ports of Calais and Boulogne. – I thought it my duty for his Majesty's service, to advise you of it; and I desire you will communicate this my letter to the Mayor of Deal, and that the neighbouring towns should have advice for assembling to their common defence; and my cruisers' signals for discovering the approach of an enemy will be their Jack flag flying at their top-mast-head, and firing a gun every half hour, and to desire they will forward the alarm.

The writer of the next letter voices his suspicion that the eagerly broadcast invasion from Dunkirk was nothing but a decoy to distract attention from the real threat which might have met with success at one point. The opportunity was once again allowed to slip past, however.

22

IS IT JUST A FARCE TO DECEIVE US?

James Henshaw to Vice-Admiral Henry Medly, Commander-in-Chief, Mediterranean.

Tower Hill, January 7, 1746

We have been alarmed for almost two months past with an invasion from Dunkirk, the formidableness of which has been trumpeted from Rome, Paris, etc., and the Pretender's youngest son, with several princes, generals, and volunteers, have been for some time at the towns on the French coast. This has put us to a vast expense, and has given us an infinite deal of trouble. Our troops are spread all along the coasts so as to be assembled with as much despatch as possible. Beacons and lighthouses are planted on every hill; the people are ordered to drive their cattle 20 miles inland. We have 26 line of battleships between Plymouth and the Nore, and great numbers of small ships, sloops, cutters, yachts, etc., continually on the French coast; the Admirals Vernon, Martin, and Mayne in the Downs; Captain Knowles on the coast of France; Captain Boscawen at the Nore; and Admiral Byng on the coast of Scotland.

After all this bustle, which still continues, we are told that it is a perfect farce, designed to amuse us and keep us at bay, whilst the stroke is really designed some other way, which time alone must set us right in. Mr Knowles tells me in a letter that he had stood into Dunkirk, Ostend, Calais, and Boulogne until the shot flew over him, and by the nearest computation he could make, there were not vessels enough to carry the necessary materials for an embarkation of 10,000 men, much less the men themselves; so that if there really was an invasion intended, it must have been with the Ferroll and Brest squadrons, and troops on board of them and large transports, and the materials, as Mr Knowles observes, were to be transported in these small embarkations. Had this been attempted before Mr Martin returned with his squadron, and before the East India and Cape Breton convoys – which together makes 17 of the line of battle ships now at home – they might have given us a world of trouble, and it is plain by the Pretender's forced marches directly for London that something of that kind was intended; otherwise his little army might have been eaten up here, where nine men in ten were resolved to expose themselves to all hazards in opposition to him. We have now 25,000 regular troops in and about London, so that we are in no want of spirits.

The Jacobite Rebellion (1745–6)

From French and pretender
Great Britain defend her
ADDITIONAL VERSE TO THE NATIONAL ANTHEM, SUNG IN LONDON THEATRES

When Cumberland had been defeated at Fontenoy and England was deprived of troops, the Scottish Jacobites, champions of the descendants of James II still smarting under the defeat of Flodden and the Union of 1707, thought their hour had struck. The Young Pretender, Prince Charles Edward, James' grandson, sailed from Nantes in July 1745 in the brig *Doutelle* with nine officers, under the protection of the French frigate *Elisabeth*, laden with arms, ammunition, money and seven hundred men. They were intercepted by the *Lion* and, as a result of a four-hour fierce fight off the Lizard, both ships were crippled and suffered severe casualties. The Prince's brig escaped and finally landed at Loch-na-nuagh, but the *Elisabeth* had to limp back to France with his vital supplies.

23

THE PRETENDER'S ESCORT SHIP IS DISABLED

Captain (later Admiral Sir) Peircy Brett (1709–81) reports to Thomas Corbett, Secretary of the Admiralty.

Lyon, Plymouth Sound, July 30th, 1745

On the 9th inst. west of the Lizard 39 leagues, I saw two of the enemy's ships. By four o'clock I was within two miles of them, they then hoisted French colours, and shortened sail, one was a man of 64 guns, and the other a small ship of 16 guns. At five I ran alongside the man of war within pistol shot, and began to engage. By six my mizzen mast and yard came down upon deck. By nine all my lower masts and topmasts were shot to pieces, so that I lay muzzled and could do nothing. The enemy did not receive much damage in his masts and yards, but his hull must have suffered greatly. At ten he sheered off, and as he was going I gave him a farewell with two of my 24-pounders, but he made no return, and in less than an hour was out of sight, and my conditon was such I could not follow him. The small ship in the beginning of the engagement made two attempts to rake me, but I soon beat him off with my stern chase.

From the beginning to the end of the engagement we kept a continual fire at each other, about the distance of a pistol shot. The *Lyon's* hull is very much shattered as well as her masts, yards, rigging, two of my guns dismounted, and 45 of my men killed and 107 wounded. The next morning at daylight I saw the enemy to the southward of me, making the best of his way to some port in the Bay of Biscay, and as the small ship was not then in company I imagine he proceeded on his voyage to the westward. It was near 24 hours after the engagement before I was in a tolerable condition of making sail. . . .

My officers all behaved extremely well except the Captain of the Marines, whom I have put under arrest, for skulking on the poop under cover of some bags that were there, for the greatest part of the engagement, which encouraged most part of his men to do the like. I was not an eye witness of his bad behaviour, else I should have treated him as he deserved, for the poop ladder being shot away, and myself wounded, rendered me incapable of climbing up. . . . As I was not so happy as to take him, [the *Elisabeth*] I have only this satisfaction left, that I spoiled his voyage.

The Prince entered Perth and Holyrood with the support of the Macdonalds, and from Edinburgh his 5,000 Highlanders, reinforced by the Gordons and Mackintoshes, swept along to Prestonpans. In a surprise attack at dawn, brandishing their broadswords behind targes, they routed Sir John Cope's dragoons who found their bayonets useless against them. The sergeant left in charge of the Highland redoubt of Ruthven defended it bravely against heavy odds.

24

NO SURRENDER WITHOUT BLOODY NOSES

Sergeant Molloy, left with only twelve men in barracks at Ruthven by Sir John Cope, sends him a report to Inverness.

Aug. 30, 1745

This goes to acquaint you, that yesterday there appeared in the little town of Ruthven, above 300 men of the enemy, and sent proposals to me so surrender this redoubt, upon condition that I should have liberty to carry off bag and baggage. My answer was, 'That I was too old a soldier to surrender a garrison of such strength without bloody noses.' They threatened hanging me and my men for refusal. I told them I would take my chance. This morning they attacked with about 150 men fore-gate and attempted to set sally-port on fire, with some old barrels and other combustibles; about two hours after, they sent to me, that two of their chiefs wanted to talk to me. I spoke to them from the parapet: – they offered conditions; I refused. They desired liberty to carry off their dead men: – I granted. They went off westward about eight this morning; but came back at night-fall. They took all the provisions the poor inhabitants had in the town; and Mrs M'Pherson, the *barrack wife*, told me they were above 3000 men, all lodged in the corn fields west of the town, last night, and their grand camp is at Dalahinny. I expect another visit this night, I am informed, with their peteraroes,[10] but I shall give them the warmest reception my weak party can afford. I shall hold out as long as possible. . . .

Alderman Pattinson, deputy mayor of Carlisle, proved less consistent: after first defying the Highland army who were threatening to put the city to fire and sword, the militia mutinied when siege guns were brought up and Pattinson surrendered the city.

25

A HERO FOR TWENTY-FOUR HOURS

Horace Walpole to Sir Horace Mann.

[1745]

For these two days we have been expecting news of a battle. Wade[11] marched from Newcastle, and must have got up with the rebels if they stayed for him, though the roads are exceedingly bad and great quantities of snow have fallen. But last night there was some notice of a body of rebels being advanced to Penrith. We were put

---

10 Obs. var. of 'pedrero' – a small gun originally used for discharging stones.
11 Marshal George Wade, aged seventy-two.

into great spirits by an heroic letter from the mayor of Carlisle, who had fired on the rebels and made them retire; he concluded with saying, 'And so I think the town of Carlisle has done his Majesty more service than the great city of Edinburgh, or than all Scotland together.' But this hero, who was grown the whole fashion for 24 hours, had chosen to stop all other letters. The King spoke of him at his levée with great encomiums; but, alack! the next day the rebels returned, having placed the women and children of the country in waggons in front of their army, and forcing the peasants to fix scaling ladders. The great Mr Pattinson instantly surrendered the town, and agreed to pay £2000 to save it from pillage. . . .

The Lord Chancellor's wife finds the hearts of the people up North 'not easily seen thro' '; they were, in fact, pretty indifferent to the rival dynasties and most of them neither helped nor combated the Scots. Lady Hardwicke is deeply apprehensive of the foreign troops, 'odious to the nation', who nobobdy thought would fight for England, and urges her son to come home with the expeditionary force to defend the country.

26

'The nation does not like foreigners'

Lady Hardwicke tells her son, Colonel Yorke, in Flanders, the British troops should return.

Sep. 3 [1745]

My dear Jo,

A letter from you makes me so happy for the time, I can't help telling you the pleasure it gives me. . . . I am not as yet able to tell you what they are doing at the other end of the Island for the intelligence from thence is like the hearts of the inhabitants, not easily seen thro' by such plain folks as myself. The young Pretender is certainly there, and joined by some of the clans, tho' I assure you it is not believed by many fools in town, and in the meantime his friends treat it as a ridiculous attempt, in hopes to lull the Government into a false security, whilst they say the French and the Spanish fleets are joined with a number of land forces ready to put on shore. You know me well enough to guess what I feel, especially living by myself as I have done this vacation. . . . What we want at present is some of our own troops; for we think you will fight for us, if you were here, and the nation does not like foreigners, especially at this time. God deliver us from all our foreign and domestic Enemies; which have made me older by ten years at least than when you left England. . . .

   Thus far I had writ when your letter came; I find you think as I do, in short, foreign troops are odious to the nation; we all think they will not fight for us, and what is saving Brussels to England, when we have left all the coast in the possession of the French, by which our own troops are prevented from coming to our assistance. For God's sake, some of you come to us, for I never saw the nation so defenceless, and to talk of Europe and her dangers when England is on the brink of ruin is nonsense. . . . I have not slept these two nights. If you can throw in your mite towards bringing over British troops do. Let Dutch and Austrians exclaim as they will, necessity has now Law. I could talk for ever on the subject. Adieu, my hearty prayers are ever attendant on you, and that we may see better times is the sincere wish of your most affectionate

M.H.

Yorke did return post-haste with Cumberland; the troops commanded by Wade and the Duke, who was soon to take over from him, were now in hot pursuit of the Highlanders under Lord George Murray who, however, managed to outmanoeuvre both. In the next letter Yorke thinks that the enemy who had retreated from Derby ought to be lured to London and defeated there, if it were not for the 'monied folks' whom the government did not want to upset. In fact, London was in a panic on 'Black Friday', December 6 (proverbial ever after), with only a small force at Finchley to protect it. However, the Pretender was dissuaded from such a desperate gamble, retired north and let slip the only small chance of victory he ever had.

27

THE 'PITIFUL LOUSY NITTY REBELS' COULD BE TRAPPED

Colonel Joseph Yorke writes to his father, the Lord Chancellor, in frustration about the way the pursuit is being handled.

Packington, Dec. 6th, 1745

My patience, as well as that, I believe, of the whole nation, is put to the stretch when one reflects that so many of his Majesty's forces should be in the field, divided into two armies, headed the one by a marshal and the other by the Blood Royal, and should remain so long without coming within reach of these brood of villains. I solemnly declare I would be content (if everybody thought as I do) to touch neither bit nor drop till we have made an end of the affair which I think might be done in two or three days, but it would be attended with some alarming circumstances, I am afraid, to people in London. . . .

In my humble opinion, the happiest thing for us would be to have them continue their march towards London, where you may assemble force enough to check twice their number, and we follow close at their heels and must infallibly undo 'em; or if you at the helm don't care to frighten, which I know such a march will do, your monied folks, there is nothing left for us to do. . . . I assure your Lordship the way we go on in at present is perdition, destroys our men and gives them [the Rebels] an opportunity of loading themselves with the tasted sweets and golden fields of plenty out of this country and increase their force to return upon us with new supplies of strength and spirits. . . .

Macclesfield, Dec. 11th

I was in great hopes we should have been up with the pitiful lousy nitty Rebels, but they never stop. Every man that can get a horse keeps him, and they ride all the way. We yesterday arrived at this place, thro' as difficult a country as ever cavalry went thro', and the snow frozed on the ground made it almost impossible to keep our legs; but what induced us to make such hasty strides after them was that, as they gave out they should halt at Manchester, we were in great hopes of coming up with their rear at least. We are now in their track and pick up here and there a private man of 'em, who has lagg'd behind. The main body marched in great confusion yesterday from Manchester and have taken the Preston road, the thing I always apprehended. Marshal Wade must now deal with 'em again but I believe the Dutch are a clog to him.

We shall be with our cavalry at Manchester tomorrow early; I pray to God we may still come up with their rear, for the cruelties they have committed are horrid, and shows what we are all to expect if they succeed. The country people are enraged against 'em to such a degree that if the country gentlemen had had the least grain of spirit to have headed 'em, they would never have come so far. The women all declare they will never marry for the future but in the army, for they are the only people that have show'd their heads and offer'd to protect them in this time of distress. The country people rose yesterday to hinder the Rebels from passing the Mercy [Mersey] at Cheadle Ford which obliged 'em to take another road. . . .

Preston, Dec. 15th

. . . The rebels have fled before us in the utmost consternation thus far, and I am convinced in my own mind 24 hours more would have decided this affair. Their horses are [so] fatigued that they can do no more, our men in high spirits, and the country all up ready to join us and assist us against the rebels, now they saw themselves supported by the King's troops. What the consequences of our returning may be, God only knows. The spirits of the soldiery and the poor country must be depressed. They may wait quietly at Carlisle for their reinforcements, refresh their people, put new life into 'em, ruin the bordering counties, and in a little while advance with fresh vigour and fury into the bowels of the land, in spite of all that Marshal Wade's army can do against 'em: whereas, had we pushed on our advantages, and put an end to this body, the French would never have returned into the island. We have lost our opportunity, and I dread only to think of the consequences. . . .

On 16 April 1746, at Culloden on Drumossie Moor near Inverness, 5,000 starving Highlanders with only 150 cavalry, tired out from a night march, mounted the last gallant tribal sword charge against 7,500 fresh English troops and 1,500 loyal Highlanders, who had breakfasted on biscuit, cheese and brandy. They were mown down by cannon grapeshot and musket volleys and the disciplined English infantry cut into their flank, this time each stabbing the man to his right who could not parry with his target. It was all over in half an hour: the rebels, hacking about wildly to the last, lost 1,500 men in the rout on the blood-covered moor, and the rest were scattered or taken prisoner. According to a witness, 'the Highlanders gave vent to their grief in wild howlings, tears flowing down their cheeks'. Feeling was bitter and 'as few prisoners were taken as possible'. The Duke, whose gallant presence was worth 5,000 men, in the words of one of his dragoons, stained his reputation by deliberate atrocities which earned him the nickname 'Butcher Cumberland' among the Scots, but were approved of by a population burning with revenge. He executed 120 and wreaked pitiless retribution on the Highlands – burning, shooting and torturing; it was not surprising that 30,000 Scots emigrated to America. The English soldiers, however, heartily disliked campaigning in the Scottish winter and clamoured to be sent back to Flanders to fight the French.

Wolfe, still only nineteen, was already a staff major and supported the harsh treatment of the rebels; although he had lost one third of his regiment in the battle, he was too humane to comply with the Duke's order to shoot a defiant wounded Highlander.

28

CULLODEN: NO QUARTER GIVEN

Major James Wolfe describes the battle to his uncle, William Sotheron.

Inverness, April 17th, 1746

The Duke engaged with the rebel army, and in about an hour drove them from the field of battle, where they left near 1500 dead; the rest, except prisoners, escaped by the neighbourhood of the hills.

The rebels posted themselves on a high boggy moor, where they imagined our cannon and cavalry would be useless; but both did essential service. The cannon in particular made them very uneasy, and after firing a quarter of an hour, obliged them to change their situation and move forward some 100 yards to attack our front line of Foot, which they did with more fury than prudence, throwing down their firearms, and advancing with their drawn swords. They were however repulsed, and ran off with the greatest precipitation, and the Dragoons falling in amongst them completed the victory with much slaughter. We have taken about 20 pieces of cannon in the field and 700 prisoners, amongst which are all the Irish piquets, and broadswords, plaids innumerable. . . .

Orders were publicly given in the rebel army, the day before the action, that no quarter should be given to our troops. We had an opportunity of avenging ourselves, and I assure you as few prisoners were taken of the Highlanders as possible. . . . May they ever be punished in the same manner who attempt the like!

Yorke's vindictive call that the clan system must be rooted out perhaps strengthened his father's determination to pass legislation annexing the Scottish estates to the Crown, proscribing the episcopalian clergy, and, rather foolishly (for the next thirty years), the tartan.

29

THE HIGHLANDERS MUST BE 'UNCLANNED, UNDRESSED, DISARMED AND TAUGHT TO SPEAK ENGLISH'

Colonel Yorke tells his elder brother Philip after Culloden how the Scots had upset their French allies by their brutality and querulous indiscipline.

Inverness, April 30th, 1746

I hope the apprehensions of the terrible Highlanders is by this time a little abated and I flatter myself that this is the last time blood will be shed in the field by fellow subjects of this island. . . .

Since the battle our time has been taken up in hunting out the Rebels who made their escape from our fury that day, and in examining the papers found in the baggage and pockets of the officers killed and taken. It is very evident that the Rebels never seem to have had any settled scheme or formed plan of operations. Disputes, jealousies, doubts of one another are on all sides plain which, with the total want of order, discipline and economy, must have made a hell upon earth. . . . The French and they were continually jarring and I am firmly persuaded, had they been numerous enough, the French would have saved us a great deal of trouble by putting an end to the Rebellion themselves; for they could not endure one another and every letter they wrote during the time they were amongst them, are filled with complaints of their brutality and total want of obedience and discipline. . . .

The Young Pretender is still lurking about in the Highlands, either in the Camerons country or in the Isles, where he first landed. When we move, we shall do our best to ferret him out, and if we can't send him to his long home, endeavour at least to rid the island of him. . . .

I long to hear you have begun to make some laws for this country, which absolutely till this time have been without any, or governed by the impositions of the Highland scoundrel chiefs. You must never expect to see a total end to the rebellious spirit of this country till the Highlanders are unclanned, undressed, effectually disarmed and taught to speak English. . . . [12]

With the progress of literacy in the first half of the eighteenth century, sailors of the lower deck and soldiers in the ranks could now express their feelings in letters. While the officers and particularly their leaders, tended to take a more detached, professional view of war and could sometimes vie with their opponents in chivalry, their men showed a surprisingly violent hatred of their enemies, in fact of all foreigners, even of the German mercenaries defending England against the Scots. Their exuberant patriotism is matched by their delight in carnage and looting.

---

12 'Bonnie Prince Charlie' made a legendary escape to eke out another forty-three years of plotting in France and Rome, sometimes hiding in London. Jacobitism with its aura of martyrdom lingered on – from the proclamation of 'James III' by striking coalminers at Elswick in 1750 until, in the First World War, the Pretender turned out to be Generalfeldmarschall Kronprinz Rupprecht von Bayern, commander of the Southern wing of the German army invading France!

EIGHT

The Seven Years' War with France (1756–63)

Britannia heard the piercing Voice of Fame . . .
Britons, exult! All Gallia trembling stands
CONTEMPORARY VERSE

In a reversal of alliances, England sided with Frederick the Great to protect Hanover, and France with Austria and Russia to destroy Prussia. The usual invasion panic seized the public, as the French army was poised to cross the Channel while the British army was in America and India to counter French moves to drive them out from all colonies. It was the policy of William Pitt, the strategist of worldwide vision, to support England's allies through a naval blockade and amphibious raids on the French ports, as a diversion from his real purpose, the conquest of Canada.

Keeping the French at Bay

They swear they'll invade us, these terrible foes . . .
Heart of oak are our ships,
Heart of oak are our men,
We are always ready . . .
DAVID GARRICK (1717–79)

Mrs Boscawen, the wife of one of the most outstanding admirals, expresses her confidence that he will be instrumental in winning the war. In fact, four years later, he destroyed the Toulon fleet at Lagos Bay when it tried to join up with the main fleet at Brest which would have constituted the most serious invasion threat.

1

'We shall yet humble France'

Mrs Boscawen writes to her husband whose return from America, which she was longing for, had been delayed.

> Portsmouth, 30th August 1755
>
> You suppose, my dearest love, that I am as impatient for your return as you can be. Indeed you can venture to suppose this much and more. You cannot be so impatient or so intent upon one point, having so many important ones to think of, as I am, who have had no other point in view these many days but our happy meeting, which has been all my thoughts by day and all my dreams by night. . . . Your last kind letter I could not read without a pain in my stomach, grief of heart and loss of sleep, for I had so *depended* on your coming day by day (having very brisk Westerly winds) that a month more seems an age, and to pass it here I cannot; this place would be most irksome after such a disappointment. For here is the sea, and here are ships; and men of war come in daily, but not the ship which my eyes have ached in looking for every day upon Southsea Common, spying for sails around St Helen's point. . . .
>
> War is most in my thoughts now, as being most my concern, since, as we are told, 'tis actually begun, the Captain here having orders to sink, burn and destroy – horrid words! God send us happily and honourably out of it, and, as my dear Admiral began the war, so God grant his noble achievements may make the peace and he himself live many years to enjoy that peace! . . .
>
> It is strongly reported that Spain is ours and will not go off to the French side. Something tells me, methinks, that we shall yet humble France and bring her Navy into this port.
>
> At least I must hope that YOU will succeed in all you undertake, and be as happy at sea and on shore as is wished by her whose study it shall always be to make you so, and who is, with inexpressible tenderness and attachment, your most affectionate, faithful wife, friend and servant,
>
> F. Boscawen

Her friend, Mrs Montagu, president of their 'Blue-stocking Assemblies', and no hero-worshipper of her own husband, is less optimistic but entertains her own private hopes.

2

READY TO BE CONQUERED BY A FRENCH MARQUIS

Mrs Elizabeth Montagu serves a warning to her husand.

> November 1756
>
> . . . France threatens us with an equal Navy by the Spring; there is a great demand for forces in America; and God knows where all this will end. As the weather is so sharp,

I do not stir from my dressing-room fire, for indeed I must hazard my health, which, like Great Britain, is in a tottering condition. If we were in as much danger of being conquered by the Spaniards as the French, I should not be very anxious about my continuance in the world; but the French are polite to the ladies, and they admire ladies a little in years, so that I expect to be treated with great politeness; and as all laws are suspended during violence, I suppose that you and the rest of the married men will not take anything amiss that happens on the occasion; nor indeed should it be a much greater fault than keeping a monkey, if one should live with a French Marquis for a quarter of a year.

Some say Admiral Byng should be hanged for his cowardice and others that he should be knighted for his gallantry. The people in general choose that he should be hanged.

The government, preoccupied with the threat to England, knew that the French were going to invade the important naval base of Minorca, but kept Fort St Philip and Admiral Byng's relief force short of supplies and men. After an inconclusive action against the French fleet of better ships, guns and crews, in which several English vessels were crippled without inflicting damage on the French, Byng, always pessimistic, abandoned the besieged island to its fate to preserve his force for the protection of Gibraltar. The vengeful outcry which rose in England led to his court martial and execution, eliciting Voltaire's puzzled comment that the English shoot admirals 'pour encourager les autres'. Walpole points an accusing finger at the real culprits. Minorca was restored to Britain in 1763 but reverted to Spain in 1802.

3

ADMIRAL BYNG, THE POLITICIANS' SCAPEGOAT

Horace Walpole describes to Sir Horace Mann how Byng was sacrificed to cover up the sins of ministers.

30 Jan. 1757

All England is again occupied with Admiral Byng; he and his friends were quite persuaded of his acquittal. The Court martial, after the trial was finished, kept the whole world in suspense for a week. . . . They pronounced this extraordinary sentence: they condemn him to death for negligence, but acquit him of disaffection and cowardice, unanimously recommending him to mercy. Not being able in conscience to pronounce that he had done all he could, they had been forced to bring him in guilty, but beg he may be spared. The discussion and difference of opinions on this sentence are incredible. Some who make him the scapegoat for their own neglects, I fear, will try to complete his fate. . . . He bore well his unexpected sentence, as he has all the outrageous indignities and cruelties heaped upon him. . . .

13 Feb.

Byng's fate is still in suspense. The King would not pardon him. They would not execute the sentence, as many lawyers are clear that it is not a legal one. At last the council has referred it to the 12 judges to give their opinion: if not a favourable one, he dies! . . . It will be difficult to persuade posterity that all the shame of last summer was the fault of Byng! Exact evidence of whose fault is was, I believe posterity will never have. The new Chief Justice and the late Chancellor pleaded against Byng like little attorneys, and did all they could to stifle truth. . . . The great doubtfulness of his crime and the extraordinariness of his sentence, the persecution of his enemies, who sacrifice him for their own guilt and the rage of a blinded nation, have called forth all my pity for him. His enemies triumph; but who can envy the triumph of murder?

17 Mar.

Admiral Byng's tragedy was completed on Monday – a perfect tragedy, for there were variety of incidents, villany, murder, and a hero! His sufferings, persecutions, aspersions, disturbances, nay, the revolutions of his fate, had not in the least unhinged his mind; his whole behaviour was natural and firm. A few days before, one of his friends standing by him, said, 'Which of us is tallest?' He replied, 'Why this ceremony? I know what it means; let the man come and measure me for my coffin.' He said, that being acquitted of cowardice, and being persuaded on the coolest reflection that he had acted for the best, and should act so again, he was not unwilling to suffer. He desired to be shot on the quarter-deck, not where common malefactors are; came out at twelve, sat down in a chair, for he would not kneel, and refused to have his face covered, that his countenance might show whether he feared death; but being told that it might frighten his executioners, he submitted, gave the signal at once, received one shot through the head, another through the heart, and fell. Do cowards live or die thus? Can that man want spirit who only fears to terrify his executioners? Has the aspen Duke of Newcastle lived thus? Would my Lord Hardwicke[1] die thus, even supposing he had nothing on his conscience?

The British East India Company was the greatest trading and empire-building corporation, whose charter for exclusive trade privilege was granted by Queen Elizabeth in 1600 and converted by James I into a permanent monopoly. Charles II permitted the Company to employ troops in war, erect forts, acquire territory, form alliances and govern with complete authority. After the dissolution of the Mogul Empire, the Company assumed increasing power, based on Bombay, Madras and Calcutta. The defence of its profitable trade against competition from the French and Dutch Companies led to armed conflict 'to vindicate the Rights and Honour of the English nation in India'.

1   First Lord of the Treasury and Lord Chancellor respectively: both cautious schemers who resigned in the crisis over the loss of Minorca and testified to Byng's guilt.

A Jacobite Incident by D. Morier, Battle of Culloden, 1746. The Highlanders' broadswords and targets proved to be ineffective against the English infantry. (Windsor Castle, Royal Library © 1993 HM The Queen)

General Burgoyne surrenders to the American militia under General Gates at Sarratoga, 1777. Engraving from the *First French Book of the War of Independence of the USA* (1783) by F. Godefroy and N. Ponce. (Bodleian Library, Oxford, 1718.d.15)

In 1756, Siraj-ud-daula, the young Nawab of Bengal, suspicious of British expansionist aims, surprised the motley garrison of 430 behind the tumble-down defences of Fort William in Calcutta with his army of 50,000 men. The 146 survivors were thrown into an 18 by 14 ft prison cell, the legendary 'Black Hole' and 123 of them died there of suffocation on 21 June, the hottest night of the summer. Such atrocities, intentional or not, tended to be blown up out of proportion to serve, in convenient revenge, for colonial annexation. Clive was appointed Commander-in-Chief of the punitive expedition which sailed from Madras to Calcutta with less than 2,000 troops in five naval vessels and six transports under Vice-Admiral Watson.

4

REVENGE FOR THE 'BLACK HOLE'

Lieutenant-Colonel (later Baron, Robert Clive, 1725–74,) outlines his aims to the Select Committee in London.

11 October 1756

. . . Every Breast here seems filled with Grief, Horror & Resentment. . . . I am now upon the point of embarking on board His Majesty's Squadron with a fine Body of Europeans full of spirit & Resentment for the Insults & Barbarities inflicted on so many British Subjects.

I flatter myself that this Expedition will not end with the retaking of Calcutta only: & that the Company's Estate in these parts will be settled in a Better & more lasting Condition than ever. There is less reason to apprehend a Check from the Nabob's Forces than from the Nature of the Climate & Country. . . . I hope we shall be able to dispossess the French. . . .

Calcutta was easily reconquered but the Nawab approached with his large army.

5

THE DISRESPECTFUL NAWAB IS TAUGHT A LESSON

Clive describes to Lord Chancellor Hardwicke how Siraj-ud-daula's army was defeated in a dawn attack in thick fog.

Calcutta, Feb. 23, 1757 (received Sept.)

. . . I have the pleasure to inform your Lordship this expedition by sea and land has been crowned with all the success that could be wished. The town of Calcutta and Fort William were soon retaken. This news brought down the Nabob himself at the head of 20,000 horse and 30,000 foot, 25 pieces of cannon with a great number of elephants. Agreeable to the Nabob's desire, I dispatched two gentlemen to wait upon him in hopes everything might be settled wtihout drawing the sword, but the haughtiness and disrespect with which he treated them, convinced me nothing could be expected by mild measures. This determined me to attack his camp in the night time, for which purpose I apply'd to vice-admiral Watson for 500 sailors to draw our cannon, and at three in the morning (Feb. 4) our little army, consisting of 600 Europeans, 800 Blacks, seven field pieces and the sailors set out for the attack. A little before daybreak we entered the camp and received a very brisk fire. This did not stop the progress of our troops who marched through the enemy's camp upwards of four miles in length. We were more than two hours in passing, and what escaped the Van was destroyed by the Rear. We returned safe to our camp, having killed, by the best accounts, 1300 men. The loss on our side amounted to 200 men killed and wounded.

This blow had its effect; for the next day the army decamped, and the Nabob sent me a letter offering terms of accommodation; a firm peace is concluded greatly to the honour and advantage of the Company, and the Nabob has entered into an alliance and is returned to his Capital of Muxadavad. . . .

The treacherous Nawab only wanted to gain time to return to the charge. On 23 June 1757, at Plassey, Clive's 800 whites and 2,100 Sepoys, with eight guns and no cavalry, faced the Nawab's 35,000 infantry and 15,000 crack horsemen, with 53 large cannon, manned by expert French gunners. Clive, installed in a hunting box in an orchard of 100,000 mango trees, had entered into a conspiracy with Mir Jafar, commander of one wing of the Nawab's army, who hovered undecidedly during the battle, awaiting its outcome. Clive's army was attacked by the Nawab's best troops under his only loyal general, Mir Madan, supported by devastating French gunfire. Luckily, the monsoon came to the rescue by flooding the French powder supply, while the English sailors covered up theirs. When Clive counter-attacked, the Nawab fled on his fastest camel and his army was routed, with the conspirators standing by idly. Plassey became the model for the nineteenth-century colonial wars by proving that a small, disciplined English force could beat a large native mob.

6

THE BATTLE THAT CHANGED THE HISTORY OF INDIA

Clive announces his victory to the Committee in Calcutta.

23rd June 1757

This morning at one o'clock we arrived at Placis Grove, and early in the morning the Nabob's whole army appeared in sight and cannonaded us for several hours, and about noon we advanced and stormed the Nabob's camp which we have taken with all his cannon and pursued him six miles, and shall proceed to Muxadavad tomorrow. Meer Jaffeir, Roydoolub, and Luttee Cawn gave us no other assistance than standing neuter. They are with me with a large force. Meer Muddun and 500 horse are killed and three elephants. Our loss is trifling, not above 20 Europeans killed and wounded.

The traitor Mir Jafar had the Nawab murdered after his capture, and succeeded him as a puppet ruler of the East India Company which wielded effective power over the whole of Bengal. Of the fabulous booty, estimated to be worth £40 million, Clive distributed £400,000 among his troops and kept £234,000 for himself. Accused later of taking bribes, the new peer (a melancholic opium addict), although cleared by Parliament, committed suicide at the age of forty-nine. In Bengal the English traders had turned into conquerors and were set to annex, gradually, the whole of India.[2]

To take off the pressure on Cumberland's army in Germany, an amphibious raid was to strike at Rochefort, held by a weak garrison. The commander, Sir John Mordaunt, too old at sixty to direct such an operation, did not know how to carry out the landing and disapproved anyway of what he regarded as a degrading 'hit and run' action. After Hawke's fleet had taken the Isle of Aix, he hesitated to attack the feeble defences of the city till the weather made it impossible; but a large number of merchant vessels were destroyed. On his return, Mordaunt was court-martialled: he was acquitted of disobedience but censored for his lack of resolution. In Germany, Cumberland was forced to capitulate and resigned.[3] Mordaunt's young quarter master was exasperated.

7

FAILURE OF THE AMPHIBIOUS RAID ON ROCHEFORT

Lieutenant-Colonel Wolfe gives his uncle a highly critical account of the incompetence and indecision of the leaders.

October 18th, 1757

Nous avons manqué un beau coup, as the prisoners told us, after we had loitered away three or four days in consultations, deliberations, and councils of war. The season of the year and nature of the enterprise called for the quickest and most vigorous execution, whereas our proceedings were quite otherwise.

We were in sight of the Isle of Rhé the 20th September, consequently were seen by the enemy (as their signals left us no room to doubt), and it was the 23rd before we fired a gun. That afternoon and night slipped through our hands, – the lucky moment

2 M. Edwardes, *Battle of Plassey*, Batsford, 1963.
3 R.Whitworth, *Ligonier*, Oxford Clarendon Press, 1958.

of confusion and consternation among our enemies. The 24th, – Admirals and Generals consult together, and resolve upon nothing between them but to hold a council of war. The 25th, – this famous council sat from morning till late at night, and the result of the debates was unanimously not to attack the place they were ordered to attack, and for reasons that no soldier will allow to be sufficient. The 26th, – the Admiral sends a message to the General, intimating that if they did not determine to do something there he would go to another place. The 27th, – the Generals and Admirals view the land with glasses, and agree upon a second council of war, having by this time discovered their mistake. The 28th, – they deliberate, and resolve to land that night. Orders are issued out accordingly, but the wind springing up after the troops had been two or three hours in the boats, the officers of the navy declare it difficult and dangerous to attempt the landing. The troops are commanded back to their transports, and so ended the expedition! The true state of the case is, that our sea-officers do not care to be engaged in any business of this sort, where little is to be had but blows and reputation; and the officers of the infantry are so profoundly ignorant, that an enterprise of any vigour astonishes them to that degree that they have not strength of mind nor confidence to carry it through.

I look upon this as the greatest design that the nation has engaged in for many years. The Court of Versailles and the whole French nation, were alarmed beyond measure. 'Les Anglois ont attrapé notre foible,' disent-ils. Alas! we have only discovered our own. . . .

Armchair strategist Walpole pours out his highly literary sarcasm on the poor results achieved by the raids on St Malo and Cherbourg. In fact, 1,300 guards and 6,000 marines landed in June at St Malo from their special craft without opposition, were joined by cavalry and artillery the next day, and proceeded to ruthlessly sack the city. The third Duke of Marlborough, finding the fortifications too strong and afraid of being cut off by French troops who were approaching – and assailed by sickness and lack of food – re-embarked after destroying about one hundred vessels of all sizes. In August, Cherbourg was actually captured and its defences dismantled. In a victory parade, some captured brass cannon were hauled along in triumph all the way from Kensington Palace to the Tower, and found their final resting place in Ligonier's garden at Cobham.[3]

8

PLAYING HIDE AND SEEK

Horace Walpole, writing to Sir Horace Mann, chides himself for dreams of glory.

Strawberry Hill, June 18, 1758

I write to you again so soon, only to laugh at my last letter. What a dupe was I! at my years to be dazzled with glory! to be charmed by the rattle of drums and trumpets, till I fancied myself at Cressy or Poitiers! In the middle of all the dream of conquest, just when I had settled in what room of my castle I would lodge the Duke of Alençon or Montpensier,[4] or whatever illustrious captive should be committed to the custody of Seneschal *Me*, I was awakened with an account of our army having re-embarked, after burning some vessels at St Maloes. This is the history, neither more nor less, of this mighty expedition. They found the causeway broken up, stayed from Tuesday night till Monday morning in sight of the town; agreed it was impregnable; heard 10,000 French (which the next day were erected into 30,000) were coming against them; took to their transports, and are gone to play at hide and seek somewhere else. This campaign being rather naked, is coloured over with the great damage we have done, and with the fine disposition and dispatch made for getting away – the same colours that would serve to paint pirates or a flight. However, the City is pleased; and Mr Pitt maintains that he never intended to take St Maloes, which I believe, *because* when he did intend to have Rochfort taken last year, he sent no cannon; this year, when he never meant to take St Maloes, he sent a vast train of artillery.

9

A CHERBOURG CANNON FOR HYDE PARK AND GUINEAS FOR THE FRENCH PAUPERS

Sept. 9

. . . This week, after bringing it by *land* from Portsmouth, they have dragged the cannon of Cherbourg into Hyde Park, on pretence of diverting a man [George II], at whom, in former days, I believe, Mr Pitt has laughed for loving such rattles as drums and trumpets. Our expedition, since breaking a basin at Cherbourg, has done nothing, but are dodging about still. Prince Edward gave 100 guineas to the poor of Cherbourg, and the General and Admiral 25 apiece. I love charity, but sure this is excess of it, to lay out thousands, and venture so many lives, for the opportunity of giving a Christmas-box to your enemies! Instead of beacons, I suppose, the coast of France will be hung with pewter pots with a slit in them, as prisons are, to receive our alms.

Early in July 1759, there was again one of the recurrent invasion scares:

We talk of nothing here but the French Invasion, they are certainly making such preparations as have never been made to invade this Island since the Spanish Armada,

wrote Lord Lyttleton. The grand design was formidable indeed: 48,000 troops were to assemble in 225 'frames' (sailing barges with a gun in the prow) with 100 supply ships and 12 naval craft. They were to sail under Marshal Soubise from Le Havre or Ostend to establish a bridgehead at

4   At Crécy, Edward III beat Philip VI in 1346, and at Poitiers, the Black Prince took his son Jean le Bon prisoner in 1356; the Duc d'Alençon was one of Queen Elizabeth's suitors and the Duc de Montpensier was another sixteenth-century courtier.

Portsmouth or the Thames Estuary, while the Duc d'Aiguillon was to be conveyed to the Firth of Clyde by the combined Brest and Toulon fleets with 24 battalions to take Glasgow and Edinburgh. A diversionary raid was to be made on Ireland. The signal for their departure was to be a wind blowing in the face of the Downs and Channel fleets, preventing them from interfering.[3]

Ligonier, now seventy-nine and still Commander-in-Chief, Master General of Ordnance and a member of the War Cabinet, mobilized the militia in the absence of the army abroad. Contrary to the usual attitude to general service, under the threat of invasion it became all the fashion to enlist in the local citizen force, but, in fact, the Navy was the only valid shield. Rodney made a bold and successful raid on the invasion base at Le Havre.

10

THEY MIGHT HAVE CARRIED OFF ENGLAND TO VERSAILLES

Horace Walpole writes to Sir Horace Mann about 'militia-mania'.

June 22, 1759

Well! they tell us in good earnest that we are to be invaded; Mr Pitt is as positive of it as of his own invasions. As the French affect an air of grandeur in all they do, 'Mr Pitt sent ten thousands, but they send fifty thousands.' You will be inquisitive after our force – I can't tell you the particulars; I am only in town for today, but I hear of mighty preparations. Of one thing I am sure; they missed the moment when 8000 men might have carried off England and set it down in the gardens of Versailles. In the last war, when we could not rake together 4,000 men, and were all divided, not a flat-bottomed boat lifted up its leg against us! There is a great spirit in motion; everybody is raising regiments or themselves. . . . I shall not march my Twickenham militia for some private reasons; my farmer has got an ague, my printer is run away, my footboy is always drunk, and my gardener is a Scotchman, and I believe would give intelligence to the enemy. France has notified to the Dutch that she intends to *surprise us*; and this makes us still more angry. . . .

Adieu! If you have a mind to be fashionable, you must raise a regiment of Florentine militia.

11

100,000 ACRES ON THE OHIO NOT WORTH 20 IN ENGLAND

July 8

I don't write to tell you that the French are *not* landed at Deal, as was believed yesterday. An officer arrived post in the middle of the night, who saw them disembark. The king was called up; my Lord Ligonier buckled on his armour. Nothing else was talked of in the streets; yet there was no panic. Before noon, it was known that the invasion was a few Dutch hoys. The day before, it was triumph. Rodney was known to be before Havre de Grace; with two bomb-ketches he set the town on fire in different places, and had brought up four more to act, notwithstanding a very smart fire from the forts, which, however, will probably force him to retire without burning the flat-bottomed boats, which are believed out of his reach.[5] I am sorry for this sort of war, not only for the sufferers, but I don't like the precedent, in case the French should land. I think they will scarce venture; for besides the force on land, we have a mighty chain of fleet and frigates along the coast. There is great animosity to them, and few can expect to return. . . .

From America we expect the greatest things; our force there by land and sea is vast. I hope we shall not be to buy England back by restoring the *North* Indies! I will gladly give them all the 100,000 acres that may fall to my share on the Ohio for my 20 acres here. Truly I don't like having them endangered for the limits of Virginia!

I wait impatiently for your last orders for the watch; if the worst comes to the worst, I can convey it to you by some French officer.

The weather is sultry; this country never looked prettier. I hope our enemies will not have the heart to spoil it! Adieu! I will tell you more soon, or I hope no more.

A tight blockade kept the French fleet cooped up in port and the raids disrupted invasion preparations. Both lowered French morale and safely kept them at bay, in the same way as Clive had frustrated Dupleix's designs in India and the capture of Louisbourg in 1758 put a stop to French ambitions to conquer the whole of America. The stage was now set for three most spectacular victories in the autumn of 1759 which enhanced British prestige, still unclouded by envy and resentment, perhaps higher than at any time in history.

'Annus Mirabilis': 1759

What makes Minden, Quebec and Quiberon Bay so 'miraculous' is that in the summer of 1759, after years of anxiety, the situation was still precarious, with one of the most serious invasion threats hanging over England, but suddenly the clouds were blown away by three memorable victories – on the continent, in Canada and at sea. Who were the men who, by their stubborn courage, accomplished such a turn of fortunes?

Wolfe, a rather priggish martinet, wrote in February 1758:

The condition of the troops [at Portsmouth] excells belief. There is not the least shadow of discipline, care, or attention. . . . Dirty, drunken, insolent rascals, every kind of corruption, immorality, and looseness carried to excess; it is a sink of the lowest and most abominable vices.[6]

---

5   Walpole was wrong: Rodney did succeed. He reported to Pitt that 'stores for the flat-bottom boats burnt with very great fury for upwards of 6 hours' and 'many of their boats were overturned and damaged by the explosions of the shells.' (G. Marcus, *Quiberon Bay*, Hollis & Carter, 1960, p. 76.)
6   C. Field, *Old Times*, 1939, p. 35.

Yet these were the same 'ideal' infantry men, in the words of Lord Wavell, who as 'cat-burglar, gunman and poacher' knew how to confound the enemy by their daring, and brought off at Minden 'one of the most surprising feats of disciplined valour in the history of war'.[7]

Wolfe had written earlier about the officers in a puritanical vein:

> There are young men amongst us that have great revenues and high military stations, that repine if they go 50 miles from home: Soup, and Venaison and Turtle, is their supream delight and joy; an effeminate Race of Coxcombs; the future leaders of our Armies, the defenders and Protectors of a great & free Nation! – Better be a savage than a gentle amorous Puppy, obnoxious to all the World, a perfect Philander.[8]

These very coxcombs and philanderers, whose character seemed to get transformed in action, inspired their men by their valour: to cite a naval example, Commodore Augustus Hervey, a notorious dandy, but fearless fighter, led personally the dare-devil night capture by a handful of men of the French admiral's yacht in Camaret Bay. Reckless enjoyment in peacetime and reckless courage in wartime often go together. It is a great mistake to assume that attitudes are always fixed: under the impact of war they may reveal different aspects of character, as Hitler was going to find out when he thought that the soft effeminate youths of Britain would be incapable of resisting the steeled men of Germany.

Minden

> *Their insolence in peace is bravery in war*
> DR SAMUEL JOHNSON

On 1 August 1759, at Minden near Hanover, Duke Ferdinand of Brunswick, Commander-in-Chief of the Anglo-Allied army, lured Marshal Contades' army from their unassailable entrenchments, covered by hills, marshes and rivers, to mount an attack. Through a misunderstood order, six British regiments, with a battalion of Hanoverian Guards, advanced prematurely straight into violent cross-fire from the French batteries. Lieutenant-Generals Earl Waldegrave and Kingsley, the heroes of Minden, steadied them to face the assault from the French cavalry in one of the most memorable feats of infantry. Contades himself paid this tribute to them:

---

7   A. Wavell, *Soldiers and Soldiering*, J. Cape, 1953, p. 122.
8   In A. Doughty, *Siege of Quebec*, 1901, VI, p. 30.

I have seen what I never thought possible, a single line of infantry break through three lines of cavalry ranked in order of battle and tumble them to ruin.[9]

This display of steadiness with musket and bayonet – one in three was killed – ranks with Fontenoy:

The anatomy of British military legend was becoming clear: the British came to admire imperturbable discipline, unshakeable courage and endurance,

even in pursuit of a tactical blunder.[10] The three letters which follow provide a continuous narrative of the battle.

12

'Not even lions could have come on'

Captain Thomas Thompson, 20th Foot, describes the gallant charge on the French cavalry in which he was wounded.

Minden Hospital, 18 August
. . . We discovered the enemy with the greatest advantage over us, being already formed in Battle array ready to receive us.

On the immediate sight of us they opened a battery of 18 heavy cannon which flanked this regiment in particular every foot we marched; their shot took place so fast, that every officer imagined the battalion would be taken off before we could get up to give a fire, notwithstanding we were then within a quarter of a mile of their right wing and absolutely running up to the mouth of their cannon in front.

I saw heads, legs and arms taken off, my right hand file of men not more than a foot from me were all by one ball dashed to pieces and their blood flying all over me, this I confess staggered me not a little, but on my receiving a contusion in the bend of my right arm by a spent musket shot, it steaded me immediately, all apprehensions of hurt vanished, revenge and the care of the company I commanded took [their] place. . . .

By this time we were within 200 yards or less of them and plainly perceived the Fusiliers, 'Stewart's' and 'Napier's' Regiments engaging an amazing number of their troops, all the time their right wing was pelting us both with small arms, cannon and grape shot, and we were not suffered to fire, but stood tamely looking on whilst they at their leisure picked us off. . . . The French charged them with at least 20 Squadrons, but by their steadiness and bravery, keeping their fire till the enemy were close up to

9 E.M. Lloyd, *Review of the History of Infantry*, 1908.
10 C. Barnett, *Britain and her Army*, A. Lane, 1970, p. 210.

them gave them such a terrible fire that not *even lions* could have come on, such a number of them fell both horses and men that it made it difficult for those not touched to retire. This charge over, a second and a third came on and were repulsed in the same manner. Now was the time the English Cavalry should have come up, every eye was looking with impatience.

Just at this time I got my wound, after having been hit three times before by spent balls, but this seared me like a red hot iron, [I] found myself fainting and quitting the Regt. after having called for a fresh officer, but found no one to supply my place. I heard the battalion fire which pleased me so much in my agony, that I stood stupified looking on them, many poor soldiers praying, begging me to come off. . . .

13

SIX ENGLISH REGIMENTS OF FOOT ROUT THE FRENCH ARMY

Lieutenant Hugh Montgomery, 12th Foot, writes to his mother.

Camp at Paderborn, 9th August

. . . The next who made their appearance were some Regiments of the Grenadiers of France, as fine and terrible looking fellows as I ever saw. They stood us a tug, notwithstanding we beat them off to a distance, where they galded [galled] us much, they having rifled barrels, and our muskets would not reach them. To remedy this we advanced, they took the hint, and ran away. Now we were in hopes that we had done enough for one day's work, and that they would not disturb us more, but soon after a very large body of fresh infantry, the last resource of Contades, made the final attempt on us. With them we had a long but not very brisk engagement, at last made them retire almost out of reach, when the three English regiments of the rear line came up, and gave them one fire, which sent them off for good and all. But what is wonderful to tell, we ourselves after all this success at the very same time also retired, but indeed we did not then know that victory was ours. However we rallied, but all that could now be mustered was about 13 files private with our Colonel and four other officers one of which I was so fortunate to be. With this remnant we returned again to the charge, but to our unspeakable joy no opponents could be found. It is astonishing, that this victory was gained by six English regiments of foot, without their grenadiers, unsupported by cavalry or cannon, not even their own battalion guns, in the face of a dreadful battery so near as to tear them with grape-shot, against 40 battalions and 36 squadrons. . . .

The sufferings of our regiment will give you the best notion of the smartness of the action. We actually fought that day not more than 480 private and 27 officers, of the first 302 were killed and wounded, and of the latter 18. I received from a spent ball just such a rap on my collar-bone as I have frequently from that once most dreadful weapon, your crooked-headed stick; it just swelled and grew red. . . .

The noise of the battle frightened our sutler's wife into labour the next morning. She was brought to bed of a son, and we have had him christened by the name of Ferdinand.

14

THE 'ENGLISH DEVILS' AND A WORRIED WIFE

An artillery officer writes to a friend from Frankenberg Camp.

Aug. 23

... The French thought to take us at a disadvantage by falling upon us as we were forming, but they unfortunately fell in with the hardy English, or, as they sometimes call us, English Devils. We drew up our ten guns close to the six Regiments on the right and there waited undiscov'd till the enemy came almost within pistol shot, like a cloud, with numbers, and when they were just a going to gallop down sword in hand amongst the poor mangled Regiments, we clapt our matches to the ten guns and gave them such a salute as they little expected. Our Balls (by the blessing of God) had the desired effect for we mow'd them down like standing Corn. We fired quick for about 20 minutes. The French fell so very fast that they did not know which way to fly for safety, but we paid no regard to their distress. This put the whole French Army into such a confusion that they all with one consent run away, tho' many of their Regiments had never been engaged. We advanced after them, having the pleasure to see them make their escape up the hills like a flock of sheep. Our Army seems as hearty and ready for action again as if they had lain all the time in St James' Park. ...

P.S. I had forgot to inform you that the morning after the battle my dear Wife came in search of me upon the field of battle with a heart full of grief thinking every corps she saw was mine. In such confusion I met her, but had some difficulty to persuade her I was really the Man she wanted. We are both very happy and enjoy all the pleasure that our unsettled life will allow of. It is the opinion of all here that had the Cavalry engag'd the French [who] run away, we had destroy'd their whole Army Root and Branch. ...

The failure of the British cavalry to pursue, to which the officer is referring, came as an unbelievable anti-climax: Lord George Sackville, their commander, disobeyed, until it was too late, Brunswick's thrice-repeated order to lead his twenty-four squadrons of cavalry in pursuit of the French army in full flight. A great opportunity to destroy it completely was missed, although ten thousand prisoners were taken and the French were driven from Westphalia right to the banks of the Rhine. The reasons for Sackville's enigmatic attitude have never been clarified; they may be found in his melancholic and insecure temperament, showing itself outwardly by arrogance and wounding irony which made him unpopular.[11] He was cashiered for cowardice by a court martial, but, as the writer of the next letter foresees, rose again to become a disastrous colonial secretary during the American War of Independence.

11 P. Mackesy, *Coward of Minden*, A. Lane, 1979.

15

A VIEW FROM THE CIVILIAN ANGLE

Mr Symmer writes to Andrew Mitchell, British plenipotentiary in Berlin and friend of Frederick the Great.

London, 14th September

How much do I wish that all this bustle in Europe were over, and that I had you here, in the quiet Cabinet of Mount street, to philosophise about Electricity and the hidden Powers of Nature. . . . I must acquaint you, that the late Successes His Majesty's Arms have been crowned with by Sea and Land, together with a certainty now of having nothing to fear with regard to an Invasion from France. . . . The only apparent difficulty is to supply the expenses of the war – not less than 18 million during the course of this year. This is a sum so immense, that there is not a nation in Europe could bear the burden of it long. Our comfort is that it must go as hard with our enemies, in consequence of which we may soon hope for Peace.

I take it for granted you are no stranger to which has been reported concerning the behaviour of Lord G. S—le at the Battle of Minden. He is stripped of all his military employments: and that when he *demanded* a Court Martial, he was told he might go to Germany to have it. In such a Country as E—d, and we are men of intrigue and abilities as Lord G., I should not be surprised if in six months hence the current runs another way.

Quebec

Brave let us fall, or honor'd if we live
FROM A POEM FOUND IN WOLFE'S POCKET

When Hawke drove back the French fleet with reinforcements for Louisbourg, its fate was sealed: Boscawen destroyed the squadron in the port and the great fortress, the principal French stronghold in America, fell to General Amherst after Brigadier Wolfe had dived into the sea at the head of his grenadiers to storm it. From there two armies converged on New France in 1759: Amherst marching north to the St Lawrence towards Montreal, and Wolfe – who was to prove himself as an imaginative tactician in his first and last command at the age of thirty-two – sailing up river to Quebec. Vice-Admiral Saunders' fleet succeeded in safely steering its 22 sails of the line and 200 army transports with 8,000 men through 300 miles of uncharted channels, under constant menace from rocks, shoals, currents and fogs, which had wrecked the 1711 expedition. Montcalm, the French commander of Quebec, had failed to block them, thinking it was impossible to pass through.

The fleet in St Lawrence cut off supplies from Quebec, but the fortifications, towering above on a great rock, ringed with steep cliffs, proved impenetrable in a three-month battle of wits during which Wolfe suffered a number of reverses despite his campaign of 'frightfulness': the city was mercilessly bombarded, the cathedral burnt down, and a priest scalped (treatment normally only reserved for Indians).[12]

16

Quebec's 'inaccessible entrenchments'

Major-General Wolfe writes to his mother a fortnight before he was killed.

Banks of the St Lawrence, August 31st, 1759

Dear Madam,

My writing to you will convince you that no personal evils, worse than defeats and disappointments, have fallen upon me. The enemy puts nothing to risk, and I can't, in conscience, put the whole army to risk. My antagonist has wisely shut himself up in the inaccessible entrenchments, so that I can't get at him without spilling a torrent of blood, and that perhaps to little purpose. The Marquis of Montcalm is at the head of a great number of bad soldiers, and I am at the head of a small number of good ones,[13] that wish for nothing so much as to fight him; but the wary old fellow avoids an action, doubtful of the behaviour of his army. . . .

I wish you much health, and am, dear Madam,

Your obedient and affectionate son,
Jam. Wolfe

17

HIS SOLDIERS' 'OVERBEARING COURAGE' DEFEATS WOLFE'S SCHEME

A volunteer serving under Wolfe writes home.

Sterling Castle in the River St Lawrence, two miles below the City of Quebec, Sept. 2
. . . General Wolfe made an attempt to land his forces west of the fall and force the enemy from their entrenchments. The enemy within their trenches threw numbers of shells at the ships, the Admiral being in person equally exposed with the meanest seamen and soldiers.

Mr Wolfe being in the first boat, soon got 2000 men ashore; and there was now the greatest prospect of succeeding, when the overbearing courage and impetuosity of

---

12 Maj.Gen. J.F.C. Fuller, *Decisive Battles*, Eyre & Spottiswoode, 1957, II.
13 Montcalm had 16,000 men and 106 guns to defend the Citadel, against Wolfe's 8,500.

the grenadiers totally defeated the General's scheme. Without orders they rushed up the hill, defended on the top with eight, or ten thousand men. Into this snare, did our soldiers, not knowing the General's intention, nor waiting his command, heedlessly throw themselves, all of them, rushing forward to support their comrades. Whilst they were labouring up the hill, descended such a shower of musquetry as is not to be described, when, providentially, one of the most heavy showers that I ever experienced fell unexpectedly, and put a stop to the firing. . . . Death is incapable of putting Britons to confusion: they made a noble retreat; our loss amounted to 400 killed and wounded.

18

TIT FOR TAT: ENGLISH PRISONERS FOR INDIAN SAVAGES, FRENCH LADIES FOR ENGLISH TARS

The same volunteer writes home.

The ravages of war are truly terrible, but may be rendered still more so, if cruelty grows wanton. Happily this is not the temper of Britons, whose natural humanity forbids their sporting with real distress. Some severity became necessary to curb the pride of an insulting enemy, and to convince them we were actually in earnest.

Those devastations drew from the Governor of Quebec a remonstrance to our commanding officer: 'that if the English did not desist from burning and destroying the country, he would give up all English prisoners to the mercy of the Indian savages'. To this threat, our spirited commander sent a reply: 'that having in his possession a considerable number of fair hostages, to the prisoners he might do as he pleased; but, the very instant he attempted to carry this threat into execution, all the French Ladies, without distinction, should be given up to the delicate embraces of the English tars.

N.B. We have at least three, if not four transports, full freighted with French females; some of them women of the first rank in this country.

Finally, Wolfe discovered an unguarded cliff, which was to pass into legend, and climbed up in pitch darkness through the overhanging woods with five thousand soldiers, while the sailors dragged up the guns and Saunders diverted attention by a feint attack on Beauport. In the desperate struggle on the ramparts of the Heights of Abraham, the French, attacking in column, were decimated by the assailants' volleys from close range and both Wolfe and Montcalm were mortally wounded; Quebec was conquered by this scientifically planned and perfectly timed combined operation.

19

BRITISH 'HONOUR AND JUSTICE'
VERSUS FRENCH 'INSOLENCE AND AMBITION'

The same volunteer writes home.

Quebec, Sep. 20

This will finish my long narrative. Be the next day recorded for ever! – A day not less fatal to the flag of insolence and ambition, than glorious to the brave men who fought in the cause of honour, justice, and Britain. In the evening of the 12th or rather a little before midnight, the shipping made a feint upon the turn of the tide as if they intended to get higher up the river; but the boats being loaded with troops, taking the advantage of the wind, stole down. The Marquis of Montcalm, who in the dark could hardly discern the motion of our larger vessels, was deceived, and discovered his mistake, being too late to redress it.

Before three o'clock in the morning, Gen. Wolfe landed at the fascine battery, erected to gall our shipping above the town, in so silent a manner, that the very sentinels were surprised upon their posts. The next difficulty he had to surmount was, to gain the ascent of a prodigous high hill, in which he succeeded, and by break of the morning dawn, the army was regularly drawn up in order of battle, within two musket shots of the town, and almost under the walls of the citadel. . . .

The centre, commanded by Gen. W. in person, the Highlanders discharging their pieces, fell in sword in hand, *indeed very unpolitely*, and made a havoc not to be described. A total rout ensued, part of the enemy fled into the woods, part into the town, and the rest fell in the field: – but alas! our brave general: He likewise fell: – crowned with conquest, he smiled in death: – His principal care was, that he should not be seen to fall: – Support me, said he, to such as were near him, let not my brave soldiers see me drop: – the day is ours: – Oh! keep it – and he died. . . .

20

WOLFE DIED SMILING

Ensign James Henderson, 28th Foot, gives his uncle an account of how Wolfe expired in his arms.

October 7th

I now have the Pleasure of writing to you from Quebeck Which Place is in His Britannick Majesteis Posesion. . . . On that Ever Memorable Day, 13th of September, the Generl Did me the Honour to Detach me with a few Graniders to take Possion of that Ground [a rise] And Maintain it to the Last Extremety which I Did. Till Both Armys Was Engaged And then the Genl Came to me and Took his Post By me. But Oh, How can I tell you My Dr Sir, Tears flow from Eyes Whill I write. That Great, that Ever Memorable Man Whos Loss Can never be Enough Regreted Was Scarce a

Moment With me till he Receved his Fatal Wound. I my Self Receved At the same time two Wounds for I Was Close to him, one in the Right Shoulder & one in the thigh. But my Cosern for him Was so Great that I Did not At that Time think of me. When the Genl Receved the Shot I Cant Hold him and Carried him of the Feild, he Walked About one Hundred yards And then Beged I Would Let [him] Sit Down, which I Did. Then I Opened his Breast, And found his Shirt full of Blood At which he smiled and when he seen the Distress I Was In, My Dear, said he, Dont Grive for me, I shall Be Happy In a Few Minutes take Care of yourSelf As I see your Wounded. But Tell me O Tell me How Goes the Battle their, Just then Came some Officers Who told him that the Freinch had civen Ground & Our trooups Was pursuing Them to the Walls of the town, he was then Lying in my Arms Just Expirin That Great Man Whos Sole Ambition Was his Country Glory Raised him[self] up on this News and Smiled in my Face. Now, said he, I die contented, from that Instant the Smile never Left his Face till he Deided. . . .

Amherst never got to the St Lawrence and, to escape the ice of the approaching winter, the fleet sailed home. General Murray stayed behind at Quebec with 7,000 men, soon reduced to 3,000 through famine and scurvy during the winter. The new French commander at Montreal, De Lévis, besieged Quebec with 9,000 men but Murray held out, losing another 1,000 men in desperate counter-attacks. Both generals were waiting for vital reinforcements from Europe: on 16 May 1760, the British Navy appeared first, and the last French Governor of Canada retreated to Montreal where he finally surrendered to the combined forces of Amherst and Murray on 8 September.

21

THE CAPITULATION OF CANADA

General (later Baron and Field Marshal) Jeffrey Amherst (1717–97) writes to his friend, Major-General Yorke.

Montreal, September 8th, 1760
I have as much pleasure in telling you Canada belongs to the King as I had in receiving the capitulation of it this day, from the satisfaction I know it will give you. The French troops all lay down their arms, and are not to serve during the war; their behaviour is carrying on a cruel and barbarous war in this country, I thought deserved this disgrace. I entered the inhabited country with all the savages and I have not hurt the head of a peasant, his wife or his child, not a house burnt, or a disorder committed; the country people amazed; won't believe what they see; the notions they had of our cruelties from the exercise of their own savages, drove them into the woods; I have fetched them out and put them quiet in their habitations, and they are vastly happy. . . .[14]

---

14 The apprehensions of the Indians were not wholly unfounded: at the time of Pontiac's Indian rebellion in aid of France, Amherst, who loathed them, had advised dissemination of smallpox among them, in retaliation for the torture of English officers.

Quiberon Bay

Come chear up, my lads, 'tis to glory we steer,
To add something more to this wonderful year:
To honour we call you, not press you like slaves,
For who are so free as the sons of the waves?
DAVID GARRICK (1759)

In the second half of 1759, the main French fleet at Brest was kept bottled up by Hawke, while other squadrons of the Navy blockaded Le Havre, the Flemish ports, and Cádiz, to prevent the French from collecting together a combined Armada to carry out their invasion projects; the Toulon fleet was destroyed by Boscawen on 19 August at Lagos Bay. The French warships were larger and more stoutly built, and this advantage had to be compensated on the British side by better seamanship and greater daring. The French always had a deep-rooted tendency to concentrate on careful, elaborate and perfectionist preparations, waiting for the ideal moment which would match their theory, and which never came – owing to the unreflective bulldog quality of the British who were always ready to charge, regardless of their chances.

The trouble with the Navy was the eternal muddle and ineptitude over providing proper victuals: while watching the French fleet in all weathers for six months – an innovation in naval strategy, made bearable for the men by sending a few ships in turn to Portsmouth for a short refreshing – Hawke had to battle with the Admiralty over food and drink, sending back bread 'full of weevils and maggots' and pouring rotten beer overboard. An officer of the *Bellerophon* wrote to the *London Evening Post*:

We have a fine Fleet, all in high Spirits, and well. I am a little surprised that you lazy, idle Fellows don't make a Motion for supplying the Fleet with fresh Beef, from Ireland, which would keep all Englishmen in good Health; they send us Beer and Water enough, but no fresh provision nor Greens for our People. If they don't chuse to come out, we shall have a four-month Cruize, and consequently, Scurvy will prevail amongst the Seamen, whom I look upon as the strength of the Nation. I wonder how a Parcel of Land-Drones can see poor Jacks suffer so.[15]

When, after long delays, ample supplies arrived, Lieutenant E. Thompson of the *Dorsetshire* wrote home:

15   Marcus, op. cit., pp. 63, 68, 171 f.

Tho' you truly think upon this fleet our lives and fortunes depend, yet to support the people in it, you have at last considered fresh provisions are necessary: – it is a pity this charitable thought did not occur sooner, – for alas! we are very sickly; besides, there is such an abuse in the provisions sent out, – that immediately on their arrival, a third part have been condemned not fit to eat.[15]

It must have been a miracle of endurance which kept starving and sick sailors in their watchdog station, tossed about as they were by the autumn gales blowing from the Bay of Biscay; in November the winds became so severe that Hawke had to seek shelter at Torbay with his weather-battered fleet. Admiral Conflans at last ventured out to the Morbihan to pick up the invasion army ready at Vannes, but Captain Duff's squadron, which Hawke had left behind to watch, alerted him. He hastily returned with twenty-one sail of the line right into Quiberon Bay, encircled by storm-foamed reefs and strewed with rock-islets and treacherous shoals, before Conflans could take refuge behind them. In the battle amid howling gales and rushing squalls, four French ships were sunk, including Conflans' flagship *Soleil Royal* which ran ashore and was burnt by the crew, and the *Thésée* which foundered because of opening the lee ports for firing the guns; the *Formidable* was captured and four other ships, although they had thrown guns and stores overboard, were wrecked in the mud of the river Vilaine, and 2,500 French sailors perished. Hawke lost only two ships in the raging sea with 300 to 400 men – it was a triumph of British seamanship. Henceforth, the fleet lay unchallenged at anchor in Quiberon Bay.

22

'I have had a long and tiresome service'

Admiral Sir Edward (later Baron) Hawke sends the news of the battle to his agent's daughter, after thirty-one weeks at sea.

Royal George, Quiberon Bay, 24th November 1759

Dear Sall,

My express being just agoing away for England, I have only time to tell you, that we got up with the French fleet off this place, and have beat them and dispersed their fleet. We have burnt two of their ships, we sunk two, and have taken the *Formidable*, a ship of 84 guns. In the evening near dark, and blowing fresh and bad weather, some of them ran away, clear out. Seven of them with two frigates anchor'd so near the shore that we could not get at them, and the second day they flung everything overboard (for fear the weather should moderate and we should be able to get at them), and got into a little harbour near the place they were lying at. There they must remain this winter at least without any thing in, and can be of no service to the French till we please to permit them. Thank God,

I am very well tho' almost starved with cold; I hope to be allow'd to go home soon, for I have had a long and tiresome service of it.

Believe me that I am truly, dear Sall, your sincere friend,

E. Hawke

In his report to the Admiralty, Hawke stressed the necessity he had been under of 'running all risks to break this strong force of the enemy' and that with 'two hours more daylight, the whole had been totally destroyed or taken'. It was the most important naval victory since 1588 and French naval power never recovered. Joseph Yorke called it 'the most decisive *Coup de Grace* we ever gave the French nation. It is next to a miracle, that upon such a Coast, with such a wind, many more of our ships did not go ahore.'[15] But the ruin of the French fleet led to their sailors turning into privateers who, from their pirate haunts at Dunkirk and St Malo, harried British merchant ships, 10 per cent of which they captured.

After years of anxiety about invasion, jubilation erupted at home and inspired a boy of five to wish to enlist at once in the Navy. This proved to be a premature resolution, however, for unlike his brother Robert who became a naval hero, Charles never went to sea. He in fact became the convivial fourth Duke of Rutland who started the day with half a dozen turkeys' eggs and died at the age of thirty-three.

23

'Take me with you'

Charles Manners (1754–87), son of Lord Granby, Commander-in-Chief in Germany, writes to Admiral Hawke after the battle.

I hear you have beat the French fleet when they were coming to kill us, and that one of your captains twisted a French ship round till it sunk. I wish you was come home, for I intend to go to sea if you will take me with you.

However discontented the sailors had been before the battle, (135,000 were lost in the war by disease or desertion, as against 1,500 killed in action[16]), their spirit revived, as usual, as soon as they were facing the enemy. Their expectation of gratitude for faithful service was bitterly disappointed: victuals became again as scarce as ever, pay was in arrear, and if Garrick's 'free sons of the waves' (who had indeed been 'pressed like slaves'!) stood up for themselves, they were mercilessly flogged (up to five hundred lashes with the cat-o'-nine-tails or even hanged. The poet's patriotic elation to feed an

---

16   C. Lloyd, *British Seaman*, 1968, p. 231.

eager public's emotions was far removed from sordid reality, but the men, though always grumbling, remained patient, long-suffering, and loyal, as their good-humoured doggerels show:

> They kept the foe from landing here,
> Which would have cost the Court full dear,
> And when they for their pay did hope,
> They were rewarded with the rope.

> Ere Hawke did bang
> Mounseer Conflang
> You sent us beef and beer;
> Now Mounseer is beat,
> We've nought to eat,
> Since you have nought to fear.[17]

Britain had now eclipsed the other four colonial powers in a 300-year struggle and her eight thousand ships dominated the oceans. Pitt wanted to make, once and for all, a clean sweep of the French and Spanish colonies, but the fear that such excess would cause worldwide envy and lead to a powerful coalition against Britain prevailed as a restraint. Both results followed all the same.

The atmosphere of euphoria at the end of the *annus mirabilis* is caught in the concluding letter.

24

GLORIOUS VICTORIES AND SUNSHINE

Horace Walpole, writing to George Montagu, reflects on the prevailing exultation.

October 21

. . . Can we easily leave the remains of such a year as this? It is still all gold. I have not dined or gone to bed by a fire till the day before yesterday. Instead of the glorious and ever-memorable year 1759, as the newspapers call it, I call it this ever-warm and victorious year. We have not had more conquest than fine weather: one would think we had plundered East and West Indies of sunshine. Our bells are worn threadbare with ringing for victories. . . . One thing is very fatiguing – all the world is made knights or generals. Adieu! I don't know a word of news less than the conquest of America. . . .

P.S. You shall hear from me again if we take Mexico or China before Christmas.

17   P. Kemp, *British Sailor*, 1970, p. 127.

In the punitive colonial expeditions, tiny disciplined forces kept large native mobs at bay, while at home the militia had to cope with recurring invasion alarms, some of them more serious than ever. On the continent, the bulldog spirit of the infantry, with their preference for the bayonet charge and sustained by the NCOs, often upset enemy tactics. Their belief in king, country and cause was absolute.

The appalling conditions and harsh treatment the sailors continued to suffer made them grumble, but they remained loyal and in good humour; they gloried in sea battles however terrifying they were and preferred them to the monotony of long eventless months at sea to keep invasion watch. Later, serious mutinies were to occur but the Jacobin agitators did not prevail for long. The touching letters sent home by very young boys who had enlisted were a new feature of the period.

The fratricidal American War was initiated and lost by the incompetence of politicians, generals and admirals; bitterly fought though widely disapproved, it evokes some aspects of the Civil War.

N I N E

The American War of Independence (1775–83)

Great empire and little minds go ill together
EDMUND BURKE (1729–97)

Prelude: Vision of the United States

We should not have run wild after a phantom of absolute power over a country whose liberty was the source of our greatness
HORACE WALPOLE

A year before his conquest of Canada, Wolfe predicted the future destiny of North America.

1

A GREAT PEOPLE WILL FILL THIS VAST SPACE

Brigadier-General Wolfe predicts to his mother the future destiny of North America.

Louisbourg, August 11th, 1758
. . . These colonies are deeply tinged with the vices and bad qualities of the mother-country; and, indeed, many parts of it are peopled with those that the law or necessity has forced upon it. Notwithstanding these disadvantages, the treachery of their neighbours the French, and the cruelty of their neighbours the Indians, worked up to the highest pitch by the former, this will some time hence, be a vast empire, the seat of power and learning.

Nature has refused them nothing, and there will grow a people out of our little spot, England, that will fill this vast space, and divide this great portion of the globe with the Spaniards, who are possessed of the other half. . . .

Five years before the outbreak of the war, Walpole wrote in a similar vein:

The tocsin seems to be sounded to America. I have many visions about that country, and fancy I see twenty empires and republics forming upon vast scales over all that continent, which is growing too mighty to be kept in subjection to half a dozen exhausted nations in Europe.[1]

Twenty years after the triumph of the *annus mirabilis*, British fortunes were again at a low ebb. Ironically, the very conquest of Canada and French America partially caused the loss of the thirteen American states: the elimination of any threat from the French to the colonists made British protection no longer necessary to them, and, on the ground that they were not represented in Parliament, they reacted violently against the imposition of taxes to subsidize imperial trade and defence ('No taxation without representation'). They had already increasingly resented discrimination against their exports and shipping in the interests of the rapidly expanding English home industries, and the function allotted to them of providing an overseas market without becoming a trade rival.

The lack of understanding in the aristocratic monarchy of old England for the feelings and aspirations of the rough Puritan democracy in the New World prevented any sensible settlement: the colonists were to be kept in subjection to Crown and Parliament by military coercion. In this civil war, both sides were divided, and opposition to the fratricidal conflict was strong; not only the Loyalists but even the Radicals wanted to stay under the Crown up to 1778, when the French seized the opportunity of taking their revenge for the loss of Canada. The war was initially supported by a large majority in Parliament and country, and George III remained adamant in his defence of the old colonies, but many prominent warning voices were raised.

Opinions on the War

The War was conceived in injustice and brought forth folly
WILLIAM PITT

The great preacher, whose Methodism was spreading among the colonists, solemnly invoked the fate of King Solomon's son Rehoboam who, by his refusal to reduce taxes, caused the secession of ten tribes into a rival kingdom.

1   H. Walpole, *Selected Letters*, Dent, 1926, p. 374 f.

2

'Remember Rehoboam! Remember Philip II! Remember Charles I!'

John Wesley (1703–91) appeals to the Earl of Dartmouth, Secretary of the American colonies who dreaded the conflict and sought an understanding but did not have 'strength equal to his wishes' (B. Franklin). Dartmouth was soon to be replaced by Lord George Germain (Sackville of Minden notoriety).

June 14, 1775

. . . All my prejudices are against the Americans, for I am an High Churchman, the son of an High Churchman, bred up from my childhood in the highest notions of passive obedience and non-resistance; and yet in spite of all my rooted prejudice, I cannot avoid thinking that an oppressed people asked for nothing more than their legal rights and that in the most modest and inoffensive manner. . . .

But waiving all considerations of right and wrong, I ask, is it common sense to use force toward the Americans? . . . They are divided among themselves? So I doubt not was poor Rehoboam informed concerning the ten tribes! So was Philip informed concerning the people of the Netherlands! No, my Lord, they are terribly united: not in the Province of New England only, but down as low as the Jerseys and Pennsylvania the bulk of the people are so united that to speak a word in favour of the present English measures would almost endanger a man's life. . . .

O my Lord, if your Lordship can do anything, let it not be wanting! For God's sake, for the sake of the King, of the nation, of your lovely family, remember Rehoboam! Remember Philip II! Remember King Charles I!

Charlestown Camp outside Boston was bleak and chilly at the beginning of the war, but Burgoyne, a vain, ambitious intriguer and perhaps a better playwright than general, provided entertainment with amateur theatricals.

3

'General Burgoyne is our Garrick'

Adjutant-General (later Marquis of Hastings and Governor of Bengal), Francis Lord Rawdon (1754–1826) pictures the austere atmosphere of camp life to his uncle, the Earl of Huntingdon.

October 5th, 1775

. . . We are beginning to build block-houses in order to maintain this post in the winter. 600 men will be the garrison here, to be relieved weekly from Boston. It is very bleak at present upon these heights, and the duty of the officers is severe. At our lines neither officer or man have the smallest shelter against the inclemency of the weather, but stand to the works all night. Indeed in point of alertness and regularity our officers have great merit. I have not seen either drinking or gaming in this camp. If anything, there is too little society among us. In general every man goes to his own tent very soon after sunset, where those who can amuse themselves in that manner, read; and the others probably sleep. I usually have a red herring, some onions, and some porter about 8 o'clock, of which three of four grave sedate people partake; we chat about different topics, and retire to our bed about 9. There is not so much entertainment in this way of life as in what you lead in London, or even what the troops in Boston enjoy, yet whilst the weather continued good we were content. For some days past it has not ceased raining; every tent is thoroughly wet, and every countenance thoroughly dull. A keen wind which has accompanied this rain makes people talk upon the parade of the comforts of a chimney corner; and we hear with some envy of several little balls and concerts which our brethren have had in Boston. . . .

We are to have plays this winter in Faneuil Hall. I am enrolled as an actor; not that I love sporting in public, but I did not think it right to refuse on this occasion. General Burgoyne is our Garrick: our ladies are but few in number, but I dare say we shall produce some good actresses. A meeting-house was proposed as the theatre, but we feared your censure at home, and were afraid it might have furnished Lord Chatham the old joke of turning the Lord's house into a den of thieves. The money collected by these performances is to be a fund for the benefit of the wives and children of such soldiers as fall in action. – Adieu, my dear Lord: I wish I was sitting with you over a bottle of claret and a good fire. . . .

There was no eagerness to volunteer for the army to fight colonist kinsmen; to fill the gap, many thousands of auxiliaries (more professional but slower) had to be leased from the petty German princes.

4

'Englishmen be the Divel for going on, but Hesse men be soldier'

Lieutenant W. Hale compares the ability of British and German troops in dealing with an agile enemy.

Philadelphia, 23rd March, 1778

. . . By the papers I find more Germans are to be hired, would to God England could raise an equal number of men, the behaviour of the Brunswickers is too recent to be forgotten; and the Hessians, who are allowed to be the best of the German troops, are by no means equal to the British in any respect. I believe them steady, but their slowness is of the greatest disadvantage in a country almost covered with woods, and against an Enemy whose chief qualification is agility in running from fence to fence and thence keeping up an irregular, but galling fire on troops who advance with the same pace as at their exercise. Light infantry accustomed to fight from tree to tree, or charge even in woods; and Grenadiers who after the first fire lose no time in loading again, but rush on, trusting entirely to that most decisive of weapons the bayonet, will ever be superior to any troops the Rebels can bring against them. Such are the British, and such the method of fighting which has been attended with constant success. . . . Hessians themselves make no scruple of owning our superiority over them, but palliate so mortifying a confession by saying 'Englishmen be the Divel for going on, but Hesse men be soldier.' They will not readily fight without being supported by their cannon which we think a useless encumbrance.

The life-long boon companion of Charles James Fox and his future Secretary for War, opposed the war as an MP yet joined the Guards to fight in it against his conviction. In deep despair over the hopeless outlook in view of the imminent American alliance with France, the fashionable socialite is abandoned by his renowned wit.

5

'Disgusted in the folly of the Cause'

Captain (later General) Richard Fitzpatrick predicts to his brother, Lord Ossory, that the Americans 'will be the first and greatest people in the History of Mankind'.

Philadelphia, January 1778

. . . I grow more and more disgusted in the folly and iniquity of the Cause in which I am condemned to serve and, if the disgrace and disappointments of this year do not somehow or other put an end to the war, I really think I cannot bear to sacrifice every feeling and principle I have to it any longer. . . .

Having been a witness to the horrors of this War has made me ten times more violent than ever against it, and I hate the Ministry more cordially than ever for having obliged me to become a sort of instrument (though a feeble one indeed) of injustice, barbarity and oppression.

My present system of politics would be to cry *peccavi* and, if possible at any rate, procure the alliance of America, after cutting off the heads of those who have been the means of losing it, but I am afraid the people of England have not sense enough to adopt so wise a measure, and if once America is an ally of France I cannot conceive of any salvation for us whatever.

There is a greatness and dignity in all the proceedings of this people that makes us contemptible indeed. I am well convinced that they will be the first and greatest people that there was an example of in the History of Mankind; our only consolation as Patriots must be that they are of English origin.

You see I am a complete enthusiast, notwithstanding which I am not a little impatient to see you again in your old *corrupted world* where I have lived so long that I have not virtue enough left to deserve to live in the New One.

All the prestige gained in 1759, about which Walpole had been so exuberant, has been gambled away by misguided incompetence. Britain faces a growing number of enemies without any friends or allies. Walpole is highly critical of the way the war is being conducted and, in a black mood, doubts he will live to see peace again.

6

'The Englishman in me feels again'
FRANCE DECLARES WAR

Horace Walpole, writing to the Revd William Mason, bemoans the vanished glories of the empire and the follies that hurry it to its dissolution.

July 18, 1778

As I was going out this evening, I was stopped in Twickenham, and told that France has declared war. What can be expected from two wars when one has been so ignominious? – With an army of 50,000 men against a rabble, and without being beaten, they have lost a whole continent, and near half that army, and retreated from place to place! Not one General has gained any reputation. Thus we have, the people, been gamed for; and some few of us against our wills.

Well; War proclaimed! And I am near 61. Shall I live to see peace again? . . . I condemn my countrymen, but cannot, would not divest myself of my love to my country. I cannot blame the French whom we have tempted to ruin us; yet, to be ruined by France! – There the Englishman in me feels again. It is difficult to be very tranquil when the navy of England is at stake. That thought annihilates resentment. I wish for nothing but victory, and then peace, yet what lives must victory cost! Nor will one victory purchase it. The nation is so frantic that success would intoxicate us more; yet calamity, that alone could sober us, is too near our doors.

My time of life, that ought to give me philosophy, dispirits me. I cannot expect to live to see England revive. I shall leave it at best an insignificant island. Its genius is vanished like its glories, one sees no hero or statesman arise to flatter hope: what is the history of a fallen empire? a transient satire on the vices and follies that hurried it to its dissolution. The protest of a few that foretold it, is not registered. . . . I will go to bed and sleep, if I can. Two years ago I meditated leaving England if it was enslaved. I have no such thought now. I will steal into its bosom when my hour comes, and love it to the last.

When the militia was called out on a French invasion alarm, Dr Johnson's pretty fourteen-year-old friend whom he called his Queen Esther ('Queeney'), sent him her comments on the discomforts she noticed on a visit to a camp. The great doctor, who had played horses with her, written rhymes for her, and was directing her studies of Hebrew and Mathematics, pontificates on the 'heroic life' there.

7

'The most important scene of human existence'
A MILITIA CAMP

Dr Samuel Johnson (1709–84) instructs 'Queeney' Thrale not to disdain military service; she later became the socialite Viscountess Keith.

London, 24 Oct. 1778

My dearest Love,

I was in hopes that your letter about the camp would have been longer, and that you would have considered yourself as surveying in a camp perhaps the most important scene of human existence, the real scene of heroic life. If you are struck with the inconvenience of the military in a camp where there is no danger, where all the materials of pleasure are supplied, and where there is little but jollity and festivity, reflect what a camp must be surrounded by enemies in a wasted or a hostile country, where provisions can scarcely be had, and what can be had must be snatched in haste by men who when they put the bread into their mouths, are uncertain whether they shall swallow it. . . .

In a camp you [see] what is the lowest and most portable accommodation with which life can be contented; what shelter it is that can be most expeditiously erected and removed. There is in a camp what human wit sharpened by the greatest [exigencies] has been able to contrive, and it gives ladies the particular pleasure of seeing evils which they are not to share.

I am, Sweeting, Your most humble servant
Sam: Johnson

Visiting militia camps became the rage among the ladies, and Georgiana, the glamorous Duchess of Devonshire, camping at Coxheath with her husband's Derbyshire Militia, set the fashion by donning her own version of military attire which reflected the atmosphere which prevailed also in speech and bearing. She presided over the ladies' mess to which only officers who had distinguished themselves in war were admitted.

8

GIRLS IN THE LIGHT HORSE AND MATRONS IN THE DRAGOONS?

Mrs Montagu writing to the Duchess of Portland, satirizes such unfeminine postures.

[1779]

As many of our modern dames want the modesty of women, I hope they will have the courage of men, and if they are as void of fear as of shame, they will easily drive the French back again if they invade us. I must own that last summer, not foreseeing the probability of an invasion, and the necessity of the young girls serving in the Light Horse, and the matrons being formed into regiments of dragoons, I was sorry to see them striding about the walks at Tunbridge with their arms akimbo, dressed in martial uniform. I was assured some of them would swear like troopers, so no doubt they will fight like men.

George III, who imposed his will on a cabinet of place-men and a bribed parliament, and regarded opposition as sedition, combined a patriotic sense of royal duty with an insular lack of imagination and a stubborn tenacity. In the next letter he thinks he must stem the tide threatening the empire whatever the risks, as caution would spell certain ruin: 'I own I wish either to get through it with spirit, or with a crash be ruined', he wrote elsewhere.

9

GEORGE III FORESEES THE LOSS OF THE EMPIRE AND BRITAIN BECOMING A POOR ISLAND

King George III (1738–1820) tells Lord North, his compliant First Lord of the Treasury (who did not call himself Prime Minister because the King completely directed policy), that independence must never be granted to America.

[11 June 1779]

... No inclination to get out of the present difficulties, which certainly keep my mind very far from a state of ease, can incline me to enter into what I look upon as the destruction of the empire. I have heard Lord North frequently drop that the advantages to be gained by this contest could never repay the expense; I own that, let any war be ever so successful, if persons will sit down and weigh the expenses, they will find, as in the last, that it has impoverished the state, enriched individuals, and perhaps raised the name only of the conquerors. But this is only weighing such events in the scale of a tradesman behind the counter: it is necessary for those in the station it has pleased Divine Providence to place me to weigh whether expenses, though very great, are not sometimes necessary to prevent what might be more ruinous to a country than the loss of money.

The present contest with America I cannot help seeing as the most serious in which any country was ever engaged. Whether the laying of tax was deserving all the evils that have arisen from it, I should suppose no man could allege; but step by step the demands of America have risen. Independence is their object; that certainly is one which every man, not willing to sacrifice every object to a momentary and inglorious peace, must concur with me in thinking that this country can never submit to.

Should America succeed in that, the West Indies must follow them, not independence, but must for its own interest be dependent upon North America. Ireland would soon follow the same plan and be a separate state; then this island would be reduced to itself, and soon would be a poor island indeed, for, reduced in her trade, merchants would retire with their wealth to climates more to their advantage, and shoals of manufacturers would leave this country for the new empire. . . .

The Path to Disaster

Everything has miscarried that has been undertaken, and the worse we succeed, the more is risked; and yet the nation is not angry!
HORACE WALPOLE (1779)

Although the colonists had originally no army or navy, the forces sent over to America proved increasingly inadequate for a long war over a vast territory, once the initial advantage had been lost through indecision and blundering. Instead of imposing a naval blockade, the fleet was only used in support of military operations which underestimated the determination and resilience of the colonists whose spirit was never curbed by the defeats they suffered.

Lord Germain, who masterminded the campaign from London, had no clear strategic concept and the forces were frittered away in dispersed actions over a huge, geographically diverse country which was difficult to control for an army, however superior, whose supply lines extended over 3,000 miles of the Atlantic, across which the rebels received mounting quantities of war materials from France, Spain and the Netherlands. An overstretched navy, whose budget had been severely cut, while the French, for the first time – owing to the absence of a continental war – were able to spend more on their navy than their army, was unable to intercept these vital shipments. Washington's Fabian tactics protracted the war until, by their own strategic mistakes, and the intervention of the French navy, the British generals were drawn into a hopeless position.

The first important battle occurred when Sir William Howe set out from Boston to storm the steep, 110 ft high Bunker Hill, defended by 1,500 inexperienced levies against 2000–3000 regulars, supported by naval guns, who, admittedly, were none too keen: 'We cannot forget that when we strike we wound a brother'.[2] The hill was carried only on the third assault against stubborn resistance by disciplined fire from strong redoubts, at a loss of one third of the attackers; at one time, Howe found himself standing up alone, with all around him killed. The volunteers, though beaten, had gained the confidence they needed to face the professionals.

A junior officer pictures the slaughter but for the general it was a fine pleasing spectacle. Both vastly exaggerate the enemy's strength.

---

2   P. Mackesy, *War with America*, Longman, 1964; also for other details.

10

Bunker Hill: a 'shocking carnage'

Lieutenant J. Waller, Adjutant of the 1st Marine Battalion, describes the desperate attack to his brother.

Charleston Heights, 22nd June 1775

Amidst the hurry and confusion of a camp hastily pitched in the field of battle, I am sat down to tell you I have escaped unhurt, where many, very many, have fallen. . . . It was a most desperate and daring attempt, and it was performed with as much gallantry and spirit as was ever shown by any troops in any age.

Two companies of the 1st battalion of Marines, and part of the 47th Regiment, were the first that mounted the breastwork: and you will not be displeased when I tell you that I was with those two companies, who drove their bayonets into all that opposed them. Nothing could be more shocking than the carnage that followed the storming this work. We tumbled over the dead to get at the living, who were crowding out of the gorge of the redoubt, in order to form under the defences which they had prepared to cover their retreat. In this breastworks they had artillery, which did so much mischief; but there they were obliged to abandon, being followed closely by the Light Infantry, who suffered exceedingly in the pursuit. The rebels had 5000 to 7000 men, covered by a redoubt, breastworks, walls, hedges, trees, and the like; and the number of the corps under General Howe did not amount to 1500. We gained a complete victory. . . .

God bless you! I did not think, at one time, that I should ever have been able to write this, though in the heat of the action I thought nothing of the matter.

11

'It was great, it was high spirited'

Major-General Sir John Burgoyne (1739–85) paints for Lord Stanley an 'animated impression' of the theatrical scene of battle.

[June 1775]

. . . The action of the 17th establishes the ascendancy of the King's troops though opposed by more than treble numbers. It comprised, though in a small compass, almost every branch of military duty and curiosity. Troops landed in the face of the enemy; a fine disposition; a march sustained by a powerful cannonade from moving field artillery, fixed batteries, floating batteries, and broadsides of ships at anchor, all operating separately and well disposed; a deployment from the march to form for the attack of the entrenchments and redoubt; a vigorous defence; a storm with bayonets; a large and fine town set on fire by shells. Whole streets of houses, ships upon the stocks, a number of churches, all sending up volumes of smoke and flame, or falling together in ruin, were capital objects. A prospect of the neighbouring hills, the steeples of Boston, and the masts of such ships as were unemployed in the harbour, all crowded with spectators, friends, and foes, alike in anxious suspense, made a background to the piece. It was great, it was high spirited, and while the animated impression remains, let us quit it. . . .

Over two years later, 'Gentleman Johnny''s attitude has changed from enjoyment of war to despondency. With reckless, futile courage in face of an enemy he held in contempt, he had attacked an American army of double his strength and suffered heavy casualties. At Saratoga he was then surrounded by 20,000 and forced to surrender with his 8,000 men. This was the turning point of the war, as it spurred France and Spain to join the fray, and the opportunity of winning it had now gone. Burgoyne felt he had been let down by Howe and made a scapegoat for Germain's mismanagement.

12

EXHAUSTION AND DISILLUSION

Burgoyne writes to his nieces after Saratoga, dejected over dissensions and tired out by hardship.

Albany, Oct. 20, 1777

My dearest Nieces,

There are few situations in a military life exposed to more personal hazard than I have lately undergone. I have been surrounded with enemies, ill-treated by pretended friends, abandoned by a considerable part of my own army, totally unassisted by Sir William Howe. . . . Under perpetual fire, and exhausted with laborious days, and 16 almost sleepless nights, without change of clothes, or other covering than the sky. I have been with my army within the jaws of famine; shot through my hat and waistcoat, my nearest friends killed round me; and from these combined misfortunes and escapes, I imagine I am reserved to stand a war with ministers who will always lay the blame upon the employed who miscarries.

In all these complicated anxieties, believe me, my dear girls, my heart has a large space filled with you; and I will bring it home, when God shall permit, as replete with affection as when I left you. . . .

While the campaign in the North ended in disaster, Howe, who had taken New York in 1776, forced Washington in the Battle on the Brandywine to retreat across the Delaware to Philadelphia which he took soon after. Washington later confessed he thought 'the game was pretty well played out', but, fatally, Howe allowed him to recover. Admittedly, he was rather short of troops to force a decision: when he had asked for 20,000, he got 2,500, as the Hessians were too dear and many of them deserted. It is interesting to speculate what would have happened had Washington been shot.

13

NOT SORRY HE DID NOT SHOOT WASHINGTON

Captain Ferguson, 70th Foot, describes how the rebel general had been at his mercy during the Battle on the Brandywine.

[September 1777]

We had not lain long when a rebel officer, remarkable by a Hussar dress, passed towards our army, within 100 yards of my right flank, not perceiving us. He was followed by another, dressed in dark green or blue, mounted on a bay horse, with a remarkable large cocked hat. I ordered three good shots to steal near to them and fire at them; but the idea disgusted me. I recalled the order. The Hussar, in returning, made a circuit, but the other passed again within 100 yards of us, upon which I advanced from the wood towards him. On my calling, he stopped; but, after looking at me, proceeded. I again drew his attention, and made signs to him to stop, but he slowly continued his way. As I was within that distance at which, in the quickest firing, I could have lodged half-a-dozen of balls in or about him before he was out of my reach – I had only to determine; but it was not pleasant to fire at the back of an unoffending individual, who was acquitting himself very coolly of his duty; so I let him alone.

The day after I had been telling this story to some wounded officers who lay in the same room with me, when one of our surgeons, who had been dressing the wounded rebel officers, came in and told us they had been informing him that General Washington was all the morning with the light troops, and only attended by a French officer in a Hussar dress, he himself dressed and mounted in every point as above described. I am not sorry that I did not know at the time who it was. . . .

Howe's successor as Commander-in-Chief, Clinton, could also only conceive of raids rather than a large-scale campaign, and, being uncertain and vain, alternated between inaction and rashness, regardless of the troops' sufferings. He defeated Washington at Monmouth Court House with 8,000 against 14,000 troops, but one hundred of his men died of heatstroke.

14

DYING OF THIRST IN SCORCHING HEAT

Lieutenant Hale describes the battle to his parents.

Neversunk, 4th July 1778

General Clinton's dispatches will acquaint you of an action on the 28th June, of which our Battalion bore the principal part. Lee, acquainted with the temper of our present Commander, laid a snare which perfectly succeeded. The hook was undisguised with a bait, but the impetuosity of Clinton swallowed it. . . . The Grenadiers were ordered to march to the heights of which the Rebels were already possessed; such a march I may never again experience. We proceeded five miles in a road composed of nothing but sand which scorched through our shoes with intolerable heat; the sun beating on our heads with a force scarcely to be conceived in Europe, and not a drop of water to assuage our parching thirst; a number of soldiers were unable to support the fatigue, and died on the spot. A Corporal who had by some means procured water, drank to such excess as to burst and expired in the utmost torments. Two became raving mad, and the whole road, strewed with miserable wretches wishing for death, exhibited the most shocking scene I ever saw.

At length we came within reach of the enemy who cannonaded us very briskly, and afterwards marching through a cornfield saw them drawn up behind a morass on a hill with a rail fence in front and a thick wood on their left filled with their light chosen troops. We rose on a small hill commanded by that on which they were posted in excellent order, when judge of my inexpressible surprise, General Clinton himself appeared and crying out 'Charge, Grenadiers, never heed forming'; we rushed on amidst the heaviest fire I have yet felt. It was no longer a contest for bringing up our respective companies in the best order, but all officers as well as soldiers strove who could be foremost, to my shame I speak it. I had the fortune to find myself after crossing the swamp with three officers only, in the midst of a large body of Rebels who had been driven out of the wood by the 1st Battalion of Grenadiers, accompanied by not more than a dozen men who had been able to keep up with us; luckily the Rebels were too intent on their own safety to regard our destruction.

The column which we routed in this disorderly manner consisted of 4000, the force on our side not more than 800. In the mean time the pursuit of this column brought us on their main Army led by Washington, said by deserters to be 16,000. With some difficulty we were brought under the hill we had gained, and the most terrible cannonade ensued and lasted for above two hours, at the distance of 600 yards. The shattered remains of our Battalion being under cover of our hill suffered little, but from thirst and heat of which several died, except some who preferred the shade of some trees in the direct range of shot to the more horrid tortures of thirst. . . .

In 1781 a French army crossed the Atlantic and came to the aid of Washington's forces who were in a state of mutiny, and De Grasse arrived from the West Indies with the French fleet. Admiral Graves with nineteen ships of the line attacked his twenty-four in the Chesapeake; owing to his rigidly formal deployment and some confusion over signals, he came off worse in the engagement and suffered heavy damage. Rather than risk his fleet again, Graves withdrew to New York to refit and left Cornwallis, who was under siege in Yorktown, to his fate. Cornwallis' works were crumbling under the bombardment by naval guns and by a powerful siege train which the 13,000 Americans and 8,000 French had installed for the assault, without any sign of Clinton's promised, but ever postponed, relief force. When half of his 8,000 men were unfit and he had no ammunition left, Cornwallis, after an abortive attempt to escape, marched them off in surrender to the befitting tune of *The World is turned upside down*: the war was virtually over. Five days later, Clinton arrived with 7,000 men.

Inept and corrupt administration of inadequate resources, the failure to coordinate army and navy, and, particularly, the dispersal of ten ships which would have made all the difference, were among the causes of the calamity; but Clinton's slow, half-hearted preparations must also share the blame. Had Cornwallis not been encouraged to expect a relief force, he might have succeeded in breaking out. In England, despair was acute; North exclaimed: 'Oh God! It is all over' and the country feared that all colonies might be lost, although there were still 30,000 men in America, and New York and Charleston were in British hands. The following excerpts from the Clinton–Cornwallis correspondence throw some light on the controversy, although the main culprit was Germain with his misconceived schemes.

15

THE SURRENDER AT YORKTOWN

General Sir Henry Clinton (1738–85) to General Cornwallis.

New York, 24 Sep. 1781

. . . Above 5000 men shall be embarked to relieve you and afterwards co-operate with you. The fleet consists of 23 sail of the line. . . .

25 Sep.

The necessary repairs of the fleet will detain us here to the 5th of next month; unforeseen accidents may lengthen it out a day or two longer. . . .

30 Sep.

. . . I have reason to hope, after assurances given me this day by Admiral Graves, that we may pass the bar by the 12th of October, if the winds permit, and no unforeseen accident happens. I shall persist in my idea of a direct move, even to the middle of November. . . .

16

General (later Marquis, Governor-General of India, Vice-Roy of Ireland) Charles Earl Cornwallis, to General Clinton.

Yorktown, 11 Oct. 1781

. . . Nothing but a direct move to York river, which includes a successful naval action, can save me. On the evening of the 9th their batteries opened, and have since continued firing without intermission, with about 40 pieces of cannon, mostly heavy, and 16 mortars. We have lost about 70 men, and many of our works are considered damaged; with such works on disadvantageous ground, against so powerful an attack we cannot hope to make a very long resistance.

15 Oct.

Last evening the enemy carried my two advanced redoubts on the left by storm. My situation now becomes very critical. We dare not show a gun to their old batteries, and I expect that their new ones will open to-morrow morning, so that we shall soon be exposed to an assault in ruined works. . . .

20 Oct.

I have the mortification to inform your Excellency that I have been forced to give up the posts of York and Gloucester, and to surrender the troops under my command, by capitulation, on the 19th, as prisoners of war to the combined forces of America and France. . . .

Our numbers had been diminished by the enemy's fire, but particularly by sickness, and the strength and spirit of those in the works were much exhausted, by the fatigue of constant watching and unremitting duty. Under all these circumstances, I thought it would have been wanton and inhuman to the last degree to sacrifice the lives of this small body of gallant soldiers, who had ever behaved with so much fidelity and courage, by exposing them to an assault which, from the numbers and precautions of the enemy, could not fail to succeed. I therefore proposed to capitulate; and I enclose the terms agreed upon. . . .

Although the event has been so unfortunate, the patience of the soldiers in bearing the greatest fatigues, and their firmness and intrepidity under a persevering fire of shot and shells that, I believe, has not often been exceeded, deserved the highest admiration and praise. . . .

Interlude: A Second Armada in the Channel

Providence has always saved us which
argument is built on this simple hypothesis,
that God made Great Britain, and the Devil
the rest of the world
HORACE WALPOLE

In the summer of 1779, perhaps the most serious invasion threat since 1066 lay over England. While the Navy, deprived of American timber for its replenishment, was dispersed in worldwide commitments, the combined Armada of sixty-six French and Spanish ships of the line set out from Corunna to secure the Channel. Around 31,000 crack troops were waiting at St Malo and Le Havre under the Maréchal de Broglie in five hundred invasion barges, laden with munitions and victuals, to land at Portsmouth and Plymouth after a naval bombardment.

Admiral Sir Charles Hardy, who as Governor of Greenwich Hospital had not been at sea for twenty years since Quiberon Bay, failed to intercept the Armada when he crossed its path in the fog near the Scilly Isles, and hastily returned from his search when he heard it was sailing up the Channel. He could not know that the French fleet had half its crews down with scurvy and was running out of food and water after seven weeks at sea owing to long delays caused by the Spanish fleet's unreadiness and adverse winds.

Taking 1588 as a model, he cautiously withdrew to Spithead with his thirty-eight ships in face of the much larger but slower Armada, but d'Orvilliers and Luis de Cordoba, the septuagenarian admirals, had no more stomach for a bold attack than Hardy at sixty-three.

In England there was justified panic: Portsmouth was guarded by only three militia regiments and some companies of invalids, and Plymouth by a garrison of 4,800 regulars with thirty-six unfit gunners to man two hundred guns. They would hardly have been a match for the picked French infantry, had it descended upon them under the protection of the nineteen French ships lying in the Sound, which, in the prevailing flurry, were rumoured to have reduced the city to ashes. Amherst, the Commander-in-Chief, misled by false intelligence spread by the French, had concentrated his scanty forces on London and the Sussex coast: all he had, apart from 30,000 only partly armed militia, were 17,500 regulars, and 3,000 invalids and Chelsea Hospital pensioners. There was the usual muddle, dissension and improvisation, while ministers retired to their safe country estates and 10,000 naval deserters jammed the Portsmouth road.

In the meantime, Vergennes, Louis XVI's Foreign Minister, who had been grooming himself to become Viceroy of Britain after the removal of the Royal family to Chambord, had altered plans to a less risky landing at Falmouth in undefended Cornwall and a spring offensive against London after consolidation in winter. However, the French fleet was by now just a floating hospital and ships began to drift back home. So, finally, the invasion on which the Spaniards had insisted in face of French doubts, had to be called off, and on 14 September the French fleet returned to Brest with nothing to show but the capture of the *Ardent* and twenty merchant vessels with 1,100 prisoners. In the event, Hardy's prudence, stigmatized as 'shameful and ignominious' in the House, was fully vindicated.[3]

17

'The moment is singularly awful'

Horace Walpole expresses his hope to the Countess of Aylesbury that the Navy may yet stop the imminent invasion and peace may be negotiated.

[late summer 1779]

... I have good reason to believe the Government knows that a great army is ready to embark at St Maloes, but will not stir till after a sea- fight which we do not know but may be engaged at this moment. Our fleet is allowed to be the finest ever set forth by this country; but it is inferior by 17 ships to the united squadrons of the Bourbons.

---

3   A. Temple Patterson, *The Other Armada*, Manchester University Press, 1960, for full details.

France, if successful, means to pour in a vast many thousands on us, and has threatened to burn the capital itself. . . . The moment is singularly awful; yet the vaunts of the enemies are rarely executed successfully and ably. We have trampled America under our feet? . . . I have seen danger still more imminent. They were dispersed. Nothing happens in proportion to what is meditated. I am seriously persuaded, that if the fleets engage, the enemy will not gain advantage without deep-felt loss, enough, probably, to dismay the invasion. Coolness may succeed, and then negotiation. Surely, if we can weather the summer, we shall, obstinate as we are against conviction, be compelled, by the want of money, to relinquish our ridiculous pretensions – for, with an inferior navy at home, can we assert sovereignty over America? . . .

'Brave Rodney for Ever'

> *Drink Rodney's health in bumpers full,*
> *He made De Grasse an April fool,*
> *Success to gallant Rodney*
> ANON.

After Quiberon Bay, the Navy had been allowed to fall into decay, and Sandwich, who tried to refurbish its striking power, became the scapegoat for previous neglect. Wastage among the crews was severe: of the 176,000 sailors recruited during the war, less than 1 per cent were killed, over 10 per cent died of yellow fever, scurvy and typhus, and nearly 25 per cent deserted. It was the only war in which the Navy was inferior to the combined enemy fleet and this created not only a very serious invasion threat but also had a vital bearing on the American War, although the French fleet was concerned above all to protect the immensely lucrative sugar and rum interests in the West Indies.

It was here that Rodney, the most successful admiral of the period, destroyed or captured a total of seventeen ships of the line with four admirals, which made the Allies more ready to conclude peace despite the British defeat in America. The reverse side of Rodney's bold determination was an unscrupulous greed for prize money, as well as boastfulness, womanizing, and, above all, a boundless vanity: the adoring women in his family knew how to flatter him.[4]

Rodney swooped down on the Dutch island of St Eustatius, the main supply depot for America, where he took two hundred contraband ships, many carrying British goods supplied to the enemy in vast quantities. He got so absorbed in appropriating as much as he could of the £4 million of booty that he let a defenceless French convoy escape.[5] In the climate of dismal news from America, London erupted over this easy success.

---

4   Rodney, in turn, carried the portraits of his 'dear girls' with him: 'They are the joy of my life', he wrote home, 'and converse with me daily. They calm my mind and ease the torment of the gout.'

5   On being transported to England, the booty was intercepted by a French squadron and lost again.

18

'Joy to you, Sir George'

Henrietta Lady Rodney (1739–1829) describes to her husband how her house was like a fair with well-wishers.

London, March 17th, 1781

Joy to you, my dear Sir George, equal to what you have given your friends at home, and, I may say, the whole nation, on your glorious successes, which, I believe, were never equalled in the annals of this or any other country!

It is totally impossible to describe my feelings on this occasion. Every countenance is lighted up with joy, every voice rings with your praises – then what must I feel who am so nearly and dearly connected?

Your express arrived on the morning of the 13th. My house has been like a fair from that time till this. Every friend, every acquaintance came, and the attention and notice I received from their Majesties were sufficient to turn my poor brain. . . .

P.S. I suppose John will not share any prize-money, as I find he was on a cruise. Captain Sterling told me that John chased him a whole night on his passage home, taking him for an enemy. I was rejoiced to hear he was so active.[6]

Rodney's crowning victory was the battle of the Saintes, islets between Guadeloupe and Dominica, in which his ships sank one and captured five of the thirty-three enemy ships, with Admiral De Grasse – the only decisive success against the French in this war. Rodney's flagship, the *Formidable*, penetrated the French line, holding its fire until the French fleet could be broken up by close-range broadsides. Rear-Admiral Hood took the pride of the French fleet, the 106-gun *Ville de Paris*, a gift from the city to Louis XV, and the finest ship afloat.

19

THE BATTLE OF THE SAINTES

Admiral Sir George (later Baron) Rodney (1718–92) sends his wife the good news.

At sea, off Guadalaloupe, April 13, 1782

The letters to my dear girls will inform you of my course to endeavour to intercept the French convoy; and though *they* escaped me, I have the pleasure to acquaint you, that they have now paid for all the insults France has offered England. . . .

---

6 Rodney's son, through flagrant favouritism, was made captain at the age of fifteen, although he was obviously not very bright; in a long naval career he was never promoted further.

The battle began at 7 in the morning, and continued till sunset, nearly 11 hours; and by persons appointed to observe, there never was 7 minutes' respite during the engagement, which, I believe, was the severest that ever was fought at sea, and the most glorious for England. We have taken five, and sunk another. Among the prizes the *Ville de Paris*, and the French admiral grace our victory.

Comte de Grasse, who is at this moment sitting in my stern gallery, tells me that he thought his fleet superior to mine, and does so still, though I had two more in number; and I am of his opinion, as his was composed all of large ships, and ten of mine only 64s.

I am of opinion that the French will not face us again this war, for the ships which have escaped are so shattered, and their loss of men so great, that I am sure they will not be able to repair or replace either in the West Indies.

I hope this joyful news will raise the spirits at home, and I do not doubt but you will meet with a gracious reception at St James's: do not forget to go. Adieu. I have had no sleep these four nights, and am at this moment looking out for their shattered fleet though mine has suffered not a little.

It is odd, but within two little years I have taken two Spanish, one French, and one Dutch admiral. Providence does it all, or how should I escape the shot of 33 sail of the line, every one of which, I believe, attacked me? but the *Formidable* proved herself worthy of her name. . . .

Rodney's fifteen-year-old daughter took up her mother's adulation: already two years earlier she had described the celebrations over Rodney's relief of blockaded Gibraltar by blowing up one and capturing six Spanish ships in a dark stormy night off Cape St Vincent:

Every body almost adores you; and every mouth is full of your praise. The Tower and the Park guns were fired last Monday; and that night and the next there were illuminations; you will see in the 'Morning Post', what fine verses they make to your praise. There are a great number of songs going about the streets, the choruses always, 'Brave Rodney for ever'. I congratulate you upon the thanks of both Houses of Parliament. I have loved Lord North ever since he spoke in the House about you. I hear the King is exceedingly pleased with you. He said at the drawing-room, that he knew when Rodney was out, everything would go well. Lord Oxford told it to mamma, at the Duchess of Chandos' last night. I have had a great many people wish me joy at the dancing academy – very pleasant it is.[7]

Now Rodney's family was acclaimed even in public.

7   G.B. Mundy, *Rodney*, I (1830), p. 261.

20

CLAPS, HUZZAS AND ILLUMINATIONS

Jane Rodney describes to her father how his victory was celebrated.

London, May 27, 1782

It is impossible to express how very happy the late good news has made us all. We are almost out of our senses with excessive joy; so is all London, and, indeed, all England. Everybody thinks it is impossible to do too much for you. Never was so glorious a battle fought. . . .

All London was in an uproar; the whole town was illuminated that night: we were at the play. When we went in, the whole house testified, by their claps and huzzas, the joy they felt at the news, and their love for you; their acclamations lasted for, I am sure, five minutes. You may judge how happy we were. . . .

A price had to be paid for victory: a young nobleman, captain of the *Resolution*, became a tragic hero, but many sailors died equally bravely and remained unsung.

21

JOKING WHILE HIS LEG WAS BEING AMPUTATED

Robert Blair, the ship's surgeon, gives the Duke of Rutland (a strong opponent of the war) an account of the death of his brother, Lord Robert Manners, aged twenty-four.

May 23, 1782

The *Resolution* sustained a severe fire from nine or ten of the French ships, in breaking through their line. Your Grace may guess my feelings when I saw Lord Robert brought down wounded, the first man. His behaviour on this, as on every other occasion, was heroism itself. A cannon shot had wounded both legs, and at the same instant he received a compound fracture of his right arm. The left leg was in such a state as to preclude all hopes of saving it, and accordingly I took it off immediately, at his own desire. It will scarcely be credited not only how undaunted he appeared but how perfectly he seemed to possess himself during an operation always dreadful, and in that situation particularly so, making jocular remarks on the operation with a smiling countenance, during its most painful steps.

It was probably owing to this composure and serenity of mind that the symptomatic fever was slight and soon over. He conversed with great cheerfulness with the officers who came to visit him and at one time talked seriously of remaining in the command as before. The same flattering appearances continued for a week. His wounds looked remarkably well, his appetite was good, and he passed his time in conversation, reading and hearing music. In short, being perfectly freed from the cares of the command, he declared that he never was easier or better in his life. I had cautioned his friends about indulging too sanguine hopes of his recovery. His Lordship perfectly knew that the chief danger – to which he was particularly liable from the uncommon irritability of his nerves – remained that of locked jaw and tetanus.

When the fatal symptoms appeared, he acquainted me of them with the utmost serenity and unconcern, said he thought it needless to take any medicines, and that he had entirely made up *his mind to everything*; this was his expression. He suffered himself, however, to be prevailed on, and fortunately the medicines necessary in the cure of this disease, if they fail, have the advantage of alleviating pain. He seemed at first to receive considerable benefit, but the symptoms soon recurred with redoubled violence, and swallowing, which had been very difficult, became impossible. His speech soon after for the first time became wild and incoherent, talking about the action and giving orders in the night; but next morning he was again sensible, and continued so and free from pain, till his dissolution, which took place just as the sun passed the meridian, without a groan or the least sign of uneasiness.

Not everyone was satisfied with the victory: although French designs on Jamaica had been frustrated, Hood, who led the van, blamed Rodney for not pursuing the shattered French fleet which had run out of powder; he thought twenty ships could have been captured. The sixty-four-year-old admiral was probably over-cautious, worn out from the battle, and racked with gout and gravel. He did not know that his successor was already on the way with orders to recall him.[8]

22

A CRITICAL VIEW

Rear-Admiral Sir Samuel (later Viscount) Hood (1724–1816) laments to Sir Charles Middleton, Comptroller of the Navy, the great opportunity Rodney missed.

Barfleur, at sea, 12th May, 1782

Oh, my dear Sir Charles, had Sir George done what he might and ought, we should all most probably have been peaceably at home by our firesides in the course of another year! How he can stand the reproaches of his own mind, if he is not perfectly callous, for doing so little, when a vast deal of honour and glory might so easily have been gathered for his poor country, almost a bankrupt in both, I cannot reconcile. The French could never have rose again this war; America would have shaken off her unnatural connection with them; Spain, in all human probability, would have seen her error, and have been glad of the first opening to have withdrawn herself; and

---

8 Rodney was superseded before his victory and, on his return, he was fêted and given a peerage, but it was the end of his naval career.

England would have been the admiration and envy of every Court in Europe. The very important and favourable opportunity that has been lost for raising Great Britain's glory is melancholy in the extreme to think of. . . .

The *Ville de Paris*'s powder was, very near exhausted, which her captain told me when he came on board, and further said he was sure it was the case of every French ship. I most pointedly told this to Sir George next morning, but he was not to be stimulated to a pursuit, which is matter of astonishment not only to me, but I believe, to nine-tenths of the captains and officers of this fleet. I have received the most undoubted intelligence that the four ships which put into Curaçao had scarce a round of powder left. . . .

Thanks to leaders like Rodney in the West Indies, General Carleton in Canada, and Warren Hastings in India, and their soldiers and sailors, the defeat in the American War of Independence did not spell the end of the empire, as George III had feared; it continued to flourish and expand but, with the ascent of the younger Pitt, the King's personal government came to an end instead, which may well in fact have saved the monarchy.

Postscript: the Siege of Gibraltar

> *If I was an epicure among the sharks, I*
> *should rejoice that General Eliott has*
> *just sent the carcasses of 1500 Spaniards*
> *down the market under Gibraltar; but I am*
> *more pleased that he saved some of those*
> *he overset*
>
> HORACE WALPOLE

Lieutenant-General Eliott's epic defence of Gibraltar, which was blockaded and besieged from 1779 to 1783 by strong French and Spanish amphibious forces, was another milestone in the defence of the empire. The most powerful assault, watched by huge crowds from the mainland, was made on 13 September 1782 by ten floating batteries, armoured with three layers of three-foot thick timber, interspersed with cork and wet sand, and considered indestructible; water reservoirs kept the wood saturated and roofs of wet hides protected it above. Their 142 guns and over 5,000 men were to smash the defences and clear a way for nearly 25,000 infantry and 2,500 cavalry, standing by in 300 transports under the protection of 44 French and Spanish ships of the line. Before the batteries were able to reduce the bastions to rubble, they were, however, themselves set on fire by red-hot shot which the garrison poured upon them, until the attempt was abandoned with great loss of life.[9]

9   T.H. McGuffie, *Siege of Gibraltar*, Batsford, 1965.

23

THE ATTACK ON GIBRALTAR

Captain (later Admiral Sir) Roger Curtis (1746–1816) of HMS *Brilliant* reports to Lord Commissioner Stephens, stressing that they had considered it their 'duty to make every effort' to save the enemy from burning and drowning.

Gibraltar, Sept. 1782

The combined Fleet of France and Spain, consisting of thirty-eight sail of the line, arrived in this bay on the 12th inst.: six sail of the line were here before. At eight o'clock in the morning of the 13th, the ten battering ships of the enemy lying at the head of the bay began to get under sail in order to come against the garrison. At ten the admiral's ship was placed about 1000 yards from the King's Bastion, and commenced his fire. Our batteries opened as the enemy came before them: the fire was very heavy on both sides; the red-hot shot were sent with such precision from the garrison, that in the afternoon the smoke was seen to issue from the upper part of the Admiral, and one other, and men were perceived to be using fire engines and pouring water into the holds, endeavouring to extinguish the fire. Their efforts proved ineffectual; by one o'clock the two were in flames. Confusion was now plainly observed among them, and the numerous rockets thrown up from each of the ships, was a clear demonstration of their great distress: their signals were answered from the enemy's fleet, and they immediately began to take away the men, it being impossible to move the ships.

I thought this a fit opportunity to employ my gun-boats and I advanced with the whole (twelve in number, each carrying a 24- or 18-pounder) and drew them up so as to flank the line of the enemy's battering-ships, while they were annoyed extremely by an excessive heavy and well-directed fire from the garrison. The fire from the gun-boats was kept up with great vigour and effect. The boats of the enemy durst not approach; they abandoned their ships and the men left in them to our mercy; or to the flames. . . .

The scene at this time before me was dreadful to a high degree; numbers of men crying from amidst the flames, some upon pieces of wood in the water, and all imploring assistance, formed a spectacle of horror not easily to be described. Every exertion was made to relieve them; and I have inexpressible happiness in informing my lords, that the number saved amounts to 13 officers and 344 men. The blowing up of the ships around us, as the fire got to the magazines, and the firing of the cannon of others, as the metal became heated by the flames, rendered this a very perilous employment; but we felt it as much a duty to make every effort to relieve our enemies from so shocking a situation, as an hour before we did to assist in conquering them. The loss of the enemy must have been very considerable. Great numbers were killed on board, and in boats. All the battering ships were set on fire by our hot shot except one, which we afterwards burnt. The admiral left his flag flying, and it was consumed with the ship. . . .

The spirit of the soldiers defending the Rock – and the empire – is caught in the concluding letter.

24

'My religion consists in firelock'

Samuel Ancell, 58th Regiment, who served throughout the siege, writes to his brother.

Gibraltar [n. d.]

I cannot, dear Brother, omit penning an entertaining conversation I had with a soldier in Irish Town yesterday. I met Jack Careless in the street, singing with uncommon glee (notwithstanding the enemy were firing with prodigious warmth), part of the old song,

> A soldier's life is a merry life,
> From care and trouble Free.

He ran to me with eagerness, and presenting his bottle cry'd, 'D—n me, if I don't like fighting: I'd like to be ever tanning the Dons: – Plenty of good liquor for carrying away – never was the price so cheap – fine stuff – enough to make a miser quit his gold.' 'Why, Jack,' says I, 'what have you been about?' With an arch grin, he replied, 'That would puzzle a Heathen philosopher, or yearly almanack-maker, to unriddle. I scarce know myself. I have been constantly on foot and watch, half starved, and without money, facing a parcel of pitiful Spaniards. I have been fighting, wheeling, marching, and counter-marching; sometimes with a firelock, then a handspike, and now my bottle' (brandishing it in the air). 'I am so pleased with the melody of great guns that I consider myself as a Roman General, gloriously fighting for my country's honour and liberty.' A shell that instant burst, a piece of which knocked the bottle out of his hand; with the greatest composure he replied (having first graced it with an oath), 'This is not any loss, I have found a whole cask by good luck,' and brought me to view his treasure.'But, Jack,' says I, 'are you not thankful to God, for your preservation?' 'How do you mean?' he answered. 'Fine talking of God with a soldier, whose trade and occupation is cutting throats. Divinity and slaughter sound very well together, they jangle like a crack'd bell in the hand of a noisy crier: Our King is answerable to God for us. I fight for him. My religion consists in firelock, open touchhole, good flint, well rammed charge, and 70 rounds of powder and ball. This is my military creed. Come, comrade, drink success to the British Arms.'

T E N

The War with Revolutionary France (1793–1802)

And Ocean, 'mid his uproar wild,
Speaks safety to this Island child!
SAMUEL TAYLOR COLERIDGE (1772–1834)

After a respite of ten years, the conflict with France was resumed: Jacobin leadership threatened to sweep away the dynasties of Europe and its *ancien régime* with the fervour of a new popular nationalism. The attack of the French Revolutionary army on the Netherlands and the Rhine Delta brought Britain into the war in 1793, in the traditional defence of the vital Channel approaches. As usual, however, the country was unprepared for war after neglecting its forces in peacetime through ingrained fear of a standing professional army. Soldiers and equipment were short, especially as half the army was in the West Indies for predatory attacks on the sugar islands.

Prelude: the Army in the Netherlands

Blows, blood, and death . . .
SHAKESPEARE, KING JOHN

There was much corruption among the dandified officers and the NCOs were the backbone of a soldiery imbued with fierce national pride. The British–Hanoverian army under the Duke of York stormed Valenciennes, and hoped to proceed to Dunkirk.

1

'I exspeck to be a Gentleman or a Cripel'

Corporal George Robertson, Royal Artillery, ready to go abroad with his family, tells his mother that their 'Bodyguard of British Heroes' is to lead the foreign allies into the field; he took part in the siege of Valenciennes.

Woolwich, February 26, 1793

Dear Mother,

I have just received orders for Germeny under the command of the Duck of York, with 2,200 foot guards. We expect to embark tomorrow to go with His Royal Highness as a Bodyguard of British Heroes. We are to lead the Dutch Prushen and Hanover Troops into the field, as there is none equal to the British Army. We are chosen troops sent by His Majesty to show an example to the other Troops, to go in front, & lead the combined army against the French which consists of 150,000 able fighten men. You may judge if we shall have anything to dow. I had the pleasure to conquer the French last war; but God knows how it will be this war. I cannot expect to escape the Bullets of my enemies much longer, as non has ever entred my flesh as yet. To be plain with you and not dishearten you, I don't expect to come off so cleare as I did last war. But it is death or honour. I exspeck to be a Gentleman or a Cripel. But you shall never see me destress you. If I cannot help you, I never shall destress you.

Dear Mother, I take my family with me. Where I go, they most go. If I leave them, I should have no luck. My wife and two children is in good health, & in good spirits, fear not for us. I hope God will be on our side.

2

'May the British flag ever flourish over the world'

Valencine, August 1, 1793

I received your kind letter and am happy to find you are yet in the land of the Living and well. Dear Mother and Townsmen, I have great news for you. On the night of the 23rd, our British Troops stormed the Outworks of Valencine, and took them; killed and wounded 500 French; our lose about ten only. The Elements was like on fire with Bomb shell. Never did my eyes behold the like before; and on the 26th, we heard a horn blow in the Town for a parley, and a flag of Truce to come upon Terms, which was agreed on; on these terms, that the British Troops shall have possession of the Town & Garrison and no other. On the 1st day of August, we enter the Town with two 6-pounders and a silk Flag at the head of the British Grenadiers. This is over. Thank God. The number killed in that time in the town is 6,000, and a number of Women and Children. The British Artillery manned a Battery of eight 12-pounders which hurt them more than all the firing troops. I commanded one of those Guns one day on the Battry, when a 24-pound shot went thro' one of my men's shoulders &

brock my Gun wheel. The blood and flesh of the man was all over my Cloas. The pipol in the Camp thought we was all gone. Mother, you cannot think how happy my wife and children was to see me return safe to my Tent. Every time I went to the Battery, I took leave of my wife & family. We staid 24 hours at a time; and when we returned, it was the same as new life to us both. . . .

I will do more yet for my King and Country's saik. My country shall never be stained by me. After things is settled hear, we exspect to march for Dunkirk, to besiege that Town & Garrison. Then we shall winter, and rest till the Spring; and then I hope for Parris. Keep a good heart at home; we will conquer our enemies, and bring them down. May the British flag ever flourish over the world. . . .

God bless you, Dear Mother, adu, adu, God bless you. I hope my Townsmen will drink sucksess to George Robertson.

Your ever loving Son,
Geo. Robertson

The French soon overran Holland, and, after a disastrous campaign, the British were forced to sail home from Bremen. The future Duke of Wellington, seeing active service for the first time, at twenty-five, is apprehensive of the outcome and finds French antics amusing but disconcerting.

3

THE ENEMY DANCES

Lieutenant-Colonel (later Field Marshal Duke of Wellington) Arthur Wesley[1] (1769–1862) describes to his cousin, Rear-Admiral Sir Chichester Fortescue, how they were entertained by the carmagnole, the dance of the French Revolution.

Ysendoom, 20th December 1794

At present the French keep us in a perpetual state of alarm; we turn out once, sometimes twice, every night; the officers and men are harrassed to death, and if we are not relieved, I believe there will be very few of the latter remaining shortly. I have not had my clothes off my back for a long time, and generally spend the greatest part of the night upon the bank of the river. . . . Although the French annoy us much at night, they are very entertaining during the daytime; they are perpetually chattering with our officers and soldiers, and dance the *carmagnole* upon the opposite bank whenever we desire them; but occasionally the spectators on our side are interrupted in the middle of the dance by a cannon ball from theirs. . . .

1   He signed his name 'Wellesley' from 1798.

Cornwall Militia regimental 'character', *c.* 1796, from a set of ten watercolours (artist unknown) for *A Peep into Camp*, published by S.W. Fores, 1797. (*Courtesy of the Director of the National Army Museum*)

The press gang at work. (*National Maritime Museum*)

Naval Miscellany

Of all the lives that e'er was lived,
The sailor's life for I . . .
CHARLES DIBDIN (1745–1814)

A budding Admiral, eleven-year-old William Parker, having joined the Navy at Spithead as captain's 'servant' in the *Orion*, wrote to his mother:

I am very happy and as comfortable as if I was at home; I think I have every prospect of doing well, particularly under the care of so good a gentleman as Captain Duckworth, who is like a father to us all and is so good as to send for some plums, and other good things, for me, and very often asks me to breakfast, dine, and drink tea with him.[2]

Fifteen months later, he took part in the battle of the 'Glorious First of June' at Ushant in which the *Orion* distinguished itself. Lord Howe, in an unorthodox move, attacked the rear of the French fleet of equal numbers (twenty-six) but larger ships, and captured seven of them after a furious two-hour battle, but the French grain convoy escaped. Captain Collingwood, who was to succeed Nelson, made this curious comment:

I observed that notwithstanding their superior strength, in one thing we had very much the advantage over them – we should have the prayers of our wives for our success, whereas they had neither wives like ours, nor prayers to offer.[3]

Twelve-year-old William Parker gives a dramatic account of the battle, which ended with a drunkards' mutiny and the captain's pardon – unusual in those days of harsh discipline and disregard for human life.

---

2 A. Phillimore, *Life of Admiral Parker*, quoted in C.R.N. Routh, *They saw it happen*, Blackwell, 1956, p. 112.
3 O. Warner, *Glorious First of June*, Batsford, 1961, p. 92. To supplement what has been said previously about women soldiers, Ann Talbot, serving her lover, a captain, as a foot-boy in Flanders, was wounded at Valenciennes, then joined a French privateer and, on capture, changed sides again and was wounded fighting as a sailor in the First of June battle. Other women stayed on board ship more or less promiscuously in the sailors' crammed quarters and gave help in battles. (Kemp, op. cit. p. 171.)

4

TEARS FOR DROWNED ENEMIES

Midshipman (later Admiral Sir) William Parker (1781–1866) describes to his father the 'Glorious First of June'.

June 17th, 1794

. . . At eight the action began, and the firing from the enemy was very smart before we could engage the ship that came to our turn to engage, and unluckily killed two men before we fired a gun, which so exasperated our men that they kept singing out, 'For God's sake, brave Captain, let us fire! Consider, sir, two poor souls slaughtered already.' But Captain Duckworth would not let them fire till we came abreast of the ship we were to engage, when Captain Duckworth cried out, 'Fire, my boys, fire!' upon which our enraged boys gave them such an extraordinary warm reception that I really believe it struck the rascals with the panic. . . .

The smoke was so thick that we could not at all times see the ships engaging ahead and astern. Our main-topmast and main-yard being carried away by the enemy's shot, the Frenchmen gave three cheers, upon which our ship's company, to show they did not mind it, returned them the three cheers, and after that gave them a furious broadside.

A ship of eighty guns contrived to send a red-hot shot into the captain's cabin where I am quartered, which kept rolling about and burning everybody, when gallant Mears, our first lieutenant, took it up in his speaking-trumpet and threw it overboard.

The French fleet then ran away like cowardly rascals. Lord Howe ordered our ships that were not very much disabled to take the prizes in tow; the ship which struck to us was so much disabled that she could not live much longer on the water, but she gave a dreadful reel and lay down on her broadside. We were afraid to send any boat to help them, because they would have sunk here by too many poor souls getting into her at once. We could plainly perceive the poor wretches climbing over to windward and crying most dreadfully. She then righted a little, and then her head went down gradually, and she sunk, so that no more was seen of her. Oh, my dear father! when you consider of five or six hundred souls destroyed in that shocking manner, it will make your very heart relent. Our own men even were a great many of them in tears and groaning, they said God bless them. Oh, that we had come into a thousand engagements sooner than so many poor souls should be at once destroyed in that shocking manner. I really think it would have rent the hardest of hearts. . . .

Most of our brave boys have undone all the good they ever did. They contrived to smuggle a great deal of liquor into the ship, and with the joy of the victory, most of the ships company got so drunk that they mutinied. They said that they would have liberty to go ashore. They released the English prisoners out of irons. Every officer belonging to the ship was sent for. The Captain almost broke his heart about it. Seven of the ringleaders were seized by the officers and twenty others, when they were put in irons; and the next morning, when they were told of their night's proceedings they all cried like children. They punished the twenty with two dozen lashes each, and the seven were kept in irons to be hung, if tried by a Court Martial; but Captain

Duckworth came on board to-day and said that, as he was of a forgiving temper, he gave them into the hands of the ship's company, that he looked up to them with love for the services they had done him. . . .

Lord Stanhope who declared himself to be a sansculotte and became known as 'Citizen Stanhope', was one of the many supporters of the French Revolution who opposed the war. Inventor of a calculating machine and a microscopic lens, he also experimented with steam-propelled ships and claimed in the Lords that he could build a vessel which would outsail the swiftest in the Navy. The first steam-powered warship, the *Demologos*, was built by the American Robert Fulton in 1814 and the Navy launched a wooden paddle-steamer of 80 hp, the *Comet*, in 1822, a year after the first Dover–Calais steamer. Here Lord Stanhope foretells this momentous development. Fortunately, the Directoire and the first Consul treated Fulton as a charlatan when he offered them models of a steamship and a 'plunging boat' for firing torpedoes. It was also turned down in England as a danger to the Navy.

5

THE STEAMSHIP – A THREAT

Charles Earl of Stanhope (1753–1816) expresses his fears to William Wilberforce, the champion of the abolition of the slave trade.

December 5th 1794

. . . This country, Great Britain, is vulnerable in so many ways, that the picture is horrid. I know (and in a few weeks shall prove), that ships of any size, and, for certain reasons, the larger the better, may be navigated in any narrow or other sea, without sails so as to go without wind, and even directly against both wind and waves.

The most important consequence which I draw from this stupendous fact is that it will shortly, and very shortly, render all the existing navies of the world no better than lumber. For what can ships do that are dependent upon wind and weather, against ships wholly independent of either!

The boasted superiority of the English navy is no more! We must have a new one. . . .

Admiral Sir John Jervis's victory at Cape St Vincent on 14 February 1797 with fifteen ships over De Cordoba's twenty-seven (with, admittedly, untrained crews) revived British spirit, and prevented a junction of the Spanish with the French fleet at Brest. At the decisive moment, Nelson in the *Captain* (74 guns), disobeying orders, kept the Spanish fleet cut in two by moving out of line ('We flew to them as a hawk to his prey', wrote Collingwood) and drawing seven Spanish ships to attack him, including the biggest in the world, the four-decker *S^a Trinidad* (136 guns), until 'not a sail, shroud or rope was left'. He boarded and burnt two ships with the cry of 'Westminster Abbey, or Glorious Victory!' and 'drove the Spaniards from deck to deck at the point of their swords and received the submission of the officers, while one of his sailors bundled them up with as much composure as he would have made a faggot.'[4] A gunner wrote:

> We gave them their Valentines in style, not that we loved fighting, but we all wished to be free to return to our homes and follow our own pursuits. We knew there was no other way of obtaining this than by defeating the enemy. 'The hotter the war, the sooner peace', was a saying with us.[5]

This wish to live at home in peace was shared by Nelson. He was to have his cottage but it was Emma, Lady Hamilton, rather than his wife who was to share it with him, and not for long.

6

'A Cottage and a piece of ground'

Commodore Horatio (later Vice-Admiral Viscount) Nelson (1758–1805) writes to his wife after the Battle of Cape St Vincent; he was made a KB and Rear-Admiral.

> *Irresistible*, Lisbon, 28th February 1797
>
> We got up here with our Prizes this afternoon: the more I think of our late Action, the more I am astonished; it absolutely appears a dream. The *Santissima Trinidad*, of four decks, lost 500 killed and wounded; had not my Ship been so cut up, I would have had her; but it is well, thank God for it! As to myself, I assure you I never was better, and rich in the praises of every man from the highest to the lowest in the Fleet. The Spanish War will give us a Cottage and a piece of ground, which is all I want. I shall come one day or other laughing back, when we will retire from the busy scenes of life; I do not, however, mean to be a hermit; the Dons will give us a little money.

At the unsuccessful attack on Santa Cruz de Tenerife on 24 July 1797, Nelson, one-eyed since the siege of Calvi, lost his right arm and almost his life, and had to return. A midshipman (the later Captain, Sir William Hoste) testifies to Nelson's courageous spirit and fatherly care which made them overcome all danger and hardship:

> Admiral Nelson, who has been a second father to me, returned on board, his right arm dangling by his side, while with the other he helped himself

4 Collingwood, *Correspondence*, 1828, p. 29 ff.
5 W.H. Long, *Naval Yarns*, 1899, p. 193.

to jump up the ship's side, and with a spirit that astonished everyone, told the surgeon to get his instruments ready, for he knew he must lose his arm, and that the sooner it was off the better. He underwent the amputation with the same firmness and courage that have always marked his character.[6]

Nelson thought his career had come to an end and he would retire to the cottage with Fanny.

7

NELSON LOSES HIS ARM

Nelson to his wife.

Theseus, at sea, August 3rd, 1797

My dearest Fanny,

I am so confident of your affection, that I feel the pleasure you will receive will be equal, whether my letter is wrote by my right hand or left. It was the chance of war, and I have great reason to be thankful. . . . Now I hope soon to return to you; and my Country, I trust, will not allow me any longer to linger in want of pecuniary assistance. But I shall not be surprised to be neglected and forgot, as probably I shall no longer be considered as useful. However, I shall feel rich if I continue to enjoy your affection. The cottage is now more necessary than ever. . . .

God bless you, and believe me

Your most affectionate husband
HORATIO NELSON

In April 1797, serious mutinies had broken out in the Channel fleet at Spithead and the Nore, in protest against the appalling conditions of life in the Navy: many seamen had been press-ganged with merciless brutality, their filthy overcrowded quarters favoured epidemics, there was no proper care for the sick, shore leave was rarely granted, food was rotten, teeming with weevils and worms, and fresh greenstuffs lacking. The net pay of a trifling £6 per annum for an ordinary seaman was in arrears for up to fifteen years (though £1 prize money might be added for every £10,000 the admiral would pocket), and savage flogging for the most petty offences often crippled a sailor for life. The men claimed they were 'kept more like convicts than free-born Britons' and elected delegates to negotiate with the Admiralty which, outraged by the idea of parleying with seamen, sent menacing orders and cut off their victuals. Delegate Henry Long's answer was significant for its unshaken patriotism:

---

6   H. Wragg, *Letters Written in War Time*, OUP, 1915, p. 198.

Dam my eyes if I Understand your lingo or long Proclamations, in short give us our Due at Once and no more at it, till we go in search of the Rascals the Enemyes of our Country.[7]

The mutineers kept on professing their loyalty to King and nation, but some threatened they might be 'forced to repose in another country'. The government blamed French Jacobin influence, but Nelson thought the mutineers' claims justified: 'I am entirely with the seamen.'

Finally, the Spithead Mutiny succeeded in wresting long-overdue reforms from the Admiralty, with the help of Lord Howe, but the republican mutiny of thirteen ships of the line in the Nore, under the red flag, was quelled by some determined officers in face of a lukewarm mob of sailors. Lieutenant Peter Bover who ordered the marines in Admiral Colpoys' flagship to fire on the delegates, killing five, described how he was then seized by the seamen, one of whom saved his and the Admiral's life:

I had 50 pistols levelled at my head, and the yard rope round my neck; one of the men by his manly eloquence procured a pardon from the delegates and there never was such expressive integrity painted in a man's countenance.[8]

Eventually, twenty-nine delegates were seized, put in irons, court-martialled and hanged in their ships, among them Richard Parker, their President. He had been a naval lieutenant in the American War who rebelled against his captain, then as a gold-ball maker he had got into the debtors' prison, and volunteered as an able seaman in the flagship *Sandwich*. Picked as leader of the Nore rebellion, he ordered the fleet to sail over to the enemy when negotiations brought no concessions, but was not obeyed by the sailors who felt greater hatred for the enemy than for those who refused to remedy their grievances. His 'Dying Declaration' throws an interesting light on the seamen's mentality and their relationship with their delegates.

8

THE MUTINY IN THE NORE

Richard Parker (1767–97) justifies himself to his best friend two days before his execution.

June 28th, 1797

A little while and I must depart from this world, and for ever close my eyes upon its vanity, deceitfulness, and ingratitude. My passage through it has been short but

7   See G. E. Mainwaring & B. Dobrée, *Floating Republic*, G. Bles, 1935, for the whole account

8   *Gentleman's Magazine* 1843, II, p. 32 ff.

chequered. My departure from it will be extremely boisterous, but I seriously assure you, upon my part, by no means unwilling.

The only comfortable reflection that I at present enjoy, is that I am to die a Martyr in the cause of Humanity. I know the multitude think hard things of me, but this gives me no uneasiness, for my conscience testifies that the part which I have acted among the seamen has been right, although not to be justified by prudence. *I ought to have known mankind better*, than blindfold to have plunged into certain destruction. Long since I had learnt that the miseries under which the lower classes groan are imputable in a great measure to their ignorance, cowardice, and duplicity, and nothing short of a miracle would ever afford them any relief. . . .

Upon the word of a dying man, I solemnly declare that I was not an original mover of the disturbances amongst those men, who have treated me so very ungratefully. Also, that I was elected by my Shipmates their Delegate without my knowledge, and in the same manner by the Delegates their President. I was compelled to accept those situations much against my inclinations by those who pushed me into them. It is well known what authority the seamen had over their Delegates, and in what a ferocious manner the Delegates were frequently treated for not according with every wild scheme which the sailors proposed to carry into practice. . . . The only instances in which the Delegates acted of themselves were in those of checking the violence and turpitude of their masters, and this God knows we had hard work to do. For not according with the preposterous ideas of the seamen, I and many more must suffer Death. Had we been as decidedly violent as they were, we need not have died like dogs, for all the force which could have been mustered would not have availed, and necessity would have obliged a compliance to our demands. Owing to the Delegates' moderation, they have been overcome, and for my own part I cheerfully forgive the vanquishers the bloody use they intend to make of their victory. I was prepared for the sacrifice, and may Heaven grant that I may be the last victim offered up in the cause of a treacherous and debased commonalty. . . .

I am the devoted scapegoat for the sins of many, and henceforth when the oppressed groan under the stripes of the oppressors, let my example deter any man from risking himself as the victim to ameliorate their wretchedness. Remember, never to make yourself the busy body of the lower classes, for they are cowardly, selfish, and ungrateful; the least trifle intimidate them, and him whom they have exalted one moment as their Demagogue, the next they will not scruple to exalt upon the gallows. . . . There is nothing new in my treatment; compare it with the treatment of most of the Advocates for the improvement of the conditions of the Multitude in all ages. Nay with reverence I write it, with the treatment of Jesus Christ Himself. . . .

It is my opinion that if the Government had not been too hasty the Portsmouth Mutiny would have been as readily overcome as that at Sheerness. The Mutineers have been accused of disloyalty, but it is a false accusation. They were only so to their ill-fated tools the Delegates. Both Army and Navy are in my opinion loyal, well attached to the ruling powers. . . . By the Laws of War I acknowledge myself to be legally convicted, but by the Laws of Humanity, which should be the basis of all laws, I die illegally. My judges were respectable, but not totally disinterested, for one of the demands had for its tendency the abridgement of their emoluments in Prize Money.

Now my dear Friend I take my leave of you. . . . Parting with life is no more than going to sleep, and God in His Mercy grant I may sleep sweetly after my worldly toils, through the merits of my Lord and Saviour Jesus Christ. Amen.

Adieu, eternally adieu,

From your dying friend,
R.P.

A few months later after the mutiny, the sailors proved that their fighting spirit had in no way cooled: in the fierce, bloody battle of Camperdown, Admiral Duncan penetrated the enemy line to cut them off leeward, contravening the fighting instructions like Howe and Nelson, and took eleven of the eighteen Dutch ships. In the heat of battle the sailors always forgot their grievances and fought ferociously for their country, conscious that it relied on them for protection.

Sidney Smith who had burnt the French fleet at Toulon in 1793, was thrown into the 'Prison du Temple' by Bonaparte in revenge when he was taken at Le Havre in 1796; French royalists freed him from Louis XVI's cell there. While Bonaparte had three thousand Turkish prisoners stabbed to death at Jaffa in 1799, Sidney Smith, who had assumed command of the Turkish fleet and army, freed the French prisoners languishing in a Turkish dungeon for galley slaves and sent them home. In the famous siege of Acre, Sidney Smith held out successfully for sixty-two days against Bonaparte's ceaseless attacks; at one point, eight hundred British seamen and marines saved the breached Turkish defences from the furious assault of much larger French forces. In St Helena, Napoleon said: 'That man has made me miss my destiny.'

9

BUBONIC PLAGUE AS 'PROOF OF DIVINE JUSTICE'

Captain (later Vice-Admiral Sir) William Sidney Smith (1764–1840) to Lord Nelson.

Tigre, the anchor of Jaffa, 30th May 1799

The providence of Almighty God has been wonderfully manifested in the defeat and precipitate retreat of the French army. . . . The measure of their iniquities seems to have been filled by the massacre of the Turkish prisoners at Jaffa, in cold blood, three days after their capture, and the plain of Nazareth has been the boundary of Buonaparte's extraordinary career.

He raised the siege of Acre on the 20th May, leaving all his artillery behind him, either buried or thrown into the sea. He seemed to have no principle of action but that of pressing forward, and appeared to stick at nothing to obtain the object of his ambition. Two attempts to assassinate me in the town having failed, recourse was had to a most flagrant breach of every law of honour and of war. A flag of truce was sent into the town, by the hands of an Arab dervise, proposing a cessation of arms for the sake of burying the dead bodies, the stench from which was become intolerable, many having died delirious within a few hours after being seized with the first symptoms of infection. It was natural that we should be off our guard during the conference; while the answer was under consideration a volley of shot and shells on a sudden announced an assault, which, however, the garrison was ready to receive; and the assailants only contributed to increase the number of dead bodies, to the eternal disgrace of the general who thus disloyally sacrificed them. The enemy had no alternative left but a precipitate retreat and the whole track between Acre and Gaza is strewed with dead bodies. The heaps of unburied Frenchmen, lying on the bodies of those whom they massacred two months ago, afford another proof of divine justice, which has caused these murderers to perish by the infection, arising from their own atrocious act. . . .

Invasion from France was always a danger while the inadequate British army was dispersed in campaigns or raids on the continent and in the West Indies. Already in 1793 General Hoche had plotted a large-scale raid to destroy London and its dockyards by landing a combined force of 100,000 men, only prevented by the royalist rising in the Vendée. In 1796 Hoche changed his plans to an infiltration of sabotage units, the release of five hundred convicts, and arms deliveries to revolutionaries in the West Country, but his 'troops' fought shy of the flat boats. December gales stopped 14,000 regular soldiers from landing in rebellious Ireland, when seventeen French ships lay for seventeen days unopposed in Bantry Bay. Finally, in February 1797, the 'Black Legion' – 1,400 gaol birds and galley convicts under the seventy-year-old Irish-American adventurer Colonel Tate – actually landed from three frigates at Fishguard to instigate a Welsh rising by bribing the poor and destroy the ports of Bristol and Liverpool. Terrified by four hundred menacing women in scarlet whittles and stove hats they took for soldiers, they surrendered to them and the hastily gathered 660 militia men of Lord Cawdor. There was a witchhunt for traitors while he conveyed the prisoners to London. He wrote to his wife:

We passed through great crowds of people where we changed horses and thro' Wales the indignation was great. The women were more clamorous than the men, making signs to cut their throats, and desiring I would not take the trouble of carrying them further.[9]

In 1798, Bonaparte organized the French 'Army of England' of 25,000 men, to be transported under cover of night from the Channel ports to England by sixty purpose-built gun boats and a large number of fishing vessels. Although he grandiloquently proclaimed 'Let us be masters of the Straits for six hours and we shall be masters of the world', he soon became chary of the

9   H.F.B. Wheeler & A.M. Broadley, *Napoleon and the Invasion of England*, 1908, I, p. 64; J.S. Kinross, *Fishguard Fiasco*, Walters, 1974.

invasion plan and decided to go for Egypt instead. Then again, in 1801, after an abortive small-scale landing by General Humbert in Ireland, a new flotilla of 631 vessels lay ready at Boulogne with 30,000 men. Nelson went over to bombard them while the Dover crowds tried to get a grandstand view from the cliffs of 'Nelson speaking to the French'.[10]

10

FRENCH INVASION BATTERIES SMASHED

Lord Nelson to Lady Hamilton.

Medusa, off Boulogne, August 4th, 1801

My dearest Emma,

Boulogne is evidently not a pleasant place this morning. Three of their floating batteries are sunk; what damage has been done to the others, and the vessels inside the pier, I cannot say, but hope and believe that some hundreds of French are gone to hell this morning; for if they are dead assuredly they are gone there. In fire or out of fire I am,

Yours,
Nelson and Bronte

The embarkation of the French army will not take place at Boulogne. Beyond this I cannot say. In my visits to the bombs in my barge, my friends think the French have been very attentive to me, for they did nothing but fire at the boat and the different vessels I was in, but God is good.

In the middle of the war, Robert Southey, who later wrote a very popular *Life of Nelson*, sailed to Lisbon with his wife, not without incurring some scares.

11

THE POET WITH A MUSKET

Robert Southey (1774–1843) tells his brother-in-law, Samuel Taylor Coleridge, of an encounter at sea that ended happily.

Lisbon, May Day 1800

Here, then, we are, thank God! alive, and recovering from dreadful sickness. I never suffered so much at sea, and Edith was worse than I was; we scarcely ate or slept at

---

10 See H.W. Richmond, *Invasion of Britain*, Methuen, 1941 for the whole account of invasion plans.

all: but the passage was very fine and short; five and a half days brought us to our port, with light winds the whole of the way, not, however, without alarm. On Monday morning, between five and six, the captain was awakened with tidings that a cutter was bearing down upon us, with English colours, indeed, but apparently a French vessel; we made a signal, which was not answered; we fired a gun, she did the same, and preparations were made for action. We had another Lisbon packet in company, mounting six guns; our own force was ten; the cutter was a match, and more, for both, but we did not expect to be taken. You may imagine Edith's terror, awakened on a sick bed with these tidings! The captain advised me to surround her with mattresses in the cabin, but she would not believe herself in safety there, and I lodged her in the cockpit, and took my station on the quarter-deck with a musket.

How I felt I can hardly tell; the hurry of the scene, the sight of grape-shot, bar-shot, and other ingenious implements of this sort, made an undistinguishable mixture of feelings. The cutter bore down between us; I saw the smoke from her matches, we were so near, and not a man on board had the least idea but that an immediate action was to take place. We hailed her; she answered in broken English, and passed on. 'Tis over!' cried somebody. 'Not yet!' said the captain; and we expected she was coming round as about to attack our comrade vessel. She was English, however, manned chiefly from Guernsay, and this explained her Frenchified language. You will easily imagine that my sensations, at the ending of the business, were very definable – one honest simple joy that I was in a whole skin! I laid the musket in the chest with considerably more pleasure than I took it out. I am glad this took place; it has shown me what it is to prepare for action. . . .

One tends to forget that war at sea did not consist mainly of the excitement of battle: the concluding letter catches the atmosphere of weeks of wearisome patrolling in all weather, with only day-dreams of glorious action.

12

'Must war reign eternal?'

Lieutenant (later Admiral) Thomas Whinyates (1778–1857) writes to his sister from a two-month cruise in the 20 gun sloop *Camilla.*

Feb. 3rd, 1800
. . . There is the same monotony, the same stupid passing backwards and forwards off Havre that used to enrage me so against Ushant; yet this excursion has been more productive of events than usual; for, we destroyed a large fighting boat full of herrings, chased two gun boats into the Caen river, and drove a lugger and some other small vessels under the shelter of two batteries, where we cannonaded them for upwards of two hours without much effect. . . .

Is there any likelihood of peace or must war reign eternal? In snowy, rainy or stormy weather I execrate the ship, the Navy and sea altogether and wish myself where, beside a snug fire, I can even experience enjoyment in the bellowing of the wind and waves –

> Let others brave the flood in quest of gain
> And beat, for joyless months, the gloomy wave.

Don't think me mad for quoting poetry: the first fine day and gleam of sunshine dispel these melancholy thoughts, and I fabricate aerial castles and almost fancy myself a Captain, Commodore or Admiral, panting for fame, carrying havock and confusion, terror and affright amongst my country's foes. But peace or war, be assured that I am extremely happy in this ship – happy in my brother officers, happy in my Captain.

The Making of the English Hero

> *Now drink the health to gallant Nelson,*
> *the wonder of the world . . .*
> ANON. (1803)

> *Glory is my object and that alone*
> NELSON

The Battle of the Nile

On his search for Admiral De Brueys' Toulon fleet, convoying Bonaparte's army to Egypt, Nelson overran it and arrived two days early at Alexandria. He returned to Sicily to load food and water, while Bonaparte slipped in after him and conquered Lower Egypt. Nelson returned, however, and on 1 August 1798 in Aboukir Bay he struck at dusk at the French fleet which was of heavier tonnage and lay anchored facing seawards under the protection of many gun-boats and the gun battery on the landside. Captain Foley in the *Goliath*, without orders, first squeezed through the enemy line to fire from the flank, followed by Captain Hood in the *Zealous*, while Nelson in the flagship *Vanguard* attacked from the outside, getting a good deal battered. Gradually he got half his force landwards and, in the night, completely massacred the French fleet which was overwhelmed by the speed and vigour of the unexpected attack. Of the thirteen ships of the line, seven were captured, three burnt, and the new 120-gun flagship *Orient* blew up after stubborn resistance, directed by the admiral, both of whose legs had been shot off. Five thousand Frenchmen died, as against two hundred, without loss of any ship, on the British side. Captain Miller of the *Theseus* describes how before 'the most grand and awful spectacle, such as formerly would have drawn tears down the victor's cheeks, pity was stifled as it rose, by the remembrance of the numerous and horrid atrocities their unprincipled and bloodthirsty nation had and were committing; and when she blew up, though I endeavoured to stop the momentary cheer of the ship's company, my heart scarce felt a single pang for their fate.'[11]

With one stroke, Nelson had cut off the French army in Egypt, thwarted Bonaparte's designs on India, and restored British domination of the Mediterranean. The secret of Nelson's spectacular feat was the independent initiative he allowed his captains whom he treated as equals: he lived among them as a comrade to infuse them with his new tactical conceptions.

13

'A Band of Brothers'

Baron Nelson of the Nile tells Admiral Earl Howe, retired and soon to die, how his victory was achieved.

Palermo, January 8th, 1799

. . . I had the happiness to command a Band of Brothers; therefore night was to my advantage. Each knew his duty, and I was sure that each would feel for a French ship. By attacking the enemy's van and centre, the wind blowing directly along their Line, I was enabled to throw what force I pleased on a few ships, and we always kept a superior force to the enemy. At 28 minutes pas six, the sun in the horizon, the firing commenced. At 5 minutes past ten, when L'Orient blew up, having burnt 70 minutes, the six Van ships had surrendered. I then pressed further towards the Rear; and had it pleased God that I had not been wounded and stone blind, there cannot be a doubt but that every ship would have been in our possession. . . .

The welcome given to Nelson at Naples was overwhelming: King Ferdinand sailed out in his gilt state galley to meet him and the population went wild with enthusiasm. Nelson knew what to expect from a letter Emma had sent him.

14

EMMA DRESSES 'ALLA NELSON'

Emma, Lady Hamilton (1761–1815), wife of the British envoy, 'delerious with joy' urges Nelson, the 'Savour of Itali', to come soon to be embraced and describes the transports of the Queen.

---

11 O. Warner, *Battle of the Nile*, Batsford, 1960, p. 110.

Naples, September 8, 1798

My dear, dear Sir,

How shall I begin, what shall I say to you. 'tis impossible I can write, for I am delerious with joy, and assure you I have a fevour caused by the agitation and pleasure. God, what a victory! Never, never has there ever been anything half so glorious, so compleat. I fainted when I heard the joyful news, and fell on my side and am hurt, but now well of that, I shou'd feil it a glory to die in such a cause. No, I wou'd not like to die till I see and embrace the Victor of the *Nile*. How shall I describe to you the transports of Maria Carolina, 'tis not possible. She fainted and kissed her husband, her children, walked about the room, cried, kissed, and embraced every person near her, exclaiming, *Oh, brave Nelson, oh, God bless and protect our brave deliverer, oh, Nelson, Nelson, what do we not owe to you, oh Victor, Savour of Itali, oh, that my swolen heart cou'd now tell him personally what we owe to him!*

The Neapolitans are mad with joy, and if you wos here now, you wou'd be killed with kindness. Sonets on sonets, illuminations, rejoicings; not a French dog dare shew his face. How I glory in the honner of my Country and my *Countryman*! I walk and tread in air with pride, feiling I was born in the same land with the victor Nelson and his gallant band. But no more, I cannot, dare not, trust myself, for I am not well. . . .

I wish you cou'd have seen our house the three nights of illumination. 'Tis, 'twas covered with your glorious name. Their were three thousand lamps, and their shou'd have been three millions if we had had time. . . . Sir William is ten years younger since the happy news. How he glories in you when your name is mentioned. He cannot contain his joy. For God's sake come to Naples soon. . . . I wou'd have been rather an English powder-monkey, or a swab in that great victory, than an Emperor out of it. . . .

Your ever sincere and oblidged friend,
Emma Hamilton

My dress from head to foot is alla Nelson. Even my shawl is in Blue with gold anchors all over. My earrings are Nelson's anchors; in short, we are be-Nelsoned all over.

About Nelson's peerage Emma wrote:

If I was King of England I would make you the most noble, puissant Duke Nelson, Marquis Nile, Earl Alexandria, Viscount Pyramid, Baron Crocodile, and Prince Victory.

Nelson was clearly flattered and delighted by such a reception.

15

'Nostro Liberatore'

Nelson describes to his wife how Emma fell into his arm and how he was fêted in Naples.

September 25th, 1798

My dearest Fanny,

The poor wretched *Vanguard* arrived here on the 22nd of September. I must endeavour to convey to you something of what passed; but if it were so affecting to those who were only united to me by bonds of friendship, what must it be to my dearest wife, my friend, my everything which is most dear to me in this world?[12] Sir William and Lady Hamilton came out to sea, attended by numerous Boats. My most respectable friends had really been laid up and seriously ill, first from anxiety and then from joy. It was imprudently told Lady Hamilton in a moment, and the effect was like a shot; she fell apparently dead, and is not yet perfectly recovered from severe bruises.

The scene in the boat was terribly affecting; up flew her Ladyship, and exclaiming, 'O God, is it possible?' she fell into my arm more dead than alive. Tears, however, soon set matters to rights; when alongside came the King. The scene was, in its way, as interesting; he took me by the hand, calling me his 'Deliverer and Preserver', with every other expression of kindness. In short, all Naples calls me 'Nostro Liberatore'; my greeting from the lower Classes was truly affecting. I hope some day to have the pleasure of introducing you to Lady Hamilton, she is one of the very best women in this world; she is an honour to her sex, and a proof that even reputations may be regained,[13] but I own it requires a good soul. Her kindness with Sir William to me is more than I can express; I am in their house. Lady Hamilton intends writing to you. May God Almighty bless you, my dearest Fanny, and give us in due time a happy meeting.

Ever your most affectionate husband,
Horatio Nelson

Intoxicated by popular enthusiasm, and urged on by Maria Carolina who was burning to avenge her sister Marie Antoinette, Ferdinand surprised the French by rushing his troops to Rome for a triumphal entry; however, when they came face to face with a French army a quarter of their number, they ran away after a few shots. The French took Naples, acclaimed in their turn by the populace, and Nelson had to escort the 'Court of fiddlers and harlots', as he called it, across a stormy sea on their flight to Palermo at Christmas; there, he lingered with Emma in open disobedience of Admiralty orders. In a despondent mood, he wrote: 'My task is done, my health is finished, and probably my retreat for ever fixed', but he still remained eager to do battle with the French.

---

12   He seemed to forget her thereafter, writing only much later and less affectionately.
13   He is referring to her past as a kept woman with two illegitimate children, at one time possibly a bar-maid and street-walker.

Among those who had sent congratulations was the wife of the First Lord of the Admiralty, a brilliant socialite, who used to call Nelson her 'bulldog', and, like Emma, had fainted on hearing of his victory.

16

'Immortalized Nelson'

Lavinia Countess Spencer showers her admiration on Nelson.

> Admiralty, 2 Oct. 1798

Joy, joy, joy to you, brave, gallant, immortalized Nelson! May that great God, whose cause you so valiantly support, protect and bless you to the end of your brilliant career! Such a race surely never was run. My heart is absolutely bursting with different sensations of joy, of gratitude, of pride, of every emotion that ever warmed the bosom of a British woman, on hearing of her Country's glory – and all produced by you, my dear, my good friend. All, all I *can* say must fall short of my wishes, of my sentiments about you. This moment the guns are firing, illuminations are preparing, your gallant name is echoed from street to street, and every Briton feels his obligations to you weighing him down. . . . I am half mad. Almighty God protect you! Adieu!

The wife of the President of the Royal Society describes their own special celebration of the event.

17

BEEF, PLUM PUDDING AND PUNCH FOR THE LABOURERS

Dorothea, Lady Banks to Miss Heber.

> Oct. 4th, 1798

. . . What a glorious Victory: it is nobly done indeed and makes all our Hearts glad. As we wish'd to have a little Festivity to celebrate, we had a Treat in the Evening. Besides all our Domestics, we invited the Labourers we usually employ, and their Wives, and gave them some Beef and Plum Pudding and Punch in the Servants' Hall, and they had a Dance in the Barn. We went to visit them and sang God save the King and Rule, Britannia, in which they all most heartily joined in chorus. . . .

The Battle of Copenhagen

Nelson's letter to Emma, written in a vein of true chivalry shortly before sailing for Copenhagen, may serve as a preamble to his next heroic exploit. It shows his dependence on the boundless hero-worship of women which Emma, better than any, knew how to supply.

18

'None but the brave deserve the fair!'

Lord Nelson to Lady Hamilton.

San Josef, February 8th, 1801

My dear Lady,

I am not in very good spirits; and, except that our country demands all our services and abilities, to bring about an honourable peace, nothing should prevent my being the bearer of my own letter. But, my dear friend, I know you are so true and loyal an Englishwoman, that you would hate those who would not stand forth in defence of our King, Laws, Religion and all which is dear to us.

It is your sex that makes us go forth; and seem to tell us – 'None but the brave deserve the fair!' and if we all fall, we still live in the hearts of those females who are dear to us. It is your sex that rewards us; it is your sex who cherish our memories. And you, my dear honoured friend, are, believe me, the *first*, the best, of your sex. I have been the world around, and in every corner of it, and never yet saw your equal, or even one which could be put in comparison with you. You know how to reward virtue, honour, and courage; and never to ask if it is placed in a Prince, Duke, Lord, or peasant: and I hope, one day, to see you, in peace, before I set out for Bronte, which I am resolved to do.

With the greatest truth, my dear Lady, your most obliged and affectionate friend,

NELSON & BRONTE

A few weeks later, he wrote to her of a simpler purpose, more befitting a rector's son:

> Cheer up, fair Emma! Peace in a cottage with a plain joint of meat, doing good to the poor and setting an example of virtue, even to King and princes.[14]

Britain imposed a blockade on the continent to disrupt French trade, but the neutral countries resented their ships being searched at sea, and, under French pressure, Russia, Sweden and Denmark formed the Northern League in December 1800. Admiral Sir Hyde Parker, with Nelson as his second-in-command, was sent to the Baltic with twenty-six ships of the line to prevent the assembly of a powerful Baltic fleet of potentially eighty-eight ships, by requesting the Danes to lease their fleet to England. When the ultimatum was rejected, Copenhagen harbour and the eighteen warships anchored there were bombarded; twelve of them were taken and three sunk. The coalition broke up.

---

14   C. Oman, *Nelson*, Hodder & Stoughton, 1947, p. 374.

In the action, Nelson again proved his ability to achieve victory by unexpected daring, regardless of loss of life. When, after slipping inside the harbour with eleven ships, he got battered by heavy gunfire from the fort commanding the entrance, Parker signalled him to withdraw, which would have been fatal. Nelson put his telescope to his blind eye, saying 'I really do not see a signal' and ignored the order. Then he started truce negotiations with the Regent – ostensibly to save the crews of the captured Danish ships from the cross-fire – which enabled his ships to escape destruction from the fortress guns and get away safely with his prizes. Nelson's second-in-command describes how desperately close the battle was.

19

'Our little Hero'

Rear-Admiral Thomas Graves (1747–1814) tells his brother about the action.

Off Copenhagen, April 3rd 1801

Yesterday was an awful day for the town of Copenhagen. 11 sail of our ships under the command of Lord Nelson attacked the floating batteries, ships, gun-vessels, and their works on shore, which lasted five hours, with as many hard blows and as much obstinacy as has ever been known, and with great loss on both sides, but finally ended in a complete overthrow of their outer defence. We have now 11 sail of their vessels in our possession. Two ran on shore, one sank, and one was blown up in action. It was certainly a most gallant defence, and words cannot speak too high of the boldness of the attack, considering all the difficulties we had to struggle with, and their great superiority in number and weight of guns. I think we were playing a losing game in attacking stone walls, and I fear we shall not have much to boast of when it is known what our ships suffered, and the little impression we made on their navy.

It was worthy of our gallant and enterprising little Hero of the Nile. Nothing can exceed his spirit. Sir Hyde Parker made a signal to discontinue the action before we had been at it two hours, supposing that our ships would all be destroyed. But our little Hero gloriously said, 'I will not move till we are crowned with victory,' and he was right, for if we had discontinued the action before the enemy struck, we should have all got aground and been destroyed. . . .

One of Nelson's closest companions highly commends his truce offer at just the right moment to save his ships, and, moreover, be thanked for his humanity.

20

NELSON IS ACCLAIMED BY THE ENEMY

Captain (later a baronet, vice-admiral and First Sea Lord) Thomas Hardy (1769–1839) praises to his brother-in-law, Mr Manfield, Nelson's political sense.

St George, Copenhagen Road, April 5th, 1801

. . . The more I see of his Lordship the more I admire his great character, for, I think on this occasion his Political management *was*, if *possible*, greater than his Bravery. The water was so shoal that two of the Line of Battle Ships got on shore before the action commenced, a third owing to the current and light winds was not able to get into Action, and his Lordship, finding his little squadron very hard pressed by the Batteries after the ships had struck, the wind not sufficient to take off his Prizes and crippled ships, he very deliberately sent a Flag of Truce on shore to say that his orders were *not* to *Destroy* the City of Copenhagen, therefore, to save more effusion of blood he would grant them a *truce* and land their wounded as soon as possible. The Prince thanked him for his great humanity and entered into a negotiation that moment which allowed him to get off all the Prizes that were not sunk or burnt, and his own ships, five of which at this time were on shore within gunshot of the Batteries.

His Lordship and myself were on shore yesterday, where, extraordinary to be told, he was received with as much acclamation as when we went to *Lord Mayor's Show*, and I really believe it would not have been a very hard business to have brought on a revolution in Denmark. We dined with all the Court, and after Dinner he had an audience with the Crown Prince for more than two hours, and I will venture to say that his Royal Highness never had so much plain truth spoken to him in his life. . . .

Nelson himself rejects the *ruse de guerre* interpretation generally given to his truce offer and claims his motive had indeed been pure humanity. He had a remarkable ability for dressing up interest as virtue, with complete conviction.

21

'RUSE DE GUERRE' OR HUMANITY?

Nelson gives Prime Minister Henry Addington his reason for sending a flag of truce on shore at Copenhagen.

8 May 1801

As both my friends and enemies seem not to know why I sent on shore a flag of truce – the former, many of them, thought it was a *ruse de guerre*, and not quite justifiable; the latter, I believe, attributed it to a desire to have no more fighting, and few, very few, to the cause that I felt, and which, I trust in God, I shall retain to the last moment, *humanity*. I know it must to the world be proved, and therefore I will suppose you all the world to me. First, no ship was on shore near the Crown batteries, or anywhere else, within reach of any shore, when my flag of truce went on shore. The Crown batteries, and the batteries on Armak and in the dockyard, were firing at us, one-half their shot necessarily striking the ships who had surrendered, and our fire did the same, and worse, for the surrendered ships had four of them got close together, and it was a massacre. This caused my note. It was a sight which no real man could have enjoyed. I felt when the Danes became my prisoners, I became their protector; and if that had not been a sufficient reason, the moment of a complete victory was surely the proper time to make an opening with the nation we had been fighting with. . . .

Epilogue

In the letters of this chapter we could discern some of the characteristics which single out Nelson as *the* English hero. First of all, he was a brilliant tactician and organizer, a born leader, trusted and loved by all, and followed blindly in the most dangerous operations. He transmitted to his men a burning passion for victory, and his invariably kind concern for them won him their devotion. His courage was not only unfailing but conspicuous when he exposed himself as a target by wearing all his glittering decorations. He was the champion of the English tradition of swift and daring attack and skilful mobility of seamanship in face of whatever odds, wresting success from the most unpromising situation through implicit trust in himself and his 'band of brothers'. He had the efficiency of Jervis without his foul temper and severity which made him disliked, and the proficiency and steadiness of Howe, 'undaunted as a rock and as silent' (Walpole), which made him respected, without the unsmiling distance of 'Black Dick'. In short, he had all the characteristics which made him worshipped as the hero *sans reproche* by many generations of Englishmen. The shy frail youth had blossomed out with the radiance of glory, his prime object in life, which electrified the nation and was reflected back on him in turn, spurring him on to further spectacular exploits. His heroic stature was enhanced by his physical handicaps: already small and delicate, he became one-eyed and one-armed, but kept on professing that 'not a scrap of that ardour with which I have hitherto served our King has been shot away'.

To consecrate the image of the hero of English legend two more elements are essential, at least in the Romantic, pre-Victorian age: he has to be killed at the height of his fame,[15] and have a spectacular love-affair – Trafalgar and Emma supplied both. The first falls into the next chapter, but Nelson's infatuation with Emma began after the battle of the Nile and was consummated when he begot their daughter Horatia in the *Foudroyant* – and promptly suffered a heart attack. A few months later, the trio went on a continental tour

15 Nelson was deeply impressed by Benjamin West's painting of Wolfe's death at Quebec.

during which Emma sang the Nelson-aria at the Esterhazy Palace in Vienna, accompanied by old Papa Haydn, and then they settled down in a *'ménage à trois'* at Merton Place, Surrey: Nelson lingering between passion and duty, amiable, complaisant Sir William professing to believe in the 'purity of Lord Nelson's friendship for Emma and me' and calling him 'the most virtuous, loyal and truly brave character', and Emma 'cramming Nelson with trowelfuls of flattery, which he goes on taking as quietly as a child is under pap'.[16] Her flamboyant effusions provided the drug his boundless vanity craved for. Yet he had once contritely written to Fanny when he nearly perished in a storm in 1798: 'I believe firmly it was the Almighty's goodness to check my consummate vanity. I feel confident it has made me a better man,' and later, humbly, to Emma: 'I am now perfectly the great man – not a creature near me. From my heart I wish myself the little man again.' Sometimes the heroics must have been a strain to him.

Earlier, Nelson had not been blind to the flaws in his character, when he wrote to Fanny a year before their marriage, in 1786:

> You are too good and indulgent. My whole life shall ever be devoted to make you completely happy, whatever whims may sometimes take me. We are none of us perfect, and myself probably much less so than you deserve.

Six months later he felt 'a moral certainty' that his sentiments for her would never change. However, after the birth of Horatia he would address Emma as 'My own dear wife, you and my country are the two dearest objects of my fond heart,' and dismiss his wife with a curt note: 'My only wish is to be left to myself; and wishing you every happiness, etc.' He remained deaf to Fanny's letter after Copenhagen and did not even read her pathetic appeals.

22

FANNY'S LAST PLEAS

Frances Lady Nelson (1761–1831) entreats her husband to come back to her.

[July 1801]

My dear husband,

I can't be silent in the general joy throughout the Kingdom. I must express my thankfulness and happiness it hath pleased God to spare your life. . . . What my feelings are, your own good heart will tell you. Let me beg, nay intreat you to believe no Wife

---

16 Lord Minto, writing in March 1802, quoted in Oman, op. cit, p. 434.

ever felt greater affection for a husband than I do, and to the best of my knowledge I have invariably done everything you desire. If I have omitted anything I am sorry for it. . . .

[Christmas]

. . . I now have to offer for your accommodation, a comfortable warm House. Do, my Dear Husband, let us live together. I assure you again I have but one wish in the world, To please you. Let everything be buried in oblivion. It will pass away like a dream. I can only now intreat you to believe I am, most sincerely and affectionately,

Your wife,
Frances H. Nelson

Nelson's infatuation with Emma was linked to the heroic posturing of glory and the enticing vulgarities of adulation which made it impossible for him to go back to a life of simple values. For that life, with his religious upbringing, he sometimes seems to have been longing: he became the prisoner of his own legend and had to act it out to the end.

The War with the French Empire (1803–15)

No parleying now. In Britain is one breath;
'tis victory or death!
WILLIAM WORDSWORTH (OCTOBER 1803)

After a mere fifteen months of peace, war broke out again in May 1803. Britain was suspicious of Napoleon's expansionist intentions once he had consolidated his empire and he refused to grant a commercial treaty; on the other hand, the continued British occupation of Malta was clearly in breach of the Treaty of Amiens – Napoleon and the first British empire just could not coexist. Britain had before been allied to the effete old social order in Europe against the new forces of Revolutionary France, but now a new nationalist spirit of resistance to French domination was beginning to grow everywhere. Britain, however, re-entered the war without any of the eagerness aroused by the revulsion against the horrors of Jacobin rule: the country wanted peace.

On the Home Front

Invaders should – bite at the dust,
But not a bit more of the island!
THOMAS DIBDIN, THE SNUG LITTLE ISLAND

Everybody was weary of war. Reluctantly and without enthusiasm, however, people were getting ready to give the service required of them and to stand grimly firm.

1

NO BOYISH PRATING BUT SULKY MANFULNESS

Francis Jeffrey (1773–1850), critic and later Lord Advocate, writing to his brother, deplores the insanity of going to war; he enlisted all the same.

Edinburgh: July 2, 1803

. . . We are all in great horror about the war here, though not half so much afraid as we ought to be. For my part I am often in absolute despair, and wish I were fairly piked, and done with it. It is most clearly and unequivocally a war of our own seeking, and an offensive war upon our part, though we have no means of offending, and in the present state and temper of Europe, I own it appears to me like insanity, There is but one ground upon which our conduct can be justified. If we are perfectly certain that France is to go to war with us, and will infallibly take some opportunity to do it with greater advantage in a year or two, there may be some prudence in being beforehand with her, and open the unequal contest in our own way. . . . In the meantime we must all turn out, I fancy, and do our best. There is a corps of riflemen raising, in which I shall probably have a company. I hate the business of war, and despise the parade of it; but we must submit to both for a while. I am happy to observe that there is little of that boyish prating about uniforms, and strutting in helmets, that distinguished our former arming. We look sulky now, and manful, I think.

The admiral's widow regrets that the French don't prefer the cash of upper-class English visitors to the guns of the admirals.

2

TOURISM, NOT WAR

Mrs Boscawen, writing to her cousin, laments over the pro-war motion of Parliament.

24th May, 1803

Yes, my dear *Cousine*, we regret the Peace. You know how heartily and sincerely we rejoiced over it. Yet the H. of Commons was unanimous last night, and if we should have a French visit it will surely find an English welcome; and even our women melting their leaden pipes into balls and bullets to supply our guns and pistols.

Alas, how I lament all this, which I had not once apprehended, concluding the sensible French would greatly prefer all our *bon ton riches* in the middle of Paris to the Admirals Howe, Jervis, Duncan, Nelson in the middle of the Ocean. It is calculated that our folks have spent a million sterling in Paris this winter. Pity to stop them.

This day was published,

AN

ADDRESS to the PEOPLE

OF THE UNITED KINGDOM OF

Great Britain and Ireland,

ON THE THREATENED

I N V A S I O N.

EXTRACTS FROM THE ABOVE WORK.

AMONG the inexpressibly dreadful consequences which are sure to attend the conquest of your Island by the French, there is one of so horrible a nature, as to deserve distinct notice. This barbarous, but most artful people, when first they invade a country in the conquest of which they apprehend any difficulty, in order to obtain the confidence of the people, compel their troops to observe the strictest discipline, and often put a soldier to death for stealing the most trifling article. Like spiders they artfully weave a web round their victim, before they begin to prey upon it. But when their success is complete they then let loose their troops, with resistless fury, to commit the most horrible excesses, and to pillage, burn, and desolate, without mercy, and without distinction. But the practice to which I particularly allude will make your blood freeze in your veins. These wretches are accustomed, whenever they prevail, to subject the women to the most brutal violence, which they perpetrate with an insulting ferocity, of which the wildest savages would be incapable. To gratify their furious passions is not however their chief object in these atrocities. Their principal delight is to shock the feelings of fathers and brothers, and husbands! Will you, my Countrymen, while you can draw a trigger, or handle a pike, suffer your daughters, your sisters, and wives, to fall into the power of such monsters?

Specimens of French Ferocity and Brutality in Wales.

It is well known that in the last War some French troops succeeded in effecting a landing in Wales. They were greatly superior to the regular force which happened to be in the part of the country where they landed: but, upon seeing, at a distance, a number of Welsh women with red cloaks, whom they mistook for soldiers, they surrendered! The following proofs of their ferocity and brutality are well attested.

A peasant whom they had compelled to assist them in landing their stores, presumed to ask for some compensation, upon which the commanding Officer drew a pistol, and SHOT THE POOR FELLOW THROUGH THE HEART.

Two Officers went to a house, in which was a woman in child-bed, attended by her mother, who was upwards of Seventy Years old. The French brutes tied the husband with cords, and, in his presence, defiled both the wife and the mother!!!

LONDON
Printed by H. Bryer, Bridewell Hospital, Bridge Street.

The Address is sold by J. DOWNES, Temple Bar; J. SPRAGG, King Street Covent Garden; J. ASPERNE, Cornhill; and J. HATCHARD, Piccadilly.
Price Two-pence each, or Twelve Shillings the Hundred, and Eighteen-pence per Dozen.

Advertisement of a twopenny booklet published by four London booksellers in 1803.

Plans for Napoleon's invasion of England. (*Bibliothèque Nationale, Paris*)

Napoleon aimed at turning Europe against Britain and subduing her through invasion. He thought if the Navy could be kept away or at bay for a few hours, a French army of 200,000 could be shipped over the Channel in 1,700 barges and occupy the West Country. He devised elaborate decoy operations to lure the Navy to the West Indies on a wild goose chase, by sending the Toulon and Brest fleets there for a rendezvous, but Nelson, Collingwood and Cornwallis always kept close to French heels. In the meantime, home defence was organized, and even if invasion had ever succeeded, it would seem highly doubtful whether the French forces could have been maintained without naval command of the Channel.

In the following letter a girl is perplexed by the confusion the expectation of a French invasion is causing.

3

EVACUATION

Jane Taylor complains to her mother about the discomforts.

[Lavenham, October 1803]
. . . Thank you for the carpet: it is quite a luxury to us, though, if we were all huddled together in a barn, expecting the French to overtake us every instant, we might be very well contented with

> An open broken elbow chair;
> A caudle cup without an ear; &c.,

yet we rather miss the conveniences we have been used to. . . .

Could you see us just now, I cannot tell whether you would most laugh at, or pity us. I am sitting in the middle of the room, surrounded with beds, chairs, tables, boxes, &c.; and every room is the same. But our brains are in still greater confusion – not knowing now what to do. Have you heard this new alarm? It is said the French are actually embarking: so we are quite perplexed. We have at length resolved to wait; but in the meantime, we shall be in the most delightful plight, for most of the things are packed up, ready to go to-morrow; and then if, after all, we must stay, it will be vexatious enough. If you find there is no foundation for the alarm, you will, of course, order us home directly. But do not fail to write, for we are quite deplorable. . . .

Pamphlets indulged in lurid descriptions of how the ferocious French savages were intent on brutally raping the women of Britain, and, by these atrocity stories, incited husbands, fathers and brothers to rush to arms in their defence. Similarly James Gillray's prints depicted 'French troops barbarously slaughtering the inhabitants of London, and Pitt bound ready for execution'. While massive Martello towers were being erected on the deserted invasion beaches, women paraded in fashionable green velvet 'rifle' dresses and clamoured to take up arms.[1] They were unafraid and defiant, and sceptical of Bonaparte's chances of success:

> It is a moment to inspire all dispositions & characters with Military ardour. I cannot say I have yet caught any of the terrors of Invasion. I do not feel that Bonaparte will make the attempt, & certainly not that he will ever succeed. I believe the spirit of preparation against him, which has so properly pervaded the whole kingdom, has made the proud Tyrant pause in awe of us.[2]

William Pitt, temporarily out of office and always the champion of firm war measures, devoted himself to the arduous training of volunteers and militia despite failing health. Worn out by the burden, worries and disappointments of twenty-two years as Prime Minister, he died two years later at the age of forty-six. The beautiful eccentric daughter of the Earl of Stanhope kept house for her uncle during the last years of his life and was his confidante; she also shared his military command.

4

PITT AS DRILL-SERGEANT AND HIS NIECE AS DRAGOON COMMANDER

Lady Hester Stanhope (1776–1839) describes their army duties to Mr Jackson, British minister in Berlin.

Walmer Castle, November 19th, 1803

At a moment when every free-born Englishman should exert himself in the defence of his country, Mr Pitt absolutely goes through the fatigue of a *drill-sergeant*. It is parade after parade, at 15 or 20 miles distant from each other. I often attend him, and it is quite as much (I can assure you) as I am equal to, although I am *remarkably* well just now. The hard riding I do not mind, but to remain almost *still* so many hours on horseback is an incomprehensible bore, and requires more patience than you can easily imagine. If Mr Pitt does not overdo it and injure his health every other consideration becomes trifling. . . . He is determined to remain acting Colonel when his regiment is called into the field. Some persons blame this determination, but I do not. He has always hitherto acted up to his character. Why should he then in this instance prove deficient? I should not be the least surprised any night to hear of the French attempting to land. Indeed, I expect it. But I feel equally certain that those who do succeed will neither proceed nor return. . . .

---

1 I.F. Clarke, *Voices Prophesying War*, OUP, 1966, p. 18 ff, and C. Emsley, *British Society and French Wars*, Macmillan, 1979, p. 112 ff, respectively.
2 Miss Iremonger, 5 Dec. 1803, *Heber Correspondence*, p. 223.

January 14th, 1804

We are in almost daily expectation of the coming of the French, and Mr Pitt's regiment is now nearly *perfect* enough to receive them. We have the famous 15th Light Dragoons in our barracks; also the Northampton and Berkshire Militia. The first and last of these I command, and have an orderly dragoon whenever I please from the former, and the band of the latter. . . . Bonaparte was said to be at Boulogne a few days ago; the officers patrolled all night with the men, which was pleasant. I have my orders how to act in case of real alarm in Mr Pitt's absence. I should break my heart to be driven up the country like a sheep when everything I most love was in danger. In short, I *would not*.

While many volunteered to defend their home soil against invasion, the rapidly expanding Navy, which had only just recovered from the mutinies, was always short of volunteers: press-gangs armed with cutlasses roamed round the ports and terrorized merchant seamen in their ships, in the streets, in ale-houses and even right up to church doors.

5

'A groan for the kidnapper!'

Commander William Cathcart (1782–1804), who had joined the Navy at the age of thirteen from Eton and was to die of yellow fever at twenty-two, describes to his father, Lieutenant-General Lord Cathcart, how he procured men in Ireland.

Le Renard, Waterford: 20th March, 1803

Having received orders to press, I kept the whole a profound secret. At dark I walked up the barracks, requested a captain's picquet to hold themselves in readiness, and ordered the guards to be reinforced. The vessels all lay in tiers off the quay of Waterford, with a gang-board to the shore. At 11 I landed the marines under their sergeant, with orders to post a sentinel at each gang-board and to patrol up and down the quay. At 12 I sent my three boats. The seamen gave the alarm from one vessel to the other and tried to escape, but were, to their astonishment, saluted with a charged bayonet by the marine at the gang-board and driven back. In four hours with three boats I had 140 men pressed. I was employed the next three days examining affidavits, liberating first mates, apprentices, sick and maimed men; so that out of 140 I only could keep 65 men fit for the service.

Last Thursday I had a narrow escape. I was pressing in the houses at night, mostly inhabited by butchers. I was informed that, armed with cleavers, knives, pikes, &c., they, to the number of 150, waylaid me, and I only escaped by going a different way down. They have sworn to do me out, as the term is here. I now live entirely on board, never being on shore except in the forenoon. I am then pelted and hissed. The expression is, 'A groan for the kidnapper!' I hope to God I shall soon be released from this state of drudgery. . . .

Having so many dissatisfied people on board, I loaded my two after guns with case shot and pointed them forwards, cause the officers to watch with their side-arms on, have four sentinels planted, and do not allow but one of them to come up at a time after sunset. I have one potato-digger in irons for abusing grossly one of the officers and saying, 'The boys were preparing their pikes to upset tyranny.' He is very drunk. Adieu!

The King, tenacious and patriotic, shows his moral and physical courage in face of the French threat; his periodic mental collapses finally led to his confinement.

6

THE SIXTY-SIX-YEAR-OLD KING WANTS TO LEAD HIS ARMY

George III tells his friend Richard Hurd, Bishop of Worcester,[3] about his plans for evacuating his family.

Windsor, November 30th, 1803

We are here in daily expectation that Bonaparte will attempt his threatened invasion; the chances against his success seem so many that it is wonderful he persists in it. I own I place that thorough dependence on Divine Providence that I cannot help thinking the usurper is encouraged to make the trial that the ill-success may put an end to his wicked purposes. Should his troops effect a landing, I shall certainly put myself at the head of my troops and my other armed subjects to repel them. But as it is impossible to foresee the events of such a conflict, should the enemy approach too near to Windsor, I shall think it right the Queen and my daughters should cross the Severn, and send them to your Episcopal Palace at Worcester. I certainly would rather have what I value most in life remain, during the conflict, in your diocese and under your roof than in any other place in the island.

The general who wrote the following letter rants against ministers' information, newspaper stories, and irksome inaction. He was to get plenty of action on the retreat to Corunna four years later.

7

MOORE DOES NOT BELIEVE IN INVASION

Lieutenant-General Sir John Moore (1761–1809) gives Mr Creevey a sober assessment of the situation.

Sandgate, 27th Aug., 1804

. . . We understand that Government have positive information that we are to be invaded, and I am told that Pitt believes it. The experience of the last 12 months has

---

3   Hurd's *Letters on Chivalry and Romance* (1762) had helped to initiate the Romantic movement.

taught me to place little confidence in the information or belief of Ministers, and as the undertaking seems to me so arduous, and offering so little prospect of success, I cannot persuade myself that Bonaparte will be mad enough to attempt it. He will continue to threaten, by which means alone he can do us harm. The invasion would, I am confident, end in our glory and in his disgrace.

The newspapers continue to mention secret expeditions, and have sometimes named me as one of the Generals to be employed. I put these upon a par with the invasion. We have at present no disposable force, and, if we had, I see no object worthy upon which to risk it. Thus, without belief in invasion or foreign expeditions, my situation here becomes daily more irksome, and I am almost reduced to wish for peace. I am tired of the confinement, without the occupation, of war.

Portentous new devices of warfare agitated the minds of inventors: after Fulton's steamships and 'plunging boats' armed with torpedoes, Congreve invented rockets which were used to batter the French invasion fleet. Some of the rockets were 'carcases', others were headed with shells filled with musket balls to burst in the air like shrapnel, both with a strong fire quantity.[4]

8

ROCKET ATTACK ON THE BOULOGNE FLOTILLA

William Congreve (1772–1828) who later succeeded his father as baronet and Comptroller of the Royal Laboratory at Woolwich, gives full technical details to Lord Thomas Grenville, First Lord of the Admiralty.

Dover, October 12, 1806
. . . The force consisted of 24 six-oared cutters, each carrying a frame for discharging two rockets at a time. They were assembled alongside the Clyde at nine o'clock in the evening. The boats were therefore able to approach very near the shore without being perceived till the first volley was fired – their astonishment must have been unparalleled – to see so many shells, as they must have supposed them to be, in the air at once without the reports of ordnance – and in fact, Sir, such was the consternation which appears to have prevailed, that tho' the drum was heard beating to arms for upwards of three hours not a shot was fired from the shore.

After a few rounds it was discovered that the place was on fire and that it burnt very fiercely in that quarter where the principal store houses were known to be;

---

4 The physician and scientist Dr Erasmus Darwin, Charles' grandfather and author of the first version of evolutionism, saw even further as early as 1791 (quoted by Clarke, op. cit.):

> Soon shall thy arm, UNCONQUER'D STEAM! afar
> Drag the slow barge, or drive the rapid car;
> Or on wide-waving wings expanded bear
> The flying-chariot through the field of air.

likewise some of the shipping must have been burnt. All our ammunition was expended without receiving a single shot from the enemy. The success of this attack has been very important, – the chimerical invulnerability of Boulogne is exploded. . . .

The enemy must be still in the dark as to the precise application of the means & mode of attack; and every precaution has been taken to prevent that publicity to them, which might open his eyes – which is certainly important, as far as it tends to increase consternation.

P.S. The number of rockets thrown was about 400 in less than half an hour.[5]

Trafalgar

And in the midst of glory died our brave Nelson
ANON. (1805)

This most famous of all English sea battles spelt the apotheosis of the English hero: a victory which established unchallenged naval domination for over a century, was won through Nelson's tactical genius, bold daring and the inspiration of brotherhood, glorified by the sacrifice of his life, into which a legendary love story was woven.

Villeneuve with the Toulon fleet, pursued by Nelson across the Atlantic, had taken refuge at Cádiz; outside, Vice-Admiral Collingwood was lying in wait. Relying on better seamanship and quicker and more accurate gunnery, Nelson issued the famous 'Nelson touch' memorandum in which he laid down the tactics for annihilating the enemy, as opposed to mere victory, by striking with superior force at the rear while cutting off the van.

His pride stung by Napoleon deriding him as a coward for seeking shelter at Cádiz, Villeneuve, against his better judgement, obeyed the order to come out and offer Nelson the long-sought opportunity for battle. Collingwood, with fifteen ships, created a gap with his flag ship *Royal Sovereign* in the rear of the Franco-Spanish fleet of thirty-three ships, while Nelson in the *Victory* led his twelve ships down the line of the van and attacked the centre next to Villeneuve's flag ship *Bucentaure*. The gallant, close-range stand of the *Redoutable*, in whose rigging the *Victory's* foreyard got intertwined, prevented Nelson from penetrating the line and cutting them off, but twenty ships, with Villeneuve himself, were captured or sunk, for no loss:

Everything seemed as if by enchantment to prosper under his direction: but it was the effect of system, and nice combination, not of chance,

5   Rockets were also used in 1807 in the Dardanelles, and at Copenhagen, on the north coast of Spain and at the battles of Leipzig and Waterloo (two rocket troops as part of artillery). They always caused greater terror than damage and fell out of favour after 1860, only to be revived with a vengeance by Hitler. (*Naval Miscellany*, IV, 1952, VIII, p. 447 ff.)

wrote Collingwood.[6] The great victory was bought at a heavy price: Nelson, conspicuous with his four shining orders of knighthood, was shot through the lungs and spine by a marksman on the mizen-top and fell into the arms of Captain Hardy, exclaiming: 'They have done for me at last'. After three hours of agony during which he anxiously followed the battle, he expired in sight of victory with 'Thank God I have done my duty' on his lips. Never has an admiral been so beloved by all his sailors, who wept profusely at his death. Nelson has ever since remained the most popular hero in English history.

9

'If I fall'

Nelson forecasts the battle, with a feeling of premonition, to his friend Alexander Davison, the government contractor.[7]

Victory [30 September 1805]

Day by day, my dear friend, I am expecting the Fleet to put to sea – every day, hour, and moment; and you may rely that, if it is in the power of man to get at them, that it shall be done; and I am sure that all my brethren look to that day as the finish of our laborious cruise. The event no man can say exactly; but I must think, or render great injustice to those under me, that, let the battle be when it may, it will never have been surpassed. My shattered frame, if I survive that day, will require rest, and that is all I shall ask for. If I fall on such a glorious occasion, it shall be my pride to take care that my friends shall not blush for me. These things are in the hands of a wise and just Providence, and His will be done. I have got some trifle, thank God, to leave to those I hold most dear, and I have taken care not to neglect it. Do not think I am low-spirited on this account, or fancy any-thing is to happen to me; quite the contrary – my mind is calm, and I have only to think of destroying our inveterate foe. I have two Frigates gone for more informa-tion, and we all hope for a meeting with the Enemy. Nothing can be finer than the Fleet under my command. Whatever be the event, believe me ever, my dear Davison, your much obliged and sincere friend,

NELSON AND BRONTE

---

6   O. Warner, *Life & Letters of Collingwood*, OUP, 1966, p. 18 ff.
7   Later jailed for embezzlement.

10

FROM HORATIO'S LAST LETTERS TO EMMA

[Off Dunnose on the way to take command off Portugal]
September 16

My beloved Emma,

We have fair wind, and God will, I hope, soon grant us a happy meeting. May Heaven bless you and Horatia. For a short time, farewell, I intreat you, my dear Emma, that you will cheer up; and we will look forward to many, many happy years, and be surrounded by our children's children.

[On his return to the Fleet, 15–20 miles from Cádiz] 1st October
I believe my arrival was most welcome, and when I came to explain to them the 'Nelson touch', it was like an electric shock. Some shed tears, all approved – it was new – it was singular – it was simple! and, from Admirals downwards, it was repeated – 'it must succeed, if ever they will allow us to get at them! You are, my Lord, surrounded by friends, whom you inspire with confidence.'

[around mid-October]
I have not a thought except on you and the French fleet, all my thoughts, plans and toils tend to those two objects, and I will embrace them both so close when I can lay hold of either one or the other, that the Devil should not separate us.

Victory [off Cádiz], October 19th
MY DEAREST BELOVED EMMA, THE DEAR FRIEND OF MY BOSOM,

The Signal has been made that the Enemy's Combined Fleet are coming out of Port. We have very little wind, so that I have no hopes of seeing them before tomorrow. May the God of Battles crown my endeavours with success; at all events, I will take care that my name shall ever be most dear to you and Horatia, both of whom I love as much as my own life. And as my last writing before the Battle will be to you, so I hope in God that I shall live to finish my letter after the Battle. May heaven bless you prays your

NELSON AND BRONTE[8]

In his 'Last Codicil', with Hardy and Blackwod as witnesses, Nelson, on sighting the enemy fleet at day break, recommended Emma as a legacy to King and Country, and in his last pocket book entry, he added to his prayer for victory: 'May humanity after victory be the predominant feature in the

---

8   Nelson's last letter was found open on his desk after his death. Emma wrote on it: 'Oh miserable and wretched Emma, oh glorious and happy Nelson'. Although she had an income of £2,000 p.a., her extravagance landed her for a year in a debtors' prison from which she was released on bail and escaped to Calais; there, she died in poverty in her early fifties, ten years after Nelson.

British Fleet'. After his crew had intoned 'God save the King', 'Rule Britannia', and 'Britons strike home', Nelson said 'I'll now amuse the Fleet' and signalled 'England expects every man will do his duty', followed by 'Close Action'.[9]

11

'England expects . . .'

Captain (later Vice-Admiral Sir) Henry Blackwood (1770–1832), of the frigate *Euryalus*, writes to his wife straight after the battle.

October 22nd, 1 o'clock at night

The first hour since yesterday morning that I could call my own is now before me, to be devoted to my dearest wife, who, thank God, is not a husband out of pocket. My heart, however, is sad, and penetrated with the deepest anguish. A Victory, such a one as has never been achieved, yesterday took place in the course of five hours; but at such an expense, in the loss of the most gallant of men, and best of friends, as renders it to me a Victory I never wished to have witnessed – at least, on such terms. After performing wonders by his example and coolness, Lord Nelson was wounded by a French Sharpshooter, and died in three hours after, beloved and regretted in a way not to find example. . . . I never was so shocked or so completely upset as upon my flying to the *Victory*, even before the action was over, to find Lord Nelson was then at the gasp of death. His unfortunate decorations of innumerable stars, and his uncommon gallantry, was the cause of his death; and such an Admiral has the Country lost, and every officer and man, so kind, so good, so obliging a friend as never was. Thank God, he lived to know that such a Victory never was before gained. Almost all seemed as if inspired by the one common sentiment of conquer or die. The Enemy, to do them justice, were not less so: they fought in a way that must do them honour. Buonaparte, I firmly believe, forced them to sea to try his luck, and what it might procure him in a pitched battle. They had the flower of the Combined Fleet, and I hope it will convince Europe at large that he has not yet learnt enough to cope with the English at sea.

Lord Nelson has left cause for every man who had a heart never to forget him. . . . I stayed with him till the Enemy commenced their fire on the *Victory*, when he sent me off. He told me, at parting, we should meet no more; he made me witness his Will, and away I came, with a heart very sad. . . . Under Lord N. it seemed like inspiration; the last signal he made was such a one as would immortalize any man, 'England expects every officer and man will do their utmost duty.' The alacrity with which the individual Ships answered it, showed how entirely they entered into his feelings and ideas. Would to God he had lived to see his prizes, and the Admirals he has taken! three in all: amongst them, the French Commander-in-Chief, Villeneuve. . . .

9   Oman, op. cit., p. 542 ff.

12

'It was a grand but an awful sight'

Midshipman R.F. Roberts to his parents.

Victory, at Sea off Trafalgar, October 22nd

I have just time to tell you that we had a desperate engagement with the enemy, and, thank God, I have so far escaped unhurt. The Combined Fleet came out of Cadiz with a determination to engage and blow us up (as the prisoners say) out of the water, but they are much – very much – mistaken. . . .

It was as hard an action, as allowed by all on board ship, as ever was fought. There were but three left alive on the Quarterdeck, the enemy fired so much grape and small shot from the rigging, there was one ship so close to us that we could not run out our guns their proper length. Only conceive how much we must have smashed her, every gun was trebly shotted for her. We hvae a great many killed and danger-ously wounded – 21 amputations. . . .

This morning the enemy are out of sight and we have the prizes in tow, going for Gibraltar. The rascals have shot away our mizen mast, and we are much afraid of our main and fore-masts. The *Royal Sovereign* has not a stick standing – a total wreck. It was she that began the action in a noble manner, engaging four of them at the same time. Two of the enemy blew up and one sank. You can have no conception whatso-ever what an action between two fleets is; it was a grand but an awful sight indeed; thank God we are all so well over it.

Admiral Nelson was shot early in the action by a musket ball from the enemy's top, which struck him a little below the shoulder, touched the rib and lodged near his heart. He lived about two and a half hours after; then died without a groan. Every ship that struck, our fellows ceased firing and gave three cheers like Noble Britons. . . .

13

'Chaps that fought like the Devil, cry like a wench'

Sam, an ex-ploughman, tells his father how everyone wept for Nelson.

Royal Sovereign [n.d.]

Honoured Father,

This comes to tell you that I am alive and hearty except three fingers; but that's not much, it might have been my head. I told brother Tom I should like to see a greadly[10] battle, and I have seen one, and we have peppered the Combined rarely; and for mat-ter of that, they fought us pretty tightish for French and Spanish. Three of our mess

---

10   Or: gradely – real, proper.

are killed, and four more of us winged.[11] But to tell you the truth of it, when the game began, I wished myself at Warnborough with my plough again; but when they had given us one duster, and I found myself snug and tight, I set to in good earnest, and thought no more about being killed than if I were at Murrell Green Fair; and I was presently as busy and as black as a collier. How my fingers got knocked overboard I don't know; but off they are, and I never missed them till I wanted them. You see, by my writing, it was my left hand, so I can write to you and fight for my King yet. We have taken a rare parcel of ships, but the wind is so rough we cannot bring them home, else I should roll in money, so we are busy smashing 'em, and blowing 'em up wholesale.

Our dear Admiral Nelson is killed! so we have paid pretty sharply for licking 'em. I never set eyes on him, for which I am both sorry and glad; for, to be sure, I should like to have seen him – but then, all the men in our ship who have seen him are such soft toads, they have done nothing but blast their eyes, and cry, ever since he was killed. God bless you! chaps that fought like the Devil, sit down and cry like a wench. I am still in the *Royal Sovereign*, but the Admiral [Collingwood] has left her, for she is like a horse without a bridle, so he is in a frigate that he may be here and there and everywhere, for he's as *cute* as here and there one, and as bold as a lion, for all he can cry! – I saw his tears with my own eyes, when the boat hailed and said my lord was dead. . . .

14

ONLY NELSON 'EXCITED REAL ENTHUSIASM IN THE ENGLISH'

Lady Elizabeth Foster tells her son in America how the news of Trafalgar was received in London.

November 29

It was in vain, my dearest Augustus, to have written to you the first days of the news of the victory of Trafalgar, for nothing that I could have said would have conveyed to you any idea of the impression on the public made by the loss of their favourite hero. Great and wonderful as the victory was, the prevailing sentiment in each mind was sorrow, was grief, for Nelson. If it was the most flattering homage that could be paid to worth, to heroism like his, it was also an honour to the nation to feel as they did. When we arrived at the Admiralty it was crowded, but every countenance was dejected. . . . A man at the turnpike gate said 'Have you heard the bad news? We have taken 20 ships from the enemy, but Lord Nelson is killed.' Illuminations followed, but the first night, as if unable to rejoice, there were none seen but on the public buildings. The two next nights they were general, but chiefly transparencies or mottos relating to the 'dear departed hero'. Nelson was the only person I ever saw who excited real enthusiasm in the English. Every day makes his victory more precious.

---

11   Wounded.

15

'Raw pork and half a pint of wine'

J. Brown, HMS *Victory*, one of the sailors attending Nelson's funeral in the crypt of St Pauls, to T. Windever, publican at the Blue Bell, Liverpool.

Chatham, December 28

. . . There is 300 of us Pickt out to go to Lord Nelson Funral. We are to wear blue Jackets white Trowsers and a black scarf round our arms and hats, besides gold medal for the battle of Trafalgar Valued £7–1 round our necks. That I shall take care of until I take it home and Shew it to you. We scarce have room to move, the Ship is so full of Nobility coming down from London to see the Ship looking at shot holes.

The French and Spanish Fleets was like a great wood which cheered the hearts of every British tar in the *Victory* like lions Anxious to be at it. Lord Nelson went round the decks and said my Noble lads this will be a glorious day for England who ever lives to see it, I shant be satisfied with 12 Ships this day as I took at the Nile. So we piped to dinner and ate a bit of raw pork and half a pint of wine. . . .

I hope youl have a full bottle in the bar for me to have a toothful for you may depend that I will break the bell ropes I will pull so hearty for its a long time since I had a good toothful. . . .[12]

Lord Collingwood, Nelson's successor, was a dark, lonely figure, equally steadfast and courageous, and concerned for his men, but a cold, reserved 'martyr of duty'. Like Nelson of his cottage, he dreamt of his garden during the long watch on the Spanish fleet at Christmas 1805 when prospects of peace were still distant:

> Then I will plant my cabbages again, and prune my gooseberry trees, cultivate roses, and twist the woodbine through the hawthorn hedge, with the desire and hope that the occasion never will recur to call me back to more important but less pleasurable occupations.[13]

Proud defiance and sentimental hero-worship, but also humanity towards a defeated enemy and a fundamentally peace-loving predilection for cottage and garden are among the permanent features of English attitudes to war.

12 The seaman's longing for a square meal is borne out by reports like that of a midshipman of 11, killed at Trafalgar: 'We live on beef which has been 10 or 11 years in the cask, and on biscuit which makes your throat cold in eating it owing to the maggots, which are very cold when you eat them! like calf-foot jelly or blomage – being very fat indeed! . . . We drink water the colour of the bark of a pear tree with plenty of maggots and weevils in it, and wine, which is exactly like bullock's blood and sawdust mixed together.' (J. Laffin, *Jack Tar*, Cassell, 1969, p. 135.)
13 Warner, op. cit., p. 97 f.

The Peninsular War (1808–14)

The first quality of the soldier is
constancy in enduring fatigue and privations.
Courage is only the second
NAPOLEON

Napoleon's imposition of the 'Continental System' in 1806 had closed the whole of Europe to British goods; only Portugal, Britain's old ally, resisted. Napoleon concluded a secret treaty with Godoy, the notorious power behind Charles IV's tottering Spanish throne, to carve up Portugal between them. Marshal Junot took Lisbon with 30,000 troops and Prince John, the Regent, fled with his fleet to Brazil under British escort. The treaty enabled Napoleon to occupy Spain and, once installed in Madrid, he treacherously made the Bourbons abdicate in favour of his brother Joseph. On 2 May 1808 the Spanish people rose in a patriotic surge and appealed for British help. Sir Arthur Wellesley, who had made his mark in the Mahratta War in India, landed with 10,000 men in Montego Bay, defeated Junot at Vimeiro and drove the French out of Portugal.

The Retreat to Corunna

What is the best test of a great general?
To know when to retreat and to dare to do it
WELLINGTON

In November 1808, after Dupont's capitulation to the Spaniards at Baylen, Napoleon himself descended on Spain to redress this humiliating reverse of French arms: with 250,000 men he routed the brave but disorganized Spanish army and entered Madrid. He then converged with three armies under Soult, Junot and himself on Sir John Moore's 20,000 men which had advanced from Lisbon to Salamanca, trying to encircle them. Relentlessly pursued by 300,000, Moore escaped encirclement by forced marches over a 250-mile track across the snow-covered mountains of Galicia.

Moore and Lady Hester Stanhope admired each other tenderly and respectfully. The pure sincerity and generous humanity of the brave, handsome general, five times wounded, might have tamed the domineering brilliance and gay mockery of the proud and unruly amazon. In his last letter to her, Moore seems to hint at an understanding which had never been spelt out. Even in his dying last words, 'Stanhope, remember me to your siste,' he remained discreet. Lady Hester confessed that she felt an 'overwhelming sense of loss', kept his bloodstained glove as a relic, and later withdrew to the rocky eagle's nest of Djoun where this first of feminist hippies held court among the Druses of Mount Lebanon. In Arab attire, complete with narghile and yataghan, and attended by her negro slaves, she devoted herself to witchcraft and magic.

16

'We are in a scrape'

Sir John Moore to Lady Hester Stanhope.

Lisbon, October 16, 1808

. . . The regiments are already marching. Pray for good weather; if it rains the torrents will swell, and be impassible, and I shall be accounted a bungler. . . I wish you were here with us. The climate now is charming; we should give you riding enough, and in your red habit, à l'Amazone, you would animate and do us all much good.

Salamanca, November 23

. . . We are in a scrape, but I hope we shall have spirit to get out of it; you must, however, be prepared to hear very bad news. The troops are in as good spirits as if things were better; their appearance and good conduct surprises the grave Spaniard, who had never before seen any but their own or French soldiers.

Farewell, my dear Lady Hester. If I extricate myself and those with me from our present difficulties, and if I can beat the French, I shall return to you with satisfaction; but if not, it will be better I shall never quit Spain.

I remain always very faithfully and sincerely yours,

JOHN MOORE

It must have been galling for the greatest trainer of British soldiers, who, at Shorncliffe Camp, had substituted the inculcation of moral as well as physical qualities for whipping and hanging, to witness how, on the terrible winter retreat to Corunna, his well-drilled troops, which later were to cover themselves with glory under Wellington, gradually became a rabble, as undisciplined as the Spaniards. The burning, looting, and rioting drunken soldiery, plagued by typhus and dysentery, caused Moore much pain and worry, and his moves were not always rational ('We are roving about the country in search of Quixotic adventure to save our honour', wrote Lord Paget). The callousness towards the many women and children with the army who perished was appalling. A commissary wrote:

A woman fell up to her waist in a bog and as she was sucked down by the slimy, ice-cold water, the man behind her walked over her head.

As soon as they were able to fight on reaching Corunna, the soldiers rallied and, at the sacrifice of his own life, Moore stood his ground against Soult's superior forces and devastating gunfire, to cover the embarkation of his exhausted army, preserving it for the day, six months later, when they would return with reinforcements under Wellesley to surprise and beat Soult near Oporto and clear Portugal of French troops.

17

RETREAT CHANGES THE ARMY'S CHARACTER

Sir John Moore reports to Viscount Castlereagh, the Secretary for War.

Astorga, 31 December 1808

. . . I have no option now, but to fall down to the coast as fast as I am able. There is not two days bread to carry the army to Villa Franca. I have been forced to push on the troops without stopping. There is no means of carriage; the people run away; the villages are deserted; and I have been obliged to destroy great part of the ammunition and military stores; for the same reason to leave the sick; in short, my sole object is to save the army. We must all make forced marches to the coast, from the scarcity of provisions, and to be before the enemy, who, by roads upon our flanks, may otherwise interrupt us. I hope to find on the coast transports for the embarkation of the troops. . . .

Corunna, 13th January 1809

I am sorry to say that the army has totally changed its character since it began to retreat; I can say nothing in its favour, but that when there was a prospect of fighting the enemy, the men were then orderly, and seemed pleased and determined to do their duty.

18

'The Last Bugle sounds'

Captain (later Lieutenant-General Sir) William Warre (1784–1853) writes a farewell letter to his parents and describes the retreat and the battle of Corunna; as ADC to Major-General Beresford he was among the last to embark.

Avanilla, Nr. Sahagun, Dec. 23, 1808

Though, as you will suppose, my beloved Parents, not a little hurried, I cannot leave this place to march towards the enemy at Saldanha, without a few lines, which although I am sure not necessary to convince you how much I feel, or how grateful for all the affection, love, and kindness I have ever received, will I am sure be a gratification in case of the worst. Should I fall, my dearest friends, do not grieve for me. It has been the fate of many and much finer fellows than I am, and I fall in a just and glorious cause, trusting to my God and my Saviour to forgive me and have mercy on my soul. At all events I have not disgraced myself or my family. That would be worse than a hundred deaths, or to lose your affection.

The Last Bugle sounds. Adieu, may every happiness attend my dearest Parents. Do not regret, I conjure you, the loss of an individual in so glorious a cause.

Sobrado, Jan. 4, 1809

We have been rather harrassed lately, having retreated from Sahagun to this place sometimes by night and forced marches. We have not halted for 22 days. . . . For myself I have fared very well compared to officers not on the Staff and men. I suppose no men ever did more, or any army, some even officers barefoot. . . . I am not yet really hardened enough to misery and wretchedness, not to be unhappy at contemplating the miseries of war in our men and the wretched inhabitants of the country. May our beloved country never be a scene of warfare. Better half of its men should die on the beach.

Barfleur, at Sea, Jan. 18

Happy in the prospect of soon seeing all my beloved friends, after our disastrous and most harrassing retreat from Lugo. We arrived at Corunna and found no transports, they arrived a few days after, but before we could embark the French attacked us on the 16th, with all their force, in our most disadvantageous position. They were repulsed by a valour which only English troops can possess, though exposed to a tremendous commanding fire of cannon. Poor Sir John Moore was killed. Our loss in killed and wounded is very great, though not so much as that of the enemy. . . .

During the night most of our army embarked. The French approached in the morning close to us. We gave them a warm reception with our 24 prs. assisted by the Spaniards, who on this occasion behaved very well. Fortunately the enemy did not fire on the town, and suffered us to embark. We were very weak, just enough to man the works, and dreaded an assault, the boats being able to take only 500 at a time, and weather very bad. However we not only got ourselves but most of the wounded in safety, though all most overcome with fatigue.

Adieu, in hopes of soon seeing you, My dearest Parents. Kindest love from your most affectionate Son,

Wm. WARRE

19

HORROR AND DISGRACE

Dr Adam Neale, an army physician, gives a clinical description of the retreat to Corunna and the embarkation.

Lugo, 5th January 1809

. . . It was a sad sight to behold the wretched state of the troops. A degree of spirit approaching to mutiny was manifest among them, owing to the excessive fatigue which they had undergone, and the disgrace, as they deemed it, of running away from the enemy. . . .

Early on the morning of the 3rd, we continued our march up to the mountain. The road is here cut through the rocks. On the summit which is the boundary of Gallicia we had to scramble through deep snows.

Broken waggons and carriages, money-carts, dead animals, and the bodies of human beings, who had perished from the inclemency of the weather during the night, strewed the way for miles. Never had I conceived, much less witnessed, so awful a scene. . . . In one baggage-waggon, which had overturned, an unfortunate soldier's wife, with several children, were frozen to death. – But why dwell on these horrors; the bare idea of which must make you shudder? . . .

Corunna, 11th January

On the morning of the 9th, amid a storm of wind, sleet, and rain, more severe than I can recollect ever to have experienced, we proceeded to Guitterez. Our poor soldiers, drenched to the skin, and covered with mud, lengthened out their line of march. I felt as if scalding drops of lead pelted my face. It was with the greatest difficulty I could keep my seat on horseback. Every human being fled, 'the fenceless villages were all forsaken'. Our soldiers absolutely lay down and died in the ditches without a struggle. Few women were now to be seen, the greater part had perished. . . .

I halted for half an hour in the rain, but was so stiff, that, on attempting to remount I fell down, and could with difficulty get on my legs. Here the troops had some salt beef and rum issued. Not having any fires to cook the beef, much of it was thrown away; but the rum was drunk greedily, and the powers of their stomachs being almost gone, I saw them fall down, after drinking it, in a comatose state. Death, I have no doubt, followed in an hour or two. . . .

at sea, January 19th

A severe engagement has taken place on the heights above Corunna. Our sick, artillery, and dragoons commenced embarking. The enemy had got possession of the heights above St Lucia, from which he opened a spirited fire upon the ships in the inner harbour. Nothing was now to be seen but the most dreadful confusion. The transports slipped their cables, and put to sea instantly; many running foul of each other, and carrying away yards, bowsprits, and rigging. Four or five ships ran aground on the rocks, and bilged. A 74-gun ship immediately stood in towards the French batteries, and opened her guns upon them. . . . Having put to sea, we saw, after it became dark, a considerable body of light streaming along the horizon. . . .

I am myself a good deal indisposed, and not much the better for being shut up in a little, noisome, damp cabin, with six other officers. Four of them are extremely ill, and generally raving all night long. Their complaints are the consequence of over-exertion; and their distempered and horror-struck imaginations are perpetually pursuing some dreadful hallucination connected with the casualties of war, famine, and shipwreck. . . . It blows so violent a gale that I can wrote no longer. Farewel.

When Moore, who had struggled on in deep gloom, expecting the worst, received his mortal wound, he muttered: 'I have always wished to die this way. . . . I hope the people of England will be satisfied', revealing how well he understood the part to be played by a legendary tragic hero.[14]

14   C. Hibbert, *Corunna*, Batsford, 1961, pp. 86, 126 for quotations, *passim* for details.

20

HOW SIR JOHN MOORE RECEIVED HIS FATAL WOUND

Captain (later Field Marshal Viscount) Henry Hardinge (1785–1856), the future Secretary of War, Governor-General of India, and Commander-in-Chief succeeding Wellington, reports home.

[n.d.]

. . . . I had been ordered to desire a battalion of the Guards to advance; I was pointing out to the General the situation of the battalion, and our horses were touching, at the very moment that a cannon-shot from the enemy's battery carried away his left shoulder and part of the collar-bone, leaving the arm hanging by the flesh.

The violence of the stroke threw him off his horse, on his back. Not a muscle on his face altered, nor did a sign betray the least sensation of pain. I dismounted, and, taking his hand, he pressed mine forcibly, casting his eyes very anxiously towards the 42nd regiment, which was hotly engaged; and his countenance expressed satisfaction when I informed him that the regiment was advancing. Assisted by a soldier, he was removed a few yards behind the shelter of a wall. The blood flowed fast; but the attempt to stop it with my sash was useless, from the size of the wound.

Sir John assented to being removed in a blanket to the rear. In raising him for that purpose, his sword, hanging on the wounded side, touched his arm, and became entangled between his legs. I perceived the inconvenience, and was in the act of unbuckling it from his waist, when he said, in his usual tone and manner, and in a very distinct voice, 'It is as well as it is. I had rather it should go out of the field with me.' Observing the resolution and composure of his features, I caught at the hope that I might be mistaken in my fears of the wound being mortal; and remarked, that I trusted when the surgeons dressed the wound, that he would be spared to us, and recover. – He then turned his head round, and, looking steadfastly at the wound for a few seconds, said, 'No, Hardinge, I feel that to be impossible'. . . .

The Iron Duke's Progress

> *O, Albuera, glorious field of grief!*
> LORD BYRON

Unlike Nelson and Moore, Viscount Wellington of Talavera (since his victory over Marshal Victor in 1809) was not cut in the heroic mould: although just as brave and patriotic as they were, he held an ignorant populace's craving for glory and hero-worshipping in contempt and pursued his campaign in the Peninsula with a steady, methodical, matter-of-fact honesty which made no concession to popular aspirations and personal vanity. The Press was his bugbear. He complained:

We are the most indefatigable writers of letters and news that exist in the world, and the fashion and spirit of the times gives encouragement to lies.

He blamed newspapers for giving away army positions, revealed in officers' letters.

21

WELLINGTON WILL NOT CURRY FAVOUR WITH THE PUBLIC

Viscount Wellington writes to his close friend John W. Croker, Secretary to the Admiralty, about the abuses of the Press.

Cartaxo ,Dec. 20th, 1810

The licentiousness of the press, and the presumption of the editors of the newspapers, have gone near to stultify the people of England; and it makes one sick to hear the statements of supposed facts which have the effect only of keeping the minds of the people in a state of constant alarm and anxiety, and of expectation which must be disappointed.

In the early part of the campaign all was alarm and gloomy anxiety; the British army was doomed to destruction and I was to be well thought of if I could bring any part of it off the Peninsula without disgrace. Then came the battle of Busaco, and nothing would then suit the editors of the newspapers but that Masséna's army should be destroyed, although it was 20,000 men stronger than mine. A combined army made up as mine, partly of recruits and soldiers in a state of convalescence, and composed of officers unaccustomed to the great operations of war, is not equal to a French army. But nothing will suit editors but that the enemy should be swept from the face of the earth. . . .

I really believe that, owing to the ignorance and presumption and licentiousness of the press, the most ignorant people in the world of military and political affairs are the people of England; and I cannot but think that I act wisely and honestly towards them to do what I think is good for them, rather than what will please them. . . . However grievous it is, and however injurious to the country, I cannot avoid laughing when I reflect upon all this folly. . . .

In spite of the small size of his army, though excellently trained and supplied, Wellington chased Masséna's three times superior forces and defeated his frontal cavalry attack by the steadfastness of the British infantry squares at Bussaco and Fuentes de Oñoro. He admitted, however, 'if Boney had been there, we should have been beaten'. Hunger and vermin caused severe suffering.

22

'Flead, bugged, centipeded, beetled'

Major (later General Sir) Charles Napier (1782–1853), a brother of General William Napier who wrote the famous history of the war, has just rejoined the army after being severely wounded; he describes to his mother the starvation he shares with Blanco, his horse.

Moita, 21st March, 1811

I make no apologies for the dirt of this note; for flead, bugged, centipeded, beetled, lizarded and earwigged, cleanliness is known to me only by name. Moreover a furze bush makes a bad table for writing on, and a worse chair, when breeches are nearly worn out with glory, oh! oh! We have very little food, which forced us to halt: Massena has thus got two days' start, but he is pursued by the cavalry and light division. . . .

Neither poor *Blanco* nor myself are much troubled with bile now. 100 miles, with only three hours' rest and hardly a bit to eat, did he carry me coming up to the army, and my fear was it would kill him; he did not even tire! He is the strongest horse ever backed. Still he thinks a bivouac the worst amusement in the world, as he gets nothing but heath and hard riding. Poor fellow. I kiss and coax him, but it don't make up for *no oats*. He is the most delightful animal that ever was, but thinks being admired by the Lisbon ladies with a full stomach, better than my affection with heath.

23

'My biscuit has run away on maggots' legs'

Alfayates, April 6th

. . . We have now, for one month, been up at 3 a.m., marching at 4, and halting at 7 o'clock at night, when we eat all we can get, from shoe soles to bread and butter. . . . We are on biscuit full of maggots, and though not a bad soldier, hang me if I can relish maggots. We suffer much in point of food, but the French are nearly cleared out of the country. Our late movement was to force the enemy from Almeida by turning their position there; they have run and the garrison will blow that place up. . . . Blanco is starving and curls his nose into a thousand wrinkles, cursing Buonaparte: there! my biscuit has run away on maggots' legs.

The enthusiastic but undisciplined Spanish army was no match for the French and was routed everywhere, but, spearheaded by 6,000 British soldiers who bore the brunt, a Spanish army under the command of Beresford checked Soult's in the bitterly fought battle of Albuera on 16 May 1811. Wellington wept over the 4,500 British casualties: 'Another such battle could ruin us', and Soult claimed he had won a victory but 'they did not know it and would not run'.[15] A lieutenant wrote after this bloody battle that the British troops 'were as composed as if they were going through their evolutions on a field day, but with a great deal more glee' and added, with insight into civilian mentality: 'I do not know what the people of England will think of the battle of Albuera. It was bravely contested, but we lost too many men. However, John Bull will like that, he would not give a pin's head for a battle in which *thousands* did not fall.'[16]

In the following account a soldier vividly describes his own experiences.

24

'Blood flowing down the hill'

A private in the Old Buffs tells how he was taken prisoner at Albuera and then escaped, 'a mere skeleton'.

[June 1811]

I was knocked down by a horseman with his lance, which luckily did me no serious injury. In getting up, I received a lance in my hip, and shortly after another in my knee. I then rose, when a soldier, striking me on the side of the head with his lance, left me, and soon another came up, who would have killed me, had not a French officer, giving the fellow a blow, told him to spare the English, and to go on and do his duty. This officer conducted me to the rear of the French lines, and here the sight that struck the eye was dreadful. Men dead, where the column had stood, heaped on each other; the wounded crying for assistance, and human blood flowing down the hill! I came to where the baggage was, where I found a vast number of my own regiment, with a good proportion of officers, prisoners like myself; numbers of them desperately wounded, even after they were prisoners!

Here then I offered up my most fervent thanks to Heaven for having escaped so safe. I remained prisoner seven days, and the whole I received from our enemy (marching six leagues every day on the road to Madrid) was three ounces of rice, nine ounces of bread, and a pound of meat. However, when on the line of march, they indulged us by entering bean-fields, using the same language to us as the Spaniards use to the swine, 'Hurrah! hurrah!' – Conceive my feelings, for believe me I cannot describe them. On the seventh evening I left them in open day-light, and after getting two miles lay down. Shortly a picquet passed close by me, but they did not see me. Soon after I arose, and though a mere skeleton, rushed forward to a hill, crossed it, and entered a corn-field where I was again alarmed by the trampling of horses. I immediately fell on my face; it again pleased Heaven to save me; they passed on, and did not observe me. I again rose, and travelled over mountains, through valleys and rivers, till exhausted by excessive fatigue, I sat down, and was

15   A. Brett-James, *Wellington at War*, Macmillan, 1961, p. 219, note 3.
16   H.M.C., Hastings, III, p. 289.

unable to rise. Here a refreshing sleep allayed my hunger, and recruited exhausted nature. I arose, and proceeded to a village, where I was received according to the Scriptures; 'I was naked, and they clothed me; hungry, and they fed me.' Such treatment I never before experienced as going through this extensive country, every person out-vying with each other so soften the hardships I had endured. In 16 days I reached Elvas, and soon after joined my regiment.

The strong fortress of Ciudad Rodrigo, which it had taken Marshal Ney twenty-five days to wrest from a Spanish garrison of raw recruits, was stormed on 19 January 1812 in a gallant but costly short siege. In the disgraceful sack which followed, a drunken soldiery (two drowned in casks of brandy), enraged by their severe casualties, went on a rampage of plunder and destruction. Brutal flogging was needed to restore discipline. William Warre, now a major, wrote home:

> Nothing could resist the ardour and impetuosity of our Troops, and in 20 minutes after the storm began they were in full possession of the town. The storming parties drove everything before them, and we scarce thought the business begun when the Hurrahs announced their glorious victory. It is quite out of my power to do justice to the heroism and gallantry of our troops. They seemed to surpass their wonted bravery and intrepid contempt of danger. Nor can I describe the awful feelings of suspense and anxiety before or during the storm.

He also found it impossible to depict 'the horrors and misery of a town taken by storm', plundered and burning: 'It was quite dreadful, and the scene beyond my pen to describe.'[17]

Worse was to come: the formidable fortress of Badajoz, whose siege had been abandoned in the previous summer, was now stormed despite terrible losses. One hundred British soldiers drowned in the ditches and many more were spiked, cut by sword-blades, or blown up by mines; in all, 2,000 died before the decisive breach was made. The lieutenant who opened the gates tells the story of the storm.

25

'I was the third man who mounted the ladder'

Lieutenant Robert Knowles writes to his father; he fell on the pass of Roncesvalles a year later, aged twenty-three.

April 7, 1812

It gives me great pleasure to be able to write to you after the bloody business on the night of the 6th. I had the hon. command of a party of 40 men of our Regiment,

17   W. Warre, *Letters from the Peninsula*, 1909, p. 223.

ordered to storm a strong outwork, defended on one side by water and a wall around it about 24 ft. in height. After being exposed for half an hour to the hottest fire I was ever under, we succeeded in placing one ladder against the wall, by which my party entered. A Corporal was the first who got into the Fort, and was immediately killed. I was the third man who mounted the ladder. On leaping into the place I was knocked down by a shower of grape which broke my sabre into a hundred pieces. I providentially escaped without any serious injury, although my clothes were torn from my back. My sword hand is much cut and bruised, which accounts for my bad writing. With the assistance of eight or ten men who had now got into the Fort, I charged along the ramparts, destroying or disarming all who opposed us. . . .

An unprecedented three days' murdering and raping followed. Lieutenant W.H. Hare wrote home that 'Lord Wellington had signified his wishes to the soldiers of bayoneting every man, which has been so fully complied with that, out of the whole garrison, which consisted of 5000 men, 200 have not escaped with their lives.'[18]

Whether they needed, and actually ever received, Wellington's encouragement, the fact is that, in the end, he was forced to hang a few men to restore order. Captain R. Blakeney describes the scene:

The infuriated soldiery resembled rather a pack of hell-hounds vomited up from the infernal regions of the extirpation of mankind than what they were 12 short hours previously – well organised, brave, disciplined and obedient British Army. The frenzied military mob were ferociously employed in indiscriminate carnage, universal plunder and devastation of every kind. The sack continued for three days without intermission.[19]

Plundering, sometimes even of their own dead, had always been a prime object of the English soldier, but such an outrage was exceptional and was to occur otherwise only in retaliatory colonial expeditions.

Not everyone was indifferent to the scenes he witnessed: Lieutenant G. Hennell was horrified by the callousness of the men 'singing and swearing while their comrades lay round them in heaps dead', which 'threw shells into my soul more formidable than the balls fired from French battries'.[20]

Robert Long went even further: he was an unusual general in so far as he detested war. He was critical of Wellington but refused the staff post at home he was offered, and was, in the end, dismissed from active service. His letter is pervaded by deep humanity in face of the horrors he had witnessed.

18   *Blackwood's Magazine*, vol. 253, April 1943, p. 271.
19   J. Laffin, *Tommy Atkins*, Cassell, 1966, p. 92.
20   *Letters*, ed. M. Glover, Heinemann, 1979, p. 19.

26

'The age of selfishness has succeeded'

Brigadier (later Lieutenant-General) Robert Long (1771–1825), writing to his brothers, repudiates military reputation as mostly a gift of fortune and chastizes the joy felt at home over the storms of Albuera and Badajoz.

Villar del Rey, 14th March 1812

. . . I am not, and never have been, a soldier in my heart. Those who follow a military life from natural predilection are, in the very execution of their duty, prosecuting their sweetest pleasures. To minds not formed in the same mould, the feelings are widely different. To me the day of Albuera was one of deep affliction. I felt pain where others found pleasure. I dislike butchery in all its forms and shapes, and of all kinds of butchery that of the human species is to me the most odious. No ambition, no love of reputation can conquer this feeling. . . . Lord Wellington talks of *expending* such and such Battalions, as you would talk of expending so much shot and powder; to him, War must have every charm that can fascinate a man's heart. He is a *thoroughbred* soldier. I make a distinction between the duty that summons every man to the field to defend his own country and rights; but Armies which are formed for other purposes (and all of them are) should be made up of Volunteers who love War as a trade. I say honestly that *I* have no business among *this* class of men, for I dislike the thing, and always have. You cannot, therefore, be surprised at my anxiety to see an end to what I abhor. I have really nothing to hope for or look to but what you call the bubble reputation, which with us, is nine times out ten, the *gift of fortune*, and, generally speaking, as easy to be lost as acquired. Ambition should be made of sterner stuff than I possess, therfore I discard it from my heart, and in all humility seek the only consolation I ever can enjoy, that of living and dying, unmolested, among those who are most dear to me.

Ribera, 20 April

. . . All the world should feel and know the curses of warfare, and they would appreciate very differently from what they do, the value of domestic peace and security. Those, whose faces gladden to the capture of Badajoz should have stood on the breach the day after the assault, and have contemplated the scene of desolation that will occasion so much joy. Had they hearts they would feel for the bravest of the brave, and curse the spirit that consigns them to premature annihilation.

As I passed along the scene of death, I observed a poor fellow scraping with his hand some dust, and throwing over the body of a comrade. I rebuked him for this slovenly operation, and desired him to get a party and bury the man properly. He burst into tears, and asked me what he could do? It was his brother, and he could not bear to see him lying thus exposed. I would to God that every Tyrant could have witnessed this scene, but had they hearts to feel it, they would not be what I have called them. But the age of philanthropy is gone, that of selfishness has succeeded, and we care not who lies in the ditch of honour provided we are not there ourselves. . . .

Wellington, with his small forces, had succeeded in protecting Portugal and keeping the war in Spain going against Napoleon's most famous marshals with 350,000 picked French troops. Now, the emperor began to withdraw some of them from Spain for the Russian campaign. On 22 July 1812, Wellington won a great tactical battle at Salamanca against Marshal Marmont in which 8,000 Frenchmen were killed and 7,000 taken prisoner.

A captain describes his private skirmishes with the señoritas.

27

ABOUT THE CONQUEST OF 'SENORITAS'

Captain (later General Sir) Edward C. Whinyates (1782–1865) writes to his sisters at Cheltenham.

Gen. Hill's Cavalry Camp, nr. Villa Garcia
20th July 1812

. . . You have been imagining, I suppose, that we are in daily combats, but I assure you we pass our time much more peaceably. There are a great many 'Senoritas', i.e. young ladies, and these (most wonderful to relate) have retained so much constancy for their French lovers, that although the English have occupied the town for a fortnight and have given almost every night balls to amuse them, they still remember their first attachments. A peasant was taken bearing the billets-doux of 17 of these Penelopes to their lovers. These epistles afforded much amusement, being written with all the warmth of Spanish passion. How long these fair may continue such unheard of fidelity is very uncertain. . . . God grant us compleat victory and that we may chastise the French for their conduct in this country. . . .

[later]

I was fortunate enough to observe a very beautiful 'Senorita' walking in an olive ground with her domestic, and being charmed with her entered into a very gallant and fascinating conversation, and having of course made some impression, I was invited into the house and afterwards taken into the garden, the sweet retreat of this Calypso, and there the sweetest flowers were culled and presented to me. I took them and bore them on my bosom as a true knight. The next day, we marched to Berlanga, where I was so much more in fortune that my 'Patrona' was more beautiful still, and I am afraid the syren of Villa Garcia was forgotten. . . .

No wonder some of the young ladies in England became anxious about their officer husbands or fiancés and tried to obtain home leave for them. Wellington got worried about their frequent absence for pleasure and stopped all home leave (he himself never went away for five years), although he was not opposed to a couple of days at Lisbon 'which is as long as any reasonable man can wish to stay in bed with the same women'.[21] Being very cold with his own wife, and preferring wolf hunting as a relaxation during the campaign, he dealt with this lady's longing for her lover in no uncertain manner; his elegant wit could sting.

28

DUTY BEFORE LOVE

Wellington replies to a plea for granting leave to a major to console his lady love.

Quinta de S. João, 27th June 1811

I have had the honour of receiving your letter and it is impossible not to feel for the unhappiness of the young lady which you have so well described; but it is not so easy as you imagine to apply the remedy.

It appears to me that I should be guilty of a breach of discretion if I were to send for the fortunate object of this young lady's affections, and apprise him of the pressing necessity for his early return to England: the application for permission to go ought to come from himself; and, at all events, the offer ought to be made by him, and particularly not be founded on the secret of this young lady.

But this fortunate Major now commands his battalion, I am very apprehensive that he could not with propriety quit it at present, even though the life of this female should depend upon it; and, therefore, I think that he will not ask for leave.

We read occasionally of desperate cases of this description, but I cannot say that I have ever yet known of a young lady dying of love. They contrive, in some manner, to live, and look tolerably well, notwithstanding their despair and the continued absence of their lover; and some have even been known to recover so far as to be inclined to take another lover, if the absence of the first has lasted too long. I don't suppose that your protegée can ever recover so far, but I do hope she will survive the continued necessary absence of the Major, and enjoy with him thereafter many happy days.

For a short time Wellington even occupied Madrid which King Joseph had evacuated. The welcome from the crowds was delirious but the soldiers, unlike the officers, had to be content with – or rather suffer – male embraces.

---

21   P. Guedalla, *The Duke*, 1931, p. 206.

29

KISSES IN MADRID – FROM THE MEN!

Private Wheeler describes the tumultuous affection with which the English liberators were received.

Madrid, 18th August 1812

We were the first regiment that entered Madrid. I never witnessed before such a scene. At the distance of five miles from the gates we were met by the inhabitants, each had brought out something, viz. laurel, flowers, bread, wine, grapes, lemonade, acquedente, tobacco, sweatmeats etc. The road presented a moving forest, from the great multitude of people carrying boughs. . . . As we approached the city the crowd increased, the people were mad with joy. They called us their deliverours, their Saviours. The air was rent with deffening shouts of 'Vivi les Angolese, Vivi les Ilandos'. Wellington was at the head of the column. When we entered the city the shouting increased tenfold, every bell that had got a clapper was set ringing, the windows were ornamented with rich drapery embroidered with gold and silver, such as is only used in great festivals when the Host is carried. The whole of the windows and tops of the houses were crowded with Spanish beauty, waving white hand-kerchiefs. . . . But amidst all this pleasure and happiness we were obliged to submit to a custom so unenglish that I cannot but feel disgust now I am writing. It was to be kissed by the men. What made it still worse, their breath was so highly seasoned with garlick, then their huge moustaches was stiffened with sweat, dust and snuff, it was like having a hair broom pushed into one's faces that had been daubed in a dirty gutter. . . .

The letters of Private Wheeler give us a unique picture of both the bright and the dark side of soldiering: of adventure and lucky turns as well as of hardship and brutality of discipline, enforced by flogging and execution; of his loyal love for the army throughout all the ups and downs, and, above all, of his regimental pride.

Soult was transferred to Germany with some of the best troops, and King Joseph and Marshal Jourdan, although still mustering 200,000 men, were no match for Wellington with a mere 90,000. Chased towards the French border, they clashed at Vitoria on 21 June 1813 and in the ensuing rout lost not only 6,000 men and 1,000 prisoners but all their 120 cannon, stores and rich money chest:

> The quantity of equipage, fine ladies, riches of every sort, guns, ammuni-tion stores, oxen, sheep, poultry, pigs, claret, champagne, brandy, gauzes, muslins, jewellery, etc. that fell into the hands of our soldiers exceeds any-thing of the kind that has happened since Darius was defeated,

wrote Colonel Barnard.[22]

---

22 *Barnard's Letters*, ed. A. Powell, 1928, p. 228.

The soldiers, however, were intoxicated with wine and loot, and many thousands dispersed into the villages. Therefore despite the military police Wellington had introduced to deal with marauders, he was unable to seize the whole of the French army. It was on this occasion that he described his men as 'vagabond soldiers', the 'scum of the earth', and declared that it was 'impossible to command a British Army'. Private Wheeler supplies eloquent proof.

30

DAME FORTUNE'S GIFTS

Private Wheeler describes the scramble for money and booty.

near Pampaluna, 1st July 1813

. . . The enemy, to use their own words, had decoyed us to Vittoria to give us a good drubbing and dance in double quick time back into Portugal again. Such was King Joseph's confidence that he had caused scaffolding to be erected for the people to see them beat the English. The tops of all churches and lofty buildings were crowded with spectators to witness our disgrace. Grand dinners were provided and wine in abundance to drink to the health of the conquering French. . . .

On the morning of the 21 June we advanced. We haversacked a few sheep and ran against an old shepherd, we soon relieved him of all he had, viz. a 4lb. loaf, some cheese and about a quart of wine. The poor old fellow cried. It was no use, we had not seen a bit of bread these 11 days. . . .

The battle now began. After sustaining their fire for some time, we dashed forward, drove them from their position in such a hurry that they left ten guns behind. Soon after this the entire French army broke up, and so precipitate was their flight that they left all their material of war on the field. The dead and dying lay scattered all around us.

As soon as we halted my comrade proposed to go and see if he could get some money, as several men had come into camp loaded with money. I met one with a handkerchief full of dollars. He was followed by about half a dozen Portuguese soldiers, one of these fellows ran in and cut the handkerchief and down went the dollars, a general scramble followed. As the Portuguese were down on their hands and knees picking up the money, we paid them off in stile with the sockets of our bayonetts. . . . After much difficulty I secured a small box of dollars, and was fortunate enough to get back safe to camp.

Heights of Eschellar, 17th July

. . . Dame Fortune has distributed her gifts in her usual way, to some money, others bread, hams, cherries, tobacco etc. This of necessity soon established a market. Now the camp represented a great fair and the money and goods soon became more equally distributed. 'Who will give 50 dollars for this pipe', 'Here is a portrait of Napoleon for 100 dollars'. Then a General's coat would fetch more dollars than it cost francs. Wine and brandy would fetch a high price. Cognac from 40 to 50 dollars per bottle.

The market son changed into a grand maskerade. British soldiers were soon to be seen in French General's and other officer's uniform covered with stars and military orders, others had attired themselves in female dresses, richly embroidered in gold and silver. . . .

Wellington put the blame for indiscipline on certain junior officers whom elsewhere he called 'gentlemen who like their ease and comfort' and become 'croakers and false prophets' – the inevitable result of the system of purchasing commissions by the younger sons of the nobility. Some of them became, in due course, the generals about whose incompetence Wellington had also cause to complain.

31

INDISCIPLINE

The Marquis of Wellington to the Earl of Bathurst, Secretary of War.

Caseda, June 29th 1813

. . . We started with the Army in the highest order; & up to the day of Battle nothing could get on better. But that event has as usual totally annihilated all order and discipline. The soldiers of the Army have got among them about a million sterling in money, with the exception of about 100,000 dollars which were got for the military chest. The night of the Battle, instead of being passed in getting rest and food, to prepare them for pursuit the following day, was spent by the soldiers in looking for plunder. The consequence was that they were incapable of marching in pursuit of the Enemy, & were totally knocked up. . . .

This is the consequence of the state of discipline of the British Army. We may gain the greatest Victories; but we shall do no good until we shall so far alter our system as to force the officers of the junior ranks to perform their duty, & shall have some mode of punishing them for Neglect.

The remnants of the French army, a disorganized mob, were driven across the frontier to Bayonne, and France was now threatened by an Anglo–Spanish invasion. Soult was again sent for to redress the situation but, after outmanoeuvring the French in the battle of the Pyrenees, Wellington first stormed San Sebastian and finally Toulouse, not knowing that Napoleon had abdicated four days earlier, on 6 April 1814. Peace had come at last.

32

MACAULAY, AGED THIRTEEN, ON THE NEWS OF PEACE

Thomas B. (later Lord) Macaulay (1800–59), a future famous historian and Secretary at War, writes a rather pompous letter to his mother.

Shelford: April 11, 1814

My dear Mama,

The news is glorious indeed. Peace! Peace with a Bourbon, with a descendant of Henri IV, with a prince who is bound to us by all the ties of gratitude. I have some hopes that it will be a lasting peace; that the troubles of the last 20 years may make kings and nations wiser. I cannot conceive a greater punishment to Buonaparte than that which the allies have inflicted on him. How can his ambitious mind support it? All his great projects and schemes, which once made every throne in Europe tremble, are buried in the solitude of an Italian isle. How miraculously everything has been conducted! We almost seem to hear the Almighty saying to the fallen tyrant, 'For this cause have I raised thee up, that I might shew in thee My power.'

Ever your affectionate son,
T.B. Macaulay

The British army's reputation, at its nadir in 1794, was now as high as ever, owing to the superiority of the British line over the French column, and Wellington's strategic and tactical brilliance which inspired confidence in his leadership despite his aristocratic haughtiness and abrasive harshness. 'Cold and indifferent, nay, apparently careless in the beginning of battles, when the moment of difficulty comes intelligence flashes from the eyes of this wonderful man; and he rises superior to all', wrote a Colonel,[23] and a soldier remarked, 'Where is Arthur? We would rather see his long nose in the fight any day than a reinforcement of 10,000 men'.

Napoleon blamed the 'Spanish ulcer' for his downfall: harrassed by guerrillas and deprived of supplies, his army dispersed over a wide inclement territory, he lost 500,000 soldiers in the Peninsula, as against 40,000 on the British side.

In spite of his tremendous success – and partly because of it – Wellington never became a hero: his caution made him go into battle only when he was sure to win, his patient administrative perseverance and low opinion of humanity, and his contempt for cant and popularity, rendered him unlovable, and no legend could grow round a general who, invariably, remained successful and unhurt.

To sum up what war meant to a soldier at the time, the last word may be with Private Wheeler:

---

23 *Letters of Colonel Sir A. Frazer*, 1859, p. 550.

What a chequered life is a soldier's on active service. One moment seeking the bubble reputation at the cannon's mouth. The next courting some fair unknown damsel, sometimes scorched alive with heat, then almost frozen to death on some snowy mountain, at one time the inmate of a palace, then for months, the sky is his only covering. Hunting the enemy like a greyhound, and in return often hunted by the enemy. . . . It is the very life of a soldier to keep moving. If we do suffer privations at times, we have some sunshiney days, and dame fortune often leads us out of difficulty and puts us into possession of all the luxuries of life.[24]

Waterloo

Foremost captain of his time . . .
O iron nerve to true occasion true
LORD TENNYSON

When Napoleon returned from Elba in 1815, Wellington was sent to Brussels to take command of a hastily assembled force of about equal contingents from Britain, Germany and the Netherlands. He described this force as 'an infamous army, very weak and ill-equipped, and a very inexperienced staff'; most of the veterans from the Peninsular War had been sent to the West Indies. Napoleon was anxious to defeat Blücher's Prussians and Wellington's force separately and as quickly as possible so as to be able to deal with the Russians and Austrians in turn: his lightning advance caught both armies by surprise while they were still forming. Wellington, enjoying himself at Brussels, seemed blissfully unaware of Napoleon's intentions. The Revd Spencer Madan wrote on 13 June:

Though I have some pretty good reasons for supposing that hostilities will soon commence, yet no one would suppose it, judging by the Duke of Wellington. He appears to be thinking of anything else in the world, gives a ball every week, attends every party, partakes of every amusement that offers. Yesterday he took Lady Jane Lennox to Enghien for the cricket match, and brought her back at night, apparently having gone for no other object but to amuse her. At the time Bonaparte was said to be at Maubeuge, 30 or 40 miles off.[25]

Even on 15 June, when Napoleon had crossed the frontier and penetrated his forward lines, Wellington kept his sang-froid and, not to cause alarm, stayed at the ball of the Duchess of Richmond till 2 a.m. Captain Bowles wrote:

24 B. Liddell Hart (ed.), *Letters of Private Wheeler*, M. Joseph, 1951, p. 97 f.
25 J. Naylor, *Waterloo*, Batsford, 1960, p. 57.

The Duke of Wellington said to the Duke of Richmond, 'I think it is time for me to go to bed'; and then whispered to ask him if he had a good map in the house. Richmond said he had, and took him into his dressing-room. Wellington shut the door and said, 'Napoleon has humbugged me, by God! He has gained 24 hours on me'. Richmond said, 'What do you intend doing?' Wellington replied, 'I have ordered the army to concentrate at Quatre Bras; but we shan't stop them there, and if, I must fight him here' (passing his thumbnail over the position of Waterloo). He then said adieu, and left. He went to his quarters, slept six hours, breakfasted, and rode at speed to Quatre Bras.[26]

Contrary to orders, Ney missed his chance of occupying Quatre Bras while the defenders were weak, and some of the English officers, still in ball dress, were only just driving up in their cabriolets as if going to the races. In the meantime, Napoleon shattered the Prussian army at Ligny but, owing to d'Erlon's shuttling between the two battles, neither was decisive. Ney, too, failed to pursue Wellington on his strategic retreat and on 17 June Napoleon lost his momentum through indisposition and a subsequent heavy downpour.

'The morning of the 18th June broke upon us and found us drenched with rain, benumbed and shaking with cold,' wrote Private Wheeler: the soldiers faced the battle hungry, thirsty, and caked in mud. The continuing thunderstorm delayed the French attack till the afternoon and allowed Wellington to deploy, his dandy officers sporting their umbrellas. Napoleon had been warned by his Peninsular generals that English troops were 'inexpugnable' by frontal attack in a strong position like Wellington's, flanked by the high points of La Haye Sainte and Hougoumont and using a ridge to shelter the troops below from artillery fire. Napoleon, however, instead of outflanking, launched an old-fashioned direct attack, relying on his 72,000 seasoned soldiers and nearly 2:1 gun superiority against Wellington's motly 67,000. After d'Erlon's infantry had been repulsed with the loss of 5,000, wave after wave of Ney's cavalry kept on assaulting the British squares in the centre without making them yield; had they been supported by infantry and horse artillery, they would have won the battle. When the British defenders of La Haye Sainte ran out of ammunition and it fell, the French fire from there at last broke some of the squares, which were surrounded by the French cavalry, and a gap was opened. At this critical point, an entire Belgian hussar regiment fled to Brussels and some of the Germans shot at Wellington when he tried to rally them: 'There was so much misbehaviour that it was only God's mercy that we won the battle,' wrote the Duke later.

Fatally, the Imperial Guard Napoleon had kept in reserve too long were not sent into the gap which Wellington was closing with exhausted troops,

26   Ibid, p. 69 f.

but were deployed against Maitland's Guards Brigade. The crisis was allowed to pass, as Zieten's Prussians had by now come up and were beginning to press hard from the flank. The five battalions of the Imperial Guard, headed by Ney and their generals with drawn swords and attacking without cavalry support, were finally driven down the hill by Maitland's counterattack at 8 p.m. when the 52nd Foot rose behind their protective slope at the signal of Wellington's cocked hat; 40,000 stormed downhill in a general advance. As the sun set, Napoleon's *Grande Armée* dissolved for ever and he fled to Paris. His brilliant strategic moves had failed through his tactical errors, the quicker than expected recovery of the Prussians whom Grouchy, by his slowness, had been unable to hold off, and, last but not least, through the steadfastness of the British squares under Wellington's leadership. The superior fire-power of the British line, converging on the head of the French column, frustrated the most heroic courage and swift dash the French could muster; they left 40,000 dead on the battlefield, and the British and Prussians 7,000 each – the 27th Inniskillings lying in their squares even in death.[27]

A captain and a sergeant, both of the First Foot Guards, describe the desperate crucial struggle when the Imperial Guard was checked and put to flight.

33

'La Garde turned'

Captain H.W. Powell on the culminating moment of the battle.

Between five and six the Emperor was so much pressed by the Prussian advance on his right that he determined to make a last grand effort, and as he had tried every other Corps without effect there only remained to him the 'Garde Imperiale'. With these he resolved to play his last stake and to ensure success. His Artillery were ordered to concentrate their whole fire on the intended point of attack. The point was the rise of our position about half-way between Hougoumont and La Haye Sainte.

There ran along this part of the position a cart road, on one side of which was a ditch and bank, in and under which the Brigade sheltered themselves during the cannonade, which might have lasted three quarters of an hour. Without the protection of the bank every creature must have perished.

The Emperor probably calculated on this effect, for suddenly the firing ceased, and as the smoke cleared away a most superb sight opened on us. A close Column of Grenadiers of la Moyenne Garde, about 6,000 strong, were seen ascending the rise *au pas de charge* shouting 'Vive l'Empereur'. They continued to advance till within 50 or 60 paces of our front, when the Brigade were ordered to stand up. Whether it was from the sudden and unexpected appearance of a Corps so near them, which must

---

27   Ibid, *passim.*

have seemed as starting out of the ground, or the tremendous heavy fire we threw into them, *La Garde*, who had never before failed in an attack *suddenly* stopped. Those who from a distance could see the affair, tell us that the effect of our fire seemed to force the head of the Column bodily back.

In less than a minute above 300 were down. They now wavered, and several of the rear divisions began to draw out as if to deploy, whilst some of the men in their rear beginning to fire over the heads of those in front was so evident a proof of their confusion, that Lord Saltoun halloaed out 'Now's the time, my boys.' Immediately the Brigade sprang forward. La Garde turned and gave us little opportunity of trying the steel. We charged down the hill till we had passed the end of the orchard of Hougoumont. . . .

34

ENSIGN PARDO'S COAT

A sergeant[28] tells a friend how he rallied his men.

When the French advanced, their cannon at the same time raked us with grape, canister, and horse-nails; and our line was so shattered, that I feared they could not stand: I was for a moment really afraid they would give way; and if they had it would have gone hard with the whole line. . . . Our loss was most tremendous. It was at this juncture that I picked up Ensign Pardo's coat, which was covered with his blood, lying on a horse. The Ensign belonged to our battalion; he was killed and stripped by some of the plunderers. I stepped about 25 paces before the line, and waved the coat, cheering the men, and telling them that while our officers bled we should not reckon our lives dear. I did this a second time, when the Imperials came up against us, and I believe it had its desired effect. I thought if anything would stimulate the men, this would be effective. An officer having just sacrificed his life for his country's safety – ours were pledged for the same. The men fought with all their might; and in half an hour, we cut all to pieces. . . . I had nothing in view but to conquer or die. I believe this was the animated spirit of the British line, and they did their duty; but no more. This our country expects, and is ever worthy of it.

The general confusion in the blinding smoke from musket powder, punctuated by the roar of the guns and the groans of the wounded, is pictured by Sir Augustus Frazer:

I have seen nothing like that moment, the sky literally darkened with smoke, the sun just going down, and which till then had not for some hours broken through the gloom of the day, the indescribable shouting of

---

28   Wellington said of sergeants: 'I have served with all nations, and I am convinced that there would be nothing so intelligent, so valuable, as English soldiers of that rank, if you could get them sober, *which is impossible.*'

thousands, where it was impossible to distinguish between friend and foe. Every man's arm seemed to be raised against that of every other. Suddenly, after the mingled mass had ebbed and flowed, the enemy began to yield; and cheerings and English huzzas announced that the day must be ours.[29]

Late at night, he summed up the emotions of the day.

35

'Days of glory, falsely so called'

Lieutenant-Colonel Sir Augustus Frazer (1776–1835) tells his wife how he took pity on French prisoners.

June 18, 11 pm

How shall I describe the scenes through which I have pased since morning? I am now so tired that I can hardly hold my pen. . . . Never was there a more bloody affair, never so hot a fire. I cannot describe the scene of carnage. The struggle lasted even by moonlight. . . . The noise, the groans of the dying, and all the horrid realities of the field are yet before me. To-day is Sunday! How often have I observed that actions are fought on Sundays. Alas! What three days have I passed, what days of glory, falsely so called; and what days of misery to thousands. The field of battle to-day is strewed with dead! Never did I see so many. . . .

I might have got a decoration for you, but the officer of the Imperial Guard who wore it, and who offered it as a prisoner, looked so wistfully at the reward of many a gallant day, that I could not think of taking it. I made an acquaintance in the field with a French lieut.colonel of the 7th Dragoons, poor fellow, sadly wounded and prisoner. How misery makes friends of all. . . .

One of the ladies at the Duchess of Richmond's ball, Major Hamilton's fiancée, gives a vivid account of how the battle appeared to the anxious women at Brussels. Many of them afterwards tended the wounded on the battlefield.

---

29   H.T. Siborne, *Waterloo Letters*, 1891, p. 293.

36

THE BACKWASH OF WAR

Miss E. Ord to her brother in Florence.

July 9th

... The landing of Bonaparte put a stop to all our gaieties; in Easter week the alarm of his intending to make a dash at this country made almost all the English families fly off to Ostend, Antwerp, and England.

This storm and all the clouds attending it soon blew over, Lord Wellington arrived, almost all the fugitives came back, Brussels became as gay as ever, and if possible pleasanter when one could avoid thinking of what was to come. Lord Wellington had delightful Balls every week, and of course military of all nations abounded at them. Troops from England were arriving every day, and I think one saw every officer almost one had ever seen or heard of. At last on the 15th of June we were all invited to a Ball at the Duchess of Richmond's, and in the middle of that Lord Wellington recevied the account of the Prussians having been attacked and beat by Bonaparte, who was advancing towards one end of the English lines as fast as possible. To give an idea of this take-leave Ball is impossible, it was too dismal; but I must not begin to talk of our feelings these three or four days or I should never be able to stop. . . .

On the 16th for several hours we had a cannonade, the concussion of which on the Air we felt as if it was close at hand. It was frightful. . . . About 12 o'clock at night, Major Hamilton, with whom we had been dancing the night before and who had not gone to bed after the Ball, had rode to the field of Battle, fought all day, had his horse killed under him with other hair-breadth escapes, and had then rode off here to tell us the news. In two hours, he started again. On the 17th, you never saw anything like the state of this town night and day. The streets jammed full of horses, waggons, artillery, soldiers, – bivouacs even in our little quiet street. . . .

Sunday the 18th we shall never forget – it was passed in a sort of stupid state of despair, enlivened by reports spread to create confusion, that French Dragoons were actually in the Town. Waggons, Baggage, &c. were overturned in the fright, the road was blocked up, and the infamous villains who had raised the cry (composed of stragglers of all nations) plundered everything at their leisure, and above half the Officers have lost everything they had; those who were left to guard taking fright and galloping off in every direction, and assuring every one the French were at their heels. Every hour brought the name of some officer either killed or wounded, that the fighting was desperate, till at last we sat looking at each other without venturing to ask any questions. Again at night Major Hamilton arrived having just walked from the field of Battle, leading a horse with two balls in it, and his poor General on it severely wounded, and himself slightly so in the head. His account was that never was there such fighting from the Duke down to the Drummer, that he feared from the Prussians not being yet in action when he left the field, and the immense superiority in numbers, particularly in cavalry, of the French, that things would not end well, and in that case Brussels could not be kept. Our manner of passing the night I leave you to guess – Anne and I never took off our clothes. By five in the morning we heard that never was there so complete a Victory. . . .

Lord Wellington was everything that he ought to be, grave, awed, astonished – making exclamations about the wonderful conduct of the Army. The scenes after such a battle fought within so short a distance have been dreadful, thousands of wounded brought in hourly. Our greatest happiness was now to be useful to the sufferers. Our whole time is taken up with our Patients, and we go and sit by the beds; you cannot think how it seems to please them. There have been 30,000 wounded in the town at one time. . . .

Pity for the defeated emperor, hitherto regarded as a 'monster', was widespread in England.

37

'Poor fellow – he is so dejected'
THE PLYMOUTH MOB CHEERS NAPOLEON

Lady Charlotte Fitzgerald tells Sir Charles Hastings how the British changed their view of their enemy when he had fallen.

Exmouth, Aug. 11, 1815

I have seen Bonaparte distinctly, I was quite close to him and witnessed his transfer from one ship to another!!! Believe me the most unwise step our government ever took was showing John Bull that Bonaparte had neither horns nor hoofs! One used to hear the epithets 'Monster', 'Rascal' or 'Roast him alive' tacked to his name, but that time is gone by, and he is now mentioned as 'Poor fellow, well I do pity him' or 'What an air of grandeur he has tho' he is so dejected.' Such are the remarks amongst the common people and in not one instance has a severe opinion been passed upon him; his appearance seems to have effaced the recollections of the British blood he has spilt and to have removed the just as well the unjust prejudice we had to this man. During his stay at Plymouth the popular tide in his favour ran alarmingly high, and one evening the mob won by his smiles cheered him with enthusiasm; after that all visitors were enjoined to preserve silence and neither to rise up in their boats or to touch their hats when he came forward. How the appearance of Napoleon could thus soften their hearts rather surprises me, as his effect on mine was so different. I went to see him admiring him through all his crimes, compassionating him as a prisoner and one whom I thought had been harshly treated since he gave himself up to the British clemency, but I came away with my heart considerably steeled against him and with many fears lest the lion should again escape from his cage! The true reason of their bringing him back to Dartmouth was, that they durst not attempt changing him from one ship to another amongst his Plymouth partizans.[30]

30 Two days earlier, Charles Lamb had written to Robert Southey: 'After all, Buonaparte is a fine fellow, as my barber says, and I should not mind standing bareheaded at his table to do him service in his fall. They should have given him Hampton Court or Kensington. . . . Would not the people have ejected the Brunswicks some day in his favour?' (*Letters*, I, p. 351.)

Wellington was filled with awestruck humility in victory, won by relying on the defensive strength of the British soldier's character, but also through a number of lucky hazards, as he was the first to admit. He wrote to his brother: 'In all my life I have not experienced such anxiety, for I must confess I have never been so close to defeat,' and when he arrived in Brussels, he was in tears over the death of most of his staff and said: 'Do not congratulate me. I have lost all my dearest friends. . . . The finger of God was on me all day – nothing else could have saved me.' Yet he also saw the battle in terms of a hard-contested school match on the playing fields of Eton.

38

AN OLD-STYLE POUNDING MATCH OF GLUTTONS

The Duke of Wellington to Marshal Viscount Beresford.

Gonesse, July 2, 1815

You will have heard of our battle of the 18th. Never did I see such a pounding match: both were what the boxers call gluttons. Napoleon did not manoeuvre at all; he just moved forward in the old style, in columns, and was driven off in the old style; the only difference was, that he mixed cavalry with his infantry, and supported both with an enormous quantity of artillery. I had the infantry for some time in squares, and we had the French cavalry walking about us as if they had been our own. I never saw the British infantry behave so well.

Curious sightseers and avid souvenir hunters descended on the battlefield, Sir Walter Scott among them. He then went to Paris and commented on the eccentricity of the rich officer dandies in the age of Beau Brummel:

All the young men pique themselves on imitating the Duke of Wellington in nonchalance and coolness of manner. So they wander about everywhere with their hands in the pockets of their long waistcoats or cantering upon cossack ponies staring whistling and strolling to and fro as if all Paris were theirs. The French hate them sufficiently for the hauteur of their manner and pretensions but these grounds of dislike against us are drowned in the detestation afforded by the other powers.[31]

However, to the soldier who received £2 11s. 4d. in prize money (when generals got £1,275 and Wellington £61,000) it was of little use that the army had become more popular than ever before. He might soon be facing

---

31   *Letters of Sir Walter Scott*, Constable, 1933, p. 95.

unemployment in the slump following the war, without any hope of social reforms in the climate of anti-Jacobin reaction.

In the next two letters, Wellington reveals his views on the much-contested truth about Waterloo and battles in general. He never gave his own account, stating: 'I should like to tell the truth; but if I did, I should be torn to pieces here and abroad.'

39

WATERLOO: FICTION AND TRUTH

Wellington to Richard Earl of Clancarty, British Ambassador to the Netherlands.

Mont St Martin (HQ nr Cambrai) 3rd Dec. 1817

. . . The truth regarding the battle of Waterloo is this: there exists in England an insatiable curiosity upon every subject which has occasioned a mania for travelling and for writing. The battle of Waterloo having been fought within reach, every creature who can afford it, travelled to view the field; and almost every one who came who could write, wrote an account. It is inconceivable the number of lies that were published and circulated in this manner by English travellers; and other nations, seeing how successfully this could be done, thought it as well to adopt the same means of circulating their own stories. This has been done with such industry that it is now quite certain that I was not present and did not command in the battle of Quatre Bras, and it is very doubtful whether I was present in the battle of Waterloo. It is not so easy to dispose of the British army as it is of an individual: but although it is admitted they were present, the brave Belgians, or the brave Prussians, won the battle.

40

Wellington to John W. Croker who wrote the history of the war.

Paris, 8th August 1815

. . . The history of the battle is not unlike the history of a ball. Some individuals may recollect all the little events of which the great result is the battle won or lost; but no individual can recollect the order in which, or the exact moment at which, they occurred, which makes all the difference as to their value and importance.

Then the faults and misbehaviour of some gave occasion for the distinction of others; and you cannot write a true history of a battle without including the faults and misbehaviour of part at least of those engaged.

Believe me that every man you see in a military uniform is not a hero; and that, although in the account given of a general action, such as that of war, many instances of individual heroism must be passed over unrelated, it is better for the general interests to leave those parts of the story untold, than to tell the whole truth. . . .

Wellington's realistic wisdom had also saved Napoleon's life (Blücher wanted to shoot him on the spot), and his counsel of moderation as Commander-in-Chief of the Allied Army of Occupation prevented the cession of French territory to Prussia. Centuries of bitter Anglo–French warfare had come to an end.

During this period reluctance to go to war on the continent increased, as awareness of the hardships of war became more acute; defending England against invasion was a different matter. Flamboyant hero worship started to fade: a cold impassive view of warfare, initiated by the Iron Duke, pointed to the future when war would begin to be viewed as an unpleasant necessity to be accomplished steadfastly and methodically. For the soldier, the excitement of battle and the promise of loot still kept their attraction despite the appalling hazards.

T W E L V E

The Crimean War (1854–6)

Now France and England are combined,
To starve him out,
That despot Russian bear . . .

ANON.

The main causes of the Crimean War were, on the British side, Russian expansionism towards Turkey, the 'sick man of Europe', and the threat it implied to trade interests in the Levant and the overland route to India; for Napoleon III, it was revival of Bonapartist prestige and leadership, and revenge for 1812 and the Russian occupation of Paris. A kind of jingoist liberalism united both countries, who had been enemies for so long, in a crusade against Czarist reaction treading down Hungarians, Poles and Turks. Suspicion of French revival and designs in Italy, and the belief that they could best be curbed by an alliance, also played an important role in British policy. Besides, the public had grown tired of forty years of peace: 'The country is eager for War,' wrote Queen Victoria to the Earl of Aberdeen, her Prime Minister, while watching the army depart, and urged him to increase it by 30,000 to meet all risks: 'Who can say it is impossible that our own shores be threatened by powers now in alliance with us?'[1]

1

THE GUARDS CHEER THE QUEEN AND EMBARK

Queen Victoria (1819–1901) tells her uncle, King Leopold I of Belgium, about the Scots Fusilier Guards parading outside Buckingham Palace.

---

1   *Letters of Queen Victoria*, III, J. Murray, 1907, p. 15.

28th February 1854

The last battalion of the Guards embarked to-day. They passed through the courtyard here at 7 o'clock this morning. We stood on the balcony to see them – the morning fine, the sun rising over the towers of old Westminster Abbey – and an immense crowd collected to see these fine men, and cheering them immensely. They formed line, presented arms, and then cheered us *very heartily*, and went off cheering. It was a *touching and beautiful* sight; many sorrowing friends were there, and one saw the shake of many a hand. My best wishes and prayers will be with them all. . . .

The Path of Disillusion

Theirs is not to reason why,
Theirs is but to do and die
LORD TENNYSON, CHARGE OF THE LIGHT BRIGADE

Despite the disappearance of the *casus belli* after the Russian withdrawal from the Turkish provinces they had occupied, the expeditionary force of 26,000 British and 30,000 French soldiers, which had assembled at Varna, and was stricken by a cholera epidemic, embarked there on 7 September 1854. The invasion fleet steamed past the shore of Eupatoria, watched by Russian officers through telescopes, and landed unopposed at the aptly named Calamita Bay on the Southern tip of the Crimean peninsula, near the naval arsenal of Sebastopol. Euphoria gradually gave way to doubt and despair.

2

THE 'PLEASURE TRIP' IS NO 'CAUSE FOR REJOICING'

Lieutenant-Colonel (Sir) Frederick Stephenson (1821–1911) tells his mother and sisters how he got 'heartily sick' of what he first thought was going to be a 'charming continental tour.'

September 14, 1854

. . . We are in the act of disembarking. There is no opposition. The sight of this fleet, numbering upwards of 200 sail, is magnificent. The whole affair is really more like a pleasure trip than anything else, and if you were to hear all the laughing and joking that is incessantly going on, you would fancy yourself just about to land at Boulogne with a charming continental tour in prospect. . . .

Nov. 2

. . . We are still hammering away at Sebastopol, the capture of which is harder work than was at first supposed. There is a spirit in this army such as I am sure was never surpassed, and I think our labours are near their close.

Nov. 7

We have fought another general action [Inkerman], which was more severe than even the one at Alma. The enemy were at length driven back and completely routed. The siege in the meanwhile is not going on as well as one could wish, for though I am now giving you an account of a most glorious victory, it has been a most sad one, and anything but a cause for rejoicing. . . .

Nov. 12

. . . How the campaign will end I do not yet clearly see, but do not be disappointed if we do not take Sebastopol. The place is stronger than people thought, and our army has proved much too small for so serious an undertaking.

Jan. 21, 1855

. . . Our army is gradually vanishing, and by the spring we shall hardly have a man left. . . .

July 21

. . . I am still on the sick list. I think we are all beginning to get heartily sick of this war, Army, Navy, and everybody. I see no prospect of a satisfactory termination, and should heartily rejoice at a peace. . . .

[He was soon sent home for recovery.]

The war was the worst organized in British history and this was perhaps its principal feature and value: a feeling of revulsion arose when the first war correspondents and photographers brought the ugly face of war home to the English public which had up to then only bathed in its heroism and glory. The sheer incompetence of the governmental and military administration was unbelievable: nothing seemed to have been foreseen and the comparison with the provision the French had made was most humiliating. Thousands of soldiers perished because of it in the harsh Russian winter.

The poetess Elizabeth Barrett Browning was an ardent admirer of Napoleon III as liberator of her beloved Italy and welcomed the alliance. At first she thought the war was being fought for the noblest ideals, but three months later she became painfully disillusioned.

3

THE WAR FOR 'THE GOOD OF THE WORLD' TURNS SOUR

Elizabeth Barrett Browning (1806–61), writing to her sister Mrs Cook, is comforted in her despondency by the Anglo–French alliance.

Florence, November 6, 1854

. . . It seems to me a most righteous and necessary war – and that's all one can say of a war, when one would say the best. The Turks are not interesting, I confess – but can we say that they should not be protected according to the bond voluntarily entered into by us? and would you stand by and see a dog, even, kicked to death? Then there are great interests involved besides the specific Turkish interests – the liberty and civilization of all Europe, and the good of the world for centuries. Therefore, hating war, I do accept the war as a necessity. A dreadful necessity certainly – it makes my blood creep to think of the agony of mind endured by thousands who have no personal part at Sevastopol, and who suffer and die doubly in those dearer to them than life. The telegraphs, from their uncertainty, add much to that sort of anguish. . . . What comforts me is the *alliance*. Nothing so good ever happened either to England or France as their union; and it is infinitely affecting to me to read the instances of friendship between them, with which the newspapers abound. . . .

February 12, 1855

. . . Robert has been frantic about the Crimea. The accounts turn one sick – and yet out of all this turning up of the fetid ground, will result, I hope, a better system of drainage. A little humiliation will teach us that we are not perfect, and that our administration is one of the most corrupt in Europe. How well and magnanimously the French have behaved! Their newspapers touch most delicately and forbearingly on our errors in organization, covering us with admiration upon other points. . . .

One of the bravest subalterns, 'with the heart of a lion and the modesty of a young girl' (Wolseley), who was decorated by the Queen with the VC at the inauguration of the new reward (open to all ranks) in Hyde Park for leading the ladder assault on the Redan, voices unexpected views on war.

4

THE ABSURDITY, AND BEAUTY OF WAR

Lieutenant (later Lieutenant-General Sir) Gerald Graham to his sister.

Before Sebastopol, 23 October 1854

. . . Excitement apart, war is the most disagreeable employment in the world, a hideous and unnatural absurdity, – a pretty general opinion – though, no doubt, 40 years hence old fogies will talk of the glorious campaign in the Crimea as the pleasantest period of their life. . . . O! War is a horrible thing, and that I have often thought when out in one of those beautiful starlit nights. To see these countless worlds shining above us in supreme indifference to our wretched little contentions and ludicrously horrible way of settling them, seemed to settle the whole war at once by reducing it to an absolute nonentity. . . . My reflections on this subject would, however, be suddenly interrupted. A bright flash would be seen like distant summer sheet-lightning. 'A shot!' calls the man on the look-out. All is silent for three or four seconds, when the report is heard simultaneously with the rushing, roaring sound of the shot or shell as it flies over our heads, or knocks one of them off, dashing on with indifference in either case. The shell thrown from a mortar is a beautiful sight at night as it rises high in the air, its fuse glowing brightly like a star; in describing a beautiful curve, it falls and fulfills its murderous errand by exploding, if correct, a few feet above the ground. . . .

On 25 October a strong Russian attack was repelled at Balaclava when Brigadier-General Sir James Scarlett (aged sixty-one) led the victorious uphill charge of the Heavy Brigade of 900 against 3,000 Russian cavalry. Characteristically, it was rather the disastrous Charge of the Light Brigade which gained immortal fame; owing to a stupid error by fumbling commanders it resulted in a heroic blood-bath without purpose. The Commander-in-Chief, Lord Raglan, was sixty-six and had not been on active service since he was Wellington's military secretary at Waterloo. He kept on talking about the French as the enemy (both he and the even more aged French Commander-in-Chief Saint-Arnaud soon died). Raglan issued a vaguely worded order to the commander of the cavalry, Lord Lucan, to recapture a few guns Turkish auxiliaries had lost. It was misunderstood and Lord Cardigan (the most hated officer in the army who lorded it in his private yacht) galloped off with his Light Brigade straight into a battery of Russian guns, amid the most devastating cross-fire. Of 673 cavalrymen only 195 returned in their saddles, and Cardigan reported unmoved: 'I have lost my Brigade'. The soldiers' wives watched both charges.

5

THE CHARGE OF THE HEAVY BRIGADE

Lieutenant (later Major-General) Richard Temple Godman, 5th Dragoon Guards, describes it to his father.

October 26, 1854

Yesterday the attack came off, and here I am, Thank God, safe and sound, though the loss of cavalry we have sustained is very severe. . . . When we got the order to advance, the Greys and Inniskillings went first, then we came in support, the charge sounded and at them went the first line; Scarlett well in front. The enemy seemed quite astonished and drew into a walk and then a halt; as soon as they met, all I saw was swords in the air in every direction, the pistols going off, and everyone hacking away right and left. In a moment the Greys were surrounded and hemmed completely in; there they were fighting back to back in the middle, the great bearskin caps high above the enemy.

This was the work of a moment; as soon as we saw it, the 5th advanced and in they charged, yelling and shouting as hard as they could split, the row was tremendous, and for about five minutes neither would give way, and their column was so deep we could not cut through it. At length they turned and the whole ran as hard as they could pelt back up the hill, our men after them and cutting them down right and left. We pursued about 300 yards, and then called off with much difficulty, the gunners then opened on them, and gave them a fine peppering. . . . The ground was covered with dead and dying men and horses, strewn with swords, broken and whole, trumpets, helmets, carbines. . . . Lord Raglan who was looking down from a hill close by sent an A.D.C. to say 'Well done the Heavy Brigade'. . . .

Owing to a mistake in an order from Lord Raglan, the Light Cavalry then charged down the valley, under fire on each side, and a battery of, I believe, 20 guns in front. They drove all before them; took the guns, cut down the gunners and then retired but were perfectly annihilated by the cross-fire. . . . It was a terrible sight to see them walking back one by one and the valley strewn with them – all for nothing. . . .

6

THE CHARGE OF THE LIGHT BRIGADE

Lieutenant Edward Phillips, 8th Hussars, describes their gallop into the guns.

. . . We advanced at a steady trot, soon to a faster pace; the guns on the flanks opened fire with shell and round shot; two regiments of infantry began firing volleys of Minie balls and almost at the same time the guns at the bottom of the valley opened with grape. In spite of this awful fire we galloped over the ground strewed with the men of the first line, and our own dropping at every yard; every sound was there, the bursting of shells, the deep dash of the round shot and the whistling of the storm of Minie balls and grape shot. We passed the Infantry, and approached the guns at the bottom of the valley, which the first line charged in the midst of a fire that swept down at them and carried off almost all the officers. We charged bang through, thus opening a way for the remnant of the first line now quite broken by their losses. There were not sufficient left and everyone made his way back through the same awful fire as before; how ever any one of us escaped the storm of shot and shell and bullet is miraculous. . . .

Muddle, Horror and Nightingale

Our men are most shamefully cheerful
under these afflicting circumstances
ENSIGN J. ADDINGTON

Charles Gordon, later of China and Sudan fame, was a daring young subaltern in the engineers. He gives an excellent summary of the conditions the army had to endure.

7

TWO THIRDS WERE SICK

Lieutenant (later Major-General) Charles Gordon (1833–85) gives a retrospective description of the scene he found when he arrived early in 1855.

[n.d.]

. . . The men lay shivering on the frozen ground. Their damp clothes froze solid. There was no firewood. They had to eat their saltpork raw. There was no tea, and nothing with which to grind the green coffee. Horses died by the hundreds. In Balaclava harbour, six miles down the steep track, there were warm clothes, blankets, tents, food & fodder in such abundance that, for want of storage space, much of it was dumped in the sea; but there were no labourers, no tools to repair the track, nor any carts or pack animals to carry up supplies if it had been repaired. . . . In mid-November the frost changed to five days of torrential rain, followed by a hurricane which sank 21 ships off Balaclava together with their precious cargoes. There were comparatively few battle casualties; but through desertion, self-inflicted wounds, gangrene, fever, cholera, dysentery, rhumatism and starvation, the British army in the Crimea was reduced by January to 11,000 effectives with 23,000 sick.

When it dawned on the public what was happening in the Crimea, thanks to William Russell's reports in *The Times* and Roger Fenton's photographs, there was an outcry against the government.

8

BEYOND HUMAN ENDURANCE

Frances Anne Marchioness of Londonderry, wife of the general, whose son was serving in the Crimea, complains bitterly to Benjamin Disraeli about the total failure of the government to make adequate provision for the Army.

[1854]

Surely there must be an hour of reckoning for this hateful Government who go to war without providing an army. It is actual murder to let this little heroic wreck of an army fight those hordes and masses of barbarians who reinforce by tens of thousands while we hardly do so with hundreds. And that wintering in the Crimea, without comforts, habitations, hardly provisions – it is all heartbreaking. I think of nothing else even in my sleep, and if I were younger I am sure I should seize on the idea of 'The Times', and get a yacht and go there. It seems to dreadful to sit at home and do nothing. . . . I have deplorable accounts – floating encampments on mud, no fresh meat even for the officers, pork and biscuit, horses dying all round, and none to be got even to bring up the supplies taken out. There seems neither care nor thought, and a total indifference as to what becomes of the wreck of this fine army, and the brave spirits who seem tasked beyond human endurance.

The silent suffering of the tough, bearded, pipe-smoking men, so much worse cared for than the French, was beyond praise.

9

THE SOLDIERS' 'PATIENCE UNDER SEVERE DEPRIVATION'

Lieutenant-General (later Field Marshal) Sir John Burgoyne, son of the dramatist-general and in command of the Engineers, writes to Sir Francis Head, author of *The Defenceless State of Great Britain* (1850).

27 December 1854

... When I compare our army with theirs [the French], I see much to admire and to follow in organization, and much to envy in their habits, and knowledge how to make themselves comparatively comfortable, when our helpless creatures are full of miseries. We find our Allies frequently singing and gay, while for months I have not witnessed so much as a smile on the face of a British soldier – who, although suffering and serious, make no complaints! The spirit and animation and resolute courage in facing the enemy have greatly exceeded all I could have thought of them. It is not individuals among them, but the great body – the masses who in the open field and in broad daylight, rush upon a most determined enemy, as the Russians certainly are, to the closest quarters. . . . And if anything can exceed the conduct of these soldiers for daring spirit in action, and patience under severe deprivation, it is that of the officers! This service in the Crimea cries shame on those who in England talk of the officers in the army as fine gentlemen, thinking of nothing but idleness and self- indulgence! . . .

General Canrobert observed with amazement that the British advanced 'as if they were in Hyde Park', and fought 'like Victoria dances'. He in turn was described by the British as 'grimacing and gesturing like an actor'. This mocking incomprehension between the allies of two future great wars was to continue.

The suffering of the private in the Crimean winter was frightful: 90 per cent of the casualties were due to cholera, typhus and pneumonia – all for a net pay of £1 a month and the prospect of getting flogged up to three hundred lashes. To keep up their spirits, the rag-bag forces played cruel practical jokes on the wretched Turks.

10

IN RAGS BUT TEASING THE TURKS

Lieutenant Temple Godman writes home.

December 17, 1854

. . . You would not recognize the British soldier again were you to see him here, unwashed and unshaven, covered with mud from head to foot, some clothed partly in Russian garments, an old sack, or some original dress made out of an old blanket, tied on with bits of string. Then alas! the Heavy Dragoon and smart Hussar, what if some of our lady friends could see us now; I don't think they would ever care much about soldiers again, with uniforms torn, and hardly to be recognized, legs bound up with hay and straw bands, some without shoes or socks.

The Johnnys [Turks] are made to do all the dirty work, that is as much as the idle rascals can be forced to do. Everyone pushes and cuffs them, especially the sailors, who make great fuss of them. They work now in the trenches and when Jack [Tar] sees a shell coming, he picks up a stone which he lets drive the Johnny, just as the shell bursts somewhere near, who feeling himself hit drops his spade, and runs about howling, to the immense delight of Jack and his comrades.

The main cause of the incredible inefficiency was divided and uncoordinated control: the War Office was responsible for the worldwide distribution of troops and for finance, the Commissariat at the Treasury for food and transport, and the Ordnance for artillery, munitions and equipment. The commander in the field could do nothing to alleviate the general disorganization of allocations, owing to a labyrinth of regulations and responsibilities. There were herds of cattle in the wrong place while the soldiers got only salt beef, plenty of coal and wood on the ships while the freezing soldiers had to eat their meat raw because there was no transport for the six miles of slush and mud between Balaclava harbour and the trenches on the heights, and the many thousands of children's stockings and left-foot boots which were delivered were a cruel mockery to the bare-footed men in the snow and ice. As usual the government shifted the blame onto the military command which, in fact, was only responsible for its own blunders. Apart from the Press, the uncensored postal service spread the dismal news at home where the attitude to war was changing rapidly: the lives of soldiers, even of humble station, began to be valued, and the disregard of basic human decencies was no longer accepted.

Captain Campbell and Lieutenant-Colonel Sterling were highly critical observers and their attitude foreshadows the new outlook.

11

THE BRITISH SOLDIER BEFORE SEBASTOPOL

Captain Colin Campbell describes to his brother-in-law, Francis Russell, and to his sister, the gloom, deadly cramps and waddling in mud, with 'none of the excitement of personal conflict'.

November 17th, 1854

. . . A deep gloom settled over the camp, partly caused by regret at the loss of so many brave fellows at the battle of Inkerman, and partly from the conviction that the siege must be raised. I find that this has spread even more amongst the men than among the officers. The thinking part of us look forward with alarm to the idea of spending a winter in this place, as our stores are already beginning to run short, and the roads are in such a state that the commissariat have the greatest difficulty in bringing our food from Balaclava. There is no blinking the fact that we who are besieging Sebastopol are ourselves a besieged army, and live in a constant state of alarm lest our rear should be attacked. The fire of the French and English batteries, which, when I came here, was kept up with great spirit has now dwindled away to almost nothing. . . .

The work for the English troops here is dreadfully hard, and is killing the men; what is most trying is what are called covering parties – large bodies of men are marched down every night to the entrenchments and remain there 24 hours, to prevent the Russians from entering the batteries and spiking the guns. Whatever the weather may be there the men have to stay, and, as their clothing is very insufficient, the men are sometimes half dead with cold. Nothing like a fire can be lit, as it would immediately bring upon us the fire of the Russian batteries. . . . The state of the trenches in rainy weather surpasses all description; the thick sticky mud is nearly a foot deep, and in it the men have to lie, as the sight of their heads above the parapet in daytime would be the signal for a shower of shot and shell. . . . We are losing four or five a day by what is put down in the returns as cholera, but is nothing but cramps brought on by lying in the wet and cold.

As long as I live I shall never forget the day of that dreadful storm, which destroyed so much of our shipping. I was in the trenches, in charge of 150 men about five miles from our camp. At about eight o'clock at night, when it was my time to go home, having been there 24 hours, I found the men dreadfully exhausted, and began to have great doubts whether I should ever be able to get them home. The extreme violence of the wind had ceased, but it was snowing fast, as dark as pitch, and the road difficult to find. However, there was nothing for it but to try; we were four hours on the road, and nearly lost our way. The snow and wind were in our faces all the way, and at one time I had to halt the men and make them a short speech, in which I told them that anyone who fell out would have to lie and die as he fell, as I could not stop to assist anyone.

This roused them up to struggle on, and I got them all to the camp; I shall never forget the scene when I got there. The snow had ceased, but the wind was still blowing violently; every tent in the regiment (except about ten) was down, and the men endeavouring to shelter themselves under the wet canvas as it lay on the ground; 160 men had been taken sick that day, and were lying crowded in the hospital tents, the whole of which had been blown over, and the sick and dying were lying under them, with horses, that had broken loose during the storm, galloping about. Ten men of our regiment died on that night. . . .

The perpetual talk amongst the men is, 'Why do they not allow us to assault?' But an engineer officer told me the other day that three weeks ago we might have assaulted with success, but that we had not a sufficient number of men to do so, and now that reinforcements had come it was too late, as the streets were barricaded, the walls loopholed, and such preparations made as would destroy an army. We might winter here if we got an immense supply of firewood and forage, but if circumstances turned out unfavourably the whole army might be annihilated. I wish we were all safe on the other side of the Black Sea, and that, I can assure you, is the general feeling in the camp. . . .

December 22

Our life is so dreary that I wonder sometimes that I am able to fill up a letter. We waddle down to the trenches every other day or night, and in the morning or evening waddle slowly back again with one or two wretched fellows killed or wounded. We acquire the gait I called waddling from the slipperiness of the ground and the quantity of clothes we have to carry.

January 17th, 1855

The want of transport has destroyed more lives and caused more misery than all other mistakes put together. I have seen our men after having come back from the trenches, and having barely time to eat some biscuit and coffee, sent off to Balaclava to bring up rations, warm clothing, blankets, etc. They would return at night after their 14-mile tramp through the mud, and throw themselves down on the floor of their tents as if they were dead, so exhausted, that even if their dinners had been got ready for them, many of them could not have eaten a morsel. Next morning probably one third of them would be in hospital, and the remainder for the trenches the following evening.

The day after the battle of Inkerman, and even before it, every man with one grain of sense could foresee that Sebastopol would not fall for months, and that we must spend the winter there. Notwithstanding, not one single preparation was made. If each regiment had been furnished with 2–300 short poles and a few entrenching tools, they could have hutted themselves in a week.

I do not think a single mule was bought, although even in fine weather we were very insufficiently supplied, and lived from hand to mouth, never being able to bring up more than one day's rations. Yet with the whole coast of Asia Minor teeming with ponies and barley, within 48 hours' sail of us, and vessels which could bring over 300 at each trip lying in the harbour, it is scarcely credible that not one single animal was brought. Our cavalry were set to work to carry biscuit, an occupation which killed the horses at the rate of about 20 a day. About the beginning of December 250 mules arrived, a set of half-starved dying animals savagely thrashed along by Poles, Bulgarians, Tartars, and every sort of blackguard. What a contrast in the French animals! They pass our camp in long lines of hundreds daily, they walk in a row, every mule as fat and sleek as if he were a pet, and stepping along cheerfully. To every three mules there is a French soldier who chats to his mules as if they were his friends. This is only one of the points in which they beat us; it is the same in everything. . . .

If I were to try to write about all the mistakes and blunders made in our different departments here, I should fill a tolerable volume. They are endless. Those in the medical department, though not worse than others, are more dreadful in their consequences. Doctors will tell you how they have been suddenly ordered on board a ship to take 300 men across the Black Sea; how the men would lie on the hard boards in every form of cholera, dysentry, and fever, with not one atom of medicine to give them, and two or three drunken pensioners to attend on them. In the morning the doctors and pensioners would go round picking out the dead from the living, and throwing them overboard. . . .

June 11

. . . Of all the dreadful places in the world, I think a battery under a hot sun and a heavy fire is the most dreadful. There is none of the excitement of personal conflict; you become blackened with smoke, and the heat and noise are almost unendurable. Then the nature of the wounds is so dreadful; you see men cut to pieces with a round shot, or blown up with a shell, so that there is no trace of there having been human beings left. I saw myself a sailor blown up by a 13-inch shell at least 40 feet high. . . . I dare say you would like to know what my own sensations were when standing on the top of the parapet. I assure you I felt neither fear nor excitement; I had almost the same feelings as I have had when long-stopping to a swift bowler on bad ground, except that there my anxiety was to stop the balls, whilst here I had every wish to let them pass. . . .

12

'They are the true England'

Lieutenant-Colonel (Sir) Anthony Sterling, Assistant Adjutant-General to the Highland Division, describes how the British soldier endured the winter and what reward he could expect.

Balaclava, 10th January, 1855

. . . Yesterday I was obliged to go on duty to the Light Division. The ground was covered with melting snow, regular slush, with hard-frozen ground underneath; so that riding was a ticklish matter. I found sad misery among the men; they have next to no fuel, almost all the roots, even of the brushwood, being exhausted. They are entitled to rations of charcoal; but they have no means of drawing it, and their numbers are so reduced, that they cannot spare men enough to bring it from Balaclava. The consequence is, they cannot dry their stockings or shoes; they come in from the trenches with frost-bitten toes, swelled feet, chilblains, etc.; their shoes freeze, and they cannot put them on. Those who still, in spite of this misery, continue to do their duty, often go into the trenches without shoes or they cut away the heels to get them on. I heard of men on their knees crying with pain. Of course there are men, and plenty of them, who will never give in, but rather die on the spot for England and duty. . . . Many of the frost-bitten men will lose their feet; the army is cruelly weakened. The French suffer little of all this: for they have plenty of organised transport.

23rd January

. . . The French have always had fresh meat and fresh bread baked every other day, for their whole army, while we have been left on salt meat and biscuit. Retribution I hope will fall sooner or later on the guilty person, whoever he may be. England will cry for her men. Let us hope that a noble revenge will be taken; the faults are to be attributed to a system which we must abandon, or we perish as a military nation. I saw yesterday 200 sick carried on board on French mules; I saw the gaunt faces; not one ever likely to do a day's duty again. . . .

26th April

. . . Blindness has smitten the ruling classes of my country, while the expense of the whole affair is something appalling. All our poor soldiers out here are, however, in the highest spirits, and ready to knock their heads against any wall behind which they can find Russians. They are the true England; stars whose brilliance will be historical when aristocratical names are forgotten, or covered with immortal shame. I believe they would fight and die to the last man rather than give in or give up. Beaten they can never be. Remember, they are not chosen; a great majority entered from poverty or misconduct. What an army would the conscription give us! . . .

4th May

. . . War is a very ugly thing, with very little lace and feather belonging to it. What we have a right to admire in war is the display of very admirable qualities in poor, uneducated, brave men, who have nothing to gain except the approbation of the company they belong to, and of their own conviction or conscience. You know how I have praised these poor peasants all along; yet they have wonderful vices – drunkenness, lying, thieving. Still they are – humanity; enduring and daring for a principle many of them, I verily do believe. . . .

8th June

. . . I hate war, as every good soldier and humane person must. The fine part of war is the British private who should have ample provision for life at the national cost, a quart of turtle and a bottle of champagne per man. They will really get 1s. per diem, when incapacitated by age or wounds, and the Crimean medal. . . .

Florence Nightingale was a formidable character: highly emotional and driven by a masochistic sense of mission. From her Hospital for Distressed Gentlewomen in Harley Street she had sailed with thirty-six nurses to the filthy barracks at Scutari where she soon had five thousand wounded on her hands; thousands were still at Balaclava, three hundred miles away, and the medical stores were stuck at Varna. Operations were performed without anaesthetics, even merely fractured limbs were amputated, and although Miss Nightingale did not believe in the existence of germs, sepsis after operations and gangrene epidemics were frequent.[2]

---

2 According to the letters of surgeon G. Lawson, ed. V. Bonham-Carter, Constable, 1968. After the war Miss Nightingale was the first to investigate scientifically the soldiers' health care and living conditions, and at St Thomas' Hospital she founded the first Training School for Nurses. Her example inspired the movement for women's professional education on an equal footing; she died as a Christian mystic at the age of ninety.

13

'It is good for us to be here'
THE LADY WITH THE LAMP

Florence Nightingale (1820–1910) tells William Bowman, the leading ophtalmic surgeon and professor of anatomy, of the appalling conditions in her 'hospital', with '40 British females more difficult to manage than 4000 men'.

November 14, 1854

. . . We had 1715 sick and wounded in this Hospital (among whom 120 Cholera Patients) and 650 severely wounded in the other building, when a message came to me to prepare for 510 wounded who were arriving from Balaclava. I always expected to end my Days as Hospital Matron, but I never expected to be Barrack Mistress. We had but half an hour's notice before they began landing the wounded. Between one and nine o'clock we had the mattresses stuffed, sewn up, laid down – alas! only upon matting on the floor – the men washed and put to bed, and all their wounds dressed. I wish I had time; I would write you a letter dear to a surgeon's heart. I am as good as a 'Medical Times'! But oh! you Gentlemen of England, who sit at Home in all the well-earned satisfaction of your successful cases, can have little Idea from reading the newspapers of the Horror and Misery of operating upon these dying, exhausted men. A London Hospital is a Garden of Flowers to it. . . .

Two of our Medical Heads are brutes and four are angels – for this is a work which makes either angels or devils of men and of women too. As for the assistants, they are all Cubs, and will, while a man is breathing his last breath under the knife, lament the 'annoyance of being called up from their dinners by such a fresh influx of wounded'! But unlicked Cubs grow up into good old Bears. . . . We have now *four miles* of Beds, and not 18 inches apart.

We have our Quarters in one Tower of the Barrack, and all this fresh influx has been laid down in two Corridors with a line of Beds down each side, just room for one person to pass between. Yet in the midst of this appalling Horror (we are steeped up to our necks in blood) there is good, and I can truly say, like St Peter, 'It is good for us to be here' – though I doubt whether St Peter had been here he would have said so. As I went my night rounds among the newly wounded that first night, there was not one murmur, not one groan, the strictest discipline – the most absolute silence and quiet prevailed – only the steps of the Sentry – and I heard one man say, 'I was dreaming of my friends at Home', and another said, 'I was thinking of them'. These poor fellows bear pain and mutilation with an unshrinking heroism which is really superhuman, and die or are cut up without a complaint.

The wounded are now lying up to our very door, and we are landing 540 more. I take rank in the Army as Brigadier General, because 40 British females, whom I have with me, are more difficult to manage than 4000 men. Let no lady come out here who is not used to fatigue and privation. Every ten minutes an Orderly runs, and we have to go and cram lint into a wound till a Surgeon can be sent for, and stop the Bleeding as well as he can. In all our corridor, we have not an average of three Limbs per man. And there are two Ships more 'loading' at the Crimea with wounded. Then come the operations, and a melancholy List is this. They are all performed in the wards – no time to move them; one poor fellow exhausted with hemorrhage, has his leg amputated as a last hope, and dies ten minutes after the Surgeon has left him. Almost before the breath has left his body, it is sewn up in its blanket, and carried away and buried the same day. We have no room for Corpses in the Wards. The Surgeons pass on to the next. . . . Among these exhausted Frames, the mortality of the operations is frightful. . . . We hear there was another engagement and more wounded, who are coming down to us. This is only the beginning of things.

Lieutenant-Colonel Sterling sees the funny side of this revered figure which Lytton Strachey was to debunk with excessive sarcasm together with other 'eminent Victorians', including the Queen herself.

14

MISS NIGHTINGALE'S HIGHLAND BRIGADE OF NURSES

Lieutenant-Colonel Sterling writes home.

Balaclava, 14th February, 1855
. . . We are going to make an attempt upon Miss Nightingale. She keeps all our men when they are discharged from hospital, and makes nurses of them, not considering that the other men are doing their duty in the trenches. I believe she has about 300 men of the Highland Brigade thus employed. There ought to be men enlisted as nurses, and the soldiers should be left to fight. . . .

26th April
. . . I beg your pardon for laughing at the Nightingale, and other birds of her feather. I believe that she has been of use. When will she go home! As Christopher Sly says, 'Would it were done!' They expect her here. Will she wear a wig or a helmet? You see, I cannot help laughing at her, as I have a keen sense of the ridiculous.

The Queen and the Glory

My whole soul and heart
are in the Crimea
QUEEN VICTORIA

Victoria said of herself: 'My nature is too passionate, my emotions are too fervent.' Her romantic exuberance, with a good shot of *naïveté*, pervades the letters she regularly wrote to her uncle, but her heart and common sense were always close to the feelings of the British people. She gained new popularity when she showed her concern for the wounded by organizing relief and personally visiting them. The frequent underlining in her letters heightens the emotional impact.

At the beginning of the campaign 40,000 Russians with 100 guns were looking down the rising banks of the river Alma, fifteen miles from Sebastopol, but they had failed to fortify their position. The Allies stormed it on 20 September 1854, suffering 3,500 casualties, but no cavalry was available for the pursuit. Sebastopol might have been taken there and then, but Saint-Arnaud, already mortally ill, prevaricated. The golden opportunity was lost when the Russians were given time to fortify the defences and bring up large reinforcements. A long winter siege began, and sickness took a much higher toll than the enemy: one day in January, before the arrival of fresh troops, only one British soldier was facing every twenty Russians, although two thirds of them regularly perished on their three-month trek south.

15

THE BATTLE OF THE ALMA

Queen Victoria to King Leopold on 'courage and desperation beautiful to behold'.

Hull, 13th October 1854

. . . We are, and indeed the whole country is, *entirely* engrossed with one *anxious* thought – the *Crimea*. We have received all the *most gratifying* details of the *splendid* and decisive victory of the Alma; alas! it was, a bloody one. Our loss was heavy, but my noble Troops behaved with a *courage* and *desperation* which was beautiful to behold. . . . Since that, the Army has performed a wonderful march to Balaclava, and the bombardment of Sebastopol has begun. Lord Raglan's behaviour was worthy of the old Duke's – such coolness in the midst of the hottest fire. . . . I feel so *proud* of my dear noble Troops, who, they say, bear their privations, and the sad disease which still haunts them, with such courage and good humour.

In the fierce bayonet combat at Inkerman on 5 November, 8,000 British and 6,000 French troops fought off the Russian attempt to roll up the right wing. Raglan gave no command and left all to the troops' initiative, for which he was duly made a Field Marshal.

16

THE SOLDIERS' BATTLE

Lieutenant Temple Godman to his father.

December 21st

. . . People express much discontent at our Field Marshal – who is never seen and seems to take things precious easy. He got his promotion for nothing but his negligence, he did not turn out at Inkerman till long after the battle began and as to commands, not one was given. Regiments, companies and small knots of men fought like devils to keep back the enemy, and all acted independently in a thick fog without orders. Such was Inkerman won *only* by the bravery of the troops engaged, and at one time we were as near beaten as possible, quite driven back and the enemy in our camp, and had they not been driven back by our men, they would soon have been able to bring the whole of their force to bear at once and then it was all up with us. . . .

When Raglan succumbed to the cholera, Victoria comforted his widow by telling her the army will be 'sadly cast down'. Her letter seems trite compared to Queen Elizabeth's to Lady Norris, though it was, perhaps, more heartfelt.

17

THE QUEEN CONDOLES

Victoria to Lady Raglan, Wellington's niece.

30 June 1855

Dear Lady Raglan,

Words *cannot* convey *all* I feel at the irreparable loss you sustained, and I and the Country have, in your noble, gallant, and excellent husband, whose loyalty and devotion to his Sovereign and Country were unbounded. We both feel *most deeply* for you and your daughters. . . . We must bow to the will of God; but to be taken away thus, on the eve of the successful result of so much labour, so much suffering and so much anxiety, is cruel indeed!

We feel much, too, for the brave Army, whom he was so proud of, who will be sadly cast down at losing their gallant Commander who had led them so often to victory and glory. . . .

Believe me always, my dear Lady Raglan,
yours very sincerely,
V.R.

The Queen was deeply moved when she distributed Crimea Medals to the common soldiers for whom she felt as if they were her 'own children'.

18

SHE SHOOK ROUGH HANDS

Victoria describes to Leopold how she came in contact with privates.

Buckingham Palace, 22nd May 1855

. . . What a *beautiful* and *touching* sight and ceremony (the first of the kind ever witnessed in England) the distribution of the Medals was. From the highest Prince of the

Blood to the lowest Private, all received the same distinction for the bravest conduct in the severest actions, and the rough hand of the brave and honest private soldier came for the first time in contact with that of their Sovereign and their Queen! Noble fellows! I own I feel as if they were *my own children*; my heart beats for *them* as for my *nearest and dearest*. They were so touched, so pleased; many, I hear, cried – and they won't hear of giving up their Medals, to have their names engraved upon them, for fear they should *not* receive the *identical one* put into *their hands by me*, which is quite touching. Several came by in a sadly mutilated state. None is more gallant than young Sir Thomas Troubridge, who had, at Inkerman, *one leg* and the *other foot* carried away by a round shot, and continued commanding his battery till the battle was won, refusing to be carried away, only desiring his shattered limbs to be raised in order to prevent too great hemorrhage! He was dragged by in a bath chair, and when I gave him his medal I told him I should make him one of my Aides-de-Camp for his very gallant conduct, to which he replied: 'I am amply repaid for everything!' *One must* revere and love such soldiers! . . .

On 8 September 1855, the British attempt to take the Redan with mostly new recruits was repelled. Their sap trenches were too far away and casualties severe on the 250 yards of open ground they had to cross; they were still exposed while they escaladed the ditch. Some got inside the Redan and, waiting in vain for reinforcements, held out valiantly for two hours before they were driven out again by the Russian reserves and mown down by the guns on their retreat. Dogged courage could not make up for the incompetence of the generals.

19

IT WAS TOO FAR

Captain Hugh Hibbert, 7th Fuseliers, describes how the attack was beaten back.

We had to advance across the open plain with guns loaded with grape and canister shot blazing away into us. As I advanced I thought every second would be my last. I could hardly see for the dust that the grape shot made in ploughing up the ground all around us – before – behind – and on each side – shells bursting over my head and fellows rolling over right and left. I seemed to bear a charmed life for nothing would hit me! My haversack was covered with blood from men who were shot near me and so was my sword. When we got to the abattis which is the last 50 yards from the Redan the fire was so heavy that no mortals could stand it and there was nothing for it but to retreat as rapidly as possible. In fact we were regularly beaten back and I saw the rascally Russians taking off their caps and jeering at us.

At the same time, launching a surpise attack from their sap trenches close to the ditch, the French under Macmahon stormed the Malakoff Tower at the hour of relief when the defenders were at dinner. In the night the Russians abandoned the whole fortress and withdrew to the north side of the port.

Camp of the Fourth Dragoon Guards in the Crimea, 1854–5. Photograph by Robertson, Roger Fenton's assistant. (*Mansell Collection*)

JUSTICE.

Justice, the call for merciless revenge for the massacres of women and children committed during the Indian Mutiny. (Punch, *12 September 1857*)

20

'It is all over now with Sebastopol'

Captain Temple Godman describes to his brother the scene inside the fortress.

Kadikoi, September 10th, 1855

. . . The events of the last few days have been so exciting. On the 8th at noon the French had sapped up over the parapet into the Malakoff. The whole place became a mass of smoke. Nearly at the same time our men stormed the Redan, but the Russians were in such force in rear, and our supports not coming up in time, our men were driven out again. Lots of men who came up with their limbs smashed, stopped and talked to us and seemed not to care the least for their wounds. The number of officers was out of all proportion to the men, these latter I may tell you did not behave quite so well as usual. I only say this as you are sure to hear reports about it, but when the country trusts its honour to *children* who know next to nothing of drill and discipline, it cannot expect such deeds as were performed by old and trained soldiers.

I was told that about 20 officers held the Redan for some minutes against masses of Russians, but the men did not support them, and nearly everyone was killed; the fighting was desperate, and when too close for muskets, they dashed each other's brains out with stones. . . . I saw the 97th march home, about 60 men out of 800, and one subaltern, but more turned up after. The officer had lost his cap and was covered with powder and dirt, and his clothes spattered with blood and torn in several places by shell. Then the 88th marched by nearly cut to pieces, six officers coming back out of 17. We saw all these men going down in the morning as cheerful as possible. . . .

In the night the Russians left the town and retreated across the bridge, I suppose they saw it was useless to remain when the Malakoff was taken. The town was now on fire all over the large buildings by the water, the ships, the docks, etc. I walked into the town by the garden battery, the strength of the place is enormous and I can't think how we could take it. I walked to a high part of the town, however, I was afraid to go further and thought it best to retreat. The Russians were springing mines with electric batteries; the houses were riddled with shot, and the burst shell was enough to pave the streets with. I never saw such a scene of havoc. . . . Just after I came out a large magazine blew up in the docks, and explosions constantly take place even now.

At one time a number of English and French were plundering when a panic took them, some said a mine was going to blow up, and others that a steamer was coming across to shell them. However away they all went, one over the other, dropped their spoil, and the men on horses rode over the men on foot, such a scrimmage you never saw – they did not stop till quite outside the town.

I then went to the Redan, and it seems to me we should never have attacked it, for it is quite commanded by the Malakoff, and could not be held when we were in, but the French said we must go at it to draw off the men from other parts. The Russians were there in heaps, and the ditch was nearly full of dead English piled one on the other, I suppose five feet thick, or more. The Redan was terribly strong, and bombproof inside. There was not a place an inch large that was not ploughed up by our shot and shell, guns, gabions; and even pieces of human flesh were scattered about, it was absolutely torn to pieces, and one mass of rubbish and confusion impossible to describe. . . . It is all over now with Sebastopol, the smoke of the town extends for miles up the country. The Fleet say the Russians are retreating but I can hardly believe it true. . . .

The Queen celebrates the victory with a bonfire at Balmoral Castle and looks back on the war in terms of national altruism.

21

A BONFIRE FOR UNSELFISH ENGLAND SAVING EUROPE

Victoria to Leopold.

Balmoral, 11th September 1855

My dearest Uncle,

The great event has at length taken place – *Sebastopol has fallen*! We received the news here last night. We did what we could to celebrate it; but that was but little, for to my grief we have not *one* soldier, no band, nothing here to make any sort of demonstration. What we did do was in Highland fashion to light a *bonfire* on the top of a hill opposite the house, which had been built last year when the premature news of the fall of Sebastopol deceived every one, and which we had to leave *unlit*, and found here on our return!

Windsor, 29th January 1856

. . . The peace negotiations occupy everyone. . . . England's policy throughout has been the *same, singularly unselfish*, and solely actuated by the *desire* of *seeing Europe saved* from the *arrogant* and *dangerous* pretensions of that *barbarous power* Russia. . . .

With Albert's best love,
ever your devoted Niece,
VICTORIA R.

The legend of Russian military effectiveness had been disproved. As an invasion of the Russian mainland was out of the question, and now unnecessary, the futile war had come to an end. The only tangible result of the peace treaty was a ban on Russian warships in the Black Sea which remained effective for fifteen years. For this, 22,000 British soldiers, and nearly twice as many French and five times as many Russians, had died – an ominous warning of the greatly increased destructiveness of war.

War correspondents and photographers had helped to bring about a fundamental change in the country's attitude towards its soldiers: for the first time they were pitied and honoured. Henceforth, the minor reverses and victories of the colonial campaigns aroused intense popular emotion; despite the prevailing jingoism, the belief in the usefulness of war began to wane.

T H I R T E E N

Queen Victoria's 'Little Wars' (1839–85)

If we are to maintain our position as a first-rate Power
we must be prepared for attacks and wars, somewhere or other, CONTINUALLY. . .
VICTORIA TO DISRAELI

Yonder's the man with his life in his hand,
Legs on the march for whatever land
GEORGE MERDITH, ATKINS

The nineteenth century was the British century: the empire quadrupled and became the largest in world history, five times the size of the Roman Empire and spanning a quarter of the globe and its population, with an area a hundred times that of the British Isles. No wonder this unprecedented success engendered a proud conviction of merit bestowed by Providence, and of a Christian vocation to rule the majority of the coloured races for their own benefit, in accordance with British institutions considered superior to all others. This sense of evangelical mission – Kipling's 'white man's burden' – blended quite naturally with commercial exploitation, based on the new technology, and with chauvinist arrogance and self-righteous militancy. Yet it must not be forgotten that the intention, if not always the effect, was humane, even if the contradiction between English liberties and colonial despotism, however sympathetic to the natives, could not entirely be covered up behind the façade of a dazzling pageant.[1]

---

1   'Double-think appeared to be a necessary part of Empire-building. It has often been said that the British Empire was acquired in a fit of absence of mind. . . . [It] may have been ruled absent-mindedly, but there was a good deal of presence of mind in acquisition.' (E. Pakenham, *Jameson's Raid*, Weidenfeld & Nicolson, 1960, p. 19.)

The Army, starved of funds, and unlike the unchallengeable Navy, tiny in view of its worldwide responsibilities, was glorified with jingoistic pride but remained poorly organized, led, fed and housed, at least until the Caldwell reforms of the 1870s instilled a measure of professionalism through abolition of the purchase of commissions, short service enlistment, and improvement of barracks and catering.

The string of little wars, none of great importance or extent, never ceased during the whole century and stirred up disproportionate passion in peaceful England, especially as owing to unpreparedness, complacency and blunder, they usually began disastrously. All, however, ended in triumph, upholding what was firmly believed to be the cause of duty and righteousness.

The incompetence of some generals in face of often primitive tribesmen was compensated by the usual courageous tenacity of the British soldier. However, these punitive expeditions, nicknamed 'Butcher and Bolt', were frequently marked by retribution of unrestrained cruelty, destruction and looting, whether to avenge a barbaric massacre or just for the fun of it. Such excesses were bound to reinforce the anti-militaristic current of conscientious objection to the empire which was gaining support: in 1876, there was considerable opposition to Victoria (who always defended the empire as if it were her personal property) assuming the title of Empress of India.

The Afghan (1839–42, 1879) and Sikh (1845–9) Wars

Hear the whizz of the shot as it flies,
Hear the rush of the shell in the skies,
Hear the bayonet's clash, ringing bright! . . .
Ah! Glory or Death, for true hearts and brave,
Honour in life, or rest in the grave
G. FLAVELL HAYWARD

The 'Army of the Indus', 21,000 men under Sir John Keane, advanced in April 1839 from Upper Sind into Afghanistan, to forestall the threat of Russian expansionism to India, and occupied Kabul on 7 August. Dost Mohammed surrendered and was replaced by the British puppet ruler Shah Shuja. The army then returned to India, leaving only 8,000 men under General Elphinstone to support the unpopular Shah and the British resident, Sir William Macnaghten. Brigadier Willshire stormed Ghazni in July and Kelat in December after driving Mehrab Khan's 2,000 men from the three hills outside and breaking the gate by gunfire.

1

'More like hounds than disciplined soldiers'

Lieutenant T.W.E. Holdsworth writes home.

Kotree, December 8th, 1839

... About three miles and a half from Kelat the fortress appeared before us, frowning defiance. The sun had just burst out, and was lighting the half-cultivated valley beneath us, interspersed with fields, gardens, ruinous mosques; while Kelat was still in the shade and seemed to maintain a dark and gloomy reserve; nor was the effect diminished when a thin cloud of smoke was seen spouting forth and curling over its battlements, followed, in a short interval, by the report of a large gun, which came booming over the hills towards us. 'Hurrah! They have fired the first shot', was the exclamation of some of us, 'and Kelat is prize-money!' ...

We could only see the citadel, which was more commanding and difficult of access than that of Ghuzni. Nearer the fort we could observe the body of cavalry drawn up, under cover of the redoubts of the hills. Gen. Willshire now ordered one of the guns to open on the horsemen, to cover the movements of the advance companies, who were driving the enemy's matchlock-men before them. The third shot went slap in among them. ... The whole affair was the most exciting thing I ever experienced. We moved steadily on, the guns from the redoubts blazing at us as fast as they could load them, but only two shots struck near us. When our artillery unshipped one of their guns they exploded their powder, and retired in the greatest disorder. ...

Capt. Outram[2] here rode up to us, and cried out: 'On men, and take the gate before they can all get in.' This acted like magic on the men. All order was lost, and we rushed madly down the hill on the flying enemy, more like hounds with the chase in view than disciplined soldiers. The consequence was, we were exposed to a most galling fire from the ramparts. ... The fugitives were too quick for us, and suddenly the cry was raised by our leading men, 'The gate is shut'. Unluckily a rush was made by the greatest part of the regiment who were so closely jammed that they could not move, exposed to the fire which the matchlock-men kept pouring in with utmost impunity. Had the artillery been less expedient in knocking down the gate, the greatest part of them would have been annihilated. ... Our men gave the general hurrah; and Gen. Willshire came up to us at his best pace, waving his hat, 'Forward, Queen's', he sung out, 'or the 17th will be in before you.' On we rushed again for the gate as hard as we could. ...

However, on entering, we found matters not so easy as we expected. The streets were very narrow and so intricate that they formed a perfect labyrinth. The men, therefore, soon got scattered about and some, I am afraid, thought of loot more than of endeavouring to find a way to the citadel. ... In a short time we found ourselves in a large courtyard with Beloochees right under the windows of the citadel. These men

---

2   After commanding the cavalry in the siege of Kelat, the future Lieutenant-General Sir James Outram, the 'Bayard of India', undertook a secret mission, disguised as an Afghan and living on dates and water.

cried out for 'mercy'; but the soldiers recollecting the treachery that had been practised at Ghuzni were going to shoot the whole kit of them, when I suddenly
received a shock, which made me think at the moment I was smashed to bits, by a
ball from a ginjall, or native wallpiece. I was knocked senseless to the ground. . . .
When I came to myself I found myself coughing up globules of clotted blood at a
great pace. I made a desperate effort, got on my legs, and soon found some of our
men, who supported me until a dooly could be brought and I was soon on my way
to the doctor. . . .

In the meantime, there had been sharp fighting in the citadel. One party reached
the place where Mehrab Khan, at the head of his chiefs who had joined his standard,
was sitting with his sword drawn. The others seemed inclined to surrender, and
raised the cry of 'Aman!' but the Khan, springing on his feet, cried, 'Aman, nag!'
equivalent to 'Mercy be d—d' and blew his match; but all in vain, as he immediately
received about three shots. . . . So fell Mehrab Khan, and died game, with his sword
in his hand, in his own citadel. . . .

At length a few survivors, being driven to their last stronghold at the very top of
the citadel, surrendered; then one loud and general 'hurrah!' proclaimed
around that Kelat was ours. . . . The loss was 140, about one in seven. My wounds
continued doing very well; I caught a low fever and I have continued to grow better ever since.

Larkhann, December 24th

I have delayed sending this till our arrival here. Now the campaign is near its close, I
feel very glad that I have been on it, as it is a thing that a man does not see every day
of his life in these times; and I consider it to be more lucky than otherwise that I have
four holes in my body as a remembrance of it; but I cannot say that I relish a longer
sojourn in India, unless we have the luck to be sent to China which I should like very
much, (fancy sacking Pekin, and kicking the Celestial Emperor from his throne). . . .

A street riot on 2 November 1841, which Elphinstone failed to quell, developed into a revolt, led by Dost Mohammed's son, Akbar Khan, against the
detested puppet ruler, bent on breaking up the tribal militia, and against the
British occupation. Elphinstone, aged and gout-ridden, had been blind to the
peril and, instead of strengthening his defences, had devoted himself to
pony races and theatricals. Although he could have held out in the Bala
Hissar citadel, he allowed himself to be humiliated and taken prisoner. He
agreed to evacuate the 700 British and 3,800 Indian troops, together with
12,000 mostly Indian civilians, including many women and children, and
sent orders to the Jellalabad garrison also to withdraw to India.

Sir William Nott, the commander of the Kandahar army, foresaw that
Macnaghten's optimistic complacency was leading to disaster. He was shot
by Abkar with the very pistol he had presented to him, and the Ghazis
hacked him to pieces and carried his head in triumph through the streets of
Kabul.

2

'Our blood must flow'

Major-General Sir William Nott (1782–1845) to his daughter.

31 January 1842

We have just heard of Macnaghten's death. Poor fellow! His end was like the rest of his proceedings from the day he entered the country. He ought *not* to have trusted those wretched half-savage people; but his system was all wrong. It has always appeared wonderful to me how Government could have employed so very weak a man. I fear his three years' doings cannot be retrieved, and that our blood must flow for it. . . . Have I not for two years in my letters told you that we were drawing down the deadly hatred of these people upon us?

At Kabul there was apprehension about Afghan faith to the treaty.

3

'All our Afghans have deserted us'

Captain (later General Sir) George Lawrence (1804–84) to Macgregor, the political agent at Jellalabad.

Caubul, Jan. 4th, 1842

. . . We have been obliged to conclude the treaty, and it is settled we march to-morrow. Whether we are attacked on the road depends on their good faith. . . . Orders have been sent to you to evacuate Jellalabad before our arrival; if, however, the treaty is broken by our being attacked, you will consider the orders cancelled, and you will use every exertion to aid us. If you could take supplies for us to the mouth of the Khybur, it would be very desirable. Keep the Scouts on the road, and give us as much intelligence as you can. You must chiefly depend on ourselves for news of us, as all our Afghans have deserted us. . . .

The trek of the army across the Khyber Pass in mid-winter became a nightmare when they were constantly harrassed by Afghan tribesmen. All but the women were gradually butchered; the last stand was made by sixty-five survivors on Gundamuck Hill against thousands of their merciless pursuers. Of the whole army only one wounded surgeon reached Jellalabad on his dying horse.

4

The 'messenger of death'

Dr William Brydon (1811–73) to his brother.

Jellalabad, Jan. 20 [1842]

Here I am safe, but not all sound, having received three wounds. My life has been saved in the most wonderful manner and I am the only European who has escaped from the Cabul army. I got on well till within 50 miles of this with the exception of losing all my baggage. I then lost the horse on which I was riding. Having taken one of my servants, who was wounded, up behind me we fell rather too far in the rear, when he was pulled off from behind, and I fell with him. I was instantly felled to the earth with the blow of a large knife which wounded me in the head. I managed however to avoid the second blow, by receiving my enemy's hand on the edge of my sword; he dropped his knife, and made off as fast as he could, and I, following his good example, managed to reach the main body, minus my horse, cap and shoe which I lost in the snow. I was then trudging along holding fast by the tail of another officer's horse, when a native told me to take his horse. I now got to the front, where I found a number of officers, who determined to push on, as the men would obey no orders, and were halting every minute. We travelled on slowly all night, fired at occasionally from the sides of the hills, and found ourselves at daybreak about 30 miles from this.

At about ten a.m. we were attacked and surrounded on all sides by horsemen: three officers were killed. I, with the remaining four, pushed on. I proceeded slowly for a short time when I saw a great many people running towards me in all directions. I waited until they got pretty close, and then pushed my horse into a gallop, and ran the gauntlet for about two miles under a shower of large stones, sticks and a few shots, in which I had my horse shot in the spine and my body bruised all over by the stones. I was now attacked by a horseman who wounded me on the knee and hand; when seeing me stoop down, he galloped away as fast as he could, thinking I suppose that I was looking for a pistol. I now proceeded unmolested, and arrived here about one o'clock quite done up, as also my poor horse, who lost the use of his hind legs, and died two days after, without even getting up after his arrival. . . .

Akbar Khan soon laid siege to Jellalabad for five months. On 10 April, three days before the arrival of Sir George Pollock's relief force, the garrison made a victorious sally. Captain R. Bruce Norton writes with characteristic contempt of the natives:

We had a splendid scrimmage and licked Akbar Khan in first-rate style. We burnt his camp getting lots of plunder and captured his four guns. The beggars opened their guns on us when within 500 yards of their camp and we rushed on with a cheer: they fled in all directions. . . . What is to be done on arrival of General Pollock heaven knows: proceed to Kabul and give these fellows a lesson they deserve?[3]

After defeating Akbar Khan Pollock advanced to Kabul on 16 September and destroyed the citadel and the bazaar in retribution for the massacre; Dost Mohammed was re-installed in a settlement which lasted until 1879. Then, to prevent Russia from gaining influence in Afghanistan, British troops once again invaded the country. After the murder of another British resident, Lieutenant-General Sir Frederick Roberts occupied Kabul and a year later relieved Kandahar, until finally peace was concluded.

5

THE VC FOR DISOBEYING ORDERS

Major (later Field Marshal Sir) George White (1835–1912) describes to his wife the battle of Charasiab for the pass dominating the access to Kabul which earned him the VC; Kabul fell without a shot.

Cabul, 15 October 1879

. . . General Baker, who was in charge of all the operations, directed me to await the development of [his] attack and to engage the enemy's artillery at 2500 yards. I thought these orders rot, and put them in my pocket. I opened fire on the hill with my rifles and ordered the guns to shell the height. I had but 100 men and taking the lead myself on foot, had the satisfaction of carrying it with the trifling loss of 7 men. . . . One lad saved my life by giving me timely warning as I was climbing a ledge to get on. I had not observed a wounded Afghan within 5 yards of me. The boy shouted 'Look out, sir!' and as I ducked my head the bullet just whistled by me where I would have been but for the undignified duck! I am sure it took 30 rounds to kill that Afghan. . . . At another place I borrowed a soldier's rifle and cleared a nest of them out by regularly stalking the leader like an ibex. He saw me just as I had covered him, and turned to bolt, but was too late. . . . It was a good sensation at the top when the men came and offered me all the spoils they had taken. I accepted a sword, and have it still. . . .

I left strong posts on all the heights I had taken, and sent a dispatch to General Roberts: 'I hold the pass to Cabul, and have all the Afghan guns'. Next morning all the HQ people rode through the gorge. Sir Fred congratulated me most warmly. . . .

The Sikhs, a sect of dissenters from Hinduism under Islamic influence in the Punjab, had a strong, well-trained army of fiercer fighting spirit than any in

3   National Army Museum, 6807–224.

India, founded by Maharaja Runjeet Singh fifty years earlier who kept a harem of 150 'Amazons' and fortified himself with raw spirit flavoured with meat juice and opium. They crossed the Sutlej river frontier to challenge the British occupants of India. In the battle of Aliwal on 28 January 1846, Sir Harry Smith led the decisive cavalry charge of his army of 12,000 against Runjur Singh's 20,000 Sikhs lined up behind their guns. The intrepid 16th Lancers were in the forefront: they tore into the enemy cavalry and dispersed it, and, after jumping the ditch, stabbed the gunners at their entrenched batteries.

6

'A thrill of ecstasy'
THE CAVALRY CHARGE

Captain Knight writes home.

[January 1846]

. . . We suddenly found ourselves in the midst of a fearfully large square of the enemy's infantry, firing at us right and left and completely surrounding us. The moment that I felt my horse leap the ditch in which their battery was placed and found myself charging into the square a proud sensation of delight came over me. Everything seemed charged into a thrill of ecstasy; and how we all escaped the deadly shower of musketry that was poured into us on all sides is wonderful.

One fellow discharged his gun right across my face and for the moment I was quite blinded by the gunpowder, and my face so blackened no one knew me. . . . Everyone who charged with the 16th must have had narrow escapes, for the bullets hissed over our heads like hail. . . . Our brave fellows fell very thickly here, and every man whose horse was killed was to a certainty slain also, for the moment those savages saw any one on the ground they rushed at him and never ceased hacking at them, till they had literally severed them to pieces with their tulwars, which were like razors. . . . After having charged through this mass of infantry we rallied and pursued the stragglers to the very banks of the river. . . .

Those who did not get away in their boats to the other bank were driven into the river where they drowned. Sir Harry Smith wrote home:

Oh, the fearful sight the river presents! The bodies, having swollen, float, of men, horses, camels, bullocks. Thousands must have perished. . . . Never was victory more complete.

Three thousand Sikhs were lost with all their guns and stores, against 580 men on the British side.[4] After a number of other hard-fought battles, the

---

4   G. Bruce, *Six Battles for India*, A. Barker, 1969, *passim*.

Sikhs finally surrendered and the Punjab was annexed to complete the Indian Empire. Peshawar was also added in retribution for Dost Mohammed's support of the Sikhs with his cavalry, which was routed at Gujrat. Queen, country and army were largely united in their conviction that annexation was justified:

> Our keeping these countries in India and elsewhere is (and always will be) because the *Native* Sovereigns CANNOT maintain their authority. . . . It is *not* for *aggrandisement* but to *prevent war* and *bloodshed*.[5]

The colourfulness of action in the exotic outposts of the empire may have excited popular imagination in the increasing drabness of everyday life in the factories and offices of England, but an officer on guard at an isolated frontier fort was equally excited by the prospect of returning to the amenities of Piccadilly. Charles Townshend commanded Fort Gupis during the tension in Peshawar on the north-west frontier. He paid a visit to the Mehtar of Chitral, between the Punjab, Afghanistan and the Hindukush. A year later he was to advance in the January snow through Ghizar (10,000 ft) to Chitral with 250 men to put down a revolt and withstand a siege in the fort. He was a spirited young officer, full of *joie de vivre* and straining nostalgically at the leash of his mountain desert, with *Vie Parisienne* pin-ups on the mud walls.

7

A VISION OF GIRLS, BRANDY AND CIGARS

Charles Townshend (1861–1924) (later Major-General Sir), writes to his sister.

Chitral, November 9th, 1893

I rode into the village at the head of a mob of 'catch-em-alive-ohs', armed to the teeth, for the King of Chitral insists on guarding me on my trip. . . . There is every appearance of a row. In fact, I don't see how we shall get through the winter without a pantomime rally up here of sorts, and I am glad to say they have reinforced me at Thayer Lasht with a gun and more troops. A row up here would suit me, as I should be in command. You can imagine me leading a charge with a cigarette case in one hand and a silver-headed cane in the other, can't you? There is actually a lady now at Gilgit. I think it awful rot and nonsense. A fellow in the Transport Corps (the fellows in that corps are *all* married) has brought his wife up. I call it turning the place into a regular Punch and Judy show! Gilgit will be getting quite suburban, and lines of dubious-looking lingerie, I suppose, hang out to dry, like you see in the outskirts of London, as you approach in the train. . . . I try to live as little as possible like John the Baptist, although I *am* in the desert. As regards being happy, one's life in Central Asia

5   *Letters of Queen Victoria*, 2nd series III, p. 43 (11 September 1879).

is bound to be like being stretched on the bed of Procrustes. . . . However, I expect the season of '95 will see me home, wearing gum boots and 'filant le parfait amour'. We 'follow fleeting fires' as some sporting men say in Tennyson.

I suppose I shall be happy when I find myself at home in the purlieus of Piccadilly. A few glasses of Monopole, delicious cigars, and a glass of that old brandy to send me along after dinner. I see all these in my dreams and *more than these*. But though I stretch out longing hands, they vanish as a vision in the night and I wake up through some blarsted bugle call in Thayer Lasht![6]

The Indian Mutiny (1857)

An Englishman's pride –
It is known far and wide –
Is the innocent always to spare.
But the vicious – ah! they
Shall remember the day
That an Englishman's vengeance was born!
WRITTEN ON THE LUCKNOW WALL

The Indian Mutiny, which has since been called a war of national liberation though it was mostly confined to Bengal, would never have stirred up people in England so much, including the Queen, if atrocities had not been committed against women and children. The sepoys who had been serving the British Empire so well became jealous of the newly recruited Sikhs and Gurkhas, and were apprehensive of losing their privileged position. Moreover, in January 1857, it became known that their Enfield rifle cartridges, which had to be bitten before being loaded, had been greased with cow and pig fat – taboo to Hindus and Moslems respectively. The disturbances which broke out at Barrackpore and Meerut could have been crushed before the rebels reached Delhi and murdered the white civilians there. Soon after, Sir Henry Barnard routed 30,000 sepoys with a mere 3,500 of his own – it was a curious fact that the sepoys only fought well under British (or French) commanders. Most provinces, and civilians in general, remained loyal or at least neutral, although opposed to reforms like the prohibition of the burning of widows (suttees) and of female infanticide, and the loss of the Brahmans' and landowners' privileges. The rebellious Bengali sepoys were largely high-caste Hindus.

As India had never been conquered as a colony but only pacified by the East India Company in succession to the Mogul Empire and in opposition to oppressive petty rulers (and the French), the Pax Britannica was widely acceptable. Even the bellicose Sikhs and Afghans, so recently conquered,

---

6 Townshend was to become notorious for his surrender of the garrison of Kut (Mesopotamia) to Turkish brutality, after a four-month siege in 1916.

remained friendly, and troops could be moved from the north-west frontier to the Ganges valley to quell the revolt against the British Raj.

Sir Hugh Wheeler who had felt so safe in his fortified camp at Cawnpore (before losing his treasury and magazine with all his guns through Nana Sahib's treachery) that he sent fifty men to reinforce Lucknow, held out for three weeks.

8

'To die like rats in a cage'

Major-General Sir Hugh Wheeler (1789–1857) writes desperately to Brigadier Sir Henry Lawrence at Lucknow two days before he and his family were massacred with the whole garrison.

> Cawnpore, June 24th, 1857
> We have had a bombardment in this miserable position, three or four times daily, for 19 days. To reply is out of question. All our gun-carriages disabled, ammunition short. British spirit alone remains; but it cannot last for ever. We have no instruments, no medicine, provisions for 10 days at farthest, and no possibility of getting any more, as all communication with the town is cut off. We have been cruelly deserted and left to our fate. Surely we are not to die like rats in a cage. . . .

When in the July heat of up to 138°F food and water for the four hundred civilians, most of them women and children, were running out, Wheeler accepted terms of surrender. The Nana betrayed the safe-conduct he had promised and, as they were embarking, all but four men were gunned down; later the women and children were hacked to pieces. The relief force under Sir Henry Havelock, which arrived too late, wreaked terrible vengeance on the rebels, massacring them in turn. Captain Wolseley, a budding Field Marshal and empire stalwart, seethed with indignation: 'The idea that a native should have dared to put his hands on an English woman was too much,' and he took a vow 'of vengeance and having blood for blood, not drop for drop, but barrels and barrels of the filth which flows in these niggers' veins for every drop of blood which marked the floors and walls of that fearful house'. Brigadier James Neill justified his indiscriminate retribution with Cromwellian unction: 'No doubt this is strange law, with the blessing and help of God. I cannot help seeing His finger is in all this.'[7] In fact the mere 'ingratitude' of the faithless 'niggers' had in itself already elicited a cruel racial revenge.

7   C. Hibbert, *The Great Mutiny, India 1857*, A. Lane, 1978, p. 212.

9

LADIES' BODIES THROWN INTO WELLS

Lieutenant William Hargood tells his parents how they took Cawnpore.

Allahabad, 26th June

. . . The whole way up I had most frightful work to set fire to villages. I am almost tired with soldiering, after seeing men hanged, and villages on fire. . . . There is a force going to leave here immediately to relieve the garrison of Cawnpore. . . .

Cawnpore, 18th July

We fell in with the enemy, who consisted of 9000 men. After 4 hours' fighting we drove them from their positions. As it was getting dark we halted to sleep upon the bare ground without food. We were all thoroughly knocked up as we had marched night and day. I came upon some muddy water which was in a rut made by cart wheels, and I though I never tasted anything so delicious. . . .

We entered Cawnpore without resistance, as the brutes have all bolted. The frightful massacre that was reported is too true. . . . Poor fellows they defended the place to the last, but, overcome by hunger, they told the Nana that they were willing to give up the place if he would allow them to go down the river in boats; he agreed to it, and, even had the wounded carried down in carts – deceitful villain – they had no sooner entered the boats, than these cowardly brutes opened fire upon them, and, those that were not shot, were cut to pieces in a most brutal manner; after their defeat on the 14th by us, the poor ladies were all killed, and their bodies thrown into wells, but the day of retribution for these inhuman savages, is at hand. . . .

Another budding Field Marshal and popular hero ('our Bobs'), born at Cawnpore, shrinks back in horror from hearing what had been done to the women, but the thought of gaining the VC soon makes him jolly again. When he gathers on the spot what actually happened, he joins in the general cry for revenge.

10

'It makes one's blood run cold'

Lieutenant Frederick (later Earl) Roberts (1832–1914) writes home.

Camp before Delhi, July 24th

. . . We are perfectly in the dark what has taken place and I positively dread to hear. . . . These poor women and children – it makes one's blood run cold to think what they have suffered. I only trust the ruffians have had the mercy to kill those that have fallen into their hands and not taken them with them. . . . Such atrocities have never, I fancy, been so universally committed. Our enemies, the Afghans and Sikhs respected our wives and children, but these cowardly wretches delight in torturing them, and yet I'll venture to say the English papers and Members of Parliament will try to excuse them and put the blame on every one else but the proper scoundrels. Don't think I am in low spirits, darling Mother, Very far from it. I could not be jollier. What I want more than any other is the V.C. Oh! If I can only manage that, how jolly I should be. . . .

> August 25th
>
> . . . We received an account of the tragedy at Cawnpore. It has excited such a feeling of horror that I would undergo cheerfully any privation in the hopes of *revenge* on these cruel murderers. . . .

> Cawnpore, October 27th
>
> . . . We arrived here yesterday. In this wretched place, our poor women were kept in a miserable house, not fit for dogs, until the evening before our troops reached Cawnpore; when they were all murdered. God knows how. The natives say that the children were hanged before their mothers, and that when all had been wounded by shots from the Sepoys, butchers were sent in to finish the bloody business. There were about 200 altogether – women and children. The floor is now strewed with clothes, shoes, etc., and the ground from the house to the well, where the remains were thrown down, is covered with locks of hair. Oh, Mother, looking at these horrible sights makes one feel very, very sad. No wonder we all feel glad to kill these Sepoys. . . .

This was no longer 'glory and honourable warfare', as a few years earlier in the Crimea. The Queen is worried.

11

'Horrors committed on the poor ladies'

Queen Victoria to King Leopold.

> Balmoral Castle, 2nd September
>
> . . . We are in sad anxiety about India . . . the horrors committed on the poor ladies are unknown in these ages, and make one's blood run cold. The whole is so much more distressing than the Crimea – where there was *glory* and honourable warfare, and where the poor women and children were safe. Then the distance and the difficulty of communication is such an additional suffering to us all. . . . There is not a family hardly who is not in sorrow and anxiety about their children, and in all ranks – India being *the* place where every one was anxious to place a son! . . .

Delhi, with its great arsenal, was the first city to be taken by the mutineers who restored the Mogul monarchy in Bengal and massacred whites and Christians. A survivor describes their ordeal, after a band of ferocious tribesmen with spears and bludgeons had captured them and stripped the ladies of their stays and clothes. A dozen of them with their colonel managed to escape and hide in a suffocating hut from which they were rescued by an old Jew who treated them to drinks and dinner till the arrival of British soldiers.

12

LAUGHING ABOUT BEING MASSACRED

Ensign Gambier to Mrs Knyvett, wife of his colonel.

. . . We were led in triumph into an open space by a bazaar. The assembled multitude who closed round us, gaping in perpetual wonderment and cracking coarse jokes on our condition and chances of life a few days ago would have salaamed and kissed our feet and crouched in abject humility to us. . . . We were taken to a fakir's hut, the object of attraction to hundreds of curious eyes, as if we were the last imported rarity into the Surrey Zoologicals. A large sheet was spread for us to lie on – 'to catch our blood' so the Colonel said, 'when they sacrificed us after we had been fattened for a day or two' with that irresistibly comic effect which made us sometimes shake with laughter, the knife, as it were, at our throats. . . .

General Sir Henry Barnard approached with a force to retake Delhi, but the military chiefs were described by Lieutenant Cadell as a 'choice collection of muffs' whose 'mismanagement almost beats the Crimea'.[8] One of them admits the failure of organization but not his own fears.

13

'Fits of weariness and prostration'

Brigadier Archdale Wilson writes to his wife.

Ridge Camp above Delhi
. . . Instead of being besiegers we were besieged, with a fair prospect of being starved out, not an attempt being made to keep open our lines of communication, to preserve our convoys and supplies, nothing was done. . . .
You are getting as unreasonable as other know-nothings who are acting on their own impatience, think a force under 2000 bayonets can easily hop over the walls of Delhi covered with heavy guns and massacre with ease the 30,000 or 40,000 men defending it, as easy as toasting cheese. We here all think the force has done wonders in keeping these fellows at bay so long. . . . I am suffering from one of my fits of weariness and prostration – very fagged. . . .

At last the siege train arrived. An officer explains lucidly what an assault implies and worries he might swear.

8   Ibid, p. 281.

14

ESCALADING MUST BE THOUGHT 'CAPITAL FUN'

Charles Ewart writes to his mother.

I believe we are to escalade. You know what that will be – rush up a ladder with men trying to push you down, bayonet and shoot you from above. But you must wave your sword and think it capital fun, bring your men up as fast as you can and jump down on top of men ready with fixed bayonets to receive you. All this is not very pleasant to think coolly of, but when the moment comes the knowledge that your men are looking to you to lead them on and bring them up with a cheer makes you feel as happy as poss. . . . It will be fearfully exciting work. I hope it won't make me swear, though that is almost allowable for you are mad with excitement and know not what you are saying. But I will strive against it with all my might.

The Cashmere Gate was blown open with powder bags and the soldiers stormed through the breach 'like a pack of hounds' but suffered heavy casualties from rebel fire through loopholed walls. They were intoxicated with vengefulness.

15

'Skivering through the Pandy'

Lieutenant Coghill writes home about the assault on Delhi.

. . . I took a bit of pistol bullet in my mouth and with a devil's yell rushed from under cover, knowing that the quicker the rush the nearer the enemy and the earlier the revenge. The musketry and jingalls poured in like rain and men kept falling on every side of me, but I thought my life charmed and they could not touch me. The groans and execrations of the wounded and dying, cursing their fate at being left outside and not being able to revenge themselves, was pitiable in the extreme. They rolled and writhed in agony. . . . I felt like a drunken man. I just remember putting my sword back and seizing the ladders and throwing them down the ditch. They were over 8 ft. long and the ditch we found 20 ft. deep. In the excitement we just dropped down and then rushed up. The brutes fought till we regularly cut and hacked our way through them with sword and bayonet. Unfortunately the first thing my sword struck in was the body of a colour sergeant of mine who was shot and fell onto it. But the next moment I was skivering through the Pandy and then another. All orders and formation was over and we cut and hacked wherever we could. I never thought of drawing my pistol but poked, thrust and hacked till my arm was tired.

Brigadier Nicholson, who was shot dead when he stormed into Delhi at the head of his men, had written a few months earlier:

Let us propose a Bill for flaying alive, impalement, or burning of the murderers of women and children at Delhi. I will not, if I can help it, see fiends of that stamp let off with a simple hanging. If I had them in my power to-day, I would inflict the most excruciating tortures I could think on them with a perfectly easy conscience. . . .[9]

The drunken soldiery sacked Delhi, and English officers relished watching the convulsions of five hundred sepoys suffering slow hanging on the gallows. At Shansi, even Indian women and children were massacred.

At Lucknow Residency, Sir James Outram's garrison of British and loyal sepoy soldiers stoutly defended hundreds of women and children against vastly superior numbers of rebels.

16

SHE RAN OUT IN HER NIGHTGOWN!

Mrs Frances Wells, a surgeon's wife, writes to her father from barracks outside Lucknow Residency.

[early April]
We were in bed and sound asleep when the women came screaming that the house was on fire. . . . Never shall I forget the horror I experienced. I tore my children out of bed and in my *nightgown* ran over to the Dashwoods' house but had I not met one of the officers who relieved me of the children I think I should have fainted. [I] saw ten sepoys placing lighted straws on the thatch. . . . Although feeling in a dreadful state I could hardly help laughing at some of the odd things that happened. One young man ran over with my brooches, rings, stays and tea caddy. . . . The sight our store room presents is most extraordinary – currants, salmon, potatoes, all baked. . . . Dear Papa, it makes me tremble to think of it. I can write no more.

After three months during which heavy shelling, sickness and famine had taken their toll, a small relief force battled their way through to the besieged Residency on 25 September, led by Sir Henry Havelock.

9   M. Edwards, *Red Year*, 1973, p. 156.

17

THE RELIEF OF LUCKNOW

Lieutenant Hargood, ADC to General Sir William Outram, writes to his parents; he died of fever six months later.

18th November

. . . We began to march with 2000 men towards Lucknow. The enemy had taken up a strong position upon the canal, with the bridge defended by guns of a very heavy calibre. My Regiment charged the bridge under heavy fire of grape and took the guns. We were now about a mile from the Residency where the garrison had entrenched themselves. The whole way was through narrow streets the houses of which were loopholed and full of men armed with muskets, and matchlocks. The 78th Highlanders with Sir William Outram and General Havelock led the charge. I was in front of everyone, and how I escaped, I cannot tell, as I was a conspicuous mark being on horseback. The Residency was at last reached, and the joy of the garrison can be better imagined than described. If we had not come in that night they say they would have been blown up, as the whole place was mined, and we enabled them to sally out and destroy the mines. Our loss was very severe, as we are as much besieged as the old garrison were. The enemy fire at us day and night. . . . There are here upwards of 600 ladies, women and children – it is quite wonderful how unconcerned they appear about shot and bullets. My poor Regiment, which came to Bengal 850 strong do not now muster 400. . . .

P.S. The following things were selling at auctions of Officers who had been killed. Brandy £5 – 3lbs. of bacon £6.10.0 – sugar 32/- a lb. – cheroots, original cost 1d, sold at 8/-.

The garrison continued to guard the Oudh Crown Jewels and the treasure of £250,000 until their surviving half were finally rescued by slow-moving Sir Colin Campbell ('Sir Crawling Camel') who routed the rebels with the help of 10,000 Gurkhas. Retribution was savage:

The first ten prisoners were lashed to the muzzle of the guns and blown to pieces, the artillery officer waved his sword, you heard the roar of the guns, and above the smoke you saw the legs, arms and heads flying in all directions. Since that time we had an execution parade once or twice a week, and such is the force of habit we now think little of them.[10]

10 Quoted in J. Morris, *Pax Britannica*, Faber & Faber, 1968, p. 137. S.N. Sen, *1857* (1957), p. XVI, comments: 'Muslim noblemen were sewn alive in pigskin and pork forced down their gullets . . . wounded prisoners were burnt alive. . . . No nation or individual can indulge in such horrible atrocities and yet claim to be civilised.'

During all this violent upheaval, which cost 11,000 British lives (9000 died of sunstroke or sickness) the empire watch went on as usual in a creepy-crawly fort of the undisturbed Punjab.

18

'They will have to wear our yoke for ever'

Lieutenant (later Field Marshal) George White describes conditions to his sister.

July 13th

We are in an old ruined native fort stowed away into places not much bigger than good-sized rat-holes in the walls, full of snakes and every other creeping thing. Three of us officers live together in a cell about 12 foot square in which the thermometer averages 100°. Our men have been very sickly lately, one going out with nearly every day. I am kept pretty busy committing them to earth. . . .

At night I dress, put on gloves and every thing lese to try to keep off musquitoes & sand flies, but to no purpose. We constantly see scorpions make their appearance from some crevice in the wall. Altogether it is a cheerful place to pass the hot weather. . . .

The niggers now say if we are not driven out of India this year that they will have to wear our yoke for ever. I fancy they will rather. . . .

The Wars in China (1857–60), Burma (1885) and Tibet (1904)

Man shooting is the finest sport of all;
there is a certain amount of infatuation
about it, that the more you kill the more
you wish to kill
WOLSELEY

The East India Company held the trade monopoly for opium and, to pay for tea and silk, started smuggling it more or less openly into China in 1829. The Chinese were just as much annoyed about this as the British were about their refusal to grant them trade equality. Sir Hugh Gough descended from gun-boats to subdue the garrison of 45,000 at Canton who, in the words of Lord Elgin on Christmas Day 1857, were 'doomed to destruction from the folly of their own rulers and the vanity and levity of ours'. The city was devastated by a round-the-clock naval bombardment.

19

'A mere child's play'

Colonel Frederick Stephenson describes the storm of Canton to his mother.

January 13, 1858

We left Hong Kong; the wretched little force of 400 bayonets, 60 sappers, 250 artillery, and 20 guns, assisted by the French and English navies were to attack a large city supposed to contain one million inhabitants. Everyone expected a tough resistance, the walls being 30 ft. high, mounted with guns, protected by detached forts which proved to be a mere child's play. . . . The next morning we were all anxiously listening for the first gun to fire from the fleets, who it was agreed should bombard the town for 24 hours; shells and rockets were shortly flying in all directions, and very soon the town caught fire. It was now time to commence landing the troops, which was done without any opposition whatever. We now proceeded to the attack of Fort Lin under fire of the walls of the town. We planted our ladders and escaladed, the enemy running away. The Braves, however, made some very plucky stands, but were all shot or bayoneted and so the Maiden City was captured. . . .

Gough proceeded with an army of 2,500 to Chinkiang which the Tartars defended stubbornly until, rather than surrender, they killed their wives and children and then burnt themselves in their houses. Now the usual looting could begin. Gough wrote home: 'I am sick of war and its fearful consequences'. Sir James Hope's flotilla of one battleship, two frigates and thirteen gun-boats sailed into the mouth of the Peiho river to force the boom and attack the formidable Taku Forts with their 600 guns which were blocking the way to Peking. The expedition ended in disaster when the landing party of 1,100 got stuck in the mud and were mown down by the fire from the forts, suffering 40 per cent casualties.

20

THE TAKU DISASTER

Midshipman (later Admiral Lord) John Fisher (1841–1920) to his mother.

June 1859

. . . We had a hard fight for it, but what could we do against such a fearful number of guns, and us poor little gunboats enclosed in such a small place, not much broader across than the length of our ship. . . . I had to fling all my arms away coming back from the forts and was nearly smothered once, only one of our bluejackets was kind enough to heave me out. You sank at *least* every step, and just fancy the slaughter going 500 yards in the face of about 30 pieces of artillery right in front of you and on each flank. It was dreadful, horrible work, but thank God I came out all right.

Despite this setback the Treaty of Tientsin legalized both the opium trade and access for merchant ships, but war started again when the Chinese blocked the way to Tientsin and wanted to revise the treaty. In the summer of 1860 Lord Elgin raised a much stronger force, consisting of 14,000 British and 7,000 French soldiers on 120 transports, escorted by 70 naval vessels; Major-General Sir James Hope Grant, complete with wife and cello, was in command. After a massive bombardment, the forts were taken by assault, despite the formidable obstacle of mudbanks, ditches, and sharpened bamboo stakes. Afterwards, Elgin noted with compassion: 'All round the Fort were numbers of poor Chinamen, staked and massacred in all sorts of ways.'[11]

The way to Peking was now open to teach the Chinese a lesson. When the expedition got near the city there was a race to the Summer Palace to get first choice in the pillage, with the French in front. Sir Gerald Graham wrote with regret: 'We were an hour late to loot; the Sikhs had been before us, and all the palaces were in flames – a fine sight.'[12] Lord Elgin had singled out the Summer Palace to be burnt to avenge the torture and murder of envoys and *The Times* correspondent, as he explained to the Foreign Secretary, Lord John Russell:

It was necessary to discover some act of retribution and punishment, without attacking Peking, and in such a manner as to make the blow fall on the Emperor who was clearly responsible for the crime.[13]

21

THE SACK OF THE SUMMER PALACE

James Bruce Earl of Elgin (1811–63), Governor-General of India, laments to his wife the damage caused by plunder.

Peking, October 7th, 1860
This morning the French and our cavalry have captured the Summer Palace of the Emperor. All the big-wigs have fled. . . . The Summer Palace is really a fine thing, like an English park but alas! such a scene of desolation. There was not a room in which half the things had not been taken away or broken to pieces. Plundering and devastating a place like this is bad enough, but what is much worse is the waste and break-

---

11   *Letters of the 8th Earl of Elgin*, 1872, p. 346.
12   R.H. Vetch, *Sir Gerald Graham*, 1901, p. 192.
13   *Victorian Military Campaigns*, ed. B. Bond, Hutchinson, 1967, p. 103

age. Out of one million pounds worth of property, I daresay £50,000 will not be realised. . . . War is a hateful business. The more one sees of it, the more one detests it.

While the Earl deplored the sack of the palace he had ordered to be burnt, the Adjutant General is sorry that for appearances' sake he could not join in the delight of plundering.

22

THE PLEASURE OF SMASHING UP AND ROBBING

Colonel Stephenson to his brother.

> Camp before Peking, October 9
> . . . The army arrived before the walls of Pekin. The formidable Tartar army has vanished, utterly panick-struck. . . . We marched as far as the Emperor's Summer Palace, literally crammed with the most lovely knick-knacks you can conceive. Fancy having the run of Buckingham Palace and being allowed to take away anything you liked, and armed moreover with a thick stick and a deep-rooted feeling of animosity to the owner, being able to indulge in the pleasure of smashing looking-glasses and porcelain, and knocking holes through pictures. . . . If I had not been Adjutant General of the Army I might have walked off with such an amount of valuable plunder as would have satisfied the most greedy: richly ornamented robes lined with costly furs, such as ermine and sable, fans, Mandarin's hats, rolls of silk, all embroidered. All these were plundered and pulled to pieces, floors were literally covered with jade ornaments, porcelain, sweetmeats. . . . If you and Julia could have been present, and had two large Exeter wagons at hand, you might have passed a most delightful morning, and enriched yourselves with all those beautiful things. Unfortunately for myself, it did not do to show too much greediness, and I had no means moreoever of carrying things away.

A lieutenant has no need for such inhibitions. He collected some valuable trophies but writes contemptuously about the 'paraphernalia of Buddhist worship'.

23

GRABBING THE EMPEROR'S STATE SEAL

Lieutenant Allgood to his mother.

> 21 October
> . . . As retribution for the murder of our poor fellows we burnt the Emperor's Palace to the ground. It will give you an idea of the extent of the conflagrations when I tell you that 3,500 men were employed for two days burning. Hundreds of buildings were reduced to ashes.

I have collected several pretty things – something, I think, for every one – from the Emperor's own rooms. I have one grand trophy – the Emperor's own State Seal.

How I shall talk to you about all these things when I return home! This is an immense city, at least 23 miles round the walls. The population must certainly be two million at least.

Our Divisional Head Quarters are in a Tibetan Temple, with scores of gods and shapes, and all the paraphernalia of Buddhist worship. Some of the gods have been displaced from the pedestals to give room for more useful furniture. They are curious places, but when you have seen one you have seen all, and they cease to interest.

Reactions at home were summed up by Sidney Herbert, Secretary of State for War: 'The public here are, I think, very pleased with the way everything has been done in China,' which would appear to include massacres, destruction of art treasures and looting. Justification was no doubt found in the firm belief in the imperial mission, based on superiority in every respect, including morality, and on disdain for the coloured races, as Colonel Stephenson wrote about the Chinese when he set out from Canton: 'The wily, slippery people, who act upon no principle, but are guided solely by events as they happen, and then submit to what they call fate,' and, with a foretaste of exotic sightseeing: 'Fancy getting up to the Great Wall, which one used to read of as a child with such wonder! If I do get up there I will certainly bring you back a brick, which I will previously throw at a Chinaman's head to enhance its interest.'[14] When Lord Elgin proceeded to the Hall of Ceremonies in the Forbidden City to meet Prince Kung, he raised his status by having himself carried on a chair of state escorted by seven hundred soldiers chanting 'God save the Queen'.[15]

The subjection of Burma was even easier, although there were some reverses. When the Burmese invaded Bengal in 1824 Sir Archibald Campbell took Rangoon from the sea in twenty minutes, and in the Anglo–Indian counter-attack Assam and the Arakan were annexed, but at the cost of 15,000 men who perished from scurvy, dysentery and malaria. In 1885, General Prendergast's punitive expediton encountered resistance from the river forts on the way to Mandalay, but King Thibaw then surrendered it without a fight; only the dacoit guerrillas delayed pacification.

14   F.C.A. Stephenson, *Letters from the Crimea*, 1915, p. 252 f.
15   E.C. Holt, *Opium Wars in China*, Putnam, 1964, p. 273.

24

'We shot them down like dogs'

Private John Meighen describes their progress up river to his sister Sarah.

Fort Minlu, December 10, 1885

I rite you these few lines hoping to find you all in good health has it leaves me at present the regiment got orders to proceed by steamer to Burma has war was declared we left calcutta and got into rangoon we had to get on large river flats and get towed up the river by small steamers their is about five large forts the first one we took was only built of mud we went on shore and captured 2 big guns and the enemy all run as soon has they seen us climbing the hills to the fort we attacked the rear while our gun boat attacked it from the river we captured it in about five ours the next day we left the flats at six in the morning when going up a narrow pass the enemy opened fire on us and we returned the fire and they run we shot them down like dogs about 150 when we got at the fort they fired on us through the port holes and General pendergrass gave the order to charge in climbing the walls when they seen us charging and cheering they left their guns and ran down the hills to the river and swimming across to the other side the blue jackets naval men was shooting them in the water the fort was in an awful state arms heads and legs lying all about where the shell had bursted and blown them to pieces we have got about 400 prisoners and we har making them bury the dead the smell of them would nock you down their is all ready more of our men dying with sickness than anythink the flats has go father up the river to manderly wher the king is I do not know when we will shift from this fort we have to go out nealy every night catching decoits their is gangs of them roving the village we got the order to shoot every decoit we catch they are a sneaking lot they come at night and fire on us when everythink is quiet we har setting fire to all the villages it has been raining for three days and fore night and we have nothing to shelter in we are like drowning rats and not much to eat nothing but boiled rice. . . .

British influence even extended to Tibet, a protectorate of the Manchu Empire, when after the Gurkha invasion of 1855 an agency was established at Lhasa. Later, however, trade relations broke down and Francis Younghusband, the imperialist mystic and explorer, led an expeditionary force to the trading centre at Gyantse. After a bloody battle at Tuna, and assaults on fortified monasteries on the way, he reached Lhasa on 3 August 1904. In the absence of the Dalai Lama who had fled, the regent signed a trade treaty.

25

'POP AND DODGE' AT TIBETAN MONASTERIES

C.G. Rawlings, a transport officer, describes the actions on the way to Lhasa.

[July 1904]

I will try and tell you something about recent events in Tibet. The first part of the march was through the steamy heat of the Teesta Valley made no pleasanter by the monsoon. From Lingtam to Jeyluk we climbed 5000 feet in six and a half miles. It was wonderful to see the way in which the mules struggled up the narrow path that more resembled badly made stairs. The climb was a very stiff one all the way up to the Jelap La Pass (14,300 ft.) and here most of us got frightful headaches on account of the high altitude. We played hockey at Tuna, which is 15,000 ft. and defeated our opponents by 20 goals to 4, but we nearly all died from it!

The next day we marched through the Red Gorge to Saotang. The Tibetans were holding the monastery at Niani. We advanced to the attack, but it seemed as if the enemy had bolted. However when we were 200 yards off they loosed off with every conceivable kind of weapon. Their shooting was very erratic, however, and, as we were very widely extended, did no damage beyond making holes in two men's clothes.

We then rushed the village, and accounted for everybody who had not bolted inside the big wall. There we sat and blazed away at the men on the walls at a range of about 150 yards. It reminded one of 'pop and dodge' on the range in hot weather! Eventually we managed to get in by a part of the wall that was broken down, the Tibetans barricading themselves in the houses. Then began house-to-house fighting of a most exciting nature. The Tibetans, having no way of escape fought like cats. We had no explosives, and some of the houses were very hard to break into. The fight continued till the General [Macdonald] called us off, and we went on into Gyantse. Here we were greeted with a royal salute from the jong as we marched into camp, and very tired and sleepy we went to bed to be lulled to sleep by the 'jinglings of the jingals in the jong'....

The Tibetans are far better shots with boulders than they are with guns, and usually seem to prefer this means of offence. One of them landed a brick on my head and sent me flying down the *khud*, and then put out his tongue and turned up his thumbs, which is the Tibetan salaam!

The next day the Taping Monastry and village was attacked and captured, the enemy losing about 100. The camp moved again, but as it was war all over deep watercuts, I moved with my *ekkas* into the Mission Compound only 1,000 yards from the jong, so it was perpetually bombarded, but being splendidly protected, it was almost as safe as London. Then an armistice was made, the Ta Lama, who is next to the Delai Lama and the Grand Secretary having arrived. Younghusband is the ideal man, and gave them a fine time of it. Nothing was agreed to, as our first condition was the giving up of the *jong*, which, of course, they would not do.

At 2.30 a.m. the following morning the troops took up their positions. A surprise was intended, but the Tibetans were found to be fully awake and ready. A perfect blaze of fire met the advancing force, but fortunately all the shots went high. The outskirts were soon captured and house to house fighting continued throughout the day.

Several attempts were made to work up the precipices. Only one spot held out a hope, and this the ten pounders finally breached. The Tibetans did not care a little for our shells, maxims, or rifles, just bending double and rushing right through a storm of bursting shells and a rain of bullets, and what's more, they nearly always got away again under cover unhit. If the fire became hot from any house, shells were poured in there, but were they silenced? not a bit. Three seconds afterwards, pop went the rifles again, sometimes through the very holes the shells had made.

At about 4.30 started the finest sight I have ever seen, the storming of the breach. Had the defenders been backed up, we should never have taken the place. Each of those men, six in number, should have the V.C., for they fought almost to the last. Every gun, about 14, 12 maxims, and many infantry poured in a cloud of shell and shot right into these men. They were at times absolutely hidden by the bursting shells and clouds of splintered rocks and stones, and yet there they worked hurling down rocks on the advancing party. Almost up the sheer precipice the plucky little Gurkhas and a few of the 7th crawled, splendidly led by two officers, right in the thick of the falling rocks urging on their men. The actual assault could only be done by one at a time, climbing on to the shoulders of another. A Gurkha climbed on the shoulders of his officer first, but got a rock on his head. Down he went. Then the officer had a try and down he came. It was at this point that the six defenders fled. Then up went another Gurkha, then one by one they clambered up, and the *jong* was won. . . .

Looting, I mean to say foraging, went on for several days all around it was back luck on the people, for there was not much left when we had finished. Everyone wants to get back to India. Personally I like this country immensely, and I would not mind stopping here for a long time. It was nasty work at first for our men are mostly criminals, the sweepings of the bazaars of India. . . .[16]

The Abyssinisan (1868), Ashanti (1874) and Zulu (1879) Wars

> *Soldiers are nothing more than grown-up*
> *schoolboys. The wild moments of enjoyment*
> *passed in the pillage of a place live*
> *long in a soldier's memory*
> WOLSELEY

Theodorus, the Emperor of Abyssinia, put the British Consul (and some missionaries) in chains, as a hostage for the extortion of arms-making machinery and personnel needed for his tribal wars. In 1868, an expeditionary force of 12,000 men under Sir Robert Napier landed in Annesley Bay, 420 miles from the 7400 ft high fortress of Magdala where the prisoners were held. After a laborious four-month trek, with elephants dragging the guns up the mountains, they were greeted by Theodore's guns high up on Fala crest and his army rushed down for a frontal assault: seven hundred natives were soon mowed down by the quick fire of the breech-loading rifles.

---

16 *Jong* = fortress; *ekka* = one-horsed vehicle; *khud* = ravine; Ta Lama = Tashi Lama.

26

THE PUNITIVE CAMPAIGN IN ABYSSINIA: BRITISH SUCCESS 'A NATURAL LAW'

A staff officer pictures the triumphal progress of the imperial force.

Antalo, 5th March 1868

If our friend 'Punch' would like to represent the Abyssinian expedition he might sketch it after this fashion. The central figure, of course, should be His Excellency Sir Robert Napier, and if a triumphal car be thought necessary for him, an Armstrong gun-carriage would supply a suitable study for it. His left hand, far in rear as much as possible out of sight, should grasp a might sabre, while the right, extended as far in front, held out a bag of dollars towards the crowd of adoring Abyssinians. In the background a train of camels, laden with gifts, might be shown trooping in long Indian file. Such a sketch would in truth portray the manner in which we are passing through the land. . . . Let it not be thought, however, that the dollars could of themselves have done the work. Our friendly relations with those around us have largely rested on the military array which we have held all the time in the background. . . . We Britons have grown so accustomed to success that we are apt to regard it as if it were a matter of course – something due to the operation of a natural law rather than the result of the right use of means. . . .

[mid-April]

. . . All of a sudden, while we were scanning with telescope the enemy's commanding position, the familiar little cloud of white smoke was seen hanging for a moment on the brow of Fahla, and a hurtling round-shot, burying itself in the ground not far from His Excellency, fell, like a declaration of war, in the midst of us; the men's feeling was expressed in a cheer for Theodore! Shot followed shot in rapid succession, and the last 5000 of the warriors of Ethiopia were soon rushing down the sides of Fahla. One might long search in vain for a finer background for a battle-piece: when suddenly the sky was overcast by a tempest; when the sound of man's puny artillery was drowned ever and again in the roll of heaven's terrible thunder; when shells from the enemy's mortars kept bursting over our heads in wreaths of smoke hardly distinguishable from the fast-descending mists; and when the hissing of our rockets was like the noise of a thousand fiery spirits rushing forth from hell; – then, in truth, the scene was grand as ever entered into the mind of a painter to conceive. But the result of such a contest could not be long doubtful. Paralysed and stricken with amazement, they yet showed no signs of defeat. When the 4th King's Own Regiment opened fire with their Sniders on the plain into which they had so foolishly descended against lines of British infantry, covered by movable artillery, ravines filled with dead. Savage bravery may avail one where only savages are engaged; but discipline will decide the conflict of armies. . . .

It was all over. Theodore freed the unharmed prisoners and sent one thousand cows and five hundred sheep as a peace offering, but refused to surrender to Napier, 'that servant of a woman'; he challenged him in vain to single combat. The fortress was blasted by naval rockets and stormed, and Theodore, rather than be taken prisoner, shot himself with the pistol Queen Victoria had given him as a 'token of gratitude'. The conclusion of the imperial lesson was celebrated by an orgy of plundered liquor.[17]

The Ashanti were a warlike race on the Gold Coast, symbolically united with their ancestors by the mystique of the sacred Golden Stool of the King which they believed to be animated with the invincible spirit of the people. In January 1873 King Koffee invaded the British Protectorate of the Cape Coast in an attempt to conquer and enslave the tribes there. Wolseley was sent out to check Ashanti ambitions: he was convinced that his mission would be beneficial to the tribes. Waiting for the arrival of reinforcements from England, he felt weary from fighting in so many campaigns and always being up against the incompetence of the upper-caste military establishment. In a mood of contemplation, his usual burning ambition for glory seems to have faded.

27

'Ambition has died out within me'

Major-General Sir (later Field Marshal Viscount) Garnet Wolseley (1833–1913) writes to his wife.

Cape Coast, 17th October 1873

. . . Any war brings one to think more seriously than when sitting at home at ease, and makes one realise how dependent we are upon Him for everything. Our life is a frail affair, the cord of which is easily and rapidly snapt at all times, whether at home or abroad. I trust that God will spare me to carry out this campaign successfully; but the personal ambition of which my very heart was at one time so full, has in great measure died out within me, and I have often of late wished that I could be taken. . . .

Advancing from Cape Coast Castle with a mere 2,400 men, half of whom soon contracted bush fever, Wolseley immediately tried to browbeat King Koffee (with forces ten times larger) into submission by threatening him with the might of his tiny Imperial army. He underestimated the King's determination, pride and cunning: he kept up an apparently amicable correspondence, addressing Wolseley as 'my good friend' while dragging out negotiations to lure the British into the deadly bush under the cover of which he kept on harrassing them in the hope of cutting them off from their base.

17   D. Bates, *The Abyssinian Difficulty*, OUP, 1979, *passim*.

28

THE IMPERIAL POSTURE

Wolseley serves notice on King Koffee Kalkalli.

January 2, 1874

King,

. . . The Queen of England has sent me as her General to demand reparation. A large force of her white troops are now on their march from Cape Coast for the purpose of invading your territory to enforce compliance with my just demands. The Queen of England has placed ample forces at my disposal to crush the Ashanti nation. She is anxious to avoid shedding more Ashanti blood. I shall therefore be prepared to make a lasting peace with you on the following terms: –

(1) that you deliver forthwith all wrongfully detained prisoners

(2) that you will pay Her Majesty 50,000 ounces of approved gold

(3) that a new treaty of peace be signed at Coomassie to which place I would proceed for that purpose with a sufficient force of white soldiers. . . .

Be warned in time to continue a hopeless struggle against an army of white men. . . .

I am, King, your true friend

G.J. Wolseley

The King professed peaceful intentions to gain time. Wolseley continued to exert pressure on him.

January 13

. . . I am glad to find from your letter that your Majesty has resolved upon peace; but before I can enter into any negotiations whatever with your Majesty, it is essential that you should convince me of the sincerity of your intentions. . . . Until these terms are complied with, I cannot halt any of my four armies. The advanced guard has already crossed the Prah, and the other three will shortly invade your Kingdom. . . . In order that peace may be lasting it is essential that your Majesty and your people should learn that you can no more prevent an army of white men marching into your territory than you can stop the sun from rising every morning.

The King released all white prisoners and promised to pay £200,000, but continued his operations. Wolseley's threats became greater.

January 24

I intend to go to Coomassie. It is for your Majesty to decide whether I go there as your friend or as your enemy. If I go there as your enemy, I shall march at the head of an irresistible English army, and I must again remind you of the consequences that this may have upon your Majesty's dynasty and upon the Ashanti Kingdom.

Wolseley assured his troops that 'Providence has implanted in the heart of every native in Africa a superstitious awe and dread of the white man that prevents the negro from daring to meet us face to face in combat,' but, at the same time, warned them that when 'surrounded on all sides by hordes of howling enemies they must rely on their own courage and discipline'.[18] He was confident but apprehensive.

29

'My trust in God is implicit'

Wolsely reflects on the planned battle to his wife.

Sartu, 30th January

To-morrow we fight, and on the result of the action everything here depends; my trust in God is implicit, and I feel we shall beat these bloodthirsty and cruel people. . . . I rejoice at the prospect of to-morrow, for it must end the business one way or another. Fighting against great odds is all very well on the plains of India or China, where you can see what you are about, but in this forest, where you can never see a hundred yards, it is nervous work, especially with a mere handful of troops and so far from their base.

Keeping up his bluff, Wolseley directed the battle of Amoafo the next day by waving his cigar, enthroned on a cane chair, carried by four tribesmen in Ashanti manner; fortunately for him, the Ashantis had only slugs and no bullets. But even so, the cross-fire from the bush caused two hundred British casualties, in addition to the two hundred sick, but the advance continued.

30

VICTORY AT AMOAFO

Brigadier Sir Archibald Alison, Bart., a one-armed Crimean veteran, writes home.

February 4

. . . Then followed one of the finest spectacles I have ever seen in war. Without stop or stay the 42nd [Highlanders] rushed on cheering, their pipes playing, their officers to the front; ambuscade after ambuscade was successfully carried, village after village won in succession, till the whole Ashantis broke and fled in the wildest disorder down the pathway on their front to Coomassie. Umbrellas and war-chairs of their chiefs, drums, muskets, killed and wounded, covered the whole way, and the bush on each side was trampled as if a torrent had flowed through it. . . .

18   A. Lloyd, *Drums of Kumasi*, Longmans, 1964, p. 88.

When the Black Watch had taken the capital and were parading through the streets, pipes playing, the stern Imperial general who had always been as good as his word, tried to conciliate the fugitive King:

> King, so you have deceived me, but I have kept my promise to you. I am in Coomassie, and my only wish is to make a lasting peace with you. I have shown you the power of England, and now I will be merciful. . . .[19]

Meanwhile, in the palace, in which bones, heads and blood from large-scale fresh human sacrifices, exacted by the fetish priests to stave off defeat, had been found, the prize agents, among them Buller (later of Boer War notoriety), were collecting their loot by candle-light throughout the night, piling up gold masks, cutlery, bracelets and nuggets. The next morning the palace was blown up and the thatched roofs of the houses set on fire until nothing remained of the capital but a heap of smouldering ruins. Then, as the rains had started, threatening to cut off escape, a hasty retreat began over tree trunks laid across streams which had swollen two hundred yards wide and six feet deep. When the army had limped back precariously to the safety of Cape Coast most of them were invalids and Buller was so sick with fever that he had to be carried in a hammock.

31

'I have really enjoyed this expedition'

Captain (later General Sir) Redvers Buller (1838–1908) writes home.

Coomassie, 5/6 February
. . . I was never so impressed with anyone as with Sir Garnet, he was cheery and cool to the last. He sent for me and said, 'Buller, is the King coming in?' 'He is at least six miles off' I said, 'and bolting'; 'Very well, I shall loot and burn Coomassie, and appoint you Head Prize Agent.' 'Thank you, sir,' I said, for there is a percentage and the loot ought to have been worth something. . . . 'Get what you can out of the Palace to- night, to-morrow I shall burn the town and return.'

14 Feb.
. . . We were run hard in Coomassie. Frightful weather, short of grub, a handful of 1500 men surrounded by a dense bush full of thousands of howling savages, and our 70 miles of communications attacked at every point, with our few Europeans going down with fever and no hammocks to carry them.

I shall be glad to get back home, as I can't help feeling that I lose energy daily. . . . I have really, though I am dull, enjoyed this expedition, and it has done me a great deal of good, but there is an end to all things. . . .

19   H. Brackenbury, *The Ashanti War*, 1874, II, p. 228.

Wolseley wrote home: 'So ended the most horrible war I ever took part in' but he was pleased with his souvenirs from the palace pillage and did not forget a present for the Queen.

32

KING KOFFEE'S COFFEE POT

Wolseley to his wife.

Cape Coast, 25/2

We have had a sale of loot taken, and I have bought King Koffee's coffee-pot – old English silver, I should say of George II, but in a battered condition. I thought, anyhow, it would be a subject for conversation at breakfast whenever we might have very stupid people staying with us. I have also the gold rattle from the King's nursery. . . . My staff have purchased the King's sword for me – very nice of them, is it not? It was presented by Her Majesty to the King many years ago. I sent home the King's state umbrella to the Queen. . . .[20]

Soldiers' letters have rarely been used with so much effect to reconstruct a campaign as those of the Zulu War of 1879.[21] Their testimony, of which only a few excerpts can be given here, brings to life the characteristic sequence of a Victorian colonial war: initial blunders resulting in tragedy, heroic resistance leading to recovery, and finally complete victory crowned by annexation.

The last Zulu king, Cetshwayo, a cruel tyrant, who had raided Natal and the Transvaal, failed to reply to an ultimatum demanding disbandment of his army: Lord Chelmsford subsequently invaded Zululand in January with an army of 5,000 British and over 8,000 Zulus opposed to their king. His centre column of 4,000 camped at Isandhlwana without digging entrenchments or forming a laager. Chelmsford was lured away with his main force, and then the Zulus attacked the remaining garrison. Colonel Durnford fatally dissipated his 1,000 British and 600 black soldiers by sending them out in

---

20 After deposing and murdering King Koffee, as he had failed to be invincible, the Ashantis retook the lost territory and left the promised indemnity unpaid, but the tribal spirit seems to have been broken and the 1896 expedition proved to be a farce without a contest. The new King kissed Sir Francis Scott's feet (he had demanded 50,000 ounces of gold) and the Gold Coast became a British protectorate. When the Governor Sir Fred Hodgson insisted on sitting on the Golden Stool as the Queen's representative, the humiliated Ashanti spirit revived and nine months of hard fighting ensued till the country was finally annexed.

21 F. Emery, *The Red Soldier*, Hodder & Stoughton, 1976.

single companies to tackle the 20,000 Zulus who were descending from their hide-out behind the hills. They had plenty of firearms and as they were advancing shield to shield in a terrifying jog-trot, they rattled their deadly assegai spears against their shields, hissing war cries.

33

'Hope that everybody clings to'

Lieutenant (later General Sir) Horace Smith Dorrien (1858–1930), who was to become one of the best generals in the First World War, describes the scene during an eclipse of the sun.

22 January

. . . A dreadful disaster has happened to us. It seems to me a pure miracle that I am alive to tell you about it.

When I arrived in camp, I found the greater part of the column gone out with the General to meet the Zulu force, so that there was really one a caretaking force left – five companies, two guns, about 600 Native Contingent, and the sick in the hospital tent. The first Zulu force appeared about six o'clock in the morning. Two companies were sent out after them. The Zulus seemed to retire, and there was firing kept up at long ranges. At about 10.30 the Zulus were seen coming over the hills in thousands. They were in most perfect order, in about 20 rows in a semi-circle round us, at least 20,000.

In half an hour they were right up to the camp. Bullets were flying all over the place, but I never seemed to notice them. The Zulus nearly all had firearms. Before we knew where we were they came right into the camp, assegaing right and left. Everybody then who had a horse turned to fly. We were completely surrounded and the road to Rorke's Drift was cut off. Everybody went pell-mell over huge boulders and rocks until we got to a deep spruit or gulley. How the horses got over I have no idea. I was riding a broken-kneed old crock which did not belong to me, and which I expected to go on its head every minute. We had to go bang through them at the spruit. Lots of our men were killed there. I was firing away at them with my revolver as I galloped along. The ground there down to the river was so broken that the Zulus went as fast as the horses, and kept killing all the way. This lasted till we came to a kind of precipice down to the River Buffalo.

I jumped off and led my horse down. Just as I was doing so the horse went with a bound to the bottom of the precipice, being struck with an assegai, I gave up all hope, as the Zulus were all round me, finishing off the wounded. However, with the strong hope that everybody clings to, I rushed off on foot and plunged into the river, which was little better than a roaring torrent.

I was being carried down the stream at a tremendous pace, when a loose horse came by me and I got hold of his tail and he landed me safely on the other bank; but I was too tired to stick to him and get on his back. I rushed on and was several times knocked over by our mounted niggers, then up a tremendous hill with my wet clothes and boots full of water. About 20 Zulus got over the water and followed us up the hill, but I am thankful to say they had not their firearms. A few followed us for about 3 miles, but I had a revolver, which I kept letting them know. They did not come in close, and finally stopped altogether.

Well, to cut it short, I struggled into Helpmakaar, about 20 miles off, at nightfall, to find a few men who had escaped entrenched in a waggon laager. We sat up all night, momentarily expecting attack. . . .

Nearly a thousand British soldiers were massacred, mutilated, and stripped, and even little boys in the band 'were hung up on hooks and opened like sheep'; only fifty-five Europeans escaped. Some men regretted they had enlisted under the influence of drink.

34

'I wish I was back in England'

Private Henry Moses writes a pitiful letter home to Pontypool.

[n.d.]

. . . I know what soldiering is now. We have marched 200 miles and haven't had a night's sleep this month. We are in fear every night, and have had to fight the Zulus, who came on us and killed 800 of our men. I wish I was back in England again, for I should never leave. It is sad times here, and we are on the watch every night with our belts buckled on and our rifles by our side. It is nothing but mountains here; all biscuits to eat. Dear father, and sisters, and brothers, goodbye. We may never meet again. I repent the day that I took the shilling. I have not seen a bed since I left England. We have only one blanket, and are out every night in the rain – no shelter. . . . Good-bye, if we never meet again, and may God be with you.

35

'Vultures tearing up the corpses'

Melton Prior returns four months later to the camp with a salvage party and describes the field of carnage.

[n.d.]

The sight I saw at Isandhlwana is one I shall never forget. In all the seven campaigns I have been in I have not witnessed a scene more horrible. . . . To come suddenly on the spot where the slaughtered battalion of the 24th Regiment and others were lying was far more appalling. Here I saw not the bodies, but the skeletons of men whom I had known in life and health, mixed up with the skeletons of oxen and horses, and with waggons thrown on their side, all in the greatest confusion, showing how furious had been the onslaught of the enemy.

Amidst the various articles belonging to them which were scattered over the field of carnage, were letters from wives at home to their husbands, from English fathers and mothers to their sons, portraits of those dear to them, and other homely little things, remembrances of the dearest associations. Skeletons of men lay on the open ground, bleaching under a tropical sun, along miles of country. The individuals could only be recognised by such things as a patched boot, a ring on the finger-bone, a particular button, or coloured shirt, or pair of socks. And this could be done only with much difficulty, for either the hands of the enemy, or the beaks and claws of vultures tearing up the corpses had in numberless cases so mixed up the bones of the dead that the skull of one man, or bones of a leg or arm, now lay with parts of the skeleton of another. The Lancers went about all over the field, often here and there quietly lifting the clothes off the skeletons, or gently pushing them on one side with their lances, to see what regiment they belonged to. I almost regretted to see this done, for it seemed like sacrilege. But this is a time of war.

36

GRAIN GROWING FROM LIFE-BLOOD

Archibald Forbes' letter is the ultimate in evoking the ravages of death in the awesome solitude of a battlefield in the African veldt; he observes bitterly how the black 'savages' show respect at least towards their own dead while the British are only concerned to salvage what they can grab.

[n.d.]

. . . In this ravine dead men lay thick, mere bones, with toughened, discoloured skin like leather covering them, and clinging tight to them, the flesh all wasted away. Some were almost wholly dismembered, heaps of yellow clammy bones. I forbear to describe the faces, with their blackened features and beards bleached by rain and sun. Every man had been disembowelled. Some were scalped, and others subjected to yet ghastlier mutilations. The clothes had lasted better than the poor bodies they covered to keep the skeletons together. All the way up the slope I traced by the ghastly token of dead men, the fitful line of flight. It was like a long string with knots in it, the string formed of single corpses, the knots of clusters of dead, where (as it seemed) little groups might have gathered to make a hopeless, gallant stand and die. . . .

But on the slope beyond, on which from the crest we looked down, the scene was the saddest, and more full of weird desolation than any I had yet gazed upon. There was none of the stark, blood-curdling horror of a recent battlefield. A strange dead calm reigned in this solitude of nature. Grain had grown luxuriantly round the waggons, sprouting from the seed that dropped from the loads, falling in soil fertilised by the life-blood of gallant men. So long in most places had grown the grass, that it mercifully shrouded the dead, whom four long months tomorrow we have left unburied. . . . The Zulus, who have carefully buried their own dead, will come back to find that we visited the place not to bury our dead, but to remove a batch of waggons. . . .

After tasting blood at Isandhlwana, 4,000 Zulus turned their fury after nightfall on the hospital at Rorke's Drift where 110 British soldiers under two lieutenants were guarding 40 sick men. Their epic all-night defence of the laagered compound earned the unique distinction of eleven VCs.

37

'My nerves were as steady as a rock'

Trooper Harry Lugg, Natal Mounted Police, was one of the hospital patients.

[n.d.]

. . . A carabineer rode into the little yard, without boots, tunic, or arms. All we could glean from his excited remarks was, 'Everyone killed in camp, and 4000 Kaffirs on their way to take the hospital – not pleasant tidings for a hundred men, you may be sure. When he came to himself a bit he said, 'you will all be murdered and cut to pieces' and the only answer he received was 'We will fight for it, and if we have to die we will die like Britishers.'

All those who were able began to throw up sacks and knock loopholes out with pickaxes and otherwise showed their war-like spirit. . . . A man rode out to see if he could see anything of them, and on going about 1,000 yards out he could see them just a mile off, 'as black as hell and as thick as grass'. 'Stay operations and fall in!' My carbine was broken, or rather the stock bent. I found a piece of rein, tied it up, and fell in with the soldiers. I thought, if I can get somewhere to sit down and pop away I shall be all right, because my knees were much swollen. I was told off in my turn to take a loop-hole, and defend the roof from fire. At about 3.30 they came on, first in sections of fours, then opened out in skirmishing order. Up came their reserve, and then they were on us. The place seemed alive with them. No orders were given, every man to act as he thought proper. I had the satisfaction of seeing the first I fired at roll over and then my nerves were as steady as a rock. I made sure almost before I pulled the trigger. There was some of the best shooting at 450 yards that I have ever seen.

Just before dark we had beaten them off with great losses, and only a few casualties on our side. . . . Before it got really dark the fiends lit the hospital thatch, which being very closely packed did not burn well. At about 10 they came on in tremendous force, sweeping the fellows before them and causing them to retreat to the store. But Providence favoured us. The thatch roof burst out in flames, and made it as light as day, and before they had time to retreat we were pouring bullets into them like hail. We could see them falling in scores. Then you could hear suppressed British cheers. They kept up the attack all night with no better luck. We knocked them down as fast as they came. At 5 a.m. the last shot was fired, and the last nigger killed; he had a torch tied on his assegai and was in the act of throwing it into the storehouse thatch, but he was 'sold'. The column came to our relief about 5.30 and real British cheers went up, I can tell you. . . .

The Isandhlwana massacre, the worst since the Indian Mutiny, caused a great shock in England, and six months later, a few days before Wolseley arrived to supersede him, Chelmsford took his revenge on the Zulus in the battle of Ulundi, burning down 20,000 huts and killing 2–3,000 for the loss of only twenty-five. It was left to Wolseley to capture Cetshwayo who was exiled to England – only to be entertained for lunch by the Queen, for, after all, he was a king and he and the Zulus were admired for their martial accomplishment.

38

CETEWAYO'S LIONS' CLAWS – 'CHARMS' FOR THE LADIES

Wolseley writes to his wife about the capture of Cetewayo.

Camp Ulundi, 29th August

Well, after more than one miss, Cetewayo is a prisoner at last. This morning early I heard the clatter of hoofs past my tent, and upon going out was greeted by a cry, 'They've caught him, sir'. My heart jumped within me when I heard the news. All my plans for the pacification of the country hinged upon his capture. As days went by, and he managed to slip through my patrols, I became nervous. Now, however, thank God, all this is past.

I have managed to secure one of Cetewayo's necklaces of lions' claws – only the highest in the land are allowed to wear such a distinction. I shall send home a few of the claws to be mounted. You must write a note with each, saying I send a little 'charm', which had formed part of Cetewayo's necklace. Baroness Coutts; Lady Constance Stanley; Lady Sherborne; Lady Cardwell; etc.

The War in the Sudan (1884–5)

Who would not die for England! And for Her
He dies . . . stern to every voice but Hers,
Obeys Duty and Death
ALFRED AUSTIN (1835–1913)

Wolseley, who had called himself 'a Jingo in the best acceptation of that sobriquet' was sent to Egypt in 1882 with 25,000 men to suppress Ahmed Arabi's nationalist rebellion against the Khedive which had caused a massacre at Alexandria. Against heavy odds he cut up the Egyptian army at Tel-el-Kebir on 12 September and established a British military presence and responsibility in Egypt. In reward he was made a full general and baron, but the Ministry of Defence and General Staff he advocated ('War is a serious business which has to be prepared for') were not set up. He praises death in battle, which he would prefer to defeat, and raves at foreigners.

39

JOHN BULL GLOATS OVER THE 'BUTCHER'S BILL'

Wolseley writes to his wife before the battle of Tel-el-Kebir.

Ismailia, 7th September 1882

. . . I long for a real success to make the world feel that England has a lot left in her, and that her soldiers' strength and courage in unaffected by the influence of Radicalism. . . . The news of our fight will have reached you with its disquietening 'butcher's bill' over which Mr John Bull rather gloats, and thinks, when the list is a long one, that he has had something for his money. And yet how much pleasanter is death from clean bullet wounds than from loathsome diseases. To be killed in the open air with the conviction that you are dying for your country, how different from rotting to death in a hospital, or dying like a consumptive girl in an artificially heated room. I am no great lover of life, but I should like to do something before I die. . . .

I have four foreigners – representatives of France, Germany, Russia, and the United States – coming to live upon me, I am sorry to say, at my expense, but they won't dine at my table. It would be unbearable to have a *bundle* of foreigners listening to all one said at every meal. . . .

10 September

. . . I have determined to attack the enemy's fortified position. I know that I am doing a dangerous thing, but I cannot wait for reinforcements; to do so would kill the spirit of my troops. . . . I hope I may never return home a defeated man: I would sooner leave my old bones here, than go home to be jeered at. . . .

When the fanatical Muslim dervishes of the Sudan, guided by the Mahdi (Messiah) annihilated an Egyptian army under Colonel Hicks Pasha in November 1883, it was decided to abandon the Sudan. Gordon, who, as Egyptian Governor-General in 1877, had tried to suppress the slave trade there, was sent to Khartoum to evacuate the Egyptian army and civilians.

40

'If I get humbled . . . '

Major-General Gordon writes to his sister.

[Cairo] 26 January 1884

. . . I leave for the Soudan to-night. I feel quite happy, for I say, If God is with me, who can or will be hurtful to me? May He be glorified, the world and people of the Soudan be blessed, and may I be the dust under His feet.

[. . . and to Colonel Ffolliott]

Khartoum, 5 March

I came up here very weak in human means, but have been much blessed by our Lord, and things will turn out for the best. It is odd to be here in this vast ruin of an empire, but my long lonely rides now bear fruit by His blessing. What a defeat Hicks's was! It is terrible to think of over 12,000 men killed; the Arabs just prodded them to death, where they lay dying of thirst, four days without water! It is appalling. What a hecatomb to death! . . . My resource is in constant prayer, to accept His will in all things without murmuring. . . . He will not dwell in a proud heart, which I have in excess; so you will know, if I get humbled and the people blessed, that my prayers are answered. . . .

Gordon declared the Sudan independent on his arrival and sent 2,500 women, children, sick and wounded to safety down the Nile. He would not leave himself and held on to Khartoum, though inwardly uncertain whether to do so until it was too late and he was cut off. Eight years before he had written from Khartoum: 'Talk of two natures in one! I have a hundred, and they none think alike and all want to rule. I never know my own mind for two days consecutively. I wish I was more decided, but alas! I cannot be so. . . .'[22]

Gladstone turned a deaf ear to the clamour for Gordon's relief and there was a fatal delay in despatching a rescue force; when it was on the way in autumn, Wolseley wanted to take it on the shortest route through the desert on camel back to 'capture' Gordon: 'Fancy a Life Guardsman clothed like a scarecrow and with blue goggles on, mounted on a camel, over which he has little control. What a picture!'[23] But he was ordered to take the longer and slower river route.

41

WOLSELEY FORETELLS THE BOER AND FIRST WORLD WARS

Wolseley, writing to his wife, rages against 'vestrymen' and 'dunghill democrats.'

Wady Halfa, 13/10/84

. . . Just off to one of the very difficult cataracts up the river to see some native boats dragged through it. A good rattling day of discomfort in the broiling sun is good for one, and prevents one from feeling age creeping on. In London one hears so much of party politics and the struggle of place-hunters; but when one gets clear away, any

---

22 *Letters of Gen. Gordon*, 1888, p. 136.
23 G. Arthur, *Letters of Lord and Lady Wolseley*, Heinemann, 1922, p. 121.

shred of concern vanishes after a few weeks spent in the Nubian deserts. If, to please the Gladstones, the Brights, and vestrymen of that ilk, the English choose to see their Empire wrecked, provided the catastrophe takes place in accordance with law and the theory of Parliamentary Government, all I can say is, they deserve to lose it.

Dongola, 10th November
I am amazed at the bickerings and dodges of professional politicians. At this distance from Westminster, Private Tommy Atkins, slaving away here amidst a thousand discomforts, seems a far more respectable person, and one of whom England should be much prouder. . . .

24th Nov.
. . . I am so tired and wearied with Mr Gladstone and his Cabinet of vestrymen, with their love of party, and indifference to the honour and greatness of England. . . . They will have their day; a dirty, dunghill sort of democratic wave is now passing over the world. Old creeds are laughed at; power and strength are scoffed at. The stump orator, poking his head out of a railway carriage, tells a man that he is a splendid fellow and the pink of wisdom as long he keeps the Prime Minister in power.

26th Nov.
. . . I have just come in from a good canter and I feel healthy and ready to fight the Mahdi but if great mortality occurs, it will be Gladstone's fault in not being able to foresee the necessity of this expedition. . . . The amount of human blood that has been shed and will yet be shed through his want of statesmanlike ability is bad to contemplate. Heaven knows I am not squeamish about taking human life, but, when taken, the action ought to be deliberate and well thought out, to limit the extent of wars and bloodshed. His action has been the reverse of this. He talks glibly about bloodguiltiness, and yet no Englishman of modern days has so much on him, not because he loves to kill, but because he cannot rule the affairs of England. Whilst he is canting on half-penny cards about the sinfulness of war, he is planting the seeds of trouble which must end in a great Boer War in South Africa, and eventually in a war in Europe.

While the General is concerned with the defence of the empire, his wife expresses more homely anxieties and puts the unspeakable in French.

42

'Don't bathe in the teeth of the crocodiles'

Lady Wolseley sends her husband her photo and chocolate cakes, together with schoolmarmish advice.

23rd September 1884
Little 'King' takes my photograph and a bag of chocolate cakes. We think a nibble of them before you start on your *rickety* camel in the morning will settle your stomach

and prevent sickness. If the journey causes them to coagulate into one large lump you must eat it out of the box with a spoon. I hope, too, you will like the photo. Please slip me out of the frame and observe the beauty of my arms, which is very remarkable! I am delighted to hear of the camel present and that he is worth £200. Long live the Khedive and the Camel – if the latter sells for a good price. A word about your spelling. Week (semaine not faiblesse) is not spelt weak, and development has not got two 'p's' or 'l's'.

You write an excellent simple style usually, but *sometimes* there is something rather *apprêtée*[24] in your sentences, a little air of writing for posterity, and remember, if you write for posterity, posterity won't keep its eye on what you write, because it will be unnatural and wanting in life. There is a sermon for you.

Nos soupçons sur la cuisinière ne sont que trop vrais! Elle est depuis sept mois dans cet état. Je la trouve très impertinente de rester chez nous si longtemps car cela pourrait arriver d'un moment à l'autre. Je l'envoie, *with an escort*, chez sa soeur qui est une femme mariée. Il parâit qu'elle serait restée jusqu'à son accouchement, si on n'avait pas fait cette découverte.

2nd October

I see to-day that you have arrived at Assuan. There may not, or may, be much fighting before you, but I think there seems plenty of danger without – crocodiles, sails catching fire, boats upsetting. I only wonder I ever close my eyes, but I *do*, and have even an afternoon nap. I read horrid accounts of the crocodiles lying like logs of wood, and snapping their crunching jaws as you tread on them. I beg you to be careful. Be as dirty as you like, but don't bathe in the teeth of the crocodiles.

23rd Oct.

. . . Sometimes I get very low and anxious thinking about you, and the Nile seems full of crocodiles and cataracts ready to eat you up. Last night many tears trickled down on the pillow.

6th November

When I get into my comfortable bed at night I think of you and all the miseries you are going through, and I feel a *wretch* for leading such a quiet, easy life while you are toiling and moiling. I wonder if the chocolate cakes and the photograph have reached you. I hope they have not been con-*fused* into one another by the heat.

27th Nov.

. . . I shall feel anxious about you till you are at Khartoum. I wish you would have a little cord ladder hanging down from your camel to climb up by in case he gets up too soon.

Meanwhile, engrossed in contemplation of the Bible (he was a fundamentalist), Gordon sat waiting for relief at Khartoum, taking comfort in brandy and chain-smoking. He bravely withstood the siege for 317 days but the Mahdi's hordes at last broke into the palace on 26 January 1885 and massa-

---

24   = affected.

cred him and his garrison. He awaited his fate on the stairs in his white cere-monial uniform with a true sense of drama: he was speared and passed into empire legend as a martyr. He seems to have known his fate all the time and to have willed it.

43

'I have tried to do my duty'

Gordon writes a last letter to his sister.

14 December, 1884

This may be the last letter you will receive from me, for we are on our last legs, owing to the delay of the expedition. However, God rules all, and, as He will rule to His glory and our welfare, His will be done.

Your affectionate brother
C.G. Gordon

P.S. I am quite happy, thank God, and I have *'tried* to do my duty.'

Emotions welled up in England and there was a shocked outcry against the government in which the Queen, always reflecting the feelings of the man in the street, joined emphatically. She fell ill for a few days when she heard the news of Gordon's death and attended the memorial service in Westminster Abbey on the 'Day of National Mourning'.

44

THE QUEEN ACCUSES GLADSTONE

Victoria expresses her grief to Sir Henry Ponsonby, her private secretary.

17.2.1885

Mr Gladstone and the Government *have* – the Queen *feels it dreadfully* – Gordon's innocent, noble, heroic blood on their consciences. *No one* who reflects on *how* he was *sent* out, how he was *refused* help, can deny it! It is awful. . . . May they *feel* it, and may they be *made to do*! It is all this that has made the Queen *ill*. . . . Her heart is with her soldiers – she *always* bid them farewell – in 1854 – in 1882. . . .

Wolseley's advance force under Sir Charles Wilson arrived two days late to save 'God's friend', as he called Gordon, now eulogized even by Gladstone as 'a hero of heroes': 'We all look very foolish,' he wrote wrily, 'To have struggled up here against immense difficulty and at the cost of great labour and then, when the goal was within sight to have the prize snatched from one, is indeed hard to bear.'[25] But already shortly before, a feeling of frustration and longing for domestic peace had overcome him when he wrote wearily to his wife, dreaming, like Nelson, of a cottage: 'A small country place with plenty of books in the house, a nice garden, with woods and heather and running water beyond, make up a picture my mind delights in dwelling upon. The centre of every such picture is you.'[26]

Colonel White, who had earned his VC in Afghanistan, writes charmingly to his 'dear little holy-minded child', as he called her, imbued with empire sentiment in child-language.

45

LAZY BLACKS AND A BLACK GENTLEMAN

Colonel George White writes to his little daughter.

In the Land of Egypt, 24th April 1885

My dear Rosie,

I know a little lady far away to whom a letter is owed since I had to dwell among the wicked Egyptians, I am sitting down on oh! such a small stool, on oh! such a hot day, to write her a letter. I am building a home on the banks of the Nile, and the black men who ought to be working very hard are sitting down under a tree doing nothing. If I go out and scold them, they don't understand me, and it makes me very hot, so I have to look on at the lazy fellows, and hope they will do a little work when the sun is not quite so hot.

We had a black gentleman to dine with us. His name is Kasm-el-Mons, and he was a great friend of Gen. Gordon's and fought for him as long as he could. He rode into our Camp with a great many followers beating drums. Some of the men were riding on donkeys, and some on camels, & some on horses. The men on horses rode as fast as they can, flourishing their spears as if they were fighting their enemies, and they all made such a grand show that the English soldiers thought it was the Mahdi come to make peace. . . . I cannot send you any more photographs, as there is not a shop within 120 miles of where I am. . . .

Your loving Father

The 'Warrior of God' was finally avenged in the blood-bath of the battle of Omdurman of 1898, when Kitchener, that other stalwart of the empire, slaughtered 10,000 Sudanese; Lieutenant Churchill and cavalry officer Haig took part in this retribution on behalf of imperial justice and morality.

25 *Wolseley Letters*, p. 167.
26 Ibid, p. 156.

F O U R T E E N

The Boer War (1899–1902)

We have had no end of a lesson: it will do us no end of good.
We made an army in our image, which faithfully mirrored its makers' ideals,
equipment and mental attitude
KIPLING, THE LESSON (BOER WAR)

Redvers Buller has gone away
In charge of a job to Table Bay;
In what direction Redvers goes
Is a matter that only Redvers knows
ANON.

British Imperialism gradually shed its missionary claim late in the nineteenth century and assumed an increasingly brutal predatoriness and vulgar jingoist stance which reached its glorified apogee with the Diamond Jubilee of Queen Victoria in 1897. The Navy's domination of the oceans safeguarded commercial prosperity and peace at home, while the empire was spreading still further over the globe and the natives were governed by the administrative and military rulers fashioned in the public schools. The British people were lulled into complacency by their providential attainment (Joseph Chamberlain proclaimed: 'I believe that the British race is the greatest of the governing races that the world has ever seen') and were unaware that the United States and Germany were increasingly challenging Britain's industrial, commercial, military, and even naval dominance. At the same time, notions of human rights and liberties (for example Gladstone's 'Remember the rights of the savage!'), in conjunction with social reforms and the evolution of a democratic society at home, engendered growing opposition to the empire. Even Disraeli had once called colonies 'millstones round our necks' and Wolseley's 'vestrymen' saw them as the cause of tyranny and war. However, sentimental popular support for the empire and pride in its civilizing mission continued unabated.

The Boer War dealt the first serious blow to the myth of an unassailable world empire and exposed the weakness of its military foundations: to the delight of gloating foreign nations, it took Britain nearly three years of muddle and humiliation, with the loss of 22,000 men (two thirds through sickness) to subdue only double that number of determined Dutch settlers, fighting with common sense military unorthodoxy against the hallowed drill of by far the largest British army ever sent abroad – a huge 450,000.

The disaster on Majuba Hill, which occurred during the reconquest by the Transvaal Boers of their independence in 1881, should have served as a warning. Sir George Colley (one of the most brilliant scholars ever to serve in the army) had climbed by night, with 650 men, the steep 2,000 ft mound overlooking the Boer laager at Laing's Nek. Although he had no guns, he thought his basin-shaped position impregnable, placed no guards and went off for his midday nap, while fifty Boers, led by a twelve-year-old boy, ascended from both sides and suddenly opened up a cross-fire from behind the boulders on the ridge. The British soldiers panicked and stampeded or fell down the precipices; only Colley remained 'as cool as on parade' and died bravely and uselessly, walking straight into the enemy. There were nearly three hundred British casualties for two dead Boers. In England public indignation about a 'treacherous massacre' through the use of 'barbarous missiles' ran high and Colley was said to have been found the next day 'stretched out exactly as the effigy of a knight lies in a cathedral'. Heroism and incompetence sometimes go together, as Wellington recognized when he said: 'There is nothing so stupid as a gallant British officer.'[1]

Colley had a presentiment of his fate.

1

'The wrong card may turn up'

General Sir George Colley (1835–81) writes an affectionate farewell letter to his wife two hours before climbing up Majuba Hill.

8 p.m., February 26, 1881

I am going out to-night to try and seize the Mujaba Hill, which commands the Boer position, and leave this behind, in case I should not return, to tell you how very dearly I love you, and what a happiness you have been to me. Don't let all life be dark to you if I don't come back. It is a strange world of chances; one can only do what seems right to one in matters of morals, and do what seems best in matters of judgement, as a cardplayer calculates the chances, and the wrong card may turn up and everything turn out to be done for the worst instead of for the best. . . .

1   J.H. Lehmann, *First Boer War*, J. Cape, 1972, *passim*.

Good night, darling. . . . How I wish I could believe the stories of meeting again hereafter; but it is no use complaining because things are not as one might wish – one must only brace oneself to meet them as they are. Think of our happiness together, and our love – not a common love, I think – and let that be a source of comfort and light to our future life, my own much-loved one, and think lovingly and sadly, but not too sadly or hopelessly, of your affectionate husband

G.P.C.

In the early stages of the war which the Boers fought for their independence and right to exploit the blacks as they pleased, Winston Churchill, who had been at Omdurman in the 21st Lancers, went to South Africa as a war correspondent and was involved in the Chiveley incident on 15 November 1899: an armoured train with a naval gun was derailed and overturned by a large stone and ambushed by the Boers. Churchill took charge of clearing the truck under a hail of shells and bullets, until he was taken prisoner. After two months he escaped through a latrine over the wall and General Joubert offered a small reward for the recapture of 'just a little newspaperman'. His letter is imbued with the spirit of chivalry, reminiscent of a seventeenth-century Cavalier.

2

WINSTON'S ESCAPE

Winston Churchill (1874–1965) writes a polite letter to the Boer Secretary of War, de Souza, before leaving the States Model Schools Prison.

December 10, 1899

Sir,

I have the honour to inform you that as I do not consider that your Government have any right to detain me as a military prisoner, I have decided to escape from your custody. I have every confidence in the arrangements I have made with my friends outside, and I do not therefore expect to have another opportunity of seeing you. I therefore take this occasion to observe that I consider your treatment of prisoners is correct and humane, and that I see no grounds for complaint. When I return to the British lines I will make a public statement to this effect. I have also to thank you personally for your civility to me, and to express the hope that we may meet again at Pretoria before very long, and under different circumstances. Regretting that I am unable to bid you a more ceremonious or a personal farewell,

I have the honour, to be, Sir,
Your most obedient servant,
Winston Churchill

Ladysmith[2] was invested by 22,000 Boers on 2 November 1899; Sir George White, VC, the veteran commander, had 12,000 regulars, including four out of five cavalry regiments in South Africa, and 1,000 volunteers, with plenty of artillery. At first, life was not too unpleasant: the Boers kept their attacks in strict office hours – they started after breakfast until the lunch break, finished at tea-time and reserved Sundays for prayers, enabling British officers to play tennis and cricket (on black soil among ditches) after church parade, and enjoy strawberry and cream teas provided by the ladies. The city, however, was crammed with refugees, and rations were soon drastically cut until they consisted almost entirely of horse and biscuit, washed down with dirty brock water which caused a typhoid epidemic.[3] The enfeebled defenders were subjected to heavy shelling, although all but 7,000 Boers gradually left for the Tugela river to bar the way to Buller's relief force. The next letter captures the atmosphere of the siege.

3

'How very like England'

Major R. Bowen continued to write every week to his wife in England although his letters could not be posted; he kept his sense of humour and knew how to console himself.

Ladysmith, Dec. 4

Dearest Missy

We are still struggling on, but have run short of drink and vegetables and the Klip River which we have to drink is more sand and mud than water. I don't believe you would let your dog drink it at home. . . . I am sick of 100 pound shells dropping in from 5 miles. The flies here are very annoying. When I come home I shall want to sleep in my clothes out on a path in the garden in a blanket, if it isn't raining I should like someone to pour a watering pot over me every now and then. And the gardener come out and shoot every hour or so in the night. A stone or the door scraper will do for a pillow. I must be up at 2.45 a.m. and stand about till 5, and then lie down again till breakfast. . . . It is marvellous how shells explode right among men and perhaps touch nobody at all. They are most alarming to nervous people but people are so used to them now that the moment they fall they run out with spades to dig them up when they don't explode. Even the women do so in the town. I suppose it will surprise you to hear that there are lots of nice looking English women. One has no idea till you come here to the Colonies how important they are, and how very like England it is after all. . . .

---

2 Named after Juana, the Spanish beauty whom Sir Harry Smith, later Cape Governor, had married in the Peninsular War.
3 A kind of horse Bovril, baptized 'Chevril', was believed to be a remedy.

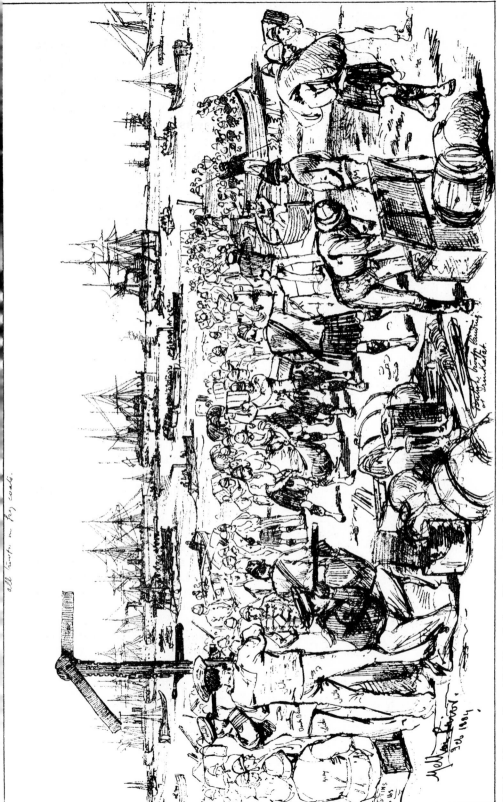

British soldiers landing at Trinkitat, Sudan. (Illustrated London News, *15 March 1884*)

Officers of the Gloucestershire Regiment in South Africa during the Boer War, 1900. (*Reproduced by courtesy of the Gloucestershire Regiment Museum*)

Buller, VC of the Zulu War, now a portly hot-tempered general of sixty, was not really up to holding independent command: by the time he had built a pontoon bridge over the Tugela, Botha had occupied the hills which dominated the twenty miles to Ladysmith. At Colenso 4,500 Boer commandos beat back Buller's 18,000 on 15 December, killing over 1,100 for a loss of forty. Always wavering between complacency and defeatism, Buller's self-doubt was only too justified: he seemed fatuously perplexed.

4

'Kismet'

General Sir Redvers Buller writes to his wife.

Colenso, 18 December

I had to have a play at Colenso, but I did not think I could get in . . . but I am all the better for it. One knows the worst at any rate – I think quite between you and me that I was lucky in not getting in as if I had I should not have known what next to do but I was very disappointed, and the more so that I had been well served. I ought not think to have got in. Kismet. Better luck next time.

On 20 January Buller's men stormed up the rocky ridges through grass burning from their shelling, only to run into cross-fire from Boers entrenched behind stone walls. Drenched by a rainstorm in a night without food and drink, they attacked in the morning but were again beaten back with heavy losses.

5

'One's sorrow is for oneself, really'

Lieutenant Frank Isherwood (1869–1915) writes to his fiancée, Kathleen Machell Smith, about fear and frustration in battle; the writer Christopher is their son.

Venter's Spruit, January 22nd 1900

A letter written actually under fire . . . We had a terribly long morning of waiting, from 3.30 a.m. to about 2 o'clock, under a burning sun and then we moved forward and got it pretty hot, 77 killed and wounded. You will of course want to know, was one frightened; personally as long as I was moving and under the excitement of getting the men together, I wasn't in the very least. One had a most 'supporting feeling', as you say, of heroism, but since then we moved on to this valley where we have sat for two days doing nothing and every now and then having shells pitched into us. You can't imagine anything so demoralizing. The awful sinking at one's stomach pit when you hear the nasty buzz, followed by a plomp and burst. Then there are nasty pieces of shell which wander about and are quite capable of taking one's head off. 'I feel dreadfully sorry for the men, having to lie out doing nothing under fire' is the polite and proper way of putting it, but one's sorrow is mostly for oneself, *really*. . . .

I wish you could see us cooking such nasty messes as we make on our little fires, and then we all lie down together as close as we can to keep warm and forget our sorrows and discomforts and see that we haven't had our boots and puttees off for a week. You see, I'm piling it on to give you that comfortable feeling you like so much.

The views of the mountains have been lovely. Extraordinary great precipices and pointed peaks all tumbled together, and the most varied lights. Sometimes they are a filmy blue, sometimes a dark mysterious purplish colour, just like the 'old master' mountain in fact, both in shape and colour. Saint Jerome would be quite in his proper background against them. This morning just at daybreak there was a rich orange ring in the sky just above them, fading away to primrose, to dark blue and then, far up above one, the southern cross shining faintly. I think the stars at daybreak are so comforting. As the day begins again and the fusillade starts and everything seems so unpleasant, they seem to say 'God's in his heaven, all's right with the world'. . . .

Jan. 27

We had a terrible time in the valley. We could see our people drive the Boers back from their trenches, and then began a terrific fire of shells which literally decimated them. The General and Staff were all wounded or killed. . . . At night they evacuated the hill and we recrossed the Tugela and came back here, having lost upwards of 1000 men for as far as I can see absolutely nothing. We are exactly as we were a fortnight ago, but they say Buller's pleased. . . . Ladysmith might have to go, we don't seem to relieve it this way. We move so slowly and the enemy move so quickly that a hundred of them seem to be in two places at once, to hold them against us. Besides which, I am sure we waste time unnecessarily. If we had only attacked the first day we crossed the Tugela, hardly any men and only one gun at most were there. . . .

You can't think how delightful the idea of our lodgings and visit to Ventnor seems out here. . . . When you're wet through and bivouacing, or sitting down to a tin of bully beef for dinner, having already had the same for breakfast and tea, it's rather refreshing to think tenderly of our comfortable home lives. An old aunt of mine, who used to give us tea when we were schoolboys at Cheltenham, almost made me cry the other day! I am afraid, you know, I'm not really built for a warrior. . . .

Buller blundered into another defeat at Spion Kop, losing 1,700 men. Although his son was killed and he himself wounded, he commented rather oddly: 'I wickedly confess I liked it very much'. He despaired, however, of breaking through to relieve Ladysmith and ordered White to surrender. As soldiers value personal courage above all in their generals, most of them continued to worship the hard-drinking jovial Buller, but as he was too brusque and confused to make his intentions clear to his staff, the officers lost all trust in him. Brigadier Ian Hamilton, later of Gallipoli fame, wrote home:

Buller is *no use*. He is indeed far, *far* worse than useless, and I write to beg you to use all your influence to get the man recalled before he does more mischief . . . generally officers and men have lost confidence in Sir Reverse as they call him.[4]

There were some of deeper insight who regarded the incompetence of a Buller only as a symptom of the inadequacy of people higher up, for which the whole system and outlook, and ultimately the nation itself, were responsible. Sir Cecil Levita put the blame for the Spion Kop disaster on:

the neglect of all but the formal elements of strategy and tactics, the incapacity to realize the value of knowledge, the disregard of difficult problems involved in scientific organisation [and] refusal to believe in the seriousness of war. What was all this but the normal intellectual and moral atmosphere in which the British Army – and indeed the whole British nation – had long lived? . . . Spion Kop was not lost by Buller, but by Aldershot and Pall Mall [War Office], by the House of Commons and by the Nation.[5]

After losing half his artillery on the exposed Tugela passage, Buller succeeded on his fifth attempt at Pieter's Hill at the cost of another 1,600 men. His reckless obstinacy at last paid off despite his slow-wittedness and tactical incompetence, and the relief of Ladysmith was now near. White had meanwhile 'kept the flag flying' precariously. He sounds depressed but rallied to repulse a bloody Boer assault two days later.

6

DUTCH HUMOUR – BUT NOT ON THE SABBATH

General Sir George White to his wife.

4th January 1900

We had a bad disappointment in Sir Redvers' reverse at Colenso. . . . Since that time I have been seedy. I got fever, my head felt like splitting. I was lying on my bed not able to raise it off the pillow when a shell from the big gun on Bulwana hit the house & carried away the room next to mine. Our house was knocked to pieces, & we have had to shift the HQ to another. . . .

My force here is terribly reduced in efficiency by disease, and there is more enteric & dysentery every day. The total of sick and wounded is 1578. The Boers occasionally treat us to a specimen of Dutch humour – e.g. about Christmas they fired a plugged

---

4 T. Pakenham, *Boer War*, Weidenfeld & Nicolson, 1979, p. 370. A Boer wrote: 'We think the British soldiers very brave men – braver than many of ours – but we place great reliance on their generals.' (K. Griffith, *Thank God We Kept the Flag Flying*, Hutchinson, 1974, p. 170.)
5 W.B. Pemberton, *Battles of the Boer War*, Batsford, 1964, p. 202.

shell into our lines which, when dug out, proved to be full of plum pudding & had cut on it the united flags of the S. African Republics and the following: 'With the compliments of the season'. . . . Some of our young officers took advantage of the quiet and safety of Sunday afternoon to play polo. The Boers entered a protest against this desecration of the Sabbath by opening fire on them. . . .

On 28 February Lord Dundonald relieved Ladysmith with three hundred troopers after 118 days of shelling, starvation and sickness; White was on the point of collapse. Private Henry Rooke, although in hospital with fever and dysentery, had lost none of his fighting spirit when he described how he helped to defeat Joubert's desperate final attempt to take the town:

> The last battle we had in Ladysmith lasted 28 hours and it was raining we was all wet through to the skin all as we had on was our thin karkie clothes we all made a galland charge on the hill. . . . i had my bayonet stuck in three of the boers at once i could hardly draw it out of them it was full of blood but can tell you that i had to do my duty for my Queen and Country.[6]

Buller is pleased with himself and sings the praises of the British soldiers, most of them former labourers and anything but robust, although of unfailing courage and endurance.

7

'I have done it under 2000'

Buller writes to his family.

Ladysmith, 3rd March

Here I am at last. I thought I was never going to get through here. We have had a hard busy time and I really have not had time to eat and sleep, much less to write. However, it is all over, thank God. We began fighting on the 14th February and literally fought every day, and nearly all every night also, till the 27th, so we had plenty of it.

I must say the men were grand: they meant to do it, and it was a real pleasure to command them. It has all seemed to me like a dream. Every day some new complication to meet, with, alas, every day the long list of killed and wounded, which is what I cannot bear. However, I thought if I got in it would cost me 3000 men, and I hope I have done it under 2000, which is something. Congratulatory telegrams are pouring in upon me, and I feel that the great British public will like it none the less because there has been a butcher's bill. . . .

I am filled with admiration for the British soldiers: really the manner in which

6   National Army Museum, 7805–65.

these men have worked, fought and endured this last fortnight has been something more than human. Broiled in the burning sun by day, drenched in rain at night, lying not 300 yards off an enemy who shoots you if you show so much as a finger, they could hardly eat or drink by day, and as they were usually attacked at night, they got but little sleep, and through it all they were as cheery and willing as could be. . . .

I marched into L.S. at the head of the whole force: a ragged-looking lot of ruffians they are, poor fellows, but fine men at that. As I passed each company of the garrison who were lining the street they gave three cheers for Sir R.B., and in the middle there was a photographer friend with his cinematograph, so I suppose it will all be in the Alhambra or some other house of entertainment as soon as may be. I should have been glad to have dispensed with it. . . .

Dearest from your rather pleased R.

Buller was still cock-a-hoop a few weeks before his dismissal at Field Marshal Roberts' insistence. Their contempt was mutual.

8

'As happy as a pig – a pretty little fight'

Buller writes to his wife about the battle of Bergendal, the last set-piece battle of the war.

30 August 1900

Here I am, as happy as a pig. . . . We had a pretty little fight, with the Field Marshal and the whole Guards Brigade looking on, so we had plenty of swagger. Certainly it went off very well and exactly as I could have wished. . . . The end cannot be far off now I do believe, but between you and me I wish the Field Marshal would move a bit quicker. He let so many chances slip. . . .

Today I had a very nice telegram from the Queen, and I hope the fight has been thought something of in England. . . .

The soldiers, constantly outmanoeuvred and ambushed by the mobile crafty Boers, felt increasingly dismal.

9

'No glitter – just bullet and dirt'

Lieutenant David Miller writes to his mother.

5 August 1901

There is so little to describe. The infantry soldier sees nothing except the men on either side of them and the enemy in front. He hears the crackle of the enemy's fire

343

somewhere – he does not know where – and he hears the whit! whit! of the bullets, and every now and then he knows vaguely some one near him is hit – he feels the smell of the powder (cordite) and the hot oily smell of the rifle. He fires at the range given, and at the given direction, and every now and then he hears 'Advance!' and he gets up and goes on and wonders why he is not hit as he stands up. That is all. Then the bullets cease to come and the action is over. . . . He marches to the chosen camping ground and perhaps goes on picket – very tired and dirty – and he does it all again next day. That is the infantry soldier's battle – very nasty – very tiring – very greasy – very hungry – very thirsty – everything very beastly. No glitter – no excitement – no nothing. Just bullet and dirt.

Hunger produced tantalizing longings. Trooper Howard wrote to his wife just before being taken prisoner:

> War is not an ennobling métier. It makes one think more of one's food than ever I did before, and I have an insatiable craving for fresh eggs à la coque and a large cup of hot coffee and some thick slices of bread and butter.[7]

Volunteers who had enlisted with 'jingoistic zeal' soon found that 'war is no blooming joke', and their 'tedious, dreary and boring' life produced increasing 'bitterness and cynicism', relieved only by drinking and looting.[8] Corporal P.T. Ross had had enough and drew up a balance sheet:

> Why I joined: to escape my creditors; patriotism; because I was sick of England; could always ride, could always shoot, thought of duty, thought of loot; 'England expects'. . . .
> Why I left: because I have changed my mind; love of England; Fed Up!!!; Patriotic Fever has run its natural course. . . .[9]

At home, at the same time, 'jingo crowds' wildly celebrated the successes: even staid stockbrokers danced with joy and threw their top hats in the air. Stirring patriotic emotionalism glossed over the cracks in society and created the illusion of national solidarity.[10]

Lord Kitchener was a bundle of energy and driving on relentlessly. His handsome ADC, Frank Maxwell, to whom he was deeply attached and liked to be teased by, describes his daily routine:

> K. is an extraordinary person. He sleeps and dreams on schemes all night, and in the morning, in pijamas and dishevelled head, gets you to work

---

7   E.W. Howard, *Theatre of Life,* Hodder & Stoughton, 1935, I, p. 284.
8   W. Nasson in *South African War,* Longman, 1980, p. 123 ff.
9   *A Yeoman's Letters,* 1901.
10 M.D. Blanch in *South African War,* p. 235.

with scale and pencil and maps, and in two hours plans are more or less complete, and orders more or less drafted. Then, being a quick-change artist, he is off and has shaved, dressed and ready to ride out to columns while you are but washing your teeth. Everything is at high pressure.[11]

No wonder, the 'Brat', as Kitchener called him, felt happy: 'It *is* a great life – war is that there is no doubt, and I do love it.' The award of the VC affects neither his modesty nor his lucidity.

10

THE MERIT OF A VC

Lieutenant (later Brigadier) Frank Maxwell (1871–1917) to his mother.

Pretoria, April 19, 1901

My dearest Mother

You must not be anxious with the fear that the V.C. will spoil me or make me proud. To those who have not been through the mill, I suppose it is difficult to realize that an action regarded worthy of a V.C. is not usually a deliberate action done in cold blood – one does not *think* about it: does not debate whether it's worth one's while doing it or not: whether there's danger in it or otherwise – Something obviously one's duty to do is there and something quite outside one's own consciousness tells one to do it forthwith. . . .

If this were not enough to prevent one becoming seized with pride (of the wrong sort) I think the knowledge of the many, many men who do far finer things left unrewarded acts as a deterrent.

Ever your most affectionate son
Frank

Kitchener felt that the Boers, whom he considered as 'uncivilized Africander savages with a thin white veneer', were not playing the game in avoiding being killed in head-on clashes in accordance with the army drill book.[12] He burnt down 30,000 farmhouses in pursuit of his scorched earth campaign, countered their guerrilla warfare, which lasted for eighteen months, by erection of blockhouses and punitive raids, and herded their women and children into nine concentration camps for 'refugees'. Around 22,000 children and 4,000 women perished there from disease, as against

---

11 F. Maxwell, *A Memoir*, J. Murray, 1921, p. 92. However, Sir Ian Hamilton thought Kitchener 'utterly out of his depth', 'knowing nothing about tactics' and just 'a master of Expedients'. (In *The Commander*, ed. A. Farrar-Hockley, 1957.)

12 A Boer prisoner said: 'We could always tell what you were going to do. You would bombard our trenches for a time. Then your soldiers would march straight at us. It was very brave but verdomd foolish.' (Pemberton, op. cit, p. 79.)

4,000 men killed in battle. Although there was no deliberate extermination attempt, the Boers accused Kitchener of genocide.[13]

Kitchener himself paints a cheerful picture of his advance to Pretoria in the Transvaal for the benefit of Lord Desborough's boys whom he was very fond of. Both fell on the Western Front in 1915.

11

THE BOERS SLINK AWAY FROM A 'FAIR FIGHT'

Major-General (later Field Marshal and Secretary for War) Lord Kitchener (1850–1916), Chief of Staff to FM Lord Roberts, writes to Julian and Billy Grenfell.

13 May 1900

Many thanks for your letters which caught me on the march here, and I read them while the guns were pounding away at the Boers who were sitting up on some hills and trying to prevent our advance. However they soon cleared out and ran before we could round them up. . . . Sooner or later we are bound to catch them, but they give a lot of trouble. The Boers are not like the Sudanese who stood up to a fair fight. They are always running away on their little ponies. We make the prisoners we make march on foot, which they do not like at all. There are a great many foreigners among the Boers, but they are easily shot, as they do not slink about like the Boers themselves. We killed a German colonel yesterday.

Now I must get back to work, so goodbye. Mind you work hard.

An amalgan of ruthless Prussian efficiency and Kiplingesque imperial heroics, Kitchener was on the way to becoming the monumental idol of virile will-power and silent impassiveness, until in 1914 he almost resembled the God of War himself, rousing the nation by the spell of his martial magic. Secretly, however, a consuming ambition haunted him with anxieties and, in his solitariness, he suffered from bouts of depression. To the Army he was linked by intuitive insight:

To make an Army effective, you must be able to feel the pulse of the whole army collectively, and instinctively to know how things will affect it as a whole. Common sense does not seem to be the best guide for understanding collective human nature.[14]

Gradually Boer resistance was worn down and the end was in sight. Kitchener's ADC captures the mood of impending victory.

13   S.B. Spies in *South African War*, op. cit., p. 161 ff.
14   25.1.1903 to Lady Salisbury. (P. Magnus, *Kitchener*, J. Murray 1958, p. 202).

12

'400 Boers laid down their arms'

Lieutenant Maxwell writes to his father.

Pretoria, March 2nd, 1902

... On arriving at Harrismith we rode and swarmed up an enormous scarped mountain, called Platberg, which stands 1000–1200 feet above the level of the surrounding country, and from the top of which we had the most glorious and extended view.... The scene was a wonderful one. Far away down in the plain – undulating, and here and there broken by great rough koppies – could be seen our people crawling about like ants, and behind them, either in black clump, or trailing in long streaks, waggons and carts and cattle. Here and there heliographs flashed, causing much excitement among our signallers, who blessed or cursed according as the sun shone, or did not. However, we hadn't been on the berg ten minutes before from 50 miles away came a twinkle, twinkle, message, which spelt out by the signaller read: '400 Boers laid down their arms this morning, and —' the sun went out, and so we got no more details....

The war ended with the annexation of the Transvaal and Orange Free State, conquered by Roberts and Kitchener with a huge army of 300,000 (against which the Boers never mustered more than 40,000) who got valuable training for the First World War twelve years later.

In the nineteenth century, the English people were convinced of their mission to civilize the natives of the empire, if necessary by teaching them a forceful lesson to safeguard the Pax Britannica. Whenever a tribe perpetrated cruelties, specially against women and children, a spirit of revenge, otherwise alien to them, could harden the hearts of the fighting men and exact a likewise retribution, joyfully administered. Some officers remarked wryly that people at home relished the newspaper reports of carnage whichever side was the victim. The Crimean War modified this attitude when its horrors were no longer veiled by a distant aura of glory: on the spot reporting and photography struck right home. While a jingoist attitude prevailed in the little wars against coloured races, the Boer War gave a foretaste of the destruction total war might inflict on a gigantic scale. Another current of opinion, lying dormant hitherto, was to erupt in 1914: there were those who believed that only war could preserve the nation from sinking into a bog of materialist ease and stagnation, and who prayed for it to come:

> Give us, O Lord,
> For England's sake,
> War righteous and true,
> Hearts to shake.

Conclusion: English Attitudes to War

It is far from easy to discern any definite trends in such an array of very personal, and therefore distinctive, expressions of views and sentiments, however much the selection of the letters and their presentation has attempted to concentrate on the essential. It is possible, however, to try to establish and evaluate recurring aspects of English attitudes to war by following their evolvement through the centuries.

Joyful bellicosity was voiced by young Robert Sidney longing to hear of 'any good wars' (1580) (p. 15), and by ensign Edmund Verney welcoming the 'brave news' that war with France, 'a blessed trade', was imminent, 'sport for us to hear that all the world were in combustion' (1630). Hessian mercenaries in the American War of Independence are said to have praised the plucky daring of Englishmen being 'the Divel for going on' and General Burgoyne, the playwright, enthused over the carnage of Bunker Hill: 'It was great, it was high spirited' (1775) (p. 190). A soldier in the siege of Gibraltar proclaimed firelock to be his religion and delighted in the 'melody of great guns' (1782) (p. 203), while a cavalry charge in the Sikh War was described as 'a thrill of ecstasy' (1846) (p. 300), and General Buller confessed to be 'happy as a pig' over the 'pretty little fight' at Bergendal in the Boer War, conducted with plenty of swagger' (1900) (p. 343). In general, however, under the impact of the ever more deadly slaughter caused by the technical progress in the manufacture of arms of destruction, such warlike zest tended to become more muted.

Boastful nationalism made Sir Francis Drake brag of 'singeing the Spanish King's beard' at Cádiz (1587) (p. 21), a seaman at Porto Bello rejoice in the fleet being 'the Cox of the Seas' in the revival of 'true British spirit' (1739) (p. 126), a corporal embarking for the continent proclaim that the British flag may ever flourish over the world (1793) (p. 206), the public at home delight in the looting of the Summer Palace in Peking in their disdainful belief in the imperial mission of a superior race over all coloured people (1860) (p. 314), a staff officer in the Abyssinian punitive expedition comment that 'Britons have grown so accustomed to success' that they regard it as 'a natural law' (1868) (p. 318), and Wolseley direct the battle of Amoafo in the Ashanti War enthroned on a chair carried by tribesmen, waving his cigar (1874) (p. 321). The jingoism of the Victorian age represented the climax of national arrogance which had been growing since Elizabethan times.

Heroism and hero worship were great features among English attitudes to war. Sir Philip Sidney, later to die of his wounds without ever losing his good humour, passed his bottle to a dying soldier with the words 'Thy necessity is greater than mine' (1586) (p. 20), the veteran standard bearer of the Royalists at Edgehill, Sir Edmund Verney, held on to the flag even in death so that his hand had to be hacked off to release it (1642) (p. 56), Lady Cowper exulted over a sixteen-year-old 'true romance hero', killed at Fontenoy (1745) (p. 140), James Wolfe expired 'smiling' at his victory of Quebec (1759) (pp. 173–4), and Sir George Rodney was glorified by his wife, daughter and the London crowds for his successes at St Eustatius and the Saintes (1781–2) (pp. 197–9). The hero of heroes, however, was Nelson: the victor of the Nile was greeted by Countess Spencer with 'Joy, joy, joy to you, brave, gallant, immortalized Nelson!' (p. 222) and as saviour of Italy by Lady Hamilton, dressed 'alla Nelson' (p. 220). Small and frail, having only one arm and one eye left, he exposed himself to enemy fire by wearing his glittering decorations; his attacks were swift and daring, his sailors adored him for the way he treated them and he had good reasons to proclaim that 'None but the brave deserve the fair!' when he wrote to Emma from Copenhagen (p. 223). Lady Foster said it was only he who 'ever excited real enthusiasm in the English' (p. 243), and an ex-ploughman wrote from Trafalgar: 'Chaps fought like the Devil, cry like a wench' (p. 243). There was never again another hero like him: Sir John Moore, receiving his fatal wound on the retreat to Corunna, remotely perhaps, and finally, with most of the nineteenth century without a hero, the last, Gordon of Khartoum, the religious mystic. Hero worship was not necessarily linked to success in war: Marlborough and Wellington, the two greatest generals, never qualified – they did not die gloriously, bearing agony without flinching. They simply won all their well-planned battles, coolly, efficiently and unromantically.

Loyalty and regimental comradeship were features which developed in the course of the nineteenth century: Nelson's 'band of brothers' of the battle of the Nile was a foretaste of things to come. Escalading the fort of Delhi was thought to be 'capital fun' if the men could look to their officers to lead them on (1857) (p. 309), while Lieutenant-Colonel Sterling expressed his admiration for the hard-suffering soldiers in the Crimea who 'have nothing to gain except the approbation of the company they belong to' (pp. 284–5). Reputation among fellow soldiers in the regiment was increasingly held dearer than life itself.

Discipline, courage and endurance were the most appraised virtues expected from soldiers and sailors at all times. Leicester commended a lieutenant for leading his troop up to the breach in the assault on the fort of Zutphen (1586) (p. 19), and the defence of besieged Londonderry by the Ulster protestants in face of bombing, starvation and fever (1689) was only possible through these qualities. The 'overbearing courage and impetuosity' of the grenadiers rushing up the hill to take Quebec was another instance, with death being 'incapable of putting Britons to confusion' (1759) (p. 172). A ship's surgeon related how young Lord Manners was joking cheerfully while his leg was being amputated after the Battle of the Saintes, before succumbing to lock-jaw (1782) (pp. 199–200), and Soult claimed victory at Albuera although the British 'did not know it and would not run', exposing themselves to casualties that made Wellington weep (1811) (p. 252). The legendary Charge of the Light Brigade was a piece of unquestioning though senseless bravery and Lieutenant-Colonel Sterling extolled the high morale of the troops inspite of their heart-rending suffering, calling them 'the true England' (1854) (pp. 284–5).

Indiscipline, looting and mutiny were the reverse side when the occasion presented itself. A sailor taking part in Anson's interception of a French convoy had greedy visions of sixty waggonloads of money having been captured and dreams of securing £1000 for himself (1747) (p. 128). Sir John Moore sadly observed how the retreat to Corunna had turned his army into a drunken rabble, burning, looting and rioting, and utterly callous towards women and children who were perishing (1808) (p. 246). In the sack of Ciudad Rodrigo the soldiers went on the rampage, too dreadful to describe, and the storm of Badajoz which had cost two thousand lives was followed by a three-day orgy of bayoneting virtually the whole garrison and of raping the women by what a captain described as 'a pack of hell-hounds' (1812) (p. 255). The stores, jewellery and money chests captured in the battle of Vitoria were estimated to have exceeded any booty since Darius and Private Wheeler grabbed a box of dollars for himself in the general scramble: it was then that Wellington called his vagabond soldiers 'the scum of the earth' – they could, of course, never have dreamt of amassing so much in the whole of their civilian lives (1813) (p. 260). While Lord Elgin deplored the plundering of the Summer Palace in Peking, one of his colonels described the pleasure of smashing up and looting (1860) (p. 313). Under Wolseley, however, the booty found in King Koffee's palace went for sale in an orderly manner, he himself purchasing the royal (Georgian) coffee pot for his wife. Generally speaking, indiscipline only occurred out of revenge or during reverses, but opportunities for looting were not easily missed.

Mutiny only rarely broke out and then under extreme provocation. Leicester warned Walsingham that his men in the Netherlands were fast deserting for not getting the pay due to them and he feared the 'foulest mutiny' (1586) (pp. 16–17). Captain Thorowgood's sailors, enraged because their pay was being withheld, seized him and refused his command (1652) (p. 83). The 1797 mutinies at Spithead and the Nore were a more serious matter, due to the appalling conditions in which the largely press-ganged sailors were being kept, 'more like convicts than free-born Britons' (pp. 211–14). Richard Parker, president of the Jacobin delegates went as far as ordering the fleet to go over to the enemy – a unique event; he was, however, disavowed by the sailors whom he had previously restrained from violence but who now shrank back from treason. Parker felt betrayed by his comrades and made a scapegoat when he was hanged.

Fear of invasion was an ever recurring theme. Already in 1462 there was apprehension of treacherous 'meddlers' ready to assist enemy infiltration and, likewise, Lord Howard entreated Elizabeth I to awake to 'villaneous treasons' around her at the approach of the Armada (p. 23). In 1599 a false rumour of a Spanish landing in the Isle of Wight caused the gates of London to be shut and the streets to be chained (pp. 36–8), and in 1744 Horace Walpole described the frantic preparations to meet the expected invasion force gathered at Dunkirk (pp. 143–4); and again, in 1779, he was alarmed at the prospect of the French army embarking from St Malo (pp. 164–5). Although some of these threats were very real, none of them actually materialized, but anxiety and suspicion were aroused by the slightest rumour.

Complacency, unpreparedness, incompetence, and blunders. Admirals Sir Edward Howard (1513) (pp. 8–9), Lord Howard fighting the Armada in 1588 (pp. 28–9), the Earl of Essex ('We eat ropes' ends and drink rain water') on the Islands Voyage (1597) (p. 36), and Blake (1655) (p. 83) complained about the unpreparedness of the fleet: no victuals, no munitions, but many leaks. There was no provision for the sick and wounded while De Ruyter was sailing up the Thames and the Medway, defenceless through lack of money (1667). The abortive amphibious landings at Camaret Bay (1694) and Rochefort (1757) were bungled, there were insufficient forces to meet the invasion threat in 1745, with London practically at the mercy of the Pretender, and, according to Horace Walpole, Admiral Byng was executed as a scapegoat to cover up ministerial incompetence (1757) (pp. 157–8). Political mistakes led to the American War of Independence (1775), mismanaged by Lord Germain, the Colonial Secretary, and ending in the humiliating surrender at Yorktown. The height of complacent incompetence was, however, reached in the Crimean War when 'neither care nor thought' had been given to the supply of stores and transport; fumbling aged generals did the rest (1854) (pp. 279–80). In the Afghan (1842) and Zulu (1879) Wars whole contingents of the army were butchered through the complacency of their leaders; on Majuba Hill (1881) General Colley left the approaches unguarded, resulting in a massacre, and the incapacity of Sir 'Reverse' Buller in the Boer war (1900) was proverbial. The historic experience of almost invariably winning the last battle was frequently at the root of initial setbacks through complacency.

Hatred of foreigners was partly linked to the obsessive fears of invasion from the mighty armies of Spain or France but the proud islanders would not tolerate provocation from any of the continentals. Blake repulsed the Dutch fleet 'to keep foreigners from fooling us' (1652) (p. 81), a seaman at Port Bello longed to cut off the ears of that 'parcel of impodent Spaniards' (1739) (p. 125), Lady Hardwick called for the return of the British troops from Flanders to protect the country against the Pretender and his French allies, distrusting the foreign mercenaries on the spot, 'odious to the nation' (1745) (pp. 150–1), and Wolseley wrote from the Sudan that he would not have 'bundles of foreigners' who had been sent as observers, listen to all one said at meals (1882) (p. 329).

Cruelty was, as we have already seen, almost invariably caused by a thirst for vengeance. Cromwell declared that it was the righteous judgement of God that all the two thousand defenders of Drogheda be put to the sword (1649) (p. 71), and Wolfe reported from Culloden that, in reprisal for an alleged Highlanders' order to give no quarter, as few prisoners as possible should be taken (1746) (p. 153). Retribution for the sepoys' massacres of women and children in the Indian Mutiny roused the relief forces to commit unparalleled brutality: Sir Henry Havelock relieving Lucknow thought 'carnage beautiful', a lieutenant described how they poured through the breach in the storm of Delhi 'like a pack of hounds' (p. 307), a brigadier proposed that the natives there would be impaled and flayed or burnt alive (p. 308), and Wolseley, then a captain at Cawnpore, called for blood vengeance: 'barrels and barrels of the filth which flows in these niggers' veins' (1857) (p. 303).

Compassion for the enemy can, conversely, be found in individual cases from the seventeenth century onwards when a more humane outlook began to appear. The occasional bridge of sentiments between royalists and puritans in the Civil War which frequently divided families and friends in different camps may be too special to be considered as they were countrymen. Sir Allen Apsley expressed indignation at the sight of enemy sailors subjected to being blown up by an English fireship in the battle of Lowestoft, commanded by an 'inhuman rogue' who deliberately ignored their begging for quarter (1655) (pp. 87–8). In the same year, John Evelyn appealed for funds to save 25,000 prisoners from starvation and plague, to avoid being 'reputed barbarians' (pp. 84–5). A midshipman described how in the battle of the 'Glorious First of June' English sailors were in 'tears and groaning' at the sight of hundreds of poor Frenchmen 'crying most dreadfully' when they were going down with their ship (1794) (pp. 208–9). After Waterloo, a lieutenant-colonel took pity on French officer prisoners, exclaiming: 'How misery makes friends of all' (p. 267), and Lady Fitzgerald told how the Plymouth mob cheered Napoleon with the words: 'Poor fellow, well I do pity him' (p. 269). Queen Victoria herself received the captured Zulu King Cetshwayo, although usually there was no compassion for coloured rebels against the British Empire.

Soldiers' critical view of civilians started with the American War of Independence: a captain proposed that the politicians whose folly had caused the war should have their heads cut off (1778) (p. 184), Wellington's bugbear was the 'presumption and licentiousness' of the press distorting the facts (p. 251), and Wolseley, campaigning in the Sudan, castigated Mr John Bull gloating over the 'butcher's bill' he likes to have for his money and raged at the bickerings and dodges of professional politicians like Gladstone and his 'vestrymen', foretelling that the 'dirty, dunghill sort of democratic wave passing over the world' would one day lead to a great Boer War and eventually to a European conflagration (1884) (pp. 329–31).

A longing for home was a noticeable development in the nineteenth century when servicemen were more likely to possess one, although the Earl of Sunderland expressed feelings of home-sickness in 1643 (pp. 51–2) and, a century later, an officer campaigning in Germany wrote nostalgically that he wished he could partake of strawberries with his baby girl (p. 136). A naval lieutenant complained about the monotony of cruising and wished himself 'beside a snug fire' (1800) (pp. 217–18), and Nelson wrote after the Battle of St Vincent to his wife of his dream of 'a cottage and a piece of ground' to retire to (p. 210) and, four years later, likewise to Emma about his longing for 'peace in a cottage with a plain joint of meat' (p. 223). In a more frivolous vein, Charles Townshend, marooned in the mountain desert fort of Chitral on the north-west frontier, had visions of girls, brandy and cigars in the 'purlieus of Piccadilly' (1893) (pp. 301–3).

Religion and prayer were the prerogative of the great, at least as far as epistolary expression is concerned. Elizabeth I reminded Lady Norris (whom she condoled for the loss of four of her sons in the Irish Rebellion) that Christian discretion should stay the flux of her immoderate grieving, as all happened by God's divine Providence (1597) (p. 35). Cromwell gave the glory of his victory at Marston Moor to God who made the enemy 'as stubble to our swords' and he told a father that his son killed in the battle was now 'a glorious saint in Heaven' (1644) (pp. 67–8). The Earl of Derby, in his farewell letter before his execution, told his brave countess that in heaven they would be free from rapine, plunder and violence (1651) (pp. 78–9). Blake turned for comfort to God when he contemplated the sad state of the fleet (1655) (p. 83), and the Duke of Marlborough blessed God for the victory of Ramillies making him the instrument of preserving the liberties of England and Europe (1706) (pp. 118–19). Wellington confessed that 'the finger of God' was on him at Waterloo as nothing else could have saved him (p. 270) and, in a quite different context, a brigadier saw 'His finger' in the retribution for the Cawnpore massacre (1857) (p. 303). Wolseley put his implicit trust in God before the Battle of Amoafo in the treacherous Ashanti forests (1874) (p. 321), and Gordon sought his resource in constant prayer 'to accept His will in all things without murmuring', wishing his proud heart to be humbled (1884) (p. 330).

Disillusionment, alienation and anti-war feeling can be discerned in a few of the more sensitive souls of past centuries, forerunners of the soldier poets in the trenches of the First World War. The Civil War, a bitter and at times painful contest between countrymen, was most apt to produce such sentiments. To Sir Thomas Knyvett, a Royalist prisoner, this fratricidal war seemed unreal, 'fit for Lunacy' (pp. 52–3), and the Earl of Sunderland, shortly before being killed at Newbury, professed feeling solitary amid the tintamarre of war (pp. 51–2). Horace Walpole, well aware of the reverse side of the glory war evokes, said he 'would not purchase another Duke of Marlborough at the expense of one life' (1745) (pp. 143–4), and Francis Jeffery proclaimed: 'I hate the business of war, and despise the parade of it' (1803) (p. 232), while Brigadier Long, horrified by the butchery at Badajoz, thought the age of selfishness had succeeded with soldiers only caring for themselves (1812) (p. 256). A lieutenant, one of the first VCs in the Crimea, considers war, excitement apart, as 'a hideous and unnatural absurdity' and, gazing at the beauty of the stars, saw it reduced 'to an absolute nonentity' (pp. 276–7), while a lieutenant-colonel considered war 'an ugly thing' he hated, 'as every good soldier and humane person must' (1854) (pp. 284–5). Even amid the vaingloriousness of jingoism, Wolseley was weary of campaigning on the Cape Coast and, feeling ambition dying in his heart, wished to be taken (1873) (p. 319).

Epilogue: Women's Attitudes in Wartime

Women's attitudes to war vary even more than men's in accordance with character, mood and circumstances.

Despondency. The countess of Sussex allayed her apprehensions in the Civil War by making jellies (pp. 55–6), old 'Gran' feared the French were coming to 'eat us all alive' (1745) (pp. 144–5), Miss Ord described the effect of the disturbing news reaching Brussels from Waterloo (1815) (pp. 268–9), and Mrs Wells expressed her horror about escaping from her burning house in Lucknow wearing nothing but her nightshirt (1857) (p. 308).

Conjugal concern for husbands away at war. Katherine Parr covered Henry VIII with a surfeit of flattery (1544) (pp. 11–12), Lady Dartmouth was concerned lest her husband, Commander-in-Chief of the Navy, missed the last moment for changing sides in 1688 (pp. 98–9), Mary II, full of anxiety for William III campaigning in Ireland, lamented being constrained at court to grin when her heart was ready to break (1690) (p. 104), and Lady Wolseley tendered her husband in the Sudan homely advice like being as dirty as he likes rather than 'bathe in the teeth of crocodiles' (1884) (pp. 331–2).

Nursing. Many women chose to devote their lives to the care of the sick and wounded. An early example is 'Parliament Joan' who was forced to beg the Admiralty Committee to refund what she had laid out for her charges, being left penniless and starving (1653) (p. 84). Two centuries later, Florence Nightingale showed such force of personality that she got away with turning three hundred convalescents of the Highland Brigade into nurses (p. 287).

Defiance. Katherine of Aragon, writing to Henry VIII campaigning in Picardy, chided English hearts for their softness over James IV's body at Flodden and sent a piece of his coat to make banners (1513) (pp. 10–11), and

Lady Harley, like the countess of Derby who withstood the puritans' siege at Lathom House, stoutly defended her castle besieged by the Royalists (pp. 62–3), while a north-country woman told of the 'brave spirits' of women beginning to rise against the Royalist 'vermin' pulling down enclosures (1642).

Soldiering. Some women went as far as enlisting in men's disguise. Ann Dismack absconded from home to follow her lover in the army and stayed on as a soldier after his death, comporting herself honourably (1657), and 'Kit' Welsh joined the army attempting to find her pressed husband and fought in Marlborough's battles, getting wounded and captured; she was finally received by Queen Anne (pp. 109–10). Lady Hester Stanhope even became acting regimental colonel of Pitt's 15th Light Dragoons, drilling her men to meet the expected invasion (1803) (pp. 234–5).

Romance with a lover abroad. Elizabeth I wrote to Essex with great affection and concern, and prays God to cover him 'under His safest wings' (1596) (p. 31). In a nostalgic mood, a lady reminded the seductive Earl of Chesterfield of their walks, by the riverside or in a grove, she would prefer to talking of the 'dismal news of death' reaching her from Sole Bay (1672) (pp. 90–1), while Nell Gwynne was in favour of war for no other reason but that the handsome future Earl of Rochester would then have to return to her from his diplomatic mission (1678) (pp. 91–2). In an even more frivolous vein, Mrs Montagu, who was later to ridicule the unfeminine postures of women in martial uniform to exhibit their enthusiasm for the American war, served notice on her husband that she was ready to be conquered by a marquis, as the polite French 'admire ladies a little in years ' (1756) (pp. 156–7).

Sources of the Letters

PART ONE: THE SIXTEENTH AND SEVENTEENTH CENTURIES

1. The Fifteenth-Century Background

1 *Paston Letters*, J. Gairdner (ed.), A. Constable, 1900, I, p. 165.

2 Ibid, II, p. 405.

3 Ibid, III, p. 103.

2. Henry VIII

1 Spont, A., *War with France 1512–13*, Naval Record Society, X, 1894, p. 49.

2 Ibid, p. 104.

3 Field, C., *Echoes of Old Wars*, H. Jenkins, 1934, p. 15 f.

4 Strickland, A., *Lives of the Queens of England*, II, 1884, p. 130.

5 Ibid, p. 132.

6 Ibid, p. 419.

7 *Henry VIII's Letters*, T. Rymer (ed.), p. 315.

3. Elizabeth I

1 *Sidney Papers*, I (1925–), p. 285 (Hist. Mss. Commission No. 77).

2 Camden Society, XXVII, p. 337.

3 *Queen Elizabeth's Letters*, G.B. Harrison (ed.), Cassell, 1935, p. 178 ff.

4 Camden Soc., XXVII, p. 427.

5 Greville, F., *Sir Philip Sidney*, 1907, p. 128.

6 Camden Miscellany, V, 1863, p. 30.

7 Ellis, H., *Original Letters Illustrative of English History*, II/3, 1827, p. 134 ff.

8 *State Papers relating to the defeat of the Spanish Armada*, I, 1894, p. 224 (Naval Record Society, X).

9 Ibid, II, p. 63.

10 Ibid, I, p. 344 ff.

11 Ibid, I, p. 364.

12 Ibid, II, p. 59.

13 Devereux, W.B., *Lives & Letters of the Devereux, Earls of Essex*, 1853, p. 219.

14 Hist.Mss.Comm., Salisbury, IV, p. 161.

15 *Queen Elizabeth Ls*, p. 245.

16 *Philip Gawdy Letters*, J.H. Jeayes (ed.), Roxburgh Club, 1906, p. 62.

17 Ibid, p. 63.

18 H.M.C., Salisbury, V, p. 290.

19 *Queen Elizabeth Ls.*, p. 250.

20 H.M.C., Salisbury, VII, p. 445.

21 Camden Soc., LXXIX, p. 56 ff.

22 *Queen Elizabeth Ls.*, p. 270 ff.

23 Camden Soc., CV, p. 39.

4. The Civil War

1 *Verney Papers*, J. Bruce (ed.), II, 1853, p. 210 ff (Camden Soc., LVI).

2 Ibid, p. 310.

3 *Cromwell Letters*, Th. Carlyle (ed.), Dent, 1908, I, p. 129.

4 Ibid, p. 135.

5 Ellis, op. cit., III/3, 1846, p. 365 f.

6 Archaeologia, XXXV, 1853, p. 315 ff.

7 Earl of Birkenhead, *500 Best English Letters*, Cassell, 1931, p. 95 f.

8 Ibid, p. 96 f.

9 *Sidney Papers*, II, p. 669.

10 *Knyvett Letters*, B. Schofield (ed.), Norfolk Record Society, vol. 20, 1949, p. 109 f.

11 Warburton, E., *Memoirs of Prince Rupert*, I, 1849, p. 400 f.

12 Rushworth, J., *Historical Collections*, VI, 1703, p. 132.

13 Verney, P., *The Standard Bearer*, Hutchinson, 1963, p. 179.

14 Ibid, p. 180.

15 Young, P., *Edgehill*, Kineton: Roundwood Press, 1967, p. 291 f.

16 Camden Soc., N.S.7, App.I, p. 203.

17 Ibid, III, p. 205.

18 Warburton op. cit., II, p. 157 f.

19 Ibid, III, p. 172 ff.

20 Wedgwood, C.V., *The King's War*, Collins, 1958, p. 490 f.

21 Warburton op. cit., III, p. 248.

22 *Verney Papers*, II, p. 85 f.

23 Camden Soc., LVIII, p. 202.

24 Strickland, op. cit., IV, p. 224.

25 H.M.C., Leyborne-Popham, 1899, p. 112.

26 Young, op. cit., p. 280 f.

27 Ibid, p. 317 f.

28 *Cromwell Ls.*, I, p. 151.

29 T. Carte, *Collection of Letters*, I, 1739, p. 56.

30 *Cromwell Ls,.* I, p. 171.

31 Ibid, II, p. 48.

32 Ibid, II, p. 174.

33 Ibid, II, p. 275.

34 *Letters of King Charles*, I, 1824, p. 230.

35 *Letters of Robert Blake*, 1927, p. 85 (Naval Record Soc., 76).

36 Blundell, W., *Cavaliers' Letters*, M. Blundell (ed.), Longman, 1933, p. 39 f.

37 De Witt, H., *Lady of Latham*, 1869, p. 140.

38 Ibid, p. 171 ff.

39 Ibid, p. 179 ff.

5. The Dutch Naval Wars, 1688 Invasion, and Wars of William III

1 *Blake Letters*, p. 158.

2 Ibid, p. 162.

3 Ibid, p. 306.

4 Gardiner, S.R., & Atkinson, C.T., *Papers Relating to the First Dutch War*, III, (1898-), p. 164.

5 Mainwaring, G.E., *United Services Magazine*, July 1918, p. 86.

6 Evelyn, J., *Diary & Correspondence*, III, 1857, p. 173.

7 Ibid, p. 184.

8 *Blake Ls.*, p. 204.

9 Field, op. cit., p. 36 ff.

10 *Works of Sir Thomas Browne*, G. Keynes (ed.), VI, 1931, p. 25 ff.

11 Wragg, H., *Letters Written in War Time*, OUP, 1915, p. 62.

12 *Letters of Philip, 2nd Earl of Chesterfield*, 1829, p. 167 ff.

13 Camden Misc., V, p. 25.

14 Ellis, op. cit., II/4, 1827, p. 130.

15 H.M.C., Dartmouth, 11th Report, App.V, 1887, p. 158 f.

16 Ibid, p. 170.

17 Ellis, op. cit., II/2, 1887, p. 278.

18 Ibid, II/4, p. 143.

19 Ibid, II/4, p. 154.

20 H.M.C., Dartmouth, p. 272 f.

21 Ibid, p. 226.

22 Ellis, II/4, p. 167.

23 H.M.C., Dartmouth, p. 232 ff.

24 Routh, C.R.N., *They Saw it Happen*, Blackwell, 1956, p. 213 f.

25 H.M.C., Dartmouth, p. 282.

26 Ibid, p. 235.

27 Charles-Edwards, T., & Richardson, B., *They Saw it Happen*, Blackwell, 1958, p. 2 ff.

28 Bowen, E., *Some Famous Love Letters*, 1937, p. 78.

29 Strickland, op. cit., VI, p. 37 f.

30 Ibid, p. 59 ff.

31 Camden Misc., VIII, p. 41.

32 H.M.C., Portland, VIII, p. 41.

33 Bevan, B., *Marlborough the Man*, Robert Hale, 1975, p. 153.

34 Laffin, J., *Women in Battle*, Abelard-Schuman, 1967, p. 83 ff.

PART TWO: THE EIGHTEENTH CENTURY

6. The War of the Spanish Succession

1 Coxe, W., *Memoirs of the Duke of Marlborough*, I, 1847, p. 83.

2 Ibid, p. 154.

3 Ibid, p. 183.

4 Ibid, p. 213.

5 Ibid, p. 231.

6 Ibid, p. 424.

7 Ibid, p. 462.

8 'Letters of Lord Orkney ', *English Historical Review XIX*, 1904, pp. 307–21.

9 *Haddock Correspondence*, Camden Misc., p. 46.

10 *Correspondence of Jonathan Swift*, H. Williams (ed.), Oxford Clarendon Press, I, 1963, p. 119 ff.

7. The Spanish War, the War of the Austrian Succession and the Jacobite Rebellion

1 *Gentleman's Magazine*, 1740, p. 183 f.

2 *Naval Miscellany*, I, p. 393.

3 Long, W.H., *Naval Yarns*, 1899, p. 23.

4 Aspinall-Oglander, C.F., *Admiral's Wife*, Longman, 1940, p. 43.

5 Wright, R., *Wolfe*, 1864, p. 13.

6 Ibid, p. 32.

7 Ibid, p. 33.

8 Ibid, p. 59.

9 Ibid, p. 43.

10 *Times Literary Supplement*, 25.8.1931.

11 H.M.C., Astley, No. 52, pp. 248, 254, 257.

12 Field, op.cit., p. 91 f.

13 *Yorke's Hardwicke Papers*, I, p. 392.

14 Ibid, p. 400.

15 *Mrs Delany Corresp.*, II, 1861, p. 353.

16 Whitworth, R., *FM Lord Ligonier*, OUP, 1958, p. 157 f.

17 *Horace Walpole Letters*, P.G. Toynbee (ed.), I, 1903, p. 291.

18 Ibid, p. 295 f.

19 *Mrs Delany*, op. cit., p. 382.

20 Beresford, J.B., *Storm and Peace*, Cobden-Sanderson, 1936, p. 59.

21 Marindin, G.E., *Our Naval Heroes*, 1901, p. 96.

22 H.M.C., Du Cane, No. 61, 1905, p. 84.

23 Naval Misc., III, p. 110.

24 *Military Anecdotes*, p. 141.

25 *Walpole Ls.*, I, p. 403 f.

26 *Yorke's Hardwicke*, I, p. 528.

27 Ibid, pp. 475, 478, 483.

28 Wright, op. cit., p. 84.

29 *Yorke's Hardwicke*, I, p. 528.

8. The Seven Years' War with France

1 Aspinall-Oglander op. cit., p. 191.

2 Ibid, p. 227.

3 Wragg, op. cit., pp. 99–101, 104–5.

4 Edwardes, M., *Battle of Plassey*, Batsford, 1963, p. 77.

5 *Yorke's Hardwicke*, II, p. 385.

6 Minney, R.J., *Clive*, Jarrolds, 1931, p. 145.

7 Wright, op. cit., p. 392.

8 *Walpole Ls.*, III, p. 143.

9 Ibid, III, p. 168.

10 Ibid, III, p. 231 f.

11 Ibid, III, p. 234 f.

12 Young, P., *The British Army*, W. Kimber, 1967, p. 72.

13 Routh, op. cit., p. 67 ff.

14 Field, op.cit., p. 104 ff.

15 Ellis, III/4, p. 412 ff.

16 Wright, op. cit., p. 553.

17 Doughty, A., *Siege of Quebec*, 1901, V, p. 14 ff.

18 Ibid, p. 20 f.

19 Ibid, p. 22 ff.

20 Lloyd, C., *Capture of Quebec*, Batsford, 1959, p. 140.

21 *Yorke's Hardwicke*, III, p. 247.

22 Long, op. cit., p. 59.

23 Moorhouse, E., *Letters of English Seamen*, 1910, p. 124.

24 Charles-Edwards & Richardson, op. cit., p. 74.

9. The American War of Independence

1 Wright, op. cit., p. 454.

2 H.M.C., Dartmouth, p. 378.

3 H.M.C., Hastings, III, p. 159 f.

4 Wilkin, W.H., *British Soldiers in America*, 1914, p. 245.

5 *The English-Speaking World*, June–July 1943, p. 246.

6 *Horace Walpole Selected Letters*, W. Hadley (ed.), Dent, 1926, p. 387 ff.

7 *Queeney Letters*, Lord Lansdowne (ed.), 1934, p. 13.

8 Temple Patterson, A., *The Other Armada*, Manchester University Press, 1960, p. 128.

9 *Correspondence of George III with Lord North*, II, 1867, p. 252.

10 Field, op. cit., p. 129 ff.

11 de Fonblanque, E.B., *Life & Correspondence of John Burgoyne*, 1876, p. 155f.

12 Ibid, p. 316 f.

13 Wilkin, op. cit., p. 154.

14 Ibid, p. 257.

15 *Clinton-Cornwallis Controversy*, II, (1888), pp. 159 f, 163, 172.

16 Ibid, II, pp. 175, 188; I, p. 510.

17 *Walpole Sel. Ls.*, p. 392 f.

18 Mundy, B., *Life of Lord Rodney*, II, 1830 p. 50.

19 Ibid, p. 250.

20 Ibid, p. 308.

21 H.M.C., Manners–Rutland, p. 55.

22 Moorhouse, op. cit., p. 143.

23 Charles–Edwards & Richardson, op. cit., p. 85 ff.

24 Laffin, J., *Tommy Atkins*, White Lion Publ., 1977 (Cassell, 1966), p. 56.

10. The War with Revolutionary France

1 Scott, A.F., *Everyone a Witness*, Martin Publ., 1970, p. 386.

2 Ibid, p. 387.

3 Maxwell, H., *Life of Wellington*, I, 1899, p. 13.

4 Walker, X.F., *Young Gentlemen*, Longman, 1938, p. 214.

5 Frischauer, P., *England's Years of Danger*, Cassell, 1938, p. XIV.

6 Dane, C., *The Nelson Touch*, Heinemann, 1942, p. 62.

7 Moorhouse, op. cit., p. 187.

8 Mainwaring, G.E., & Dobrée, B., *Floating Republic*, F. Cass, 1966, p. 273 ff.

9 Barrow, J., *Sidney Smith*, I, 1848, p. 307.

10 Bowen, op. cit., p. 325.

11 *R. Southey Letters*, 1912, p. 24.

12 Whinyates, F.T., *Family Records*, II, (1894–6), p. 40 f.

13 Moorhouse, op. cit., p. 210.

14 Sichel, W., *Emma, Lady Hamilton*, 1905, p. 490.

15 *Dispatches & Letters of Nelson*, N.H. Nicolas (ed.), III, 1845, p. 130 f.

16 Wragg, op. cit., p. 199.

17 *Heber Letters*, R.H. Cholmondeley (ed.), Batchworth Press, 1950, p. 184.

18 *Nelson Letters*, p. 12.

19 Frischauer, op. cit., p. 112.

20 Moorhouse, op. cit., p. 236.

21 Wragg, op. cit, p. 188.

22 Oman, C., *Nelson*, Hodder & Stoughton, 1947, p. 468.

PART THREE: THE NINETEENTH CENTURY

11. The War with the French Empire

1 Scoones, W.B., *Four Centuries of English Letters*, 1883, p. 423.

2 Aspinal-Oglander, op. cit., p. 195.

3 Wragg, op.cit., p. 245.

4 Duchess of Cleveland, *Life & Letters of Lady Hester Stanhope*, J. Murray, 1914, pp. 54, 56 ff.

5 Naval Miscellany, I, 1902, p. 320.

6 Wheeler, H.F.B., & Broadley, A.M., *Napoleon and the Invasion of England*, I, 1908, p. XIII.

7 *Creevey Papers*, H. Maxwell (ed.), I, 1860, p. 29.

8 Naval Misc., IV, 1952, p. 447 ff.

9 Moorhouse, op. cit., p. 265.

10 Ibid, p. 285.

11 Ibid, p. 288.

12 Ibid, p. 293.

13 Ibid, p. 302 f.

14 Foster, V., *The Two Duchesses*, 1898, p. 250.

15 Lloyd, C., *British Seamen*, Collins, 1968, p. 296 f.

16 Cleveland, op. cit., p. 74 ff.

17 *Letters from Portugal and Spain*, 1809, p. 104 f.

18 Warre, W., *Letters from the Peninsula*, 1909, pp. 46, 48, 50.

19 *Ls. from Portugal and Spain*, pp. 302 ff, 309 ff, 324 ff.

20 Moore, J.C., *The Campaign of Sir John Moore*, 1809, p. 358.

21 Brett-James, A., *Wellington at War*, Macmillan, 1961, p. 203 ff.

22 Napier, W.F.P., *History of the Peninsular War*, I, (1828–40), p. 164 ff.

23 Ibid, I, p. 166.

24 *Military Anecdotes*, p. 240.

25 *Letters of Robert Knowles*, 1913, p. 59 f.

26 *Correspondence of R.B. Long*, T.H. McGuffie (ed.), Harrap, 1951, p. 171 ff.

27 Whinyates, op. cit., pp. 246, 257.

28 Scoones, op. cit., p. 392.

29 *Letters of Private Wheeler*, B. Liddell Hart (ed.), Michael Joseph, 1951, p. 90 ff.

30 Ibid, p. 115 ff.

31 Brett-James, op. cit., p. 267 ff.

32 Trevelyan, G.O., *Macaulay's Life & Letters*, I, 1876, p. 50.

33 Charles-Edwards & Richardson, op. cit., p. 163 f.

34 *Mil. Anecdotes*, p. 122.

35 *Letters of Sir Augustus Frazer*, E. Sabine (ed.), 1859, p. 546 ff.

36 Gore, J., *Creevey's Life & Times*, J. Murray, 1934, p. 85 f.

37 H.M.C., Hastings, No. 78 (1928–), p. 307.

38 *Letters of Eminent Persons*, Wilmott (ed.), p. 414.

39 Brett-James, op. cit., 323 f.

40 Ibid, p. 319.

12. The Crimean War

1 *Letters of Queen Victoria*, A.C. Benson & Viscount Esher (eds.), J. Murray, 1907, I, p. 17.

2 Stephenson, F.C.A., *Letters from the Crimea*, F. Pownall (ed.), 1915, pp. 100, 106 f, 110 f, 123 f, 148 f.

3 Barrett Browning, E., *Letters to her Sister*, L. Huxley (ed.), 1929, pp. 206, 213.

4 Veitch, R.H., *Life, Letters & Diaries of Sir Gerald Graham*, 1901, p. 41 ff.

5 *The Fields of War: A Young Cavalryman's Crimea Campaign*, P. Warner (ed.), J. Murray, 1977, p. 73 ff.

6 Baring Pemberton, W., *Battles of the Crimean War*, Batsford, 1962, p. 109 f.

7 Chevenix Trench, C., *Gordon*, Allen Lane, 1978, p. 16.

8 *Letters of B. Disraeli to the Marchioness of Londonderry*, Macmillan, 1938, p. XXI.

9 Wrottesley, G., *Life & Correspondence of F.M. Sir John Burgoyne*, II, 1873, p. 169 ff.

10 *Fields of War*, op. cit., p. 109 ff.

11 Stephenson, op. cit., pp. 15, 69, 87, 238.

12 Sterling, A., *Highland Brigade in the Crimea*, 1895, pp. 150, 164, 241, 246, 270.

13 Cook, E., *Florence Nightingale*, 1913, p. 183.

14 Sterling, op. cit., pp. 180, 241.

15 *Queen Victoria Ls.*, III, p. 63.

16 *Fields of War*, op. cit., p. 112 f.

17 *Queen Victoria Ls.*, III, p. 164 f.

18 Ibid, p. 161 f.

19 Veitch, op. cit., p. 202 f.

20 *Fields of War*, op. cit., p. 179 ff.

21 *Queen Victoria Ls.*, III, pp. 180 f, 215.

13. Queen Victoria's 'Little Wars'

1 *Campaign of the Indus*, A.H. Holdsworth (ed.), 1840, pp. 106–30 *passim*.

2 Nott, Sir W., *Memoirs & Correspondence*, J.H. Stocqueler (ed.), 1854, p. 407 f.

3 Kaye, J.W., *History of the War in Afghanistan*, II, 1890, p. 358.

4 *Journal of the Society for Army Historical Research*, vol. 51, (1973) no. 27, p. 181 f.

5 Durand, M., *Life of F.M. Sir G. White*, Blackwell, 1915, I, p. 202.

6 Bruce, G., *Six Battles for India*, A. Barker, 1969, p. 168 f.

7 Sherson, E., *Townshend*, Heinemann, 1928, p. 18 ff.

8 Diver, K.H.M., *Honoria Lawrence*, J. Murray, 1936, p. 492.

9 *Journal Soc. Army Hist. Res.*, vol. 43, (1965), p. 197.

10 Roberts, F.S., *Letters Written During the Indian Mutiny*, Macmillan, 1924, p. 27 ff.

11 *Queen Victoria Ls.*, III, p. 246.

12 Hibbert, C., *The Great Mutiny, India 1857*, Allen Lane, 1978, p. 117.

13 Ibid, p. 282.

14 Ibid, p. 297.

15 Ibid, p. 304.

16 Ibid, p. 220.

17 *Journal Soc. Army Hist. Res.*, vol. 43, p. 204 ff.

18 Durand, op. cit., I, p. 70 ff.

19 Stephenson, op. cit., p. 196 f.

20 Holt, E.C., *Opium Wars in China*, Putnam, 1964, p. 243 f.

21 *Letters of the 8th Earl of Elgin*, 1872, p. 361.

22 Stephenson, op. cit., p. 272 f.

23 Allgood, G., *China War 1860* (Letters & Journals), 1901, p. 59.

24 National Army Museum, 6705/4a.

25 *Light Bob Gazette*, vol. 12, no. 4, 1904, p. 8 ff.

26 *Blackwood's Magazine*, vol. CIII, 1868, I, p. 728.

27 Arthur, G., *Letters of Lord and Lady Wolseley*, Heinemann, 1922, p. 11.

28 Brackenbury, H., *The Ashanti War,* 1874, II, pp. 46 ff, 54 f.

29 Arthur, op. cit., p. 17.

30 Brackenbury, op. cit., II, p. 215 f.

31 Melville, C.H., *General Sir Redvers Buller*, Edward Arnold, 1923, I, p. 77.

32 Arthur, op. cit., p. 18.

33 Emery, F., *The Red Soldier*, Hodder & Stoughton, 1976, p. 88 f.

34 Ibid, p. 95.

35 Ibid, p. 114.

36 Ibid, p. 114 f.

37 Ibid, p. 132 f.

38 Arthur, op. cit., p. 43.

39 Ibid, p. 75 ff.

40 Gordon, C.G., *Letters to his Sister*, 1888, pp. 374, 391.

41 Arthur, op. cit., pp. 126, 130 ff.

42 Ibid, p. 140 ff.

43 *Gordon Ls.*, p. 384.

44 *Queen Victoria Ls.*, 2nd ser. III, p. 607.

45 Durand, op. cit., I, p. 298.

14. The Boer War

1 Butler, W., *Life of General Sir G.M. Colley*, 1899, p. 367 f.

2 Churchill, W.S., *London to Ladysmith*, Longman, 1900, p. 176.

3 Griffith, K, *Thank God We Kept the Flag Flying*, Hutchinson, 1974, p. 146 f.

4 Pakenham, T., *The Boer War*, Weidenfeld & Nicolson, 1979, p. 240.

5 Isherwood, C., *Kathleen and Frank*, Methuen, 1971, p. 61 ff.

6 Durand, op. cit.

7 Melville, op. cit., I, p. 206 f.

8 Pakenham, op. cit., p. 370.

9 Farwell, B., *The Great Boer War*, Allen Lane, 1977, p. 372.

10 National Army Museum, 7402–31.

11 Magnus, P., *Kitchener*, J. Murray, 1958, p. 171 f.

12 *Frank Maxwell, A Memoir*, J. Murray, 1921, p. 92.

Index of Letter Writers